Valerij Tomarenko

Through the Client's Eyes

How to Make Your Translations Visible

Weiterbildungs- und
Fachverlagsgesellschaft
Fachverlag
BDÜ

Valerij Tomarenko

Through the Client's Eyes

How to Make Your Translations Visible

Die Deutsche Bibliothek – CIP Einheitsaufnahme

Valerij Tomarenko: Through the Client's Eyes
How to Make Your Translations Visible

ISBN: 978-3-946702-03-0

verlegt von der BDÜ Weiterbildungs- und Fachverlagsgesellschaft mbH, Berlin,
einem Unternehmen des Bundesverbandes der Dolmetscher und Übersetzer e. V. (BDÜ)

Lektorat: Kasia Trojanowska
Gestaltung/Satz: Thorsten Weddig, Essen
Titelbild: Prostock-studio/stock.adobe.com
Druck: Schaltungsdienst Lange oHG, Berlin

With meaningful differences difficult to find, prospects look for signals in seemingly trivial differences... In fact, much of effective service management can be described as the careful management of the seemingly inconsequential.

The first two rules of communicating about services: Make the service visible, and make the prospect comfortable.

People will trust their eyes far before they will ever trust your words... What do your visibles say about the invisible thing you are trying to sell? Watch what you show.

— Harry Beckwith, *Selling the Invisible*

■ ■ ■

L'admiration pour la forme passe avant toute compréhension du contenu.

— Kacper Kowalski, *Effets secondaires*

Foreword: A new outlook on typography, a new outfit for translators

Every translation must be made physically accessible, that is to say, in writing – whether on paper or in digital form on a screen. Both modes of presentation have this in common: our translations possess an intrinsically graphic nature. Even if your client just wants to deliver an intermediate product which will ultimately serve as a medium of target-cultural communication, and even if it will be converted to graphic form later by a graphics professional, you're still generally expected to deliver your translation in typographic form. More often than not, direct clients expect a translation to be in its final layout as a default.

Until the mid-1980s, the term "typography" was largely *terra incognita* in translation circles. This changed when the first desktop publishing programs and the WYSIWYG ("What You See Is What You Get") software made it possible to display text in proportionally spaced font on screen and in print. This led to an increasing democratisation of writing, a development that had far-reaching consequences for today's culture. Typography became both a fourth cultural technique and the signature of our time.

By replacing the typewriter as a writing tool with computers and DTP, translators followed in Johannes Gutenberg's footsteps, so to speak. That resulted in a new end-to-end process and a fundamentally new product – a translation ready for print or publication, both in terms of verbal and visual content.

For the translation profession, this allows us to step outside the image of a pure "language mediator", which the public associates more with simple recording and recoding of verbal messages – a future computer will mediate between languages almost as well, but also faster and more efficiently. This may afford translators the opportunity to tap into a more complex and nuanced career field in the production of target-cultural means of communication.

This means that the traditional understanding of the profession will have to be expanded. Translators will have to take into account that they are links in a production chain bringing together experts from different sectors who are dependent on each other while creating content. This also means that translators will have to arm themselves with the knowledge, skills, and insights they will need to consciously utilize visual elements that go beyond mere "typographic writing". That approach is what Valerij Tomarenko is describing in this book.

What makes "good for print" good for translators? By reading the book, you will see the benefits in many ways. Among other things, a keen eye for typography helps the translator to highlight the quality of their work. To visibly stand out from competitors. But also, more importantly, to help their clients to stand out in the marketplace – through compelling, tangible communication.

Speaking of typography and communication... Typography can be regarded as a semiotic phenomenon. Elements of typography and their use are known to be culture-specific. Different meanings are assigned to typographic signs in different cultures, and different conventions govern how they are used.

So the layout and typography of source and target texts, or rather of source- and target-cultural means of communication, must always be kept in mind throughout the translation process, from the time the job is evaluated, through design and execution of the translation, and finally, its revision and "imprimatur" ("good-to-print"). Especially when producing the target-culture communication medium in the source culture or a third culture, the translator is responsible for compliance with the typographical conventions of the target culture and thus for the orthotypographical correctness of the translation – the new target-culture content.

I wish you new insights and enjoyable reading.

Dr. Jürgen F. Schopp
University of Tampere (Finland)

Author of *"Gut zum Druck?": Typografie und Layout im Übersetzungsprozess*, Tampere, 2005

Preface

A translator today may be overwhelmed by a plethora of advice they're offered. From quick answers to questions on online forums, to webinars, books and comprehensive CPD courses, the range of subjects covered includes both specific, translation-related topics and general business knowledge and tips. It is debatable what is more important for a translator's commercial success: the quality of her translation or her entrepreneurial acumen. Whatever the relationship between specialist expertise and more generally applicable skills, high-quality translation is a product of the mastery of the subject matter and writing excellence, but it cannot be achieved without communication skills and a problem-solving mindset.

Chris Durban, author of *The Prosperous Translator*, gave "the hottest tip ... for translators looking to build their business" that is ingeniously simple: "become a better translator". In the context in which this advice was given, it clearly refers to the competence of a translator as a producer, less a service provider, and least of all, an entrepreneur. But whatever the relation between the product of translation and the producer's soft skills, the quality of translation may not be immediately apparent to the client. The challenge of working directly with clients often comes down to this simple fact: none too often, your clients rely on factors extraneous to their judgement simply because they cannot judge the product quality themselves. That is, to a greater or lesser extent, true of any company that deals with partners and clients in a global market and has to communicate with them in multiple, to varying degrees unfamiliar, tongues.

Other factors cannot be justifiably termed extraneous, since they refer to the characteristics of translation as a project, not a product. Nevertheless, they determine to a large extent whether your clients are likely to take a favourable view of your work. These are the most demanding project constraints – time and cost – that don't necessarily relate to the quality of the translation (but do relate to the translator's service).

Being a better translator is not tantamount to being seen and valued as a better translator by your client. To a certain extent, this book attempts to show how to close this gap. Apart from hard facts, such as project constraints, and somewhat subjective quality considerations, your clients' perception of your work (and, obviously, its value) is largely influenced by your communication. There is a whole discipline devoted to this area, called customer relationship management (CRM). However, it must not be the only source of your competitive advantage if you hope to combine your professional, quality-driven focus with the goal of commercial success. Your translation is meant to be a vehicle of communication for your client, but at the same time, **it also serves as a vehicle of communication for you, the translator**. The result of your work might be a duplicate of your client's document in another language, but it also bears your own specific mark. It is this mark that can convey your marketing message and help build a relationship with your client. The idea behind this book was to help **make the quality of your work as a translator more visible to your client**.

The vast amount of advice offered to translators means that some of it is repetitive. It seems to me that translators spend too much time talking to one another. Insights from other industries may at first seem like an unusual idea, but sometimes they turn out all the more valuable. Given that, as translators, we deal with communication in the broadest sense, what other industry can assist us better than communication design? My experience in working with and for publishing houses, as well as branding, marketing and advertising agencies has taught me a lot about my own business, not only in terms of producing better translations aimed at overcoming cultural and language barriers for my clients, but also in terms of improving my own business communication. If you believe that "customer orientation" is not just an empty phrase from business speak, greater insight into visual communication and graphic design can set you on the path to becoming a better translator.

They say the middle way is the only way that could fail to bring you to Rome, so this book doesn't aspire to provide a "middle of the road" approach. Instead, it can teach you to make better use of your available resources, including design software,[1] both for your clients' projects and for your own marketing purposes. What I hope for the most is that it can help you strengthen your sense of customer orientation by teaching you to look at your translation and your business through your client's eyes. "**Show, not tell**" might be the most important, if deceptively trivial, piece of advice that this book has to offer. But to apply it successfully, we need to stop seeing ourselves as "simply translators" and step beyond the confines of our job description.

1 Throughout the book, I recommend a number of programs and tools I consider useful in translation work. I am not invested in any of these tools and software, and all the references are based solely on my experience as a user.

Contents

1 The verbal and the visual, or why bother

1.1 Is this book for me?

Translators today come in different guises. Apart from the differences in specialisation, they vary in terms of their place in the value chain.

Translators whose digital deliverables are **ready for publication**, for instance in the form of high-resolution PDF files for print or website content files, are rare, but they are probably the most knowledgeable in terms of both verbal **and visual** content. In fact, I think they already know a lot of what this book is about. Nevertheless, it will help them to structure their knowledge and brush up on some translation-relevant skills. If they outsource a portion of their translation work, such as for multilingual projects, and have to rely on colleagues they collaborate with, they can apply some of the tips in the book to better communicate across the whole production chain. An important component of their work is related to **editing**. This is not in the sense of rewording the verbal content of translated materials, but rather with a purpose of reconciling various idiosyncrasies in terms of typography and general layout in order to prepare the translation for publication or release.

Still, a vast majority of professional translators working for direct clients produce materials **ready to be used**. These translators deal predominantly with corporate documentation. For lack of a better term, I would classify all kinds of documents (on paper or in electronic format) that a company develops and uses in their daily communication and business transactions as "**corporate paperwork**".

Corporate documents are business letters, contracts and agreements, prospectuses, press releases, financial documents and reports, as well as customer-facing newsletters, articles in professional journals or internal employee magazines. Most of these documents contain text *and* graphics. The more of the latter, the more marketing-oriented (more visual and less verbal) the communication. This is especially true of corporate brochures – many of them look like "image brochures", not only because they are set to promote a company's image in the metaphorical sense.

Nonverbal content, however, is not limited to marketing. Once chaste, **financial** or **business** reports increasingly incorporate figures (numbers) presented as figures (illustrations). A table with numerical data may be part of a supportive Excel spreadsheet, embedded in a Word or PowerPoint document as a non-editable image. Some workflows and techniques featured in this book will be especially useful for translators who regularly deal with PowerPoint presentations for their direct corporate clients.

On the other hand, **legal translators** who work on agreements and contracts totally stripped of any visual elements may also discover new ways around familiar software tools, such as Microsoft Word. Finally, even translators whose scope of work is limited to translating segments of texts via CAT (computer-assisted translation) tools, usually for **translation agencies** as clients, can benefit from developing a better understanding of the basic principles of design as well as grasping the client's perspective to improve their marketing skills and strategies.

No matter how different all these translator specialties are, one common denominator is certainly **professional competence**. On translators' forums I have come across several attempts to define a professional translator as "someone who has full command of translating technologies, the linguistic and cultural mindsets of their working languages, the knowledge of the specific subject matter they specialise in...", or as "someone with a serious approach to translation, who treats it like a business... who spends time, [and puts] money and effort into personal and professional development". That is all true, but at a risk of stating the obvious, I would like to define professional translators as those who **work for their clients**. This point is important, if we agree that customer orientation is key to ensuring professional success. In our case, customer orientation has much to do with understanding the client's views and concerns.

Translation buyers – our clients – need translators to bring the message across; to help them in turn to **communicate** with their clients, partners and target audience. Paradoxically, many translators who are brilliant communicators on behalf of their clients, seldom know how to use their communication skills to their own advantage. Sometimes, they can have "full command of translating technologies, the linguistic and cultural mindsets of their working languages, the knowledge of the specific subject matter", but show only lacklustre communication skills and lack ideas for promoting their own translation business.

That is why specific practices, recommendations and tips handled in this book go hand in hand with more general business and marketing advice. I have written this book for professional translators eager to improve their **methodical** competence along with their **technical** skills.

■ ■ ■

Some ten of fifteen years ago, a popular advertising slogan in Germany that for some reason often adorned the sides of moving companies' trucks was *Unsere Leistung ist unsere Werbung* ("Our work is our best advertisement"). I believe that a product indeed can promote its creator (or translator, in our case). What this book aspires to do is help a professional translator present her products in such a way that the translation itself, irrespective of whether the client can read or understand the language, will speak volumes about and for the translator. This isn't about delivering effective marketing pitches. In the words of Harry Beckwith, "the core of service marketing is the service itself".[2] The idea of the book is to help translators become more aware of how the client perceives and "reads" the translation, so that the translator can use the client's perspective as a competitive advantage, to stand out from the crowd and achieve greater success.

Nonverbal elements of a translation can sometimes reveal more about the value and quality of a translator's work than their language output itself. They can assist language professionals in becoming more expressive and articulate when communicating for and with their clients. However, effectively dealing with typography, layout and graphic design should not be an end in itself; rather, it should be a starting point for becoming a better translator.

2 Harry Beckwith. *Selling the Invisible: A Field Guide to Modern Marketing* (Grand Central Publishing, 2012).

1.2 My share of Ps

Chris Durban believes that two qualities are crucial in order to excel as a translator: mastery of a subject (specialisation) and writing skills ("better than those of 98% of the general population"[3]). Both non-negotiable, these qualities are ultimate markers of excellence in our profession. For me, they constitute what I simply call Professionalism. Why with a capital P? Let me explain.

Business literature is full of acronyms that are supposed to help us remember ideas easily. Sometimes, the abbreviation gets stuck in your mind, even if what it stands for is long forgotten. SWOT analysis is perhaps an exception, since "strengths, weaknesses, opportunities, threats" are easy to remember, but to spell out TEAM as "together each achieves more", or keep in mind all the SMART objectives, is more difficult, whereas the "five Ms" of management, "four Cs" of marketing or various alphanumerical combinations of Ps always seem open to different interpretations. To make things more exciting, I decided to update the definition of four Ps (originally meaning "price, product, promotion and place") and make it more applicable to translation business.

So, in "translator's four Ps", the first P stands for Professionalism. I don't have much to add to the essential qualities stated above (mastery of subject + outstanding verbal skills), however, I believe that a translator's success also to a large extent depends on her project-oriented approach and, accordingly, project-oriented mindset. Every translation job is a project, since the activity it requires usually varies in scope, has a set time span and serves to create a unique product, service or outcome.

The project management triangle describes a well-known combination of three types of constraint: scope, time and cost. The relationship between these determines, from the client's viewpoint, the choice of a particular supplier, and from the supplier's viewpoint, is critical for the translator's performance and the quality of translation.

Project-oriented approach, my second P, doesn't mean "lowering your quality standards" in order to produce "fit-for-purpose", but perhaps subpar, work. The idea is to bear in mind that your client needs your services only to

---

3 In: Jane Fox. "Bulk versus premium translation: insight from Chris Durban" [blog]. *Between Translations*, published 6 January 2014 <http://foxdocs.biz/BetweenTranslations/bulk-versus-premium-translation-chris-durban> accessed 21 August 2018.

communicate (or receive) a specific message, which can be seen as a project purpose. Your service itself is always related to a certain scope (of work to be done), time (in the form of a deadline) and cost (ideally, in relation to the message's worth for the client).

Along with Professionalism and Project-oriented approach, I consider **Personality** to be a crucial asset in the arsenal of a professional translator. On the one hand, Personality stems from the first two Ps – Professionalism and Project-oriented approach. On the other hand, and more importantly, it is any combination of characteristics that add a distinctive individuality and make you and your products stand out. Like each translation job is a unique project, all translators produce different results. Translators don't just replace words and phrases of the source language text with their equivalents in the target language, but rather interpret the meaning of the original in their own, individual way. No matter what efforts are taken and technical means used to reduce variability, translation will always come out different, not only due to the translators' distinct individual characteristics, but also because each translation is influenced by its specific purpose, its target audience and context. Without this variation, no new value can be created. Over-zealous attempts to maximise consistency lead to a constant repetition of what has already been said. As a result, new translations of existing material might be consistent with the old ones, but would be in no way consistent with new content. If the content to be translated seeks to stand out and attract attention, for instance marketing copy, it is not in line with your customer's expectations when a new translation is compiled from the repeatedly used and recycled material.

If you are an ambitious professional translator, it is in your interest to create new value through developing your individual and distinct "handwriting", based on mastery of the subject matter and your verbal skills. You need a visible and recognisable identity to differentiate yourself and become less interchangeable, of all things. "Be professional – but, more importantly, be personable"[4] – is the advice that aspiring translators should take to heart.

Personality does not reveal itself only in the **translation as a product** (e.g. in the form of an individual style), it shows up in other ways as well. Personality as the third P may also relate to a translator's **service**. Whereas time in the project management triangle is an ever-growing priority (and deadlines are getting shorter), dealing with time constraints may be regarded as an important part of a professional's personality. It means higher productivity

4 Beckwith, *Selling the Invisible*.

or speed in terms of service, but it also becomes apparent in communication with clients.

Today, the primary medium of communication in the translation industry for enquiries, requests for quotations and questions about a project is email. A fast response time might be crucial, even if to inform your client about your unavailability for the job. (As I am writing these lines, I receive an email from a fellow translator; here is an excerpt: "Can you help? I'm having trouble finding a Russian translator for this. I had one lined up, but he translated the wrong part and then disappeared...". So much for communication!)

A term that is perhaps a little over-used when speaking about communication and marketing is *branding*. As a translator, you can try to create your brand in order to communicate your values, that is to say your first three Ps. However, you don't have much of an opportunity to use your brand other than in your communication. To be more specific, you can hardly use your brand to **brand your products**. Chris Durban's idea about translators signing their work in order to take responsibility and due credit (and become more visible as a result) deserves every support (read more about it on p. 141), but a lot of corporate paperwork that you get to translate does not offer much room for acknowledging your part or including your credentials.

The quintessential idea of branding is to generate and promote a set of associations that a client makes with you as a professional translator, and with your products and services. Unless you're a literature translator, putting your brand on your every deliverable may be an unrealistic idea. But even with corporate paperwork, you can still use your brand in communication with clients *and* communicate your brand identity in your translations in a non-explicit way. This is how **Packaging** comes into play.

Packaging is the fourth element in my mix of Ps. Since what I call Packaging is the subject and raison d'être of this book, for the moment I shall confine myself to a couple of preliminary thoughts.

As far as the result of your work as a translator is a *verbal product*, it also features certain attributes of a more formal, less meaning-related nature. Later we will see that the way you handle your translation may be different from the way your client perceives your product and your services. In fact, it is your client's perception that you must become aware of if you consider customer orientation as a crucial success factor. If it sounds too abstract at the moment, the next chapters are going to be more specific and hands-on.

But first let us recap what constitutes my four Ps of translation:

1. **P**rofessionalism	Professional competence, specialisation, mastery of subject matter and outstanding verbal skills
2. **P**roject-oriented approach	Awareness of the project criteria and constraints, adding value through customer orientation
3. **P**ersonality	Pairing your professional qualities with your individuality to create difference and engage with your clients
4. **P**ackaging	Creating a visual, that is nonverbal, identity for your verbal products, appealing to the perception of your client, making the product speak for itself

Packaging is about appealing to your client's perception and making your translation speak for itself. It is also about enhancing your visibility as a translator. If we believe that the saying "Our work is our best advertisement" makes sense, it is Packaging where it fully applies.

Another term that could be used instead of "packaging" is "presentation". However, the key concept to understand here is that both "packaging" and "presentation" need to be seen from the perspective of the client. It is your client's **perception** – another p-word – that you have to understand in order to communicate the value of your products, engage with your clients and prospects, and eventually make a difference.

1.3 At the airport, in flight, at a desk

Checks and balances, an important part of the US Constitution, is a traditional way to describe the separation of powers to help ensure that no one branch – legislative, executive, judicial –abuses its powers. Whereas the word "balances" is self-explanatory, etymologists argue about which meaning of the word "checks" originally prevailed – to curb and limit or to watch, examine, review and verify. If we stick to the idea of checks as a scrutiny, and strip off all the political connotations and etymologies going back to Montesquieu and Adam Smith, "checks and balances" would be a perfect expression to describe our clients' attitude and perception as regards translation, all puns intended.

Checks and balances are what we ourselves, sometimes unconsciously, do the whole time when dealing with languages and translations.

In one of my recent jobs as an interpreter I had to take a 2-day trip from Hamburg in Germany to the Russian city of Ekaterinburg. On the day I came to the Hamburg airport, the connecting train station was full of new welcome billboards promoting the city to visitors. The ads had a clear structure – a glittering image of one of the city's landmarks, a bilingual headline and the logos of the campaign's sponsors. The positioning of the English translation, underneath the message in German, was begging for a comparison of the source and target lines.

Translation of slogans is an art in itself. Most visitors who were capable in both languages probably noticed the apparent mismatch between the German "Schlafen können Sie auch zuhause" ("If you wanted to sleep, you could have just as well stayed at home") and the English equivalent ("The time of your life!") on one of the billboards:

I can imagine that quite a few people frowned at this variation in meaning as another case of "something lost in translation" or a product of some linguistically challenged German advertisers. But I can also imagine a few who would explain the discrepancy as a result of reasons of design which prevailed over the desire to remain true to the original German message: the English version could have originated from the understandable preference for a shorter headline.

Another opportunity for checks and balances presented itself on the following day, when we flew back from Ekaterinburg on an UTair plane. UTair Aviation is a regional Russian airline. I had met their officials in Germany on a previous job, but it was my first time on board a UTair plane, and I got curious about the in-flight magazine and other printing materials that I found in the seat pocket in front of me.

For the sake of those readers who don't speak Russian and who see the Russian text only as a series of Cyrillic characters with no meaning, the aircraft safety features card of this Russian airline is a good example to illustrate a translation buyer's perspective. I believe that many translators sometime in their career had got to know clients who, having received a translation, played a game of "spot the difference".

The picture below illustrates two nonverbal discrepancies between both language versions. You may notice that a couple of words lost their uppercase letters in the translation. You may also notice that one translated line is obviously lacking a word that sticks out through quotation marks and two initial capital letters (possibly a mistype of the kind that autocorrect is always trying to fix):

On closer look, you may discover a resemblance between the company name and the Russian characters in inverted commas (this could be a reason for tweaking your autocorrect settings if you work for this company):

UTair / “ЮТэйр”

The fact that the second character (T) is identical in both cases is also revealing. Although the rest of the Russian alphabet wouldn't make much sense here either, you would be correct to conclude that “ЮТэйр” is the company's name written with Cyrillic letters. Of course, this alone wouldn't explain the missing company name in the English line (but something is always lost in translation, as we all know).

On the contrary, the irregularity in capitalization (ВЗЛЕТ, ПОСАДКА / take-off, landing) seems to be made up for by a consistent pattern of such word pairs, also appearing overleaf:

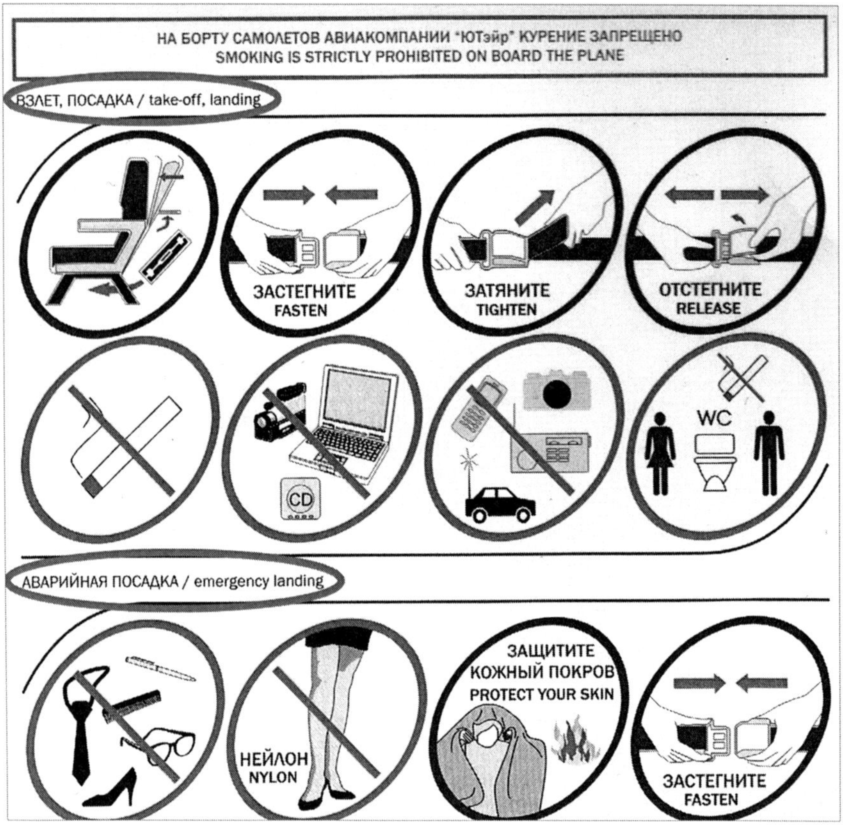

As soon as we notice that apparent irregularities tend to be repeated with a certain consistency, the impression of arbitrariness or possible faults disappears. So, if something happens to get lost (or changed) in translation, making your translation lose (or change) it consistently may help you look a better translator! Jokes aside though, we will see later that repeatability is in fact perceived as consistency and hence, a sign of professional competence.

The "spot the difference" game doesn't only apply to bilingual documents. The next example was compiled from excerpts of a Hungarian translation that I had to adapt for a user's guide. Translating a German manual into Russian and laying out translations in other languages, I had plenty of opportunities for checks and balances, on a par with my client who was quite fond of playing "spot the difference".

CPAP = Pozitív nyomású spontán légzés
CPAP lélegeztetés során a spontán légzéssel belélegzett gáz 100% oxigént tartalmaz.

A kilégzési szelep szétszerelése
Fordítsa el 90°-kal az óramutató járásával ellenkező irányban a fedőrészt = kinyitás és eltávolítás.
134 °-os forró gőzben sterilizálhatja.

Karbantartás után
Lásd az alábbi részeket:

- „Összeszerelés", 23. oldal.
- „A lélegeztető készülék elektromos táplálása", 24. oldal.
- "Gáz csatlakoztatása", 29 oldal.

A telepek töltésekor a környezeti hőmérséklet 0°C és 35 °C között legyen!

A lélegeztetési idő meghatározása
A nyomáscsökkentő mérőóráján mért palacknyomás: 200 bar.
Az oxigénpalack űrtartalma: 2,5 liter.
Rendelkezésre álló gázmennyiség:
2,5 L x 200 bar = kb. 500 l

IPPV módban, légzésfrekvencia 10/perc, VT = 1 Liter
Perctérfogat = 10/perc x 1 L = 10 l/perc
Működési idő = Sűrített gázmennyiség [L]
(MV +1*) [l / perc]
Ha az Oxylog készüléket »**Air Mix**« módba kapcsolja, a gázfogyasztás kb. 50 % kal csökken, és a működési idő kb. 90 percre nő.

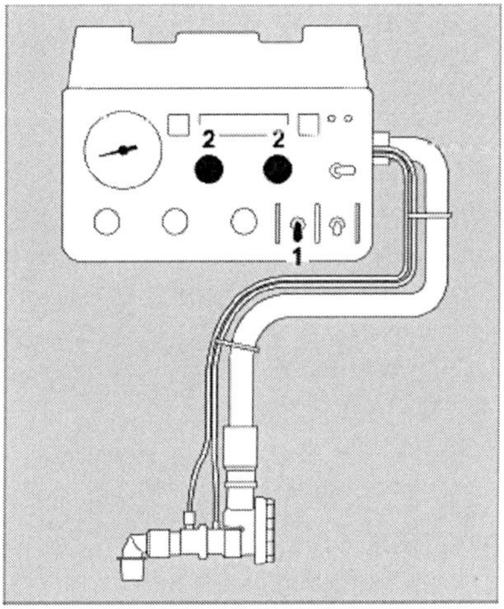

This Hungarian translation is a perfect showcase for checks and balances in monolingual translations. Without knowing a word in Hungarian, you can still compare obvious similarities and find a lot of minuscule differences.

Should the degree symbol be separated from the numeral or not?

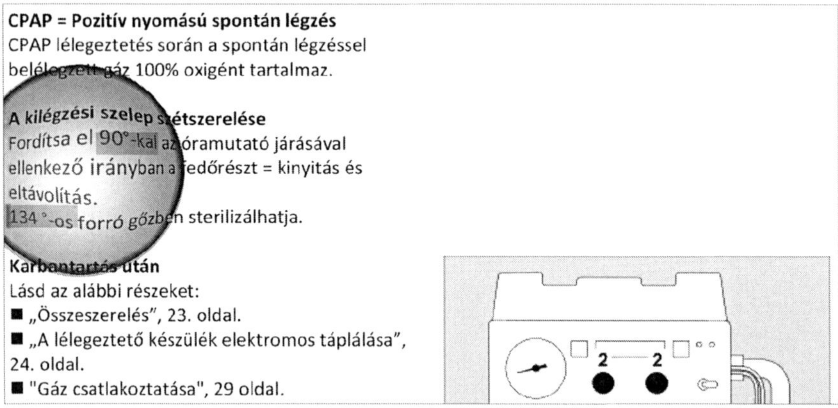
CPAP = Pozitív nyomású spontán légzés
CPAP lélegeztetés során a spontán légzéssel
belélegzett gáz 100% oxigént tartalmaz.

A kilégzési szelep szétszerelése
Fordítsa el 90°-kal az óramutató járásával
ellenkező irányban a fedőrészt = kinyitás és
eltávolítás.
134 °-os forró gőzben sterilizálhatja.

Karbantartás után
Lásd az alábbi részeket:
■ „Összeszerelés", 23. oldal.
■ „A lélegeztető készülék elektromos táplálása",
24. oldal.
■ "Gáz csatlakoztatása", 29 oldal.

Does it mean anything that a universal measurement unit is not uniformly capitalised, both when given in full and when abbreviated, or that sentences of a similar structure don't always end with a full stop? Which format is preferable, "l"-slash-"perc" or "l"-space-slash-space-"perc"? Does it really matter?

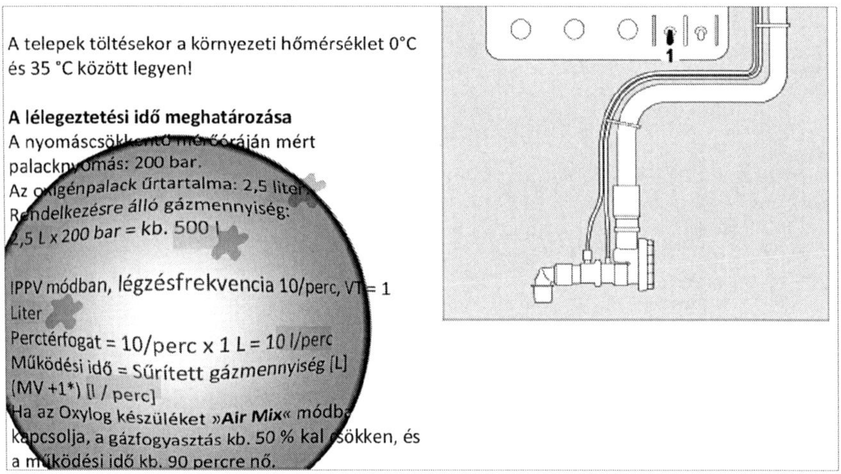
A telepek töltésekor a környezeti hőmérséklet 0°C
és 35 °C között legyen!

A lélegeztetési idő meghatározása
A nyomáscsökkentő mérőóráján mért
palacknyomás: 200 bar.
Az oxigénpalack űrtartalma: 2,5 liter
Rendelkezésre álló gázmennyiség:
2,5 L x 200 bar = kb. 500 L

IPPV módban, légzésfrekvencia 10/perc, VT = 1
Liter
Perctérfogat = 10/perc x 1 L = 10 l/perc
Működési idő = Sűrített gázmennyiség [L]
(MV +1*) [l / perc]
Ha az Oxylog készüléket »**Air Mix**« módba
kapcsolja, a gázfogyasztás kb. 50 % kal csökken, és
a működési idő kb. 90 percre nő.

A professional proofreader or editor will soon notice that, typography-wise, the whole translation text is consistent only in that it is teeming with inconsistencies (percent symbols with and without space, the same for degrees Celsius, non-uniform quotation marks):

CPAP = Pozitív nyomású spontán légzés
CPAP lélegeztetés során a spontán légzéssel belélegzett gáz 100% oxigént tartalmaz.

A kilégzési szelep szétszerelése
Fordítsa el 90°-kal az óramutató járásával ellenkező irányban a fedőrészt = kinyitás és eltávolítás.
134 °-os forró gőzben sterilizálhatja.

Karbantartás után
Lásd az alábbi részeket:
■ „Összeszerelés", 23. oldal.
■ „A lélegeztető készülék elektromos táplálása", 24. oldal.
■ "Gáz csatlakoztatása", 29 oldal.

A telepek töltésekor a környezeti hőmérséklet 0°C és 35 °C között legyen!

A lélegeztetési idő meghatározása
A nyomáscsökkentő mérőóráján mért palacknyomás: 200 bar.
Az oxigénpalack űrtartalma: 2,5 liter.
Rendelkezésre álló gázmennyiség:
2,5 L x 200 bar = kb. 500 l

IPPV módban, légzésfrekvencia 10/perc, VT = 1 Liter
Perctérfogat = 10/perc x 1 L = 10 l/perc
Működési idő = Sűrített gázmennyiség [L]
(MV +1*) [l / perc]
Ha az Oxylog készüléket »**Air Mix**« módba kapcsolja, a gázfogyasztás kb. 50 % kal csökken, és a működési idő kb. 90 percre nő.

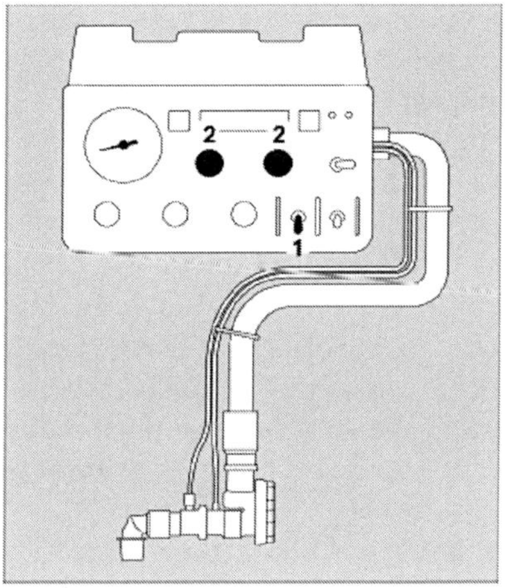

All these might be small matters of typography and writing style, nitpicky details that have no relevance for the users of the manual. They will have no impact on their understanding and most will probably not even notice them. There is only one problem – our client, for some reason, seems to care more about the looks than the function.

But can we reasonably presume that our clients – executives, lawyers, doctors, engineers, financial and marketing people – are really so preoccupied with design? Let's see.

1.4 Asymmetry and alignment

It is hardly a case of style over substance. Rather, our clients' attitude towards our translations relates to the well-known problem of so-called information asymmetry. The concept is used to describe market situations where one party in a deal has more or superior information on the subject of transaction than the other party. For instance, the seller of a used car usually knows more about it than the buyer. Unbalanced information makes the bargaining parties act on assumptions and breeds distrust, which is seen as a potential cause of market failure.

The concept of information asymmetry is occasionally used in relation to translation quality, since a translation buyer is supposed to be unable to immediately evaluate the quality of a translation. Clients hire translators either to translate a foreign language document into their own language (usually because they lack specific knowledge to interpret the original text) or to produce a translation for their own clients, business partners and so on. In the latter case, they have to rely on this third-party feedback, whether given directly or implicit, to judge whether the translation has succeeded.

In both cases, both the client's original document and the translation are known to the translator, yet the client does not necessarily have the **same level** of knowledge about the source text or about the translator's deliverable. Apart from a relatively small number of clients who themselves are native in the source or target language or have a good command of both, the language proficiency of the majority of translation clients is, actually, the reason translators exist. The feedback I once received from a new employee of my regular client, a major market research company, says it all: "Thank you very much for your translation, but I just realised I have no idea what it says. What should I do about it?!"

Information asymmetry is at its most acute when sending a request for a quote or hiring a translator for the first time. After the translation successfully achieves what it was meant to accomplish, checks and balances become mostly irrelevant and the translator's service is self-propelling, living up to the slogan "our work is our best advertisement".

However, we have all probably met or heard about those ever-worrisome clients with a tendency to always ask their more knowledgeable colleagues (or any native speakers at hand) to take a look at the delivered translation. Occasionally, they might even fall back on Google Translate for a back-translation of some critical passages. You can never be too careful, especially when dealing with something that you do not fully understand yourself.

Information asymmetry implies that one party **lacks knowledge**. If we take translation *into* a foreign language, our client's knowledge can be roughly grouped into the following areas:

	Original document	**Translator's deliverable**
How it looks	Known to client	Known to client
What it says	Known to client	???

In case of translation *from* a foreign language, it will be the intersection of the original document and what it says that is to a certain extent unknown to the client. In all cases, though, there will always be an area that we can call a blind spot and where we can put our question marks:

	Original document	**Translator's deliverable**
How it looks	Known to client	Known to client
What it says	???	Known to client

That does not sound much like an insight, does it? However, there is another problem with information asymmetry in translation. This problem is largely unknown to translation clients and largely unknown and unrealised by translators themselves, who can no longer see the wood for the trees.

Technical writing becomes increasingly more vivid and graphic. The same goes for all corporate communications. "A picture is worth a thousand words" is a popular adage not only among marketing professionals, who target their audience with compelling visuals, but everywhere in the corporate world, whether communicating with management or internal clients company-wide. Legal documents are perhaps the only area that remains largely unaffected by the general trend towards a less textual and more artistic, visually appealing and punchy presentation style. Whereas PowerPoint continues its triumphal march throughout our clients' corporate offices, translators are becoming more and more alienated from the visual look and feel of the communication that they are supposed to enable and facilitate. Since the advent of the first CAT tools, translators have tended to deal with purely textual content. Their perception is increasingly limited to extracted, separated and fragmented pieces of text. With no access to a larger, visible context, translators are losing sight of the "big picture", fail to correctly understand and interpret isolated text fragments or simply miss a point or two, and so the amount of what "always" gets lost in translation is growing.

Here's an example. I had to seriously rework my initial translation of a corporate brochure of a premium office supplies manufacturer after I saw the images that were going to accompany the text. A few passages about plain manila paper and vanilla paper tablecloths radically changed their meaning when I saw them set against a backdrop of colourful ice cream cones branded with the company's logo and colours, surrounded by colourless cones of plain vanilla ice.

Translators who get most of their work from intermediary translation agencies are particularly at risk of becoming visually challenged. Form and content are becoming inseparable in corporate communications, yet more and more translators receive prepared CAT files from translation agencies where typography and images are replaced with tags. Sometimes, complex text is cut into fragments and divided among several translators, so the lack of visual content goes alongside the lack of context as such.

"We don't see things as they are, we see things as we are", said Anaïs Nin. New technology and workflows dramatically narrowed the translator's field of vision. No matter how complex and interrelated the relationship between form and content, most translators think they have no business getting involved with anything beyond the translation of pure textual content into an "editable", that is "overwritable" (with Word or CAT tools), form. The nonverbal is non-existent or indiscriminately pegged as "design", that is to say something beyond the translator's area of expertise.

This tunnel vision runs contrary to and undermines the second P in my four Ps formula (project-oriented approach). Without an awareness of translation as part of a more complex whole, translators overlook that their deliverables are relevant only in a certain context; never an end unto itself, but always a medium combined with other parts and elements to serve a higher purpose.

All in all, the problem of information asymmetry for translation clients is aggravated by another information asymmetry on the part of translators:

	Original document	**Translator's deliverable**
How it looks	Known to translator?	Known to translator (unknown to translator if working with fragmented text?)
What it says	(Only partially) known to translator?	Known to translator (or only partially known? – see above)

The client may be unaware of the inner workings of the translation industry or of design agnosticism of their translator. However, when dealing with a translation into a foreign language, the client's opinion of the translation is inadvertently influenced simply by the way the translation looks. With asymmetrical knowledge of what the translation actually says, checks and balances boil down to a series of visual comparisons and alignments.

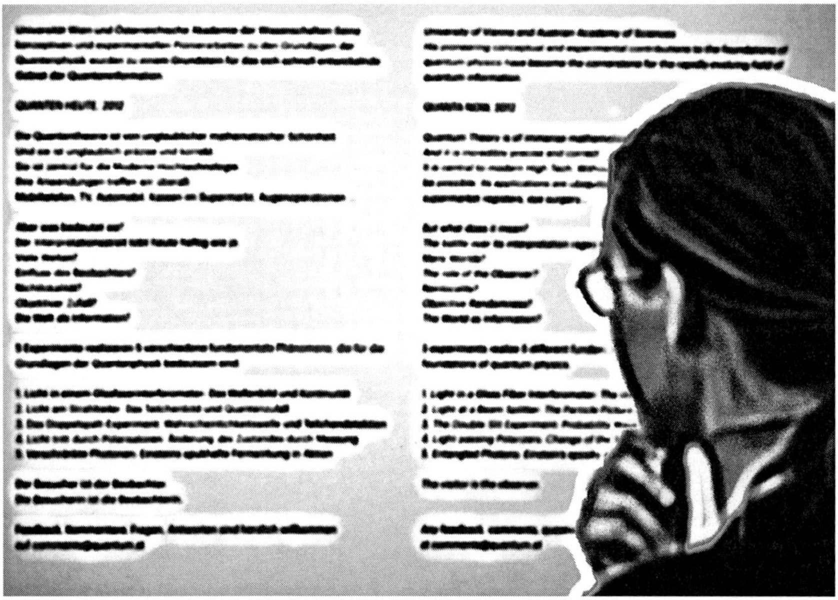

Translators take care of the content, but are frequently judged by the form. If customer orientation is to be taken seriously, it presupposes an insight into the perception of our clients. Translators do not have to forsake their professional identity of (verbal) content workers. They can remain oblivious to the matters of design, but to be more successful as translators, they might benefit from adopting a wider perspective, a more panoptic view, and learn to see their translation through the eyes of their client. Above all, they need to understand one thing: **how the translation looks determines how the client feels about it**.

With no or not sufficient knowledge of the meaning either of the original or of the translated document, the client is particularly observant and sensitive to seemingly slight, probably insignificant details that would go unnoticed by someone who is able to tell what exactly the document says. Still, if a visual check reveals irregularities and discrepancies, it is likely that the content is also not free from less obvious, less superficial inadequacies. In the worst case, it is these fine details that are telltale signs of serious inconsistencies or even errors.

Many comparisons and alignments take place, if only to compensate for the information asymmetry inherent to translation. It may be interesting to note that information asymmetry is part of our everyday life. Virtually every new deal that we make means dealing with lack of knowledge and uncertainty. When grocery shopping, we are first exposed to the look and feel of products that we are going to buy. We study their packaging. In fact, how the product looks, sometimes the design of its packaging, determines how we feel about it. Translation is no different in this respect.

That accounts for the fourth P in my formula and for my choice of terminology. Unlike grocery products, translation "packaging" is not a promising cover for what's inside. Rather, the term embraces all formal, nonverbal elements of a product that essentially comprises verbal content. These formal, nonverbal elements function to a large extent as packaging, since they compensate for the asymmetric knowledge and blind spots in our clients. They may be used for marketing as well. Essentially, though, they are part of the communication where content and form can barely be separated.

So what exactly does translation packaging mean? Is it all about "layout and design"? In the next chapters we will take a closer look at the kind of packaging a translator can provide to enhance the value of their translation and eventually gain a competitive edge, becoming a better, more successful translator.

1.5 Eyes on the dots

Every day, translation agencies and everyone listed as an outsourcer on translation job boards is flooded with spam from all kinds of applicants. The success rate of unsolicited applications is probably about zero, the worth for the recipient nil, but it is hard to block and filter all the spam emails, so some of them do get read before being sent to the waste bin.

Notwithstanding all the warnings and admonishments from the translator community, many applicants still attach their CVs as PDFs or unprotected Word documents. Sometimes, the contrast between what the wannabe translators say and how their pitches look like is astounding. "Dedicated to quality and accuracy", "with 10+ years experience in translating, editing and proofreading", "working in all major formats including Word, PowerPoint, InDesign, Trados, HTML and many others".

The exact data and wording differ, but visually, a good many CVs look like this:

Working Experience	• 2007 Action Against Hunger SP **Translator** • "Escuela de los Padres", Venado Tuerto, Santa Fe: 08-2006, Substitute Teacher of English. • 2009-2010 IEPALA SP **Translator** • 2000-2008 Oakley College Las Palmas de Gran Canaria **Translator & Interpreter** **(Business, Marketing, Finance, Education,...)** **Bursar** **Human Resources Manager**

If you click the *Show/Hide* button to display nonprinting characters – such as spaces, tabs and paragraph returns – the text will be even more revealing of the qualifications and skills that the author lays claim to:

Working Experience¤	• → 2007······Action·Against·Hunger·······················SP¶ ·······Translator → ¶ • → "Escuela·de·los·Padres",·Venado·Tuerto,·Santa·Fe:·08-2006,·Substitute·Teacher·of·English.¶ • → 2009-2010 → IEPALA·······················SP¶ ·····Translator··¶ • → 2000-2008 → Oakley·College → Las·Palmas·de·Gran·Canaria¶ ···············**Translator·&·Interpreter·**(Business,·Marketing,·Finance,·Education,...)¶ ·····**Bursar·¶** ······**Human·Resources·Manager¶**

There is not much difference between how the usually anonymous addressee of a spammy job application and our client, the recipient of a delivered translation, perceive what they get to see on paper or, in most cases nowadays, on screen. Translation is about language, and "**typography is what language looks like**".[5] If you are a "talented linguist" with a "passion for languages", how come you don't care about how your **language looks**? If you are "highly computer literate" and proficient in MS Office, SDL Trados and "HTML", why do you show the opposite with your less than rudimentary keyboarding skills?

Of course, most established translators would never produce a text with such carelessness. Yet many professional translators would identify with the statement "I'm a translator, not a graphic designer". For the majority of language professionals, pretty much everything that has to do with "how language looks" falls under the category of "design".

"Good translators always put themselves in their readers' shoes", wrote Corinne McKay in *101 Things a Translator Needs to Know*.[6] Less metaphorically, the implication is that good translators should try and look through the eyes of their clients. Clients, as we have now learnt, often don't know what the text says, yet cannot help but notice what it looks like. If we agree that good translators are customer oriented, that alone should be enough reason to pay a little more attention to what is lumped together under the hazy term "design".

5 Ellen Lupton. *Thinking with Type: A Critical Guide for Designers, Writers, Editors, & Students* (Princeton Architectural Press, 2010).

6 WLF Think Tank. *101 Things a Translator Needs to Know* (WLF 101 Publishing, 2014).

Maybe on reading this you think, "let the professionals do their job". Well, I certainly won't try to convince you of the benefits of dabbling in an area that takes professionals years to master. What I am going to show you in the next chapters though is that it pays for a translator-not-a-graphic-designer to become more typography literate and aware of matters beyond purely verbal content.

You don't have to become a designer to be a better translation professional. Paying attention to visual details that many translators attribute to the competence of a graphic or layout designer won't compromise your first P (professionalism). Looking after details beyond the verbal content relates to customer orientation as well as to the second P, project-oriented attitude. It is a holistic, customer- and project-oriented perspective which helps see translation through the eyes of the client – as part of a larger and complex whole, where content and form are interrelated in achieving successful communication.

Another reason for translators saying they are just "translators, not graphic designers", is a sloppily formatted source text, a plague of many translators and a sign of the client's obvious blindness to matters of "design". Occasionally, debate is stirred over the question of the extent the translator should improve the source document, whether going the extra mile is worth the effort and whether it will be appreciated by the client. I, too, struggled with these questions but I have now adopted a workflow that both makes the translation process more efficient and achieves better translation results.

Translators think they should primarily care about the meaning of words, not the way they look. However, if we spare some thought as to the purpose of typography and design, we might notice that it is not simply about making text more attractive. Whereas translators process and recreate messages, these volatile units of communication, typography and design help to convey them in a clearer and more understandable way. There is a clear interdependence between content, typography, visual design, usability and user experience.

The CV excerpt above does not do a convincing job because content and form clearly contradict each other. The saying that "a picture is worth a thousand words" might be somewhat trite, but many studies have shown that visual appeal plays a crucial role in forming impressions and opinions about persons, products, print media and websites. When torn between content and form that are at odds with each other, the preference is usually given to the look and feel. It is the nonverbal form which more often than not gains the upper hand over the verbal content, compels attention and stimulates recall. When visual and verbal cues compete, like in the picture below, what do you think works more convincingly?

Good design and typography are not about fancy colours, but about clarity and impact. What might be even more important is that **good design builds credibility and trust**. Studies in which participants were asked to rank websites have shown that well-designed sites appeared "more professional" and hence "more trustworthy".[7] Good design that increased credibility and inspired trust had an overwhelming influence on the customers' opinion. What was found was that to user perception, visual appeal was more important than usability and content.

As translators, we deal with verbal meanings and writing styles, but it is the nonverbal factors that affect the decisions and preferences of our clients, more often than we are aware of. Whereas clients cannot assess writing skills of somebody who translates into a foreign language, translation quality is often measured in terms of accuracy and attention to detail. A sense of accuracy and precision is well conveyed through the look and feel of the translator's texts. Regardless of whether your client has any idea about what your text actually says, your translation may look reliably thorough and precise; or careless and unkempt.

Another aspect that invites controversy is a mismatch between how we perceive ourselves and how others perceive us. This age-old problem isn't limited to the realm of personality and social psychology. The way we understand our professional selves as translators is not necessarily in tune with how our

7 For instance, "Consumer feelings and behaviours towards well designed websites" by Natalia Vila and Inés Kuster (in Information and Management, 2011, 48: 166–177) and "Informing security indicator design in web browsers" by Pan Shi and colleagues (in *Proceedings of the 2011 iConference, Seattle, Washington, USA, February 08–11*, 2011: 569–575).

clients see our tasks. The statement that became a motto of this chapter is an abbreviated quotation from a post I once came across in an online group for translators. "Dammit, I am a translator not a graphic designer" was what a translator wished she'd replied to a client who had asked her to incorporate a logo in the translation. The logo was sent to the translator separately as a low-res image. Judging from the comments under the post, most translators sided with the author and shared her frustration at dealing with "incompetent" clients. Although I understand problems arising from clients' unawareness of what working with PDF files means, in this specific case I'm inclined to regard the request to add a logo as a sign of confidence and trust in our profession. The client trusts a translator to create a better output than the original version itself.

Since both content and form produce communication, the juxtaposition "translator vs. graphic designer" would be lost on many clients. A client does not need a translator only to translate, but to help bring the message across and achieve a desired effect on the translation recipient. I believe that a translator is expected to think and act together *with* the client, keeping in mind all factors that serve the purpose of successful communication. Given that verbal content is a dedicated area of expertise, it is meaningless if not conveyed with adequate visual means.

Thinking beyond the narrow confines of sentences and phrases may be regarded as an opportunity for generating added value and ensuring a competitive edge. We may have different opinions on whether dealing with graphic elements belongs to the scope of professional practice of a translator, but sometimes it is not our opinion of what our profession entails, but that of our client's, that matters most. Any discussion of professionalism makes sense only if we consider how professionalism is perceived by our clients and how we can enrich this perception and align it with our vision.

I hope I have shown that for a product or service to be perceived as professional, it needs to *look* professional. However, what makes (or does not make) our translations professional-looking and inspires trust is not necessarily "design". We should take a closer look at what translators tend to label as "design" to get a clearer idea about how we can use it to benefit our profession.

1.6 Redefining design

Whether we deal with editable texts or graphic images, both are the result of a process initiated by our client. "The soul never thinks without a picture", as Aristotle is believed to have said, and the germ of an idea that has grown to end up as a "source file" was probably quite a mess. For it to become articulate, that is comprehensible by others, this mess needed to assume structure. That is the primary function of design – to shape an amorphous concept, whether visual or verbal, into something firm and graspable by the intended audience.

I think it is largely irrelevant whether our client sets out to write a business proposal, a product description, an editorial or a financial report. The process always stems from loose ideas, meanders through a chaos of thoughts, pauses at drafts, sketches and outlines, verbal and pictorial, and ultimately arrives at an orderly structure with ideas sorted and put into a sequence, rules of logical reasoning applied, and patterns of recognition carefully selected. A similar process is set into motion by a graphic designer after a so-called design brief. The client provides the information that the designer has to process and shape for it to be communicated to a target audience. The designer's task is now to disentangle and visualise all the client's ideas and suggestions in order to effectively bring the message across.

It is worth repeating that the purpose of design is not to add some pop and make things look punchier or nicer, but to communicate with the client's audience, that is to **translate** the client's words into something that brings clarity, makes meaning and facilitates a desirable effect, for instance, motivates the audience to take action. Even if we can metaphorically call this process "translation", the differences between a graphic designer and a translator are obvious. Whereas the designer's task is to find a visual form for verbal content, translators are confined to the verbal. This verbal content is already hard set and pre-formed, and a brief similar to that for design or copywriting is highly unusual. Our task is not to create something essentially new from cluttered and unstructured information, but to reproduce existing text using words and expressions from another language.

So, then, what is the point of the comparison? And what can graphic design teach translators?

To begin with, the process of reproduction of verbal content is not about replacing words and expressions of the source language with their counterparts from the target language. In order to make the document intelligible for the intended recipient and produce the desired effect, a translator may need to rewrite the original content, refining and reshaping the client's ideas as far as is appropriate.

With the exception of translation for purely scientific reasons, your clients need your translation only as a means of reaching their goal, for instance persuade the consumer of the benefits of their products, substantiate a corporate decision, make instructions in a user's manual clearer or use the information received from an international business partner. As long as you are aware that your work as a professional translator is instrumental for your client, it might help to think of yourself as a verbal designer who works creatively within given constraints.

Similar to design, translation is ordered and funded by clients, but it serves the needs of end users, not necessarily your direct clients. As a translator, you put yourself to work in the service of your client, but you may be able to produce a more suitable deliverable if you keep in mind and visualise the actual recipient of your work. For a typical client, a translation needs to fulfil a purpose – called *skopos* in academic circles. Therefore, translation quality, like the quality of design, is closely associated with its effectiveness and can be measured in relation to a desired outcome – sales figures, effects on decision-making or problem-solving, or positive feedback from the target audience.

A document usually arrives for translation without additional information similar to that in a design brief. Some translators routinely ask for more detailed instructions and more context, most importantly the purpose and intended audience. Yet, more often than not, an explicit "translation brief" is superfluous – a translator can infer most information from the source document itself. I am not sure which will appear more professional to your client – asking additional questions or relying on your experience and common sense. In some cases, a request for specifications can be a sign of a serious, professional approach. On the other hand, the purpose of a, say, press-release is so obvious that too much enquiry can undermine your credibility as an experienced professional who is capable of independent thinking and empathising with the client's perspective. My experience is that before you start to ask questions, it is wise to have a closer look at the document and do some background research. According to Eric Karjaluoto, author of one of the best books on graphic design,[8] **"discovery"** i.e. gathering data and becoming fa-

---

8 Eric Karjaluoto. *The Design Method: A Philosophy and Process for Functional Visual Communication* (New Riders, 2013).

miliar with the situation, is the first stage of the design process. Discovering a verbal design brief in the source document itself will benefit your translation and your interaction with the client.

1.7 Backstage

It has become commonplace to stress the importance of specialisation for a translator's success. However, our specialisms have one thing in common: whereas our clients use their specialist knowledge for their immediate goals (to report to the board of directors, elaborate a contract, conduct a research study etc.), we apply it only as mediators to **help them communicate** more effectively.

Specialising allows you to be on the same page as your client. "When you do your job well, you become transparent", says Eric Karjaluoto.[9] Like designers, translators are backstage workers. Like designers, they are out there to enable communication – and to facilitate outcomes.

As much as is written about the importance of CPD and acquiring specialist knowledge and skills in particular, I don't remember seeing a recommendation for communication design on a translator's CPD list of disciplines. As communication is the core of our business, I consider **communication knowledge and skills** to be of paramount importance for translators, along with expertise in select areas. Since communication is the very foundation of design, you can learn a lot from it to become a better – and more successful – translator.

Alongside the benefits for the quality of your work, being savvier about design and more attentive to the appearance of your source material also helps to get a better idea about your client. Seemingly small details may reveal much about a company's culture, their preferences and priorities. Not only is being sensitive to your client's style beneficial for your translation; it makes you a more competent partner, with a better understanding of your client's communication needs.

Finally, being familiar with design will benefit your own communication. Translators may underestimate the significance of small details, yet clients notice them all the more readily. While any out-of-place detail may be costly in terms of the trust in your product, inconsistent and sloppy communication may jeopardise your credibility on the whole. When you use email to respond to a request for a quote, confirm an assignment or deliver your translation, you actually engage in communication with your client. This is where "packaging" is most at work.

9 Karjaluoto, *The Design Method*.

As much as I support the idea of signing one's translation, in most cases it is only the packaging that provides an ideal opportunity to mark your work and apply branding. Here again, knowledge of how communication design works can be of great help. The word "design" is a bit of a misnomer, if the first thing that comes to your mind is appearance rather than purpose and function. However, before developing a visual identity, a designer needs to make clear what the brand stands for.

Appearance is a derivative of a number of things. For a translator, visual identifiers lie not so much in the "creative" frills and extras that supposedly help to stand out from the crowd, as in a translator's deliverable itself. It is valid both for the "product" (translations and translation-related services) and for the "packaging" (communication with the client): the absolute key to visual brand identifiers of a translator is **consistency**. Whereas packaging may communicate the core values of your brand (you may or may not use a logo and a slogan – it matters less than is generally believed), the product itself should be a statement of your professionalism and personality.

Again, achieving consistency is one of the basic functions of design. A designer proceeds from chaos and randomness to order and control. The logic of design is to establish patterns, create building blocks, and structure the initial mess into a cohesive form. A well-executed design implies that nothing is left to chance and everything is purposeful.

Design works through rules and regularities. Of course, breaking rules to capture attention may create a powerful impact. However, for rules to be broken, they first need to be established. Consistency and paying attention to every little detail create the impression of order, whether it will be creatively disturbed or not. "Getting the little things right is what sets professionals apart from amateurs... Small things such as misspelled words and improper use of quotation marks instantly make you lose credibility." This advice from Garr Reynolds[10] is meant primarily for graphic designers who deal with visual language rather than with verbal language in a conventional sense. To paraphrase it for translators, misspelled words or punctuation errors can be replaced with typographic errors and inconsistencies as a result of thoughtlessness about how the translated material will eventually look like. If you care enough about getting through to your audience in a professional manner

10 Garr Reynolds. *Presentation Zen Design: Simple Design Principles and Techniques to Enhance Your Presentations* (New Riders, 2013).

as a translator, you should be just as meticulous and consistent about your graphics and typography as about your verbal content.

The second part of this book, "Working with words", deals mostly with the rules of typography and practical workflows to achieve consistency and a professional appearance in your work. The result of your work is a verbal product that you should be more in charge of and better able to make it speak compellingly for itself.

Most books on design are written to help designers visualise ideas. The idea of this book was to help translators make the quality of their verbal products more visible. Although it is not explicitly about marketing for translators, implementing the principles of communication design will enhance your visibility as a translator as well.

The third part, "Working with images", focuses on graphic design practices and techniques which can be used by translators. Considering that translated texts are only one element in the complex communication processes of our clients and that the source documents are becoming increasingly more visual as well as verbal, the need is growing for translators to be able to apply those skills to their work.

■ ■ ■

The purpose of this first part of the book was to show the interdependence of the visual and the verbal in today's communication, where the role of a translator is simultaneously that of a language expert, knowledge worker and outcomes facilitator. It was also an attempt to convince a typical "translator-not-a-graphic-designer" of the significance of design literacy in addition to specialist knowledge and verbal skills.

I am aware that some things are best left in the hands of professionals. As much as I am convinced that knowledge of visual communication will enrich your work as a translator and help improve your marketing efforts, I think your relationship with design may mostly be limited to **adaptive**, rather than creative design techniques. The focus of a translator's creativity remains in the verbal sphere. Most of the time, graphic design skills find use when adapting texts in a more complex, mixed-media type of documents or when dealing with texts as graphics. If you ever decide to engage in creative design, such as for your website, your business cards, letterheads and other stationery, it will be a good idea to start with exploring the relationship between the visual and the verbal. Finding a right image as a possible backdrop for your text may present an interesting creative opportunity and a memorable result.

It may be worthwhile to pay more attention than usual to how design elements are used, for example, in the communication of other companies, starting with but not limited to translation companies, individual translators and other freelancers. I refer to the practice of analysing what works and what doesn't as "reverse engineering".

Stock photography of friendly young people of different races ("our multicultural staff"), bridges ("connecting cultures") or an earth globe decorated with countless flags could be considered prominent examples from the translation industry's list of marketing don'ts. Instead of visual clichés, it might be more opportune to try to find a visual metaphor or counterpoint.

Communication design teaches how to distil the essence of a verbal message into visuals, how to make abstract concepts clearer and make messages stick. While the function of graphic design today is "to communicate efficiently and effectively utilizing words and pictures",[11] a translator, working backstage for their client, helps to make communication effective and efficient.

Basic knowledge of graphic design lies well within the grasp of anyone who professionally deals with corporate communications. The good news is, you don't need to be a graphic designer to use this knowledge. It just helps to learn to think like a designer and to apply your learning to your field of work.

11 Cited from: Tatjana Vukic. "Stefan Sagmeister creates with open perception". Osocio Academy, published 2 April 2012 <https://osocio.org/message/stefan-sagmeister-creates-with-open-perception/> accessed 12 December 2018. Stefan Sagmeister is one of the most prominent graphic designers today and co-founder of the design studio Sagmeister & Walsh.

2 Working with words

2.1 Rules of typography

After all the arguments made in the previous chapters, advocating the importance of typography would be like pushing at an open door or – hopefully – preaching to the converted. So let's get down to business and see what there is to learn about typography. The tough question is where to start.

Typography comes with a great deal of rules and recommendations, which may differ substantially depending on your specific language or your client's style guide. What is considered perfectly acceptable in the source text might violate certain conventions of the target language (think punctuation). IT companies are prone to invent funny lowercase acronyms, but, at the same time, capitalise each hardware or software feature when describing their products. The syntax of numbers and units varies depending on whether we translate a scientific publication or a financial report (number and unit with or without a space, unit following a number or vice versa etc.). A corporate style guide might let an infringement on generally accepted standards slip if it helps the company's publications to stand out and catch the fancy of the target group, but sometimes a style guide is created with only one language in mind and that spells trouble for translators.

The challenge of this chapter is to find some universally applicable concepts that will help a translator see the wood behind the trees. Instead of trying to memorise long and tedious lists of dos and don'ts, why not identify a few logical, practical principles of how to use typography to our (and our clients') benefit? If "typography is what the language looks like",[12] visual clarity and consistency should translate to distinction and quality of our language services, help effectively bring the message across and convince the client of the value we have delivered.

To focus on the most basic and logical concepts means, on the one hand, identifying general, language-neutral rules and constraints that are immune to subjective or historical irrationality. On the other hand, some of these conventions are definitely a matter of taste. Typography and graphic design are interrelated. Using or failing to use certain style elements is usually dictated

12 Lupton, *Thinking with Type*.

by a person's taste. It is the awareness of both the objective principles and "soft standards" of typography that marks the difference between a reckless copyist of the client's idiosyncrasies and a meticulous translator, mindful of every detail that may affect the overall result.

So where to start? The problem of style guides presented as lists of dos and don'ts is a certain lack of orderly structure and sequence. To produce a more cohesive guideline, it would be a good idea, once again, to disengage ourselves from the verbal content and have a closer look at the visual outcome that we generate. This may be a downright silly question, but has it ever occurred to you that, as a translator, you create 2D products? Whether you produce texts for print or screen use, you arrange easily recognisable graphic elements along two dimensions, vertically and horizontally. We will use this flatness as a starting point to laying out a set of rules (or recommendations) on the basis of three essentials: the **graphic elements** (typeface and character format), their **horizontal order** (syntax, words and sentences within paragraphs) and their **vertical structure** (series of paragraphs, page layout and pagination).

2.2 Setting type

With the rise of desktop publishing, the term "typeface" became somewhat outdated and the distinction between "typeface" and "font" inessential.[13] As translators, we are lucky not to have to care about choosing the "right" typefaces. If your working languages rely on the Latin script, you probably don't pay much thought to the typeface predetermined by the original document or the default setting in your software.

Choosing fonts is usually left to graphic design professionals. As translators, it will pay us to know the distinction between basic font types (like serif vs. sans serif) and have some general idea about standard font formats (TrueType, OpenType and PostScript). If you are engaged in multi-language projects, it may benefit you to know that the OpenType format, based on Unicode, can be read across different platforms and supports Eastern European, Greek and Cyrillic character sets in addition to the primary Latin set. The choice of typeface for a document is usually determined by convention, preference and taste.

The general guideline for **using fonts** boils down to "less is more". If two or more typefaces are used within one document, each one should have a distinct function, for instance, one typeface for body text, another one for headings. Using only one typeface and introducing variety by adjusting the font size is preferable to using any combination of different typefaces. However, if two or more typefaces are used, they should provide a clear contrast, the most typical example being a combination of a serif type with a sans serif type. Coexistence of two or more similar typefaces rarely makes sense.

What Joseph Sugarman wrote in his classic *Adweek Copywriting Handbook* over a decade ago, holds true today:

> The most important role a typeface has is to allow the greatest comprehension possible, and the second role, less important by far, is to convey the image of a company [...]. Fancy type might look elegant to the type

13 For the sake of simplicity, it is a good idea to think of typeface as the actual design of a set of characters, and of font as a physical carrier of the designer's creative work. Usually, each typeface is embodied in a family of fonts, different in size, weight, spacing and style (e.g. bold, italic, condensed).

designer, but if it can't be read it has no value. It's like talking to a foreigner and finding the words difficult to understand.[14]

A translator's minimum survival kit is similar to an absolute beginner's guide to choosing wine. Basically, we have two wine varieties (red and white) to go with regular dishes and all the rest for special occasions (rosé for summer picnics, champagne as an aperitif, dessert wine for, well, dessert time). Carrying the analogy over to typography, we are properly serviced with one of the two basic varieties of typefaces (serif and sans serif) for any regular texts and all the fancier and trickier rest for special, if any, occasions (calligraphic, handwritten, typewriter and other "design" fonts).

It is also worth knowing that serif fonts are considered to be easier to read in print (e.g. Bodoni, Garamond and Times), whereas sans serif fonts are supposed to make text more legible on screen (e.g. Helvetica, Futura, Arial and Calibri). The trend to go paperless – think before you ink! – is expected to continue. For those who are looking for more in-depth information, Ellen Lupton's *Type on Screen: A Critical Guide for Designers, Writers, Developers, & Students*[15] may be more practical than the probably most widely respected, classical treatise on typography by Robert Bringhurst.[16]

The next thing that we need to streamline our understanding of is **character formats**. In a typeface family, the standard upright font (also called Roman) is usually complemented with other varieties (such as bold and italics or, more rarely, semibold, lightface, thin and other versions). Multiplied by various other style attributes or effects (e.g. small caps or wide letter-spacing), this yields a multitude of combinations. It is exactly where the principle "less is more" is essential and should be generally applied. The golden rule is to avoid redundancies. There is no need to try to achieve the effect of emphasis by using several methods simultaneously. In other words, if you want to highlight key words or phrases in a sentence, it is not a good idea to use a combination of bold and italics. Either-or is almost always better than both-and. Think of bold and italics as mutually exclusive and try to limit the use of any special character format to a bare minimum – consistently, with a pre-defined purpose in mind.

14 Joseph Sugarman. *The Adweek Copywriting Handbook: The Ultimate Guide to Writing Powerful Advertising and Marketing Copy from One of America's Top Copywriters* (Wiley, 2006: p. 113).

15 Ellen Lupton. *Type on Screen: A Critical Guide for Designers, Writers, Developers, and Students* (Design Briefs, 2014).

16 Robert Bringhurst. *The Elements of Typographic Style: Version 4.0*, 20th Anniversary Edition (Hartley and Marks Publishers, 2013).

Italics are most widely used for emphasis in fiction and journalism. Among American writers, J.D. Salinger, for instance, is especially known for his sensitive use of italics to make written words sound with the same emphasis as if they were spoken. In professional, technical and scientific literature italics are mostly reserved for titles of books, films etc., for words from Latin and other languages, and for specialist uses in nomenclature and mathematical or statistical symbols. It is also common to italicise image captions, often in combination with a smaller font size.

Italics look better with a serif font. When using a sans serif, it is better to forego italics and use boldface instead. Boldface draws attention by contrasting lighter and heavier weights of the same typeface, and makes stand-alone words and expressions look darker than the surrounding text. It is appropriate for somewhat stronger emphasis than italics and especially to accentuate the structural elements of a complex text, such as headings. Ideally, boldface should be used for better readability and orientation: it helps the reader find relevant sections in a document consisting of several chapters and identify important keywords.

It is worth bearing in mind that underlining words to add emphasis is often considered a throwback to the typewriter era. Other formatting relics are expanded letter spacing (e.g. for headlines or emphasis[17]) and, as the ultimate holdover from a bygone era, double spacing between sentences (two spaces after a full stop). Much the same applies to capitalisation of whole words other than acronyms (compare using all caps in "netiquette", where it is considered equivalent to "rudeness and yelling").

A less intrusive way of marking emphasis in type is by using small caps (also known as petite caps). However, various guidelines for print publications reserve small caps for acronyms, especially those longer than three letters (thus, you can come across USA in all uppercase, but NATO in small caps in the same sentence). Typographically sophisticated programs such as QuarkXPress or InDesign can be set up to automatically convert acronyms to small caps. It is also usual to apply small caps for initialisms such as BC, AM/PM, a word or a few words at the beginning of a new chapter, or keyboard shortcuts in technical manuals ("use Control+Shift+K for italics"). If you cannot ensure that your client won't change the format of your translation, using small caps

17 The technical term for the distance from one character to the next throughout a whole sentence or paragraph is "tracking". The amount of space between two characters in a single word is called "kerning".

(as well as most other special character formats) is risky: when working on a Word document, for an acronym to be set in small caps, you have to apply the small caps effect to lowercase letters. As a result, after importing this document to another software environment or changing styles, your acronym will be rendered in lowercase and thus may get lost among all the regular, not-abbreviated words (it will stick out as a misspelled word, eventually).

Even such a seemingly small matter like the use of small caps may become a subject of much debate among editors and design professionals, if we consider the manifold aspects of using acronyms and abbreviations, for instance the plural form (Should the -s ending be a lowercase letter?), using small caps for headings or subheadings (If there is an acronym in the heading, should it be set in normal capital letters to avoid confusion, as an exception?) or at the beginning of a new sentence or paragraph (Should the first letter be uppercase?). As translators we don't have to make all these editorial and design decisions. However, we may need to apply them when working on our own products, be it emails, invoice templates, resumes, texts for our own websites and other marketing material.

In Microsoft Word (which is probably the text editor of choice for 99% of all translators), the small caps character attribute is hidden in the *Font* menu. Here, a few character styles are called "effects" and this is a very apt term. Like with all other effects, the general rule is to use them sparingly. If the purpose is emphasis, then the more frequently they are used, the less attention they are given, the weaker their effect. Therefore, don't overemphasise.

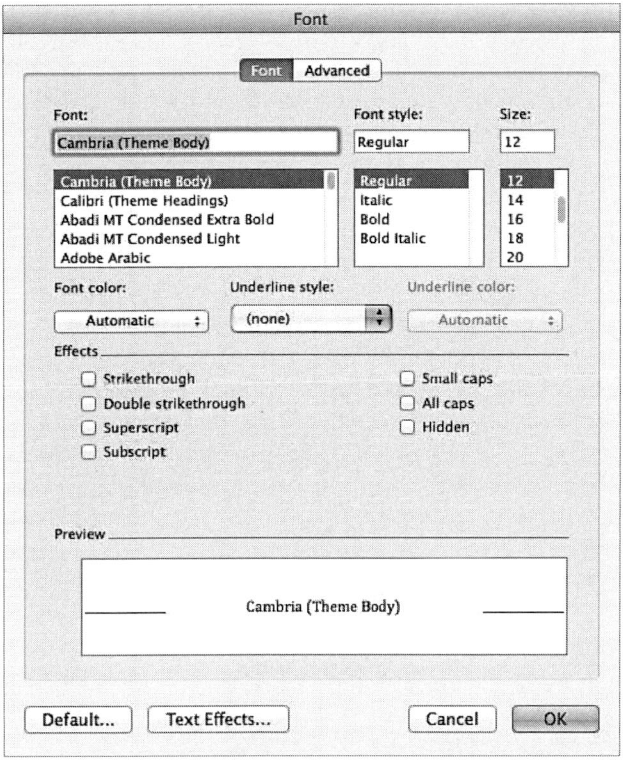

Let me stress again that, for the impression of well-designed content, a logical hierarchy of styles is crucial, as is rigorous consistency in using any style variations. This also improves usability of content, since a clearly recognisable structure of formal attributes enables better orientation. In the words of Alina Wheeler, "intelligent typography supports information hierarchy".[18] Practically speaking, when applying typographic styles, always try to consistently assign each style to a dedicated function, otherwise stick with the basic, neutral format.

Another subject in relation to typefaces and character formats is especially relevant for translators. Sometimes, our translations are used not on their own, but as part of bilingual or multilingual content, with various language versions running parallel or section-wise, one after another. This calls for using different fonts or character styles to set off different language versions with

18 Alina Wheeler. *Designing Brand Identity: An Essential Guide for the Whole Branding Team*, 3rd Edition (Wiley, 2009: p. 133).

a nice counterpoint, in particular when they are not juxtaposed in columns, but alternate continually within the running text. A possible solution could be a combination of a regular character style for the first language and italics for the second one (for the sake of symmetry, occasional italics in the first, regular typeface text could be rendered in Roman type in the second language). If the typeface family to be used comprises several varieties in terms of weight and width (e.g. black, medium, demi, condensed, light) along with the ubiquitous bold and italic fonts, it may be more elegant to combine the regular and the thin fonts, or use different colours or colour shading if appropriate.

I discovered a fittingly mundane example of a combination of two fonts from the same typeface family in a Berlin hotel, where all signage was bilingual, with German texts set consistently in bold type and English text in regular type. The example is minimalist (and in line with the minimalist design philosophy of the hotel, including the uncapitalised German pronoun "Sie"). However, the same principle works well with corporate brochures and many kinds of bilingual or trilingual marketing publications.

When talking about typefaces and fonts, we usually mean the visual design of characters that comprise a typeface. These characters are not only letters of an alphabet, but also include numerals, symbols, special signs and punctuation marks. Some of them in particular deserve a translator's attention.

It is a good practice to have at hand a list of Alt codes for special characters, that is symbols which are generated by holding down the ALT key (OPTION key on a Mac) and typing in a three-digit code with the numeric keys on your keyboard. The most common codes can be easily memorised. I personally tend to use ALT+124 for a vertical bar or ALT+0150 for an en-dash. In my experience, it is always better to insert a proper character instead of using a quick and dirty shortcut, as these can backfire. Finding the proper code for the plus-minus sign (±) may take a couple of seconds longer than entering the plus sign (+) with one stroke of the keyboard, selecting it and hitting the shortcut for underline. However, there is no guarantee that your mock symbol won't turn to a plain plus sign if a copy of your translation is pasted as unformatted text.

Similarly, some symbols can be easily confused. For example, the diameter symbol can be mistaken for the Scandinavian letter "Ø" (or vice versa) and you will find a surprising misprint after changing the type. Real-life mistakes like falling for email spoofing have been known to be caused by misidentification of alphanumeric symbols such as the uppercase letter O and the numeral 0, so it may be wise not to shrug off these examples as oddities or typographical hair-splitting.

The list of AutoCorrect symbols in Word will help you identify the typographic symbols which the software inserts as you type. Some of these substitutes can be very useful, others may strike you as less practical, but it is good to be aware of this function. For instance, each time you type three dots to intentionally leave something out, the program replaces them with an ellipsis symbol (...).

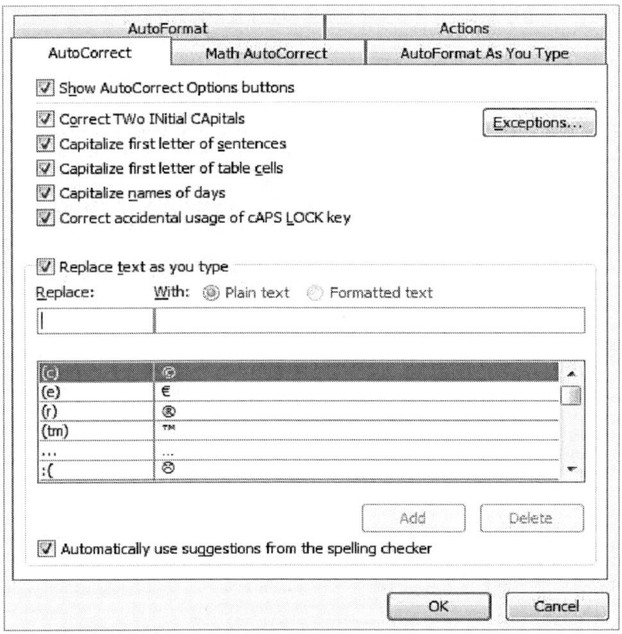

Proper symbols are definitely preferable over makeshift solutions, however common the latter may be. A good example are fractions. The most common ones, such as ½, ¼, have their own Alt codes and are represented with typographically smaller numerators and denominators. The same goes for superscripts and subscripts – think of the H2O or m3 that result from subscript and superscript formatting (using the regular 2 or 3 with the subscript or superscript effect) instead of selecting numerical characters such as ² and ³ which have their own codes.[19]

In my experience, translators make most frequent use of Alt codes for horizontal strokes (hyphens and dashes) and non-breaking spaces. The usage varies considerably, depending on the working language. As a rule of thumb, a **hyphen** (the shortest horizontal line) joins single words to produce compound words and has no space on either side. For cases other than hyphenation, a **dash** (a longer line) is used as a punctuation mark, to separate parts of a sentence. Dashes vary in width: the shorter, most common one is called an *en-dash*, since its width equals that of the uppercase letter N, and it has space on either side. The longer one is called an *em-dash* and, in traditional typesetting, had the same length as the letter M.

Today, an en-dash with spaces on both ends increasingly overtakes its longer counterpart. Rules of punctuation in general and rules for using hyphens and dashes in particular can be expected to become even more simplified in the future in any language, mainly due to the growth in electronic publications. In an anecdotal case, a British author reported that Amazon removed his professionally edited book from sales because it contained too many hyphens! I'm sure that the use of hyphens and dashes (hyphens are automatically converted into en-dashes by AutoCorrect when you type a space and a hyphen) is syntactically correct and typographically acceptable, provided it is consistent. Again, we cannot overestimate the importance of consistency for the visual appeal of our verbal products.

It is less essential and less known that spaces also come in various sizes. Most translators I know use the default shortcuts for non-breaking space (CTRL+SHIFT+SPACEBAR or ALT+0160), for instance to keep together digits and measurement units. A non-breaking space is sometimes called a whitespace character. I learned from graphic designers that some of them used to take any regular character and change its colour to that of the background, usually white, as a workaround in programs where no non-breaking spaces were

19 It might seem odd that superscript 2 (exponent 2, square, second power) is represented by ASCII code 253, whereas superscript 3 (exponent 3, cube, third power) has ASCII code 252. However, you won't probably have to use the Alt codes, at least in Word, since both superscripts have very convenient default keyboard shortcuts: CTRL+ALT+2 for ² and CTRL+ALT+3 for ³.

possible. However, a whitespace character is just a blank space punctuation mark for dividing words in text.

Besides the non-breaking space (character code U+00A0 in Unicode, an encoding standard invented to improve and extend ASCII), there is also thin space, used primarily as a separator in numbers greater than a thousand. In Word (depending on the version) thin space may be entered by clicking *Insert → Symbol*, opening the *Symbol* gallery and typing its character code: U+2009 (Unicode). There are spaces that are even thinner than U+2009, for instance U+200A (hair space), U+202F or U+FEFF (zero-width no-break space). You can also assign your own shortcut to the selected space by customising your shortcut buttons.

With horizontal strokes and non-breaking spaces, we have entered the field of punctuation. The idea of this chapter was to start with universally applicable, language-neutral typographic conventions. However, punctuation rules vary from language to language. Think of upside-down question marks and exclamation points at the beginning of a sentence in Spanish or the use of space before a punctuation mark such as a colon in French. The use of quotation marks also differs between languages and even within the varieties of the same language, such as double marks in American English and single marks (called "inverted commas") in British English. It gets more complicated when we consider combinations of different kinds of quotation marks, like those for direct speech, titles, expressing irony or rendering a quote (also "air quotes"). The Czech linguist and translator Daniel Šebesta looked at variations in punctuation across languages in an entertaining presentation delivered at the 2009 conference of the American Translators Association.[20]

Unfortunately, there is no one-size-fits-all recipe for dealing with punctuation. You have to study and apply specific rules for your working language, and we will look at those later, when we discuss how to integrate general principles of typography in a translator's workflow (see "Make typography rules work for you", p. 47). We will now explore the nonverbal conventions of the horizontal dimension, that is rules and recommendations for building sentences and paragraphs.

---

20 Daniel Šebesta. "Why punctuation needs translating: selected chapters in orthography and typography across languages". Presentation at the 50th Annual Conference of the American Translators Association (ATA), New York, 31 October 2009. For my Russian colleagues, I would like to recommend an excellent tutorial by Natalie Shahova, the translator of *Eats, Shoots and Leaves* by Lynne Truss and *Is That a Fish in Your Ear?* by David Bellos: N.G. Shahova. *Perevodim sluzhebnye znaki* [Translating punctuation] <http://www.rvalent.ru/Shaxova4_2007.pdf> accessed 21 August 2018.

2.3 There is no justification for (full) justification

As a holistic process, professional translation does not mean replacing words with words, one after another, but comprehending, interpreting and rendering a client's ideas with the verbal means of another language. As a translator, you recreate whole fragments of the source text in your working language, using different words and phrases, and building new syntactic structures such as sentences and paragraphs. While a sentence may be meaningless if taken out of context, a paragraph is a "distinct section of a piece of writing, usually dealing with a single theme and indicated by a new line, indentation, or numbering".[21] Or it should be, in any case.

Typographically, a paragraph is a fragment of text contained within two paragraph marks, also called pilcrows (¶). These are what you produce when pressing the Enter key in Word or other text processing programs. In practice, however, you may still come across texts where paragraph marks were used as substitutes for line breaks, to split a paragraph into lines neatly arranged on a page. In my experience, the nonprinting character for a line break is relatively little known and rarely used. Therefore, it is not that unusual that the text you are asked to translate turns out to have been written by someone with little appreciation of the difference between soft and hard returns[22] (line vs. paragraph breaks), or someone who simply doesn't trust the software to accomplish line wrapping[23] on its own.

Ironically, the more design-minded the author of the source document, the more likely it is that the document will contain too many inadvertently created paragraphs. This occurs even more often in such typographically sophisticated programs as InDesign or QuarkXPress, let alone PowerPoint, since pressing the Enter key, the spacebar or the tab key is a quick way to fix a formatting issue in the layout.

---

21 *Oxford Dictionary of English* (online) <https://en.oxforddictionaries.com/definition/paragraph> accessed 12 December 2018.

22 The Enter key once replaced the carriage return key of a typewriter, hence the term "return" is still used synonymously with a line break.

23 This feature is particularly beneficial for responsive design, with line length adapting automatically to the width of the viewing area (e.g. when browsing a website on a mobile device or changing the font size in an e-book reader).

If you copy content from a PDF file and paste it into a Word document, you will end up with a number of lines separated with paragraph returns. Technically, it is a series of paragraphs. You will have a hard time overwriting these fragments and joining them to produce a "distinct section of a piece of writing". Similarly, if you use a CAT tool for translation, you will have to deal with too many meaninglessly broken segments. Bear with me, as we will talk about preventing having to deal with a poorly formatted text during the translation process (p. 158). For the time being, let's just keep in mind that it is nonprinting characters, such as manual hard and soft breaks, that serve as paragraph delimiters. These are nonverbal and usually not visible elements that determine paragraph formatting and help shape the visual appearance of meaningfully organised content.

Whereas punctuation makes horizontal lines of words clearer and more understandable in a sentence, line breaks and paragraph returns control the vertical flow of the whole text. In this regard, they act similarly to punctuation, relating to larger "distinct sections of a piece of writing".

Besides carriage returns, paragraphs can be visually delimited by spacing. In today's casual writing and in many printed publications, spacing that separates one paragraph from another is often achieved by two paragraph returns, with the second pilcrow used to insert a blank line. Although text editors such as Word provide more refined methods to create a gap between paragraphs, these remain largely unused. The downside of using an empty line to divide paragraphs is having too much space between paragraphs after copying and pasting a document from Word into another program (e.g. an HTML editor such as Wordpress), where you will have to manually remove the excess blank lines.

Indiscriminately wide gaps between two consecutive paragraphs and, on the other hand, between a heading and the following paragraph of body text may indicate that the author doesn't give much thought to the logical appearance of the text. In a document intended for print it is simply an indication of poor design. It would be logical to expect a closer connection between a paragraph heading and text but, when poor design prevails, it bears on vertical spacing. This example from a Russian brochure is conspicuous with erratic, indiscriminately set gaps between headings and paragraphs:

Инвестиционный климат

Одним из безусловных привлекательных моментов для международного бизнеса является устойчивое финансовое положение Свердловской области.

В 2011 году журнал «Форбс» определил Свердловской области второе место среди наиболее инвестиционно-привлекательных регионов России, а в 2012 году Екатеринбург занял 6-е место в «тридцатке лучших городов для бизнеса-2012» по версии того же издания.

Кроме того, в очередной раз «Стэндарт энд Пурс» подтвердило установленный ранее позитивный кредитный рейтинг Свердловской области, присвоив ему оценку «Дабл Би Плюс» (прогноз изменения рейтингов – «Стабильный»).

Свердловская область располагает значительными инновационными ресурсами, которые могут быть использованы для производства новой высокотехнологичной продукции, конкурентоспособной на российском и мировом рынках.

Свердловская область в цифрах и фактах

На Среднем Урале добывается и производится 97% российского ванадия, 55% бокситов, 55% асбеста, 56,4% талька и стеатита, 12% каолина (белая глина), 10% меди, 10% железной руды

На Малышевском изумрудно-бериллиевом месторождении — крупнейшем в Европе, сосредоточено 86% запасов изумрудов России

Индустриальные парки

В настоящее время в Свердловской области реализуются три проекта по созданию индустриальных парков с государственным участием: индустриальный парк «Богословский», площадью в 110 гектаров, индустриальный парк «Новоуральский» — 256 гектаров и химический парк «Тагил» — 140 гектаров.

Выход резидентов на площадки индустриальных парков планируется в 2014–2015 годах. Кроме того, на территории Свердловской области создано 12 технопарков, резидентам которых предоставляются меры государственной поддержки, в том числе субсидии на возмещение затрат, связанных с производством и реализацией инновационной продукции на условиях 50/50.

Свердловская область в цифрах и фактах

Вклад Среднего Урала в суммарный валовой региональный продукт РФ – 2,8%.

Вклад Среднего Урала в объем отгруженной промышленной продукции РФ – 3,8%.

В Свердловской области производится 17% российских турбин, 37% буровых установок, 32% прокатного оборудования, 39% грузовых вагонов, 15% отопительных радиаторов, 27% стальных труб, 12% стали, 21% железной руды, 11% проката черных металлов, 10% чугуна, 5% электроэнергии.

Туризм

В 2013 году 8 регионов России в рамках межрегионального туристского форума «Большой Урал» заключили соглашение о продвижении туристических продуктов под единым брендом «Большой Урал» — это Свердловская, Тюменская, Челябинская, Курганская области, Республика Башкортостан, Пермский край, Ханты-Мансийский автономный округ – Югра и Ямало-Ненецкий автономный округ. Инициатором создания и объединения регионов под единым туристическим брендом выступила Свердловская область, которая является центром туризма на Урале.

A simple way to prevent this and to achieve intelligent typography, that is typography that "supports information hierarchy",[24] would be to use uniform

24 Wheeler, *Designing Brand Identity*: p. 133.

and consistent formats for any repetitive structural elements such as headings, running text and footnotes. If used consistently, even a minimalist set of paragraph attributes, such as those provided in Word, will do. Here, you can adjust spacing before and/or after paragraphs (usually in 6-point increments):

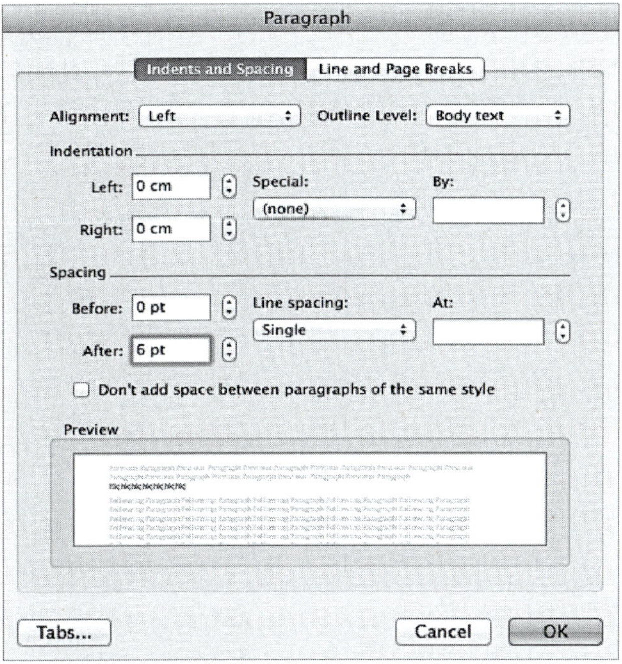

These options are helpful if you want to build a clear structure and highlight the logical relationships between "building blocks" of content, such as headings and running text, sentences to introduce a series of items and bulleted or numbered lists, images and captions etc. Consistent vertical punctuation and hence, intelligent typography, provide for more readable content.

Vertical punctuation is not limited to blank lines and spacing between paragraphs. A very traditional way to separate paragraphs is indentation. Whereas popularity of indents is clearly dependent on language-specific conventions and style guides, the general rule – avoid redundancies – holds true in all cases. First-line indents make spaces between paragraphs redundant. Therefore, a good typography rule is to **either** indent first lines **or** use extra space between paragraphs. Just as using both bold and italics means overemphasising on the horizontal level, combining indentation with extra paragraph spacing is vertical tautology.

In classic typography and professionally designed publications you will often find that the **first paragraph in a chapter** has a different format. It has been a century-long tradition to start a new chapter with a distinct first letter, often much taller than the surrounding text, set in decorative type, and extending upwards or downwards the main line of text. Whereas fancy ornamentation has all but disappeared,[25] the tradition to use **initials** to provide a visual cue, mostly as **drop caps**, lives on.

Drop caps are rarely used in Word (which was developed for composing office documents, not lay out books), although the *Drop Cap* options are still there:

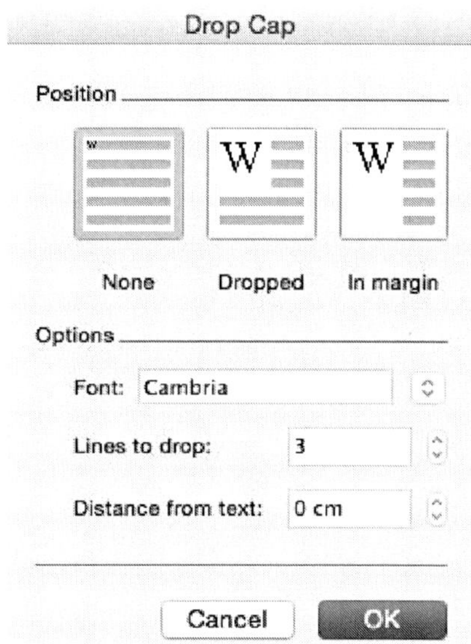

In InDesign, it is just as easy to create drop caps using the control panel. Here you can specify not only the number of lines for the character to sink (three lines in the example below), but also the number of characters to drop (this will be repeated each time the paragraph style with drop caps is applied):

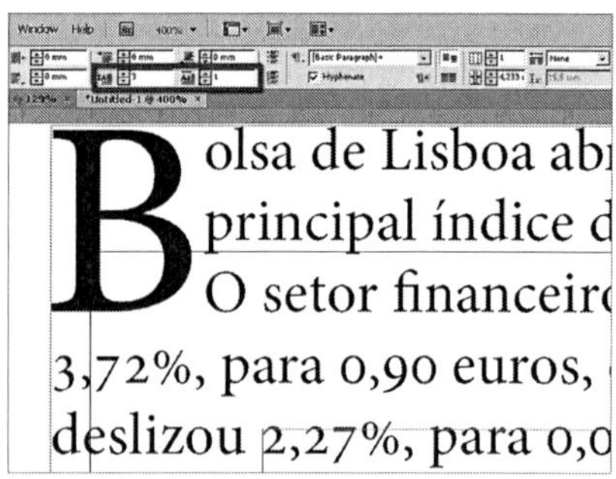

25 It has not gone away completely, as there are still books that are set in unusual, highly stylised type with ornamental words or letters, but it is no longer common practice.

InDesign allows you to create complex paragraph styles and automate their use, thus ensuring consistency. Besides drop caps, it is also common in professionally typeset publications to signal the beginning of a new section with a series of small caps. If these small caps follow the drop cap, they provide a smooth transition from the large first character to the lowercase running text, so that the first line does not look isolated. In InDesign, you can "nest" the small cap character style and set a number of words to apply this nested style to:

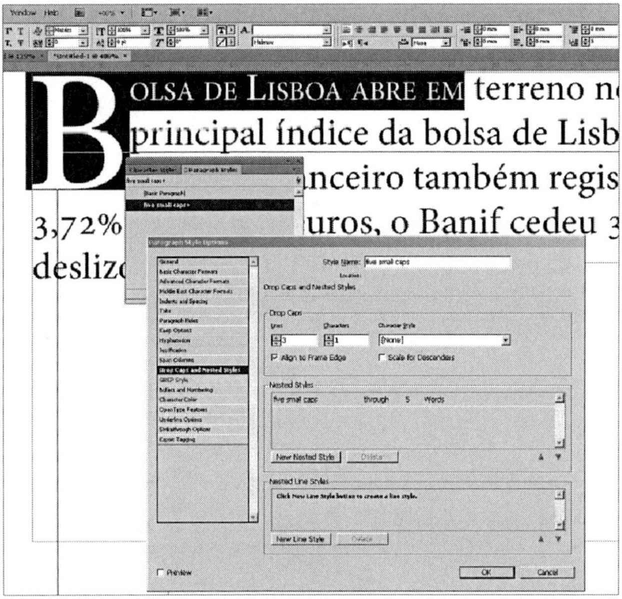

If all those options look overwhelming to you, they are only meant here as an illustration of the plethora of possibilities available to a typography-savvy professional. As a translator, you are not expected to create original design, but you are better off with some basic knowledge of how the original design was created and what purpose certain design elements have, in case your translation needs to be adapted to the original visual context.

You probably won't have to deal with elaborate typography on a routine basis, even when working for advertising agencies, but the idea of **setting off the first paragraph** is still useful, regardless of whether you ever use drop caps or complex nested styles. Professional typography is about discretion and avoiding redundancy that, among other things, means using each tool only in accordance with its purpose.

A very economical and elegant way of making the first paragraph stand out and accentuate the impression of page hierarchy is simply to forego indentation. It may be useful to remember that professional designers prefer **not to indent** the first paragraphs. This may be unusual in casual business writing, but press releases and legal documents acquire additional visual appeal through subtle and refined details that reveal a clear and coherent structure. The picture compares a more conservative, slightly old-fashioned layout with a centred heading as typical of "serious" print publications (left) and casual, business-type, non-indented paragraphs with a left-aligned heading (right):

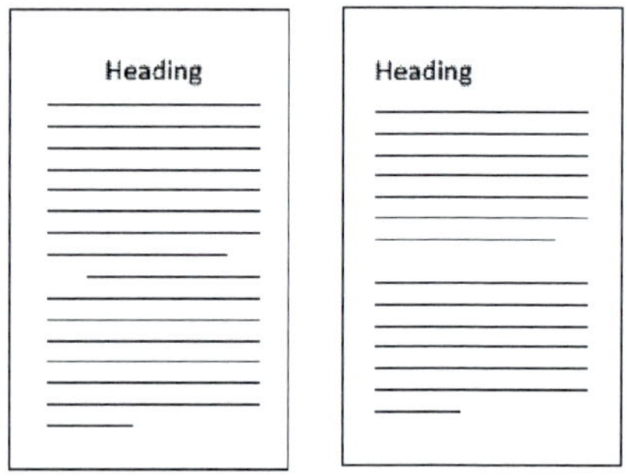

The practical takeaway is simple: don't indent the first paragraph after a heading or at the beginning of a section and don't use indentation when separating paragraphs with blank lines or extra space.

Among other visually effective means to break up the monotony of the text and divide up the paragraphs is indenting entire paragraphs (), using asterisks, dividing lines, borders, shading and frames. In technical manuals, it is also common to highlight safety-related chunks of text with signal words and alert symbols. The effectiveness of such salient warnings usually stands in inverse relation to their frequency. That is why ubiquitous "Warning", "Caution" or "Important" signs tend to be seen as nagging and sometimes nonsensical elements. As such, they get no more notice than other vertical punctuation devices, page numbers or blank lines. CAT tools seem to be predestined for translating user guides and owner's manuals, especially those designed and typeset in FrameMaker, where formalised templates enhance the repetitiveness of content. However, in order to draw attention to important messages and real hazards, less consistency could be an advantage:

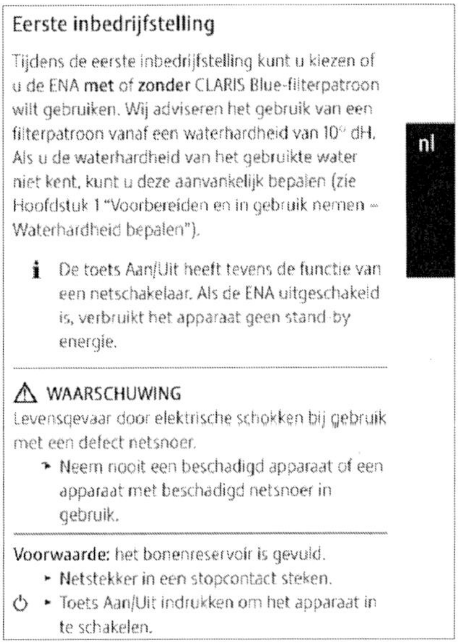
Eerste inbedrijfstelling

Tijdens de eerste inbedrijfstelling kunt u kiezen of u de ENA **met** of **zonder** CLARIS Blue-filterpatroon wilt gebruiken. Wij adviseren het gebruik van een filterpatroon vanaf een waterhardheid van 10° dH. Als u de waterhardheid van het gebruikte water niet kent, kunt u deze aanvankelijk bepalen (zie Hoofdstuk 1 "Voorbereiden en in gebruik nemen – Waterhardheid bepalen").

nl

i De toets Aan/Uit heeft tevens de functie van een netschakelaar. Als de ENA uitgeschakeld is, verbruikt het apparaat geen stand-by energie.

⚠ WAARSCHUWING

Levensgevaar door elektrische schokken bij gebruik met een defect netsnoer.

- Neem nooit een beschadigd apparaat of een apparaat met beschadigd netsnoer in gebruik.

Voorwaarde: het bonenreservoir is gevuld.

- Netstekker in een stopcontact steken.
- Toets Aan/Uit indrukken om het apparaat in te schakelen.

However far-fetched the term "vertical punctuation" may seem, punctuation means using spacing and signs to disrupt the flow of words and build sentences for the text to make more sense. Typographical devices such as blank lines or indentation also help to understand the content by joining sentences into separate blocks, one underneath another. Therefore, they serve a similar purpose. Other devices are used to add shape to these fragments. Since they are delimited by paragraph returns, I prefer to regard them as paragraphs regardless of their role in the layout of a page (e.g. title, subheading, tagline, running headers and footers, image captions).

The shape of a paragraph depends largely on three factors: leading, paragraph width (line length) and alignment. Sometimes, translation clients are particularly anxious that the number of pages of the translated document doesn't exceed that of the source text or that the translation fits exactly to the layout of the page. Their usual request is to make the font size smaller or reduce the line spacing to fit more lines on the page. From the viewpoint of typography, this well-intended advice is often misguided. The ideal relationship between font size, line height and line width is called a golden ratio. This relationship was adopted by software engineers, resulting in relevant default settings for text on screen. For this reason, default settings are almost always preferable to "quick and dirty" adjustments, when only one parameter such as line spacing is tweaked.

In typographic language, line spacing is called "leading". When type was set by hand, operators of printing presses used special strips cut from lead to provide for an adequate gap between rows of metal letters. Hence the pronunciation – /ledding/, not /leeding/. Adjusting the default leading helps to quickly fit the text into a narrow space. PowerPoint text boxes are particularly tempting in this regard. However, to produce a visually pleasing and orderly result, it is always a good practice to modify line spacing consistently. Little else makes the page look like it was poorly designed than inconsistent line spacing between paragraphs.

When dealing with PowerPoint flowcharts, you can easily minimise the effort needed to achieve uniform line spacing, if you hold down the SHIFT key as you select the text boxes, click the *Line Spacing* button and set the number to apply to text in all the selected frames. Whether or not it is worthwhile to go the extra mile depends on the quality of the source slide. Introducing consistent line spacing in the translation may be not worth the effort, if the whole slide (or an entire presentation) requires a major overhaul:

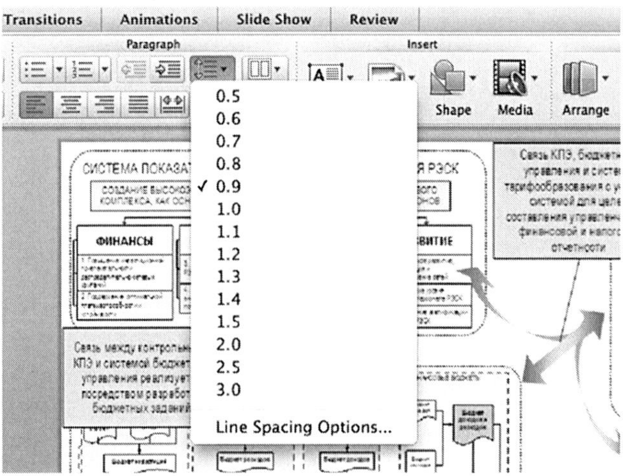

Paragraph width is also a factor that is best left as default or as set in the source text. Today, you can never be sure whether your text will reach its recipient on paper, on screen or on a mobile device. With fluid online layout and responsive design, line length ceased to be a static number. The general rule is that both too long and too short lines hamper the readability of the text.

In the 1950s, famous Swiss typographer and graphic designer Emil Ruder found that the "sweet spot" for line length lies somewhere between 50 and 60 characters. Paragraph widths in excess of 80 characters make it difficult for a reader to track back to the start of the new line. That is probably one of the reasons why the standard line of text in German-speaking countries is equal to 55 keystrokes. This "sweet spot" is supposedly also one of the reasons that most our documents still retain portrait page orientation, even if they are mostly viewed on screen in landscape mode.

Of the three factors that define the appearance of a typical plain vanilla paragraph, that is spacing, width and alignment, the last is the most revealing in terms of design literacy of its creator. Of the four text alignment options – left, centre, right and (full) justification – you are always best off with the first one, flush left. Centred text works best for short titles, headlines or for poems and songs. It is also common to centre texts in table cells, although text in the first column still looks better when left aligned. Centred text boxes are fine in PowerPoint presentations. It is good to know that both in Word table cells and in PowerPoint textboxes you can control vertical alignment of the text and complement the horizontal centre alignment with the vertical one (right-click the text box, choose *Format Text → Text Box* and set the option in the *Vertical Alignment* list). Centre alignment can also be applied to good effect in running headers and footers, for instance for document titles or page numbers. This has the advantage of removing the need to take care of alternating odd and even pages.

Similarly, flush right (in left-to-right languages) is best used for small amounts of information that is supposed to fall out of the flow of the running text and sit close to the right-side margin on a page or screen. Perhaps the most typical application is setting a date on a business letter. Using multiple left-side tab stops to shift short pieces of text to the right margin creates an unprofessional look and is likely to cause layout problems in translation, so it's best to use text alignment options to properly set the selected lines or paragraph.

Full justification is difficult to apply successfully and works best in narrow text columns. Aligning paragraphs along both the left- and right-hand side page margins, when done improperly, can produce so-called "rivers" and "islands", sudden unaccountable gaps in the flow of lines. They not only look visually displeasing, but also cause legibility issues and distract the reader's attention. The shorter the justified column, the more irregular the spacing between the characters and words can get. In my experience, form and content go hand in hand: sloppily formatted texts happen to be just as carelessly worded and formulated. The most awkward translations I ever came across also stemmed from sources with a preference for justified paragraphs:

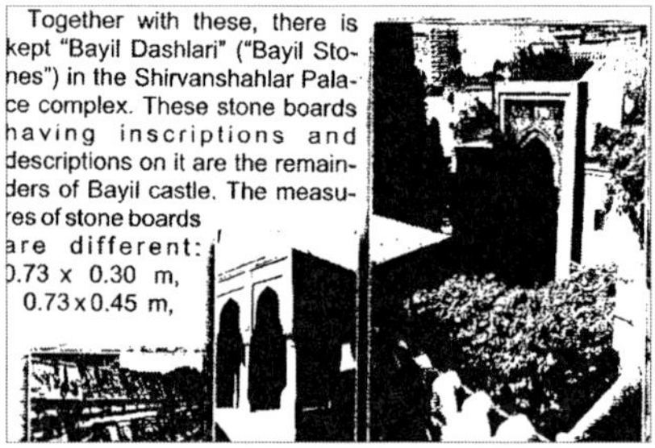
Together with these, there is kept "Bayil Dashlari" ("Bayil Stones") in the Shirvanshahlar Palace complex. These stone boards having inscriptions and descriptions on it are the remainders of Bayil castle. The measures of stone boards are different: 0.73 x 0.30 m, 0.73 x 0.45 m,

Shape and meaning are interdependent. Writing faults or stylistic shortcomings become ever more evident when choosing inappropriate formatting. In the era of responsive design and mobile devices, paragraph justification does a disservice both to the author and to the reader. The poor translation of a legal document below was first viewed by a client on her smartphone (being a speaker of German doesn't make it more readable):

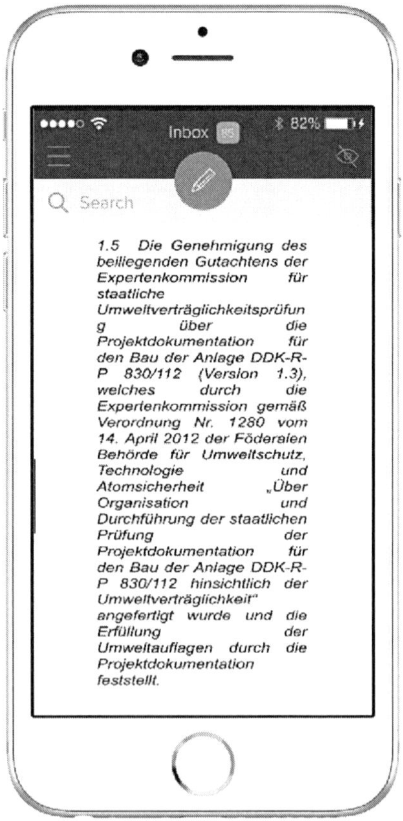

1.5 Die Genehmigung des beiliegenden Gutachtens der Expertenkommission für staatliche Umweltverträglichkeitsprüfung über die Projektdokumentation für den Bau der Anlage DDK-R-P 830/112 (Version 1.3), welches durch die Expertenkommission gemäß Verordnung Nr. 1280 vom 14. April 2012 der Föderalen Behörde für Umweltschutz, Technologie und Atomsicherheit „Über Organisation und Durchführung der staatlichen Prüfung der Projektdokumentation für den Bau der Anlage DDK-R-P 830/112 hinsichtlich der Umweltverträglichkeit" angefertigt wurde und die Erfüllung der Umweltauflagen durch die Projektdokumentation feststellt.

Of course, paragraph justification has its place in professionally designed publications. It remains the alignment of choice for printed books, newspapers, magazines, brochures, and many more. Justified text has a most formal, official feel. The problem of disturbing islands of white space and irregularly stretched words is usually fixed with hyphenation. However, if you deal with documents for internal use within your client's company, you are always better off choosing the left-side alignment instead of full justification. With electronic documents, you cannot predict whether your client's device will have the same hyphenation as yours. Therefore, any soft line breaks you have carefully set when working in your text editor are likely to be lost after your translation is imported into the client's software. In most cases, you don't know and cannot control how your translations will be displayed.

Even if you consider full justification to be more symmetrical, "orderly" and perhaps even "prettier" than the flush-left, ragged-right alignment, it is worth remembering that design is supposed to make text more useful and readable, not just "pretty". The danger of full-text justification is that it can make the text both less legible and less pleasing to the eye.

Enric Jardi, a Spanish graphic designer, said that "In a perfect world, all text should be unjustified and range left".[26] There is also a saying that "symmetry is the art of the poor". Whichever argument works best, if the only design lesson to be drawn from this book would be to "try to see your translation through the eyes of your client and avoid justifying everything", I'd consider my mission halfway accomplished.

Another issue that bodes ill for translators is incorrect use of tab stops or tabs, as they are universally called. It is only half as bad to use tabs to indent paragraphs (set the first line indent properly instead). But whenever multiple tabs, set by default at half-inch intervals, are employed to align text columns, sometimes together with multiple space characters, the translator is in trouble.

26 Freelance Web Designer. "Typography: common myths and mistakes" [blog]. Freelance Web Designer HK <https://www.flashdesigner.com.hk/blog/typography-common-myths-and-mistakes> accessed 21 August 2018.

A source document may look innocent enough, like this part of a technical inspection form:

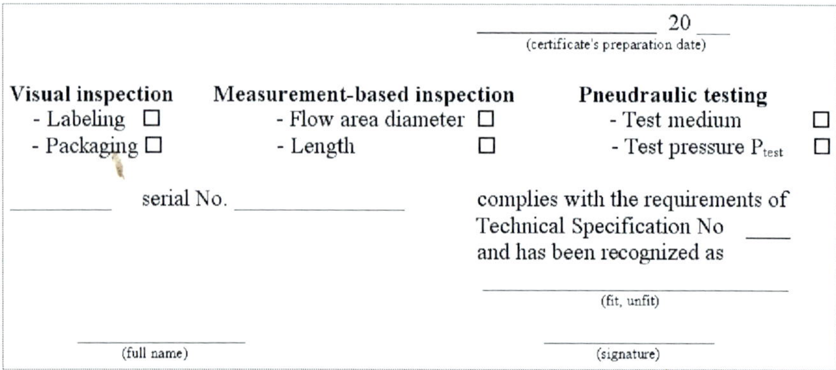

________________ 20___
(certificate's preparation date)

Visual inspection
- Labeling ☐
- Packaging ☐

Measurement-based inspection
- Flow area diameter ☐
- Length ☐

Pneudraulic testing
- Test medium ☐
- Test pressure P_{test} ☐

________ serial No. ______________ complies with the requirements of Technical Specification No ____ and has been recognized as

____
(fit, unfit)

________________ (full name)

________________ (signature)

But click on the *Show All Nonprinting Characters* button:

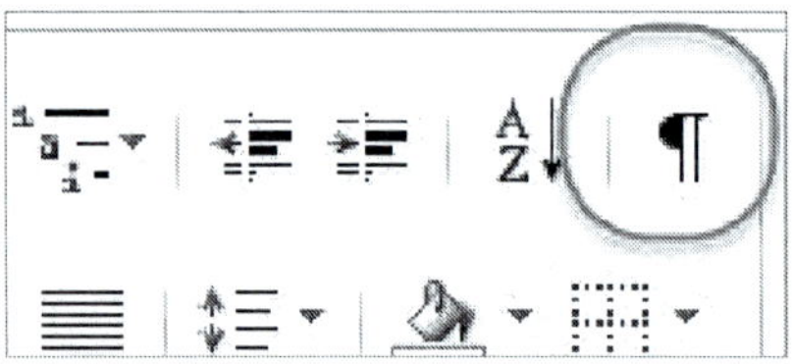

Now you will see the creative method behind this outcome:

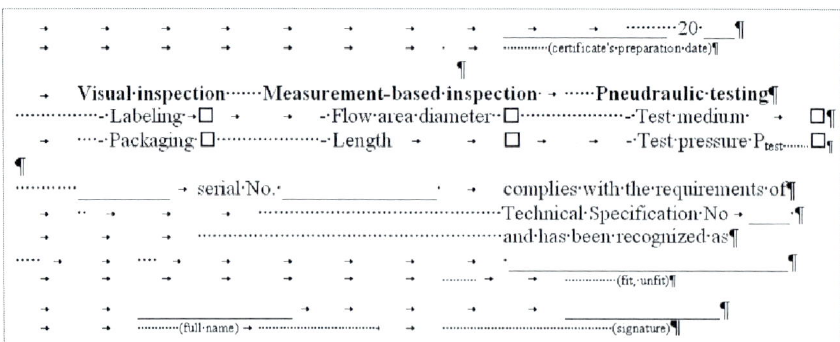

__________ ··········20·___¶
············(certificate's·preparation·date)¶
¶
Visual·inspection·······**Measurement-based·inspection**· ······**Pneudraulic·testing**¶
·················-·Labeling·☐ -·Flow·area·diameter··☐·····················-·Test·medium· ☐¶
·····-·Packaging·☐····················-·Length ☐ -·Test·pressure·P_{test}·······☐¶
¶
··········· __________ serial·No.·______________· complies·with·the·requirements·of¶
··Technical·Specification·No ____·¶
···and·has·been·recognized·as¶
····· ···· · ________________________¶
········ ···············(fit,·unfit)¶
________________ ________________¶
···········(full·name) ···························· ··(signature)¶

You cannot teach the author of this document the proper way to tackle tab stops. Neither is it much use to explain that your translation can be longer or shorter than the source, therefore it can wreck the source format. Before we get down to handling such troublesome source documents in the following chapters, here is a simple way to think about tabs. The word "tab", a short form of tabulator key of a typewriter, is cognate with "table" or "tabular". Typists used tabs to create columns of text or numbers. Today, this job can be done easier with **tables**. Tables protect your layout and keep the text structure intact, no matter how long or short the text will be when translated or edited. You don't have to create tables each time you want to shift a piece of information to a certain horizontal position. You can use tabs for that, but keep in mind that, if need be, you can easily preserve the column alignment in Word by converting your text to a table:

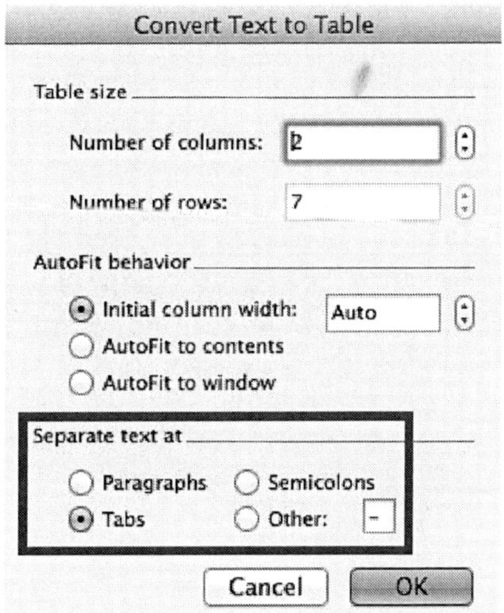

Separating text at tabs creates a table where each tab will mark a column. Converting the technical inspection form in the above example to a table would result in a mess with too many empty, superfluous columns. Therefore, whenever you use tabs to move a piece of text to the right, avoid redundancy and use only as many tabs as potential text columns. In practical terms, it means that before you press the tab button, you should first choose the points to set your tabs on the ruler above the page (if you need to make the ruler visible, go to the *View* menu and enable it from there). The default tabs are left-aligned. However, it is good to remember that for columns that will contain numbers, whether in a financial statement or a technical data sheet, right or decimal alignment may be more appropriate. Centre-aligned tables don't work well with numerals, because it is easier to compare numbers and identify relevant data if they are properly aligned. The "fit-for-purpose design" also contributes to the general impression of accuracy and, on the nonverbal level, instils more trust in your translation.

Whether you work on your own documents in Word or deal with layout constraints in the source document, it is generally a good idea to make more use of tables. You may have never heard of the rule of thirds or photographic composition, but the chances are the viewfinder of your camera or the display of your mobile phone is divided into areas with very fine fixed hairlines. It is something you can take a visual cue from when arranging your text on the page, especially if the document contains visible or imaginary columns (like in the example above).

Of course, you don't need frames or black solid borders around your table cells. In fact, it's best to think of your table as a set of guides positioned at regular or unequal intervals vertically and horizontally across the page. In graphic design, such a set of guides is called a "grid". The most typical application for grids is to define columns of text on a page, but the most important function is to provide consistency and lend structure in order to make content easily accessible and legible. The grid design helps readers to get their bearings on the page.

Now that we have covered both the horizontal and vertical dimensions of arranging text on a page, it's time to consider how knowledge of page layout can help a translator.

2.4 For more depth in translation

My earlier statement about translators dealing with 2D products cannot be seriously upheld. As soon as your text spans several pages, it acquires some literal or virtual depth. The third dimension stands for volume, both in the sense of virtual space and in the sense of a book or another type of printed work. If you think that the third dimension is not of much relevance to our products, try to imagine a world where leafing through pages has given place to scrolling on a screen (some may argue it could happen any time soon, but many of us would probably disagree). Though as translators we already spend far more time scrolling than leafing through pages, our work still preserves a certain depth, especially if we work on publications aimed for print. Despite all the paperless trends of our time, it is unlikely that discrete, clear-cut pages, on paper or screen, will be completely replaced by a digital equivalent of an ancient Egyptian roll. Most of the time, as soon as you open a new document, whether consciously or not, you define the borders of a new spatial unit. When stapled together, these units result in an orderly three-dimensional object, even if it numbers but a few pages. When you open a *New Blank Document* in Word, your first two dimensions are usually set by default, as the size of a page. The default settings direct that you start working on a document with all pages of a uniform layout and size. For print design, however, it is a **two-page spread**, rather than a single page, that is considered to be the main unit.

In Word, to get to the layout settings of the spread, you go through *Format* to *Document* to *Layout*. The picture in the preview changes from one page to a two-page spread when you select *Different odd and even* under *Headers and Footers*:

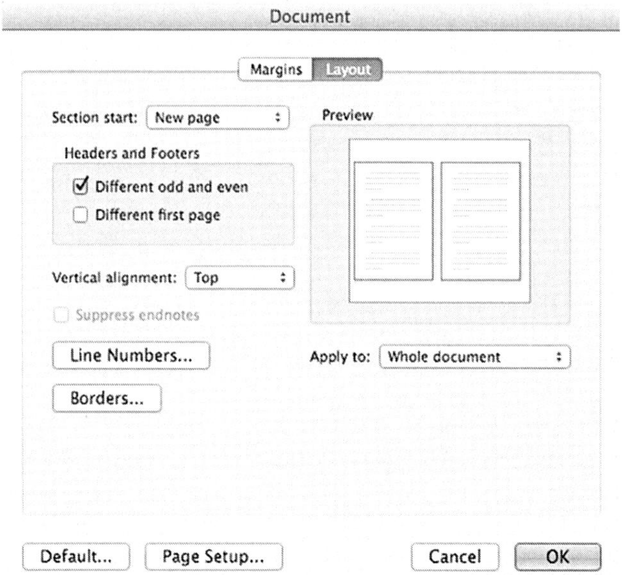

Another way to activate a two-page layout is to tick off the check box for *Mirror margins* in the menu tab *Margins*:

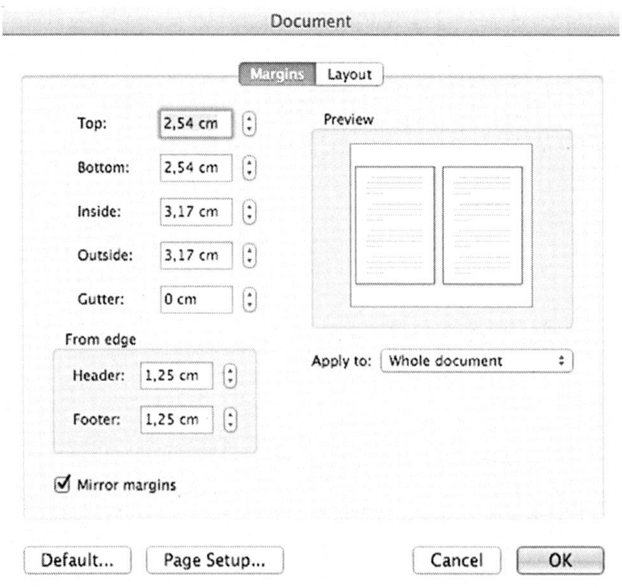

Microsoft Publisher and the newer versions of Word also provide the possibility to edit and create master pages.[27] Software originally created for desktop publishing (DTP), such as Adobe FrameMaker and InDesign, makes the handling of master pages even more comfortable. In FrameMaker you can give your publication a highly professional, consistent appearance with master pages and page layout options which, for instance, automatically make each new chapter start on the right page:

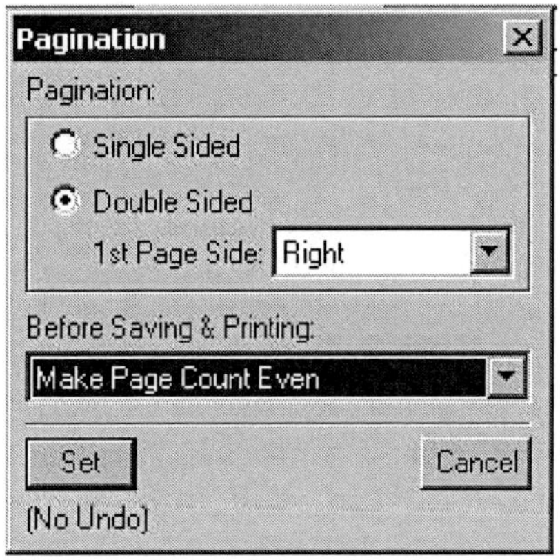

In InDesign, you can easily manage pages and spreads in a dedicated *Pages* panel:

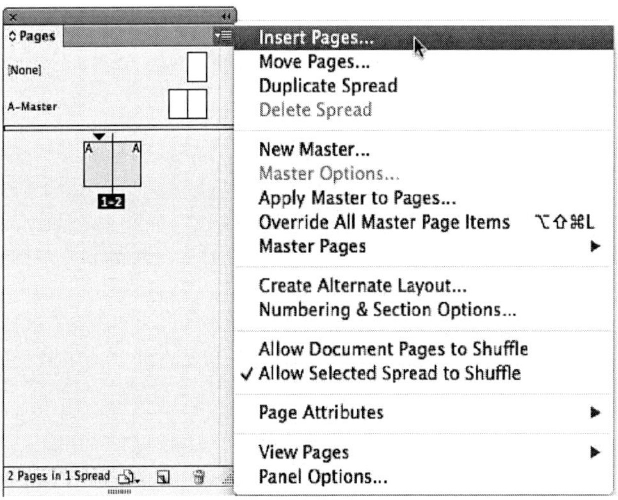

The question of how this applies to translators (who are not supposed to make changes in the layout provided by the client) is not as clear-cut as it appears.

27 If you work in PowerPoint, you will be familiar with managing slide masters, but the master page capability of Word is relatively unknown. To access this functionality, you need to activate the Publishing Layout in the View menu and click the Master Pages tab in the lower-right corner of the document window.

There are at least two reasons why page layout knowledge may be useful to a translator. Your customer's layout might be far from perfect. In extreme cases, it can be done in a rush, without respect for formatting, or ignorant of the effect that language changes are going to have on the whole document. This is often the case when working on documents extracted from PDF files. In many cases, it is not possible to produce a usable source for translation without adjustments to the original layout. This is the first reason why a layout-savvy translator is a useful asset for the client. There is added value in a translator who can transform a sloppy input into a clean, consistent, professional-looking copy that, as a bare-bones minimum, does not replicate the flaws of the original file. The second, more important reason is that even some basic layout knowledge can make the translation process easier for the translator if their source document has a messy, botched up layout. I'm writing this having completed a translation of a hundred-page Word document generated from a source PDF file by the client. There were pages with multiple section breaks, tabs, text frames and columns that violated the flow of text, running footers that moved to the top of the next page, since they had been set as formatted text, not as footers. The choice was to either stick to the original layout and try to clean up the mess after completing the translation, or adjust the layout proactively and make the translation a simple and smooth job.

So, what is the minimum that is worth knowing about layout?

Page size and orientation are usually set. They are mostly best left as they are, though there are instances when adjusting the size and orientation is more reasonable than having to deal with the idiosyncrasies of the source document. One such instance is when the page layout of the document to be translated leaves a lot to be desired. It doesn't happen often, but occasionally the page size and margins seem to have been chosen against all logic and reason. The layout of the source document is so arbitrary that printing on paper could be a problem, for example when margins are too narrow or the page size is defined by apparently random values. When the page settings are a result of negligence or accident on the part of the client, the preferred solution is to adjust the source document when preparing it for translation, rather than adjusting the layout of the translation. If there is no explanation for the page size of the source document, there might be no reason to leave it as is, as long as the effort boils down to replacing the accidental layout with a more fitting, functional and well-established pattern. A standard paper size with standard margins will remove any arbitrariness and make the translated document more usable. This may simply mean restoring the default settings: A4 (210 mm × 297 mm) or US Letter (8.50" × 11.00") for paper size and 2.54 cm

(1″) or 3.17 cm (1.25″) for margins. This alone will clean the file of all erratic elements that can negatively affect the workflow and the final result.

Design is about ordering disorder, to borrow the title of another design book,[28] and about making things more useful and functional. If making simple text changes can improve the translation process and help us to better communicate with the client, I see no reason to blindly reproduce the faults of the input in the translator's output.

Another case that calls for changing the page format is when the source document will be incorporated in the final result. Perhaps the most typical example is a bilingual document in which the source text is preserved in one of two or more parallel columns. I believe that bilingual documents are easier for a reader to take in when they are set in **landscape format**. This is to do with line length, which should ideally be set at 50 to 60 characters. Dividing a portrait-oriented page into two columns leaves room for short lines only, which might be uncomfortable to read, whereas the landscape format improves the width of a paragraph in a single column. Similarly, if the text invites comments (such as a draft), landscape orientation with wide margins may be preferable to a portrait orientation. British artist Richard Jolley has drawn a funny, minimalist cartoon with two buildings, one high, the other low and squat. The sign on the tall building reads "National portrait gallery", the sign on the other one – "National landscape gallery". Should we ever want to build a gallery collection of our translations from all the paperwork that we process on a daily basis, we could probably put enough material together to fill several "portrait" galleries, but our "landscape" gallery would stay nearly empty.

Even though in the overwhelming majority of cases page layout remains beyond the control and focus of the translator, these examples help raise awareness of the importance of presentation. A translator can achieve a noticeable improvement over the source document, the raw material for the translation, with very limited means. At the same time, she can showcase the value of her work.

After size and orientation, the next important element that defines page layout are margins. Much of how printed content is perceived depends on the white space that surrounds the printed area. Generally, it is good practice to not shy away from empty space and refrain from cramming too much on a page. Designers often argue the case of giving the text "more room to

28 Khoi Vinh. *Ordering Disorder: Grid Principles for Web Design* (New Riders, 2010).

breathe". Wide margins tend to elevate the significance of the printed word and make reading more comfortable and pleasant.

If you ever thought about signing your translations but wondered how to incorporate your imprint in a translated document, it might be a good idea to make the design of the margins a starting point for creating a brand template. Whitespace margins alone can build a frame that provides a branded look, a certain visual identity that makes your translations more recognisable, even if you are not explicitly identified as the author (we will return to this question in the chapter "What I think about when I think about signing", p. 141). Extra wide margins cause the text block to appear more prominent. The left- and right-side margins do not necessarily have to be equal[29] – asymmetry can be visually more interesting, provided it is not so subtle that it looks inadvertent. To prevent the impression of a layout error, it is recommended to emphasise, perhaps even exaggerate, the asymmetrical look and make margins unambiguously unequal. Besides setting different left and right margins (different at least by 1"), it is also a good idea to enlarge the white space at the bottom of the page (enlarging the space at the top may cause the text to look sagging).

It is certainly not that I encourage presenting your translations as if they were poetry, with a verse or two on an otherwise empty page (or deliver translations in a format different from that of the source document). Whenever a translator decides not to stick to the layout of the original, it should be a voluntary decision that has some tangible benefits for the resulting document, for the client or the client's audience and, finally, for the translator's work process. Having said that, it is worth reiterating than becoming aware of the possibilities of framing the translation is in itself beneficial for the translator. Don't dismiss presentation, it is something that can add value to your product and let your work stand out above competition. Other aspects of presentation or packaging (the four Ps) will be continued in the chapter on signing (p. 141). There we will go into more detail about developing a brand template as a backdrop for your translations. In the meantime, let us consider a few other elements that are important to the layout of a multi-page document.

29 Typographers use the term "gutter" when they refer both to the gaps between columns and to the inside margins in the middle of a two-page spread. These extra-large margins are provided for the binding of books and magazines. Though the left and right margins have different widths on a single page, the spread remains symmetrical, with the gutter margins set on the outside of the left page (called "verso" in traditional typography) and the inside of the right page (called "recto").

Headers and footers form the interface between whitespace margins and the content on the page. They keep documents organised and provide the reader with visual cues to help orientation. On the one hand, these titbits of information are clearly verbal and meaningful, and on the other hand, they serve as a frame for the text and images in the main area on the page. In Word, headers and footers belong to page margins: as per default settings, the distance from the edge to the first line is smaller than the page margins:

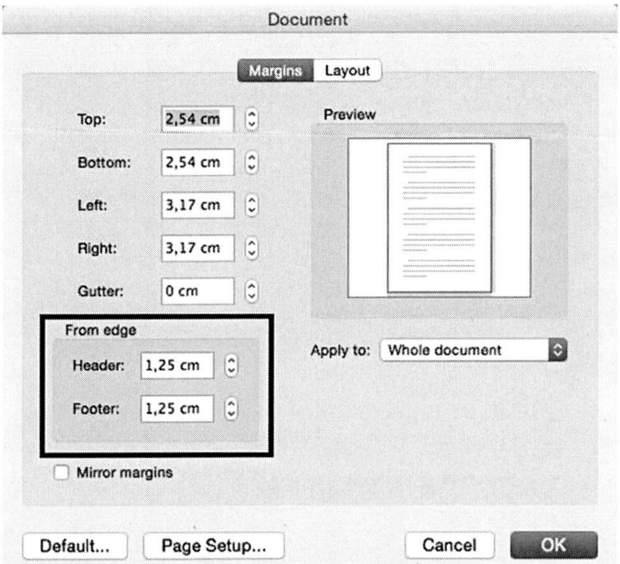

A multi-line header and footer would shift the top margin downwards and the bottom margin upwards, respectively.[30]

Running headers and footers contain typical document identifiers such as page number, date, version or file name and path. Conveniently, the software offers variables that will update this "meta information" automatically. Whereas it is fairly easy to insert the most typical data about the document in the headers and footers using the *Page Numbers* or *Autotext* functions, there are also some more advanced and less known techniques that are particularly useful for working on large documents.

30 In contrast to footers, footnotes belong to the main area of the page, since footnotes are placed above white space margins (you can also place footnotes at the end of a section, if you choose *Beneath Text instead of Bottom of Page as Location* in the *Footnote* and *Endnote* menu).

For instance, if your document consists of chapters, it would help your readers navigate it (and would produce a more professional look) to have chapter titles instead of the document title given on each page. To insert the chapter title in the header, you should first select the actual title in your text (it is probably the heading in the first line of the current document section) and apply the most appropriate style from the styles gallery, e.g. *Heading 1*:

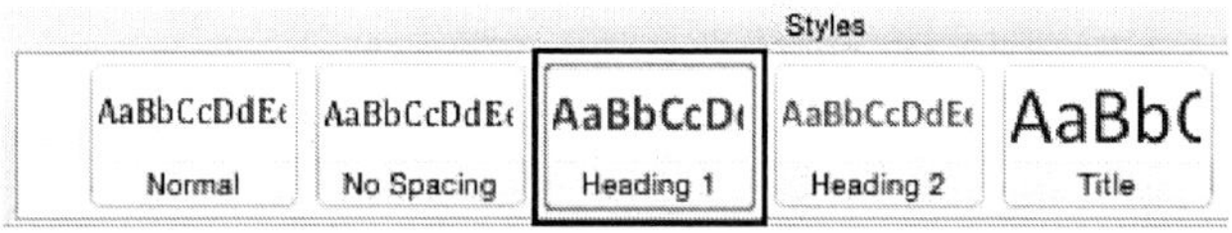

Now place the cursor in the header area and open the *Insert* menu. Click on the *Field* function and identify *StyleRef* among *Field Names* (the menu might look different depending on your Word version):

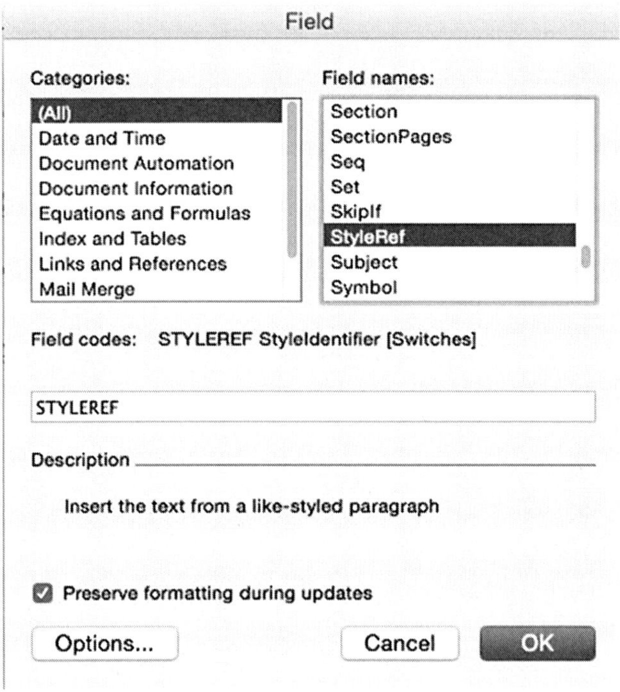

Click on *Options* and open the *Styles* tab. Then, from the list of available styles you can choose *Heading 1* and, with a click on the *Add to Field* button, assign it to the *StyleRef* field:

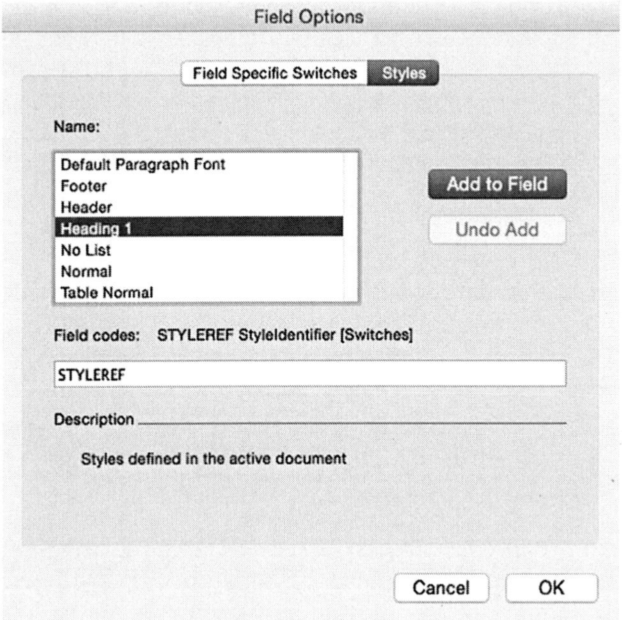

The chapter title will appear at the cursor point in the header area.

There is a simpler way to display chapter titles in headers on a page. You can place the cursor wherever you want the chapter title to appear and press CTRL+F9. In the grey area between the curly { } brackets, type *Styleref "Heading 1"* (or simply *Styleref 1*) and press F9 to update the display.

Whereas automatic functions are quite convenient, a typography-savvy translator should keep in mind that conventional rules aim at breaking the automatism. For a truly professional look, it is recommended to omit running headers on chapter and section opening pages, in the prelims, and on pages that contain only illustrations and tables, but no text. The same exceptions apply to blank pages: no running headers or footers, no page numbers. Traditionally, only the left-hand side page of a two-facing spread can be blank, with chapter openings always on the right side of a spread. Right-hand pages are always odd-numbered, usually starting with 3. Nowadays, though, I observe a trend towards simplification. Classical rules that demand an interruption of the software's automatism are increasingly being disregarded. Making no differentiation for front pages is a conspicuous example of this trend. Almost every PowerPoint presentation that I get to translate seems to have no numbering exception for the first slide, however untoward it may appear in terms of traditional design.

The same applies to Word, the most common software used for office paperwork. Ever more often, companies use Word to lay out complex, multi-page documents – technical manuals, operator's guides, training handbooks, bulky contract documents. Facing pages disappear. But even if you stay with Word and never use any DTP software (QuarkXPress, FrameMaker or InDesign), producing a properly designed, publication-grade document actually does not require that much effort. All it takes can be described in this straightforward procedure:

1. Go to the *Header and footer* menu. Find the options for *Different First Page* and *Different Odd & Even Pages*. If you select both checkboxes, you will have a *First Page Header/Footer*, an *Even Page Header/Footer*, and an *Odd Page Header/Footer*. If you check only the *Different First Page* option, you'll end up with a *First Page Header/Footer* and a *Running Header/Footer* for the second and subsequent pages.
2. Unlink the headers and footers that you want to be different by turning off the *Same As Previous* setting in each section.
3. Use section breaks (*Page Layout* → *Breaks*) for new sections, i.e. each time one of the subsequent pages should have a different header or footer. Word provides four different types of section breaks and the newer versions also contain clear explanations for each:

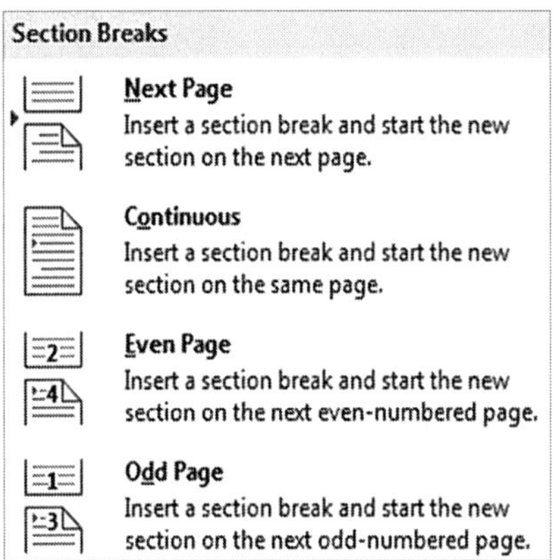

Using *Even Page* or *Odd Page* means that Word may automatically insert a blank page, for instance for a new section to start on the right-hand side of a spread.

As a translator, I often deal with clients' documents that could easily be improved in terms of layout. Sometimes, a client goes to great lengths to apply proper formatting: a document of more than 100 pages may have several chapters, numbered tables, a table of contents and dedicated styles for headings or captions. The document is obviously meant for print – a user's manual for a product, a complex contract with multiple appendices as separate chapters. Yet even such carefully formatted documents will often have headers and footers with the document title and page numbers always on the right side of the page. It may be tempting (and require only a little effort) to make page numbers alternate between the left- and right-side pages. However, such adjustments require a second thought.

If the document is not going to be printed as duplex (double-sided, front and back), it is no help to find page numbers missing on the right side of half the pages. An alternative could be to centre page numbers, which would result in a clean, symmetrical look, whether on paper or on screen, such as when scrolling through a PDF in two-page view. Another alternative would be to deliver two variants for the client to compare and choose from. There is no one-size-fits-all approach and each case should be considered independently.

As always, anything you do depends on the type of document, its purpose, whether it's appropriate to introduce modifications in general, and so on. Most colleagues would probably argue that they don't feel at liberty to introduce any changes to the layout – the client's instructions were to translate and they may not be confident using a design tool. But my argument is that "strict adherence to instructions is the most subtle form of sabotage", as a very demanding client once told me. A little effort goes a long way. In many cases, it is the small details that matter most.

There is a certain minimum of layout adjustments that I consider mandatory. Whenever I come across purported headers and footers – for instance, when document title or page numbers are not set in the header or footer area, but are repeatedly copied-and-pasted within the body text throughout the document – I think it is a must to replace them with actual headers and footers and delete the dummy ones. This will guarantee a clean, uniform layout, as the author of the document had probably intended. I would eliminate page numbers on title pages, too, provided the lead position of these pages is beyond doubt. Then, all elements that were supposed to look the same, such as headlines, subheads, captions, boxes or notes, may be standardised. The best way to do that is to use styles instead of character or paragraph formatting. In Word, style formatting is an extremely useful tool to ensure consistency and utilise automation. Paradoxically, it is also a tool rarely used, along with *Paste Special* (for copying text that should automatically adapt to the format of the target environment) or *Format Painter* or *Paintbrush* (for applying the original format to the pasted content). Other minimum style adjustments are related to page break control. Instead of beginning a new page by of a series of line breaks, you would be better served with a proper page break.

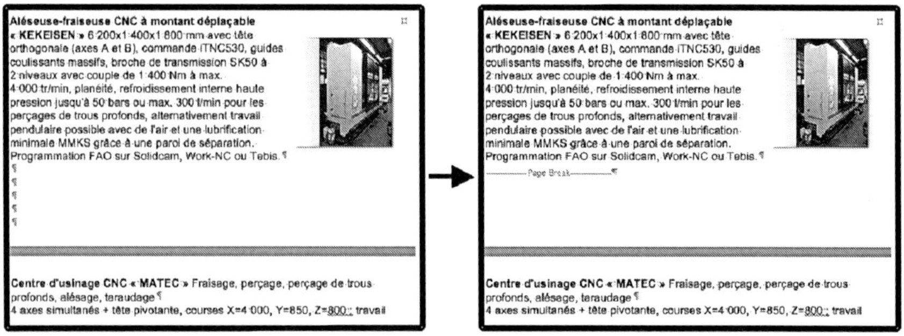

The length of your translated text will inevitably differ from that of the source document. Text overflows may create ill-placed page breaks, unforeseen empty spaces or unintentional blank pages. Setting and adjusting manual page breaks when preparing the source text for translation (like in the picture above) might be a good option, but it cannot prevent one of the most conspicuous signs (or is it sins?) of poor pagination: **widows and orphans**.

Widows and orphans are single lines appearing at the bottom and top of a page. They are either the first line of a paragraph at the bottom of a page that is then continued on the following page or the top-of-the-page, odd, one-line remains from the last paragraph of the previous page. There is no consensus which is which, but usually the first line is called a widow and the last line an orphan.[31]

An even uglier specimen of the same species is a page break between the subtitle and the body text. The next image is an illustration of such a breach on the left side, whereas the bottom of the right page is a typical example of a widow line:

31 Whereas in Russian both are usually called висячая строка ("hanging line"), the German language uses more expressive terms: a widow is a Schusterjunge ("cobbler's boy") and an orphan is a Hurenkind ("son of a whore").

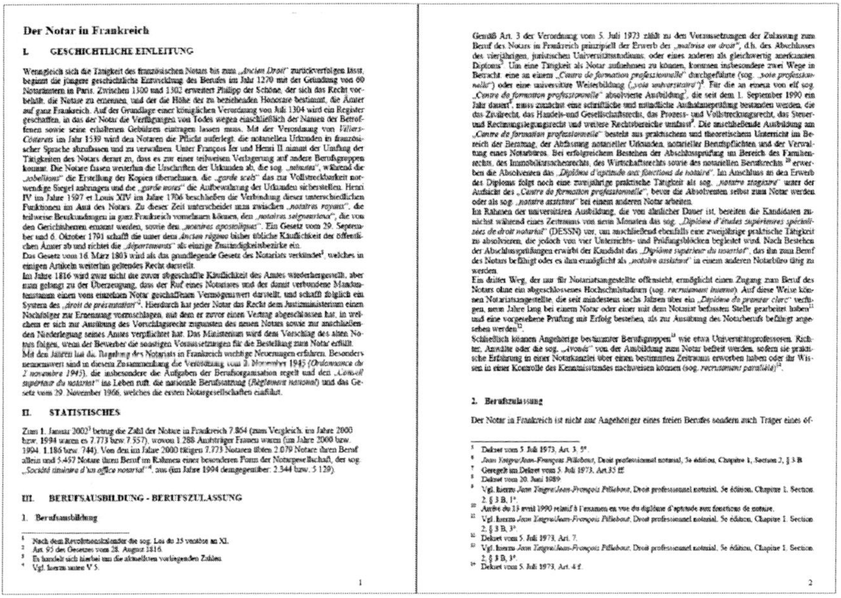

Der Notar in Frankreich

I. GESCHICHTLICHE EINLEITUNG

Wenngleich sich die Tätigkeit des französischen Notars bis zum „Ancien Droit" zurückverfolgen lässt, beginnt die jüngere geschichtliche Entwicklung des Berufes im Jahr 1270 mit der Gründung von 60 Notarämtern in Paris. Zwischen 1300 und 1302 erweitert Philipp der Schöne, der sich das Recht vorbehält, die Notare zu ernennen, und der die Höhe der zu beziehenden Honorare bestimmt, die Ämter auf ganz Frankreich. Auf der Grundlage einer königlichen Verordnung von Juli 1304 wird ein Register geschaffen, in das der Notar die Verfügungen von Todes wegen einschließlich der Namen der Betroffenen sowie seine erhaltenen Gebühren eintragen lassen muss. Mit der Verordnung von *Villers-Côtterets* im Jahr 1539 wird den Notaren die Pflicht auferlegt, die notariellen Urkunden in französischer Sprache abzufassen und zu verwahren. Unter François Ier und Henri II nimmt der Umfang der Tätigkeiten des Notars derart zu, dass es zur einer teilweisen Verlagerung auf andere Berufsgruppen kommt. Die Notare fassen weiterhin die Urschriften der Urkunden ab, die sog. „*minutes*", während die „*tabellions*" die Erstellung der Kopien übernehmen, die „*garde scels*" das zur Vollstreckbarkeit notwendige Siegel anbringen und die „*garde notes*" die Aufbewahrung der Urkunden sicherstellen. Henri IV im Jahre 1597 et Louis XIV im Jahre 1706 beschließen die Verbindung dieser unterschiedlichen Funktionen im Amt des Notars. Zu dieser Zeit unterscheidet man zwischen „*notaires royaux*", die teilweise Beurkundungen in ganz Frankreich vornehmen können, den „*notaires seigneuriaux*", die von den Gerichtsherren ernannt werden, sowie den „*notaires apostoliques*". Ein Gesetz vom 29. September und 6. Oktober 1791 schafft die unter dem *Ancien régime* bisher übliche Käuflichkeit der öffentlichen Ämter ab und richtet die „*départements*" als einzige Zuständigkeitsbezirke ein.
Das Gesetz vom 16. März 1803 wird als das grundlegende Gesetz des Notariats verkündet[1], welches in einigen Artikeln weiterhin geltendes Recht darstellt.
Im Jahre 1816 wird zwar nicht die zuvor abgeschaffte Käuflichkeit des Amtes wiederhergestellt, aber man gelangt zu der Überzeugung, dass der Ruf eines Notariates und der damit verbundene Mandantenstamm einen vom einzelnen Notar geschaffenen Vermögenswert darstellt, und schafft folglich ein System des „*droit de présentation*"[2]. Hierdurch hat jeder Notar das Recht dem Justizministerium einen Nachfolger zur Ernennung vorzuschlagen, mit dem er zuvor einen Vertrag abgeschlossen hat, in welchem er sich zur Ausübung des Vorschlagsrecht zugunsten des neuen Notars sowie zur anschließenden Niederlegung seines Amtes verpflichtet hat. Das Ministerium wird dem Vorschlag des alten Notars folgen, wenn der Bewerber die sonstigen Voraussetzungen für die Bestellung zum Notar erfüllt.
Mit den Jahren hat die Regelung des Notariats in Frankreich wichtige Neuerungen erfahren. Besonders nennenswert sind in diesem Zusammenhang die Verordnung vom 2. November 1945 (*Ordonnance du 2 novembre 1945*), die insbesondere die Aufgaben der Berufsorganisation regelt und den „*Conseil supérieur du notariat*" ins Leben ruft, die nationale Berufssatzung (*Règlement national*) und das Gesetz vom 29. November 1966, welches die ersten Notargesellschaften einführt.

II. STATISTISCHES

Zum 1. Januar 2002[3] betrug die Zahl der Notare in Frankreich 7.864 (zum Vergleich: im Jahre 2000 bzw. 1994 waren es 7.773 bzw. 7.557), wovon 1.288 Amtsträger Frauen waren (im Jahre 2000 bzw. 1994: 1.186 bzw. 744). Von den im Jahre 2000 tätigen 7.773 Notaren übten 2.079 Notare ihren Beruf allein und 5.457 Notare ihren Beruf im Rahmen einer besonderen Form der Notargesellschaft, der sog. „*Société titulaire d'un office notarial*"[4], aus (im Jahre 1994 demgegenüber: 2.344 bzw. 5.129).

III. BERUFSAUSBILDUNG - BERUFSZULASSUNG

1. Berufsausbildung

[1] Nach dem Revolutionskalender die sog. Loi du 25 ventôse an XI.
[2] Art. 95 des Gesetzes vom 28. August 1816.
[3] Es handelt sich hierbei um die aktuellsten vorliegenden Zahlen.
[4] Vgl. hierzu unten V 5.

1

Gemäß Art. 3 der Verordnung vom 5. Juli 1973 zählt zu den Voraussetzungen der Zulassung zum Beruf des Notars in Frankreich prinzipiell der Erwerb der „*maîtrise en droit*", d.h. des Abschlusses des vierjährigen, juristischen Universitätsstudiums, oder eines anderen als gleichwertig anerkannten Diploms[5]. Um eine Tätigkeit als Notar aufnehmen zu können, kommen insbesondere zwei Wege in Betracht: eine an einem „*Centre de formation professionnelle*" durchgeführte (sog. „*voie professionnelle*") oder eine universitäre Weiterbildung („*voie universitaire*")[6]. Für die an einem von elf sog. „*Centre de formation professionnelle*" absolvierte Ausbildung[7], die seit dem 1. September 1990 ein Jahr dauert[8], muss zunächst eine schriftliche und mündliche Aufnahmeprüfung bestanden werden, die das Zivilrecht, das Handels-und Gesellschaftsrecht, das Prozess- und Vollstreckungsrecht, das Steuer- und Rechnungslegungsrecht und weitere Rechtsbereiche umfasst[9]. Die anschließende Ausbildung am „*Centre de formation professionnelle*" besteht aus praktischem und theoretischem Unterricht im Bereich der Beratung, der Abfassung notarieller Urkunden, notarieller Berufspflichten und der Verwaltung eines Notarbüros. Bei erfolgreichem Bestehen der Abschlussprüfung im Bereich des Familienrechts, des Immobiliarsachenrechts, des Wirtschaftsrechts sowie des notariellen Berufsrechts [10] erwerben die Absolventen das „*Diplôme d'aptitude aux fonctions de notaire*". Im Anschluss an den Erwerb des Diploms folgt noch eine zweijährige praktische Tätigkeit als sog. „*notaire stagiaire*" unter der Aufsicht des „*Centre de formation professionnelle*", bevor die Absolventen selbst zum Notar werden oder als sog. „*notaire assistant*" bei einem anderen Notar arbeiten.
Im Rahmen der universitären Ausbildung, die von ähnlicher Dauer ist, bereiten die Kandidaten zunächst während eines Zeitraums von neun Monaten das sog. „*Diplôme d'études supérieures spécialisées de droit notarial*" (DESSN) vor, um anschließend ebenfalls eine zweijährige praktische Tätigkeit zu absolvieren, die jedoch von vier Unterrichts- und Prüfungsblöcken begleitet wird. Nach Bestehen der Abschlussprüfungen erwirbt der Kandidat das „*Diplôme supérieur du notariat*", das ihn zum Beruf des Notars befähigt oder es ihm ermöglicht als „*notaire assistant*" in einem anderen Notarbüro tätig zu werden.
Ein dritter Weg, der nur für Notariatsangestellte offensteht, ermöglicht einen Zugang zum Beruf des Notars ohne ein abgeschlossenes Hochschulstudium (sog. *recrutement interne*). Auf diese Weise können Notariatsangestellte, die seit mindestens sechs Jahren über ein „*Diplôme de premier clerc*" verfügen, neun Jahre lang bei einem Notar oder einer mit dem Notariat befassten Stelle gearbeitet haben[11] und eine vorgesehene Prüfung mit Erfolg bestehen, als zur Ausübung des Notarberufs befähigt angesehen werden[12].
Schließlich können Angehörige bestimmter Berufsgruppen[13] wie etwa Universitätsprofessoren, Richter, Anwälte oder die sog. „*Avoués*" von der Ausbildung zum Notar befreit werden, sofern sie praktische Erfahrung in einer Notarkanzlei über einen bestimmten Zeitraum erworben haben oder ihr Wissen in einer Kontrolle des Kenntnisstandes nachweisen können (sog. *recrutement parallèle*)[14].

2. Berufszulassung

Der Notar in Frankreich ist nicht nur Angehöriger eines freien Berufes sondern auch Träger eines öf-

[5] Dekret vom 5. Juli 1973, Art. 3, 5°.
[6] *Jean Yaigre/Jean-François Pillebout*, Droit professionnel notarial, 5e édition, Chapitre 1, Section 2, § 3 B.
[7] Geregelt im Dekret vom 5. Juli 1973, Art.35 ff.
[8] Dekret vom 20. Juni 1989.
[9] Vgl. hierzu *Jean Yaigre/Jean-François Pillebout*, Droit professionnel notarial, 5e édition, Chapitre 1, Section 2, § 3 B, 1°.
[10] Arrêté du 13 avril 1990 relatif à l'examen en vue du diplôme d'aptitude aux fonctions de notaire.
[11] Vgl. hierzu *Jean Yaigre/Jean-François Pillebout*, Droit professionnel notarial, 5e édition, Chapitre 1, Section 2, § 3 B, 3°.
[12] Dekret vom 5. Juli 1973, Art. 7.
[13] Vgl. hierzu *Jean Yaigre/Jean-François Pillebout*, Droit professionnel notarial, 5e édition, Chapitre 1, Section 2, § 3 B, 3°.
[14] Dekret vom 5. Juli 1973, Art. 4 f.

2

The best way to control pagination in Word is by using the *Line and Page Breaks* options in the *Paragraph* menu. Killing widows and orphans is a very economical and effective way of producing a typographically clean copy that will stay clean after changes such as adding or removing text and, of course, translating it. The four *Line and Page Breaks* options have similar, but also some different, slightly complementary, functions:

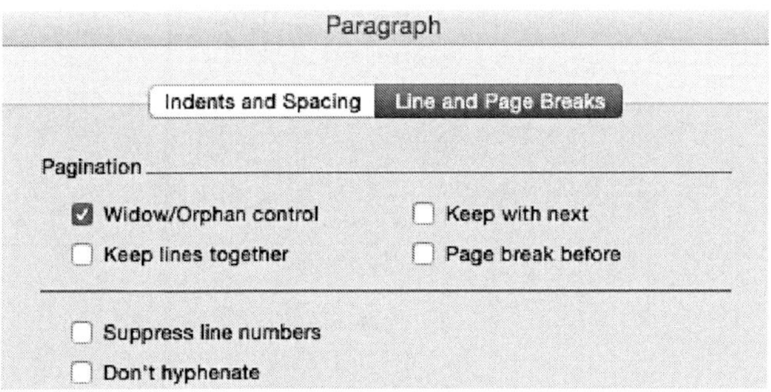

The purpose of *Widow/Orphan control* is to prevent single lines from appearing at the top or bottom of pages. *Keep lines together* is used to eliminate page breaks within a paragraph, so that the whole paragraph, if its lines don't fit in a column or on a page, will flow to the top of the next page. *Keep with next*

prevents a page break between the current paragraph and the next one (this option will keep headings together with the following body of text), whereas *Page break before* forces a new paragraph to start at the top of the page.

Whereas it is appropriate to have the checkbox *Widow/Orphan control* checked by default, the three other options won't work if applied indiscriminately throughout the whole document: you cannot keep all paragraphs on the same page and it makes little sense to have a page break before the start of each new paragraph, too.

InDesign has a few more options to tweak pagination. To define the way InDesign should handle page breaks, you need to display the *Paragraph* panel and reveal the hidden options:

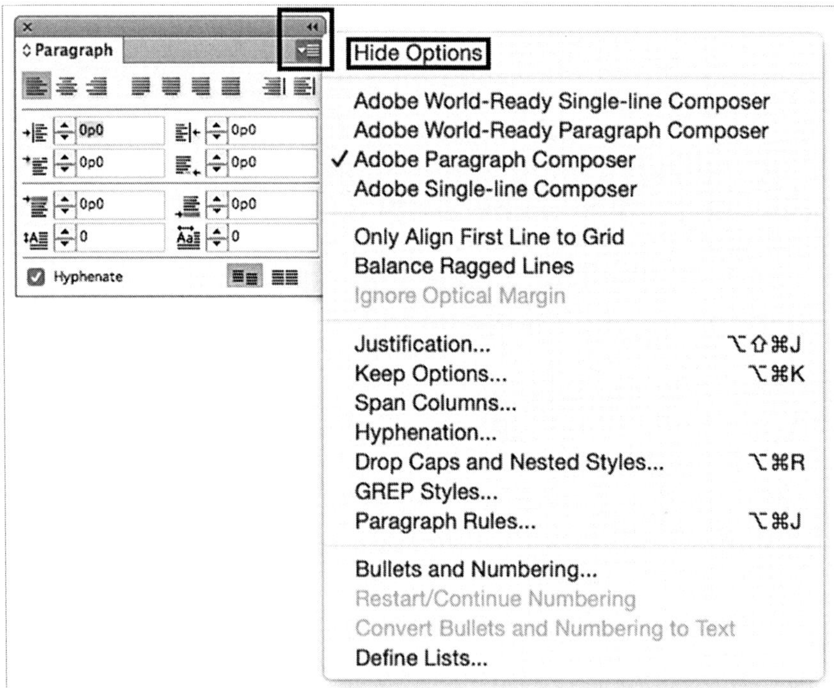

From here, you can choose your *Keep Options*:

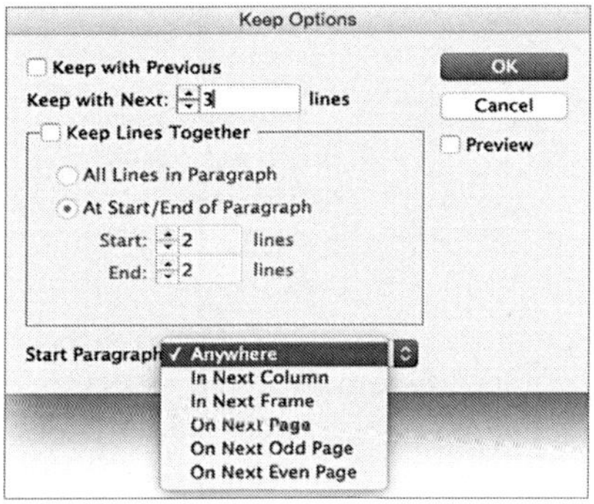

QuarkXPress has a similar feature called *Keep Lines Together*. The *Paragraph Attributes* palette conveniently groups together the most typically used options:

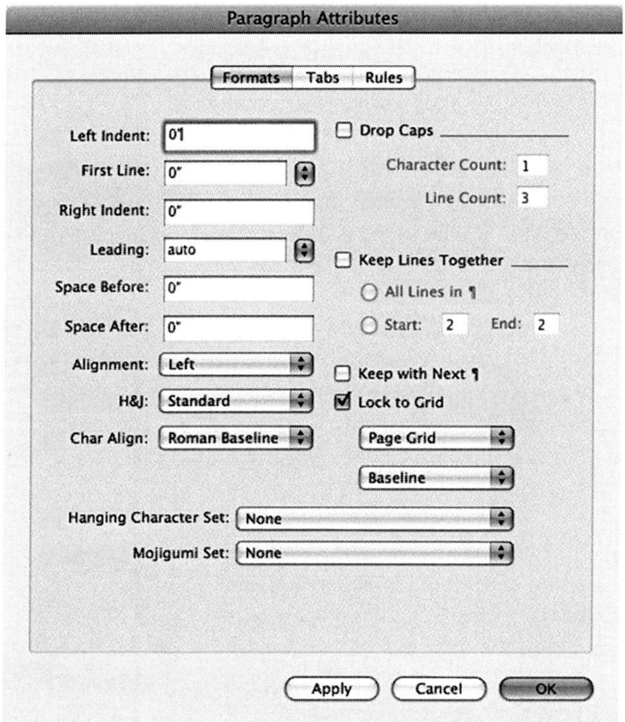

In comparison to these programs, Microsoft Word features are more limited, but they are sufficient for typical use. There are, however, a few less known aspects to controlling pagination in Word.

If a document is constructed as, or contains, a table covering several pages, inserting a manual page break will split the table into separate tables. This may damage the document structure – disrupting the numbering or causing the loss of header rows that were set to repeat at the top of each page. Therefore, to achieve a page break and keep the table whole, you should use the *Page Break Before* command *(Format → Paragraph → Line and Page Breaks → Page Break Before*) instead of inserting a manual page break (*Insert → Break → Page Break*). However, you cannot force a page break in a table cell consisting of several lines:

Obowiązujące zasady lokalne	Wymagana dokumentacja
• PSZ mogą zostać włączeni w świadczenie koniecznych usług konsultanckich (badania, udział w radach doradczych, szkoleniach i spotkaniach edukacyjnych), gdzie: Przedstawione na piśmie usługi zostały z wyprzedzeniem uwiarygodnione; • Opłata jest zgodna z realną wartością rynkową świadczonych usług; • Współpraca zostanie z wyprzedzeniem	Przed wykonaniem usług: • Umowa na świadczenie usług konsultanckich PSZ • Pismo dotyczące zakresu usług (jeżeli Umowa Ramowa zawierająca szczegółowe dane dotyczące poszczególnych usług nie została załączona) • Powiadomienie pracodawcy (jeżeli dotyczy)

In the illustration above, an attempt to insert a manual page break, for example before "• Współpraca zostanie z wyprzedzeniem" in the left column will tear apart the first and the second rows, so that the whole entire row will jump to the top of the next page. One way of stopping table rows from splitting across pages is to use the *Allow Row to Break Across Pages* option (*Table Properties → Row*), but this setting does not influence manual pagination from within cells, and the *Page break before* command won't work either. Adding multiple line breaks until the line will flow to the next page is not a sustainable option (changes in text length will cause shifts in pagination), but currently it seems to be the only workaround for managing page breaks inside Word table cells.

The *Keep with Next* feature is very useful to keep a picture on the same page together with its caption, which can sit above or below. First, select your figure together with the paragraph symbol behind it (or just the paragraph symbol alone) and the caption paragraph, and then go to *Format → Paragraph*. On the *Line and Page Breaks* tab, tick the checkbox next to *Keep with Next*, and that's it!

Picture¶

For a more professional approach, try using the *Caption* style for picture titles. Position your cursor where you want to place your picture title, click on *Insert* and choose *Caption* (in older versions of Word this feature may be called *Insert Caption* or found among *References* options: *Insert → References → (Insert) Caption*). Note that in the *Caption* style the *Keep with Next* option is not active, since it makes sense to have the checkbox unselected by default only if pictures are placed below captions, which is rarely the case.

Managing pagination is similar to managing punctuation. In the previous chapter I drew a parallel between punctuation on the horizontal level and those nonverbal measures that are used to help organise the vertical flow of the content. Both conventional and graphical, "vertical" punctuation serves to meaningfully structure verbal content and make the document clearer for the reader. In a figurative sense, page breaks, when used judiciously to keep what belongs together on the same page, form the third dimension of punctuation. Many professional, quality-oriented translators make smart use of non-breaking spaces, for instance to keep together units and values of measurement. Few give thought to smart paragraph composing and smart pagination, though the benefits – both for translators and their clients – outweigh the effort.

The last point I would like to mention with regard to complex, multi-page Word documents is using styles. Styles ensure homogenous formatting throughout the document. They help make a document look consistently structured, which improves its usability – the text is easier to read and looks visually more appealing. For those who prepare and translate complex documents, such as technical manuals or training materials, it is just as important that styles save our time.

The next chapter will present a typical example of the benefits of working with styles.

2.5 Design in practice: real-life lessons

If you're still at a loss of how the techniques shared so far can improve your translation business, the **case studies** in this chapter may be of interest. The two examples were actual translation jobs I worked on while writing the previous chapter. The first case shows the type of straightforward formatting that a translator may or may not introduce when translating a client's document. The second case picks up exactly where the previous chapter ended – benefiting from Word styles when working on complex technical documentation.

Case example 1. How to deal with Russian customs

My client is a big German company that orders materials from a Russian supplier.[32] The Russian Customs Authority asked both to confirm the delivery of recent shipments. The work I usually receive from the client comprises all kinds of documentation, starting from company brochures, advertorials and press releases, through technical manuals and specifications to short pieces of business correspondence. The letter from the Russian Customs started like this:

FEDERAL CUSTOMS SERVICE

FEDERAL
Customs Service

Уважаемый Генеральный директор!

В связи с расследованием дела № 123456789, возбужденного 01.01.2016 на основании приказа таможенной службы, прошу Вас предоставить копии документов, подтверждающих факт поставки, приема и оплаты продукции (коносаменты и платежные поручения), отправленной на следующих судах: «Лебедь-3» дата отгрузки 01.08.2015, «Щука-8» дата отгрузки 02.09.2015, «Йеллоу субмарин» дата отгрузки 03.10.2015, «Октопус Норд» дата отгрузки 04.11.2015, «Броненосец Потемкин» дата отгрузки 05.12.2015.

Также прошу сообщить, осуществлялись ли Вашей компанией поставки продукции, перечисленной в приложении № 001/002-003, заказчикам, перечисленным в приложении № 002/003-004, а именно:

There is nothing sophisticated in terms of verbal content. In fact, this is a rather trivial example of a translation job, where the addressee only needs to

32 All names, dates and business details have been changed and are fictional for illustration purposes only.

get the information, no frills attached. The client received the letter and the corresponding forms from the customs directly and I provided the German translation on the same day. However, the Russian supplier also had the letter translated into German by a translation agency in Russia, and emailed the translation to my client.

The translation (shown here in English for illustration purposes) read like this:

FEDERAL CUSTOMS SERVICE

FEDERAL
Customs Service

Dear General Director,

In connection with the investigation of case No. 123456789, which was initiated 01 January 2016 on the basis of an order from the customs service, I ask you to please provide copies of documents confirming the delivery, acceptance, and payment of the products (bills of lading and payment orders) that were shipped on the following vessels: Lebed-3, shipped on 01 August 2015; Shchuka-8, shipped on 02 September 2015; Yellow Submarine, shipped on 03 October 2015; Octopus Nord, shipped on 04 November 2015; and Battleship Potemkin, shipped on 05 December 2015.

Please also indicate whether your company delivered the products listed in Appendix No. 001/002-003 to the customers listed in Appendix No. 002/003-004, namely:

Considering the actual content of the document, you cannot expect much difference in various translations, provided the content is rendered accurately and completely in each one. My translated document differed in wording and sentence structure, but these differences were irrelevant. A more important difference was nonverbal. For the purpose of illustration, I won't change anything aside from formatting in the above translation to show this small difference. (The example is not only fictionalised, but also significantly shortened: the original letter comprised several pages, and the formatting shown below was applied consistently throughout the translation.)

FEDERAL CUSTOMS SERVICE

FEDERAL
Customs Service

Dear General Director,

In connection with the investigation of case No. 123456789, which was initiated 01 January 2016 on the basis of an order from the customs service, I ask you to please provide copies of documents confirming the delivery, acceptance, and payment of the products (bills of lading and payment orders) that were shipped on the following vessels:

- Lebed-3, shipped on 01 August 2015;
- Shchuka-8, shipped on 02 September 2015;
- Yellow Submarine, shipped on 03 October 2015;
- Octopus Nord, shipped on 04 November 2015;
- Battleship Potemkin, shipped on 05 December 2015.

Please also indicate whether your company delivered the products listed in Appendix No. 001/002-003 to the customers listed in Appendix No. 002/003-004, namely:

It is an easy guess that the client preferred this version to that of the translation agency. However small, the difference in formatting has made the document more usable. Most translators I know would probably have left the layout of the source document unchanged. This simple case brings into question the old rule that a translator should keep the formatting as is and never mind the style.

Case example 2. If it ain't broke, don't fix it?

The client is a medium-sized German manufacturer of pneumatic tools. The manual to translate was a rather voluminous Word file of more than 100 pages. I outsourced this rush job to a colleague, an English to Russian translator I have a long-standing relationship with, and took up the editing myself.

In my experience, the majority of clients are similar to translators in their attitude to document layout and formatting. Both can be rather particular and hard-judging about stuff they receive from each other, but they turn a blind eye on the shortcomings and irregularities in paperwork they themselves have created. Try as we might to encourage the client to proactively consider future localisation needs, most documents are still created without translation in mind. Moreover, direct clients from other industries are not necessarily much savvier in terms of layout, typography or even basic Word skills.

At first sight, the manual looked decently formatted, with chapter headings and subheadings. However, the way this neat appearance was achieved was not helpful for a translator. Here is a short excerpt from the table of contents that, if we take a closer look at the formatting marks used, was generated as though the author had used a typewriter – with spaces and dots, not tab stops and leaders:

```
5. Maintenance .................................................... 167

    5.1 General ................................................... 167
    5.2 Maintenance intervals ..................................... 169
    5.3 Dust bags ................................................. 171
    5.4 Filter cassettes .......................................... 174
```

After clicking on the *Show/Hide* ¶ button:

```
¶
5.·Maintenance·....................................................·167¶
¶
    5.1·General·...................................................·167¶
    5.2·Maintenance·intervals·.....................................·169¶
    5.3·Dust·bags·.................................................·171¶
    5.4·Filter·cassettes·..........................................·174¶
¶
```

I present this case here to add a how-to tutorial on using styles to create a table of contents. But what is perhaps more important is that this example is less about formatting and more about **choices** that a translator has to make when faced with a problematic source document.

The choice that my colleague had was to replace dots with dot leaders:[33]

```
¶
5.·Техническое·обслуживание·.....................→.....................·169¶
¶
    5.1→ Общие·положения·........................→.....................·169¶
    5.2→ График·техобслуживания·.................→......................171¶
    5.3→ Замена·пылесборных·мешков·..............→......................173¶
    5.4→ Замена·кассетных·фильтров·..............→.....................·177¶
```

33 "Dot leaders" is one of the formatting options in the *Tab* menu, particularly suitable for creating tables of contents:

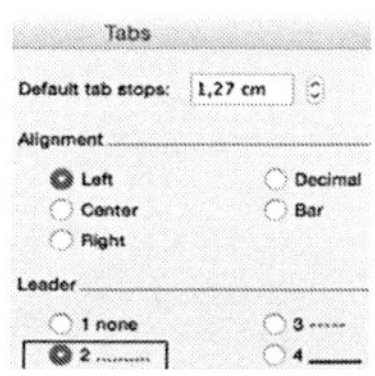

The choice to "leave it as it is" would have been obvious. And just as obviously, it wouldn't work: shorter or longer headings would disturb the alignment of page numbers. To leave the table of contents as it is, a translator has to at least add new dots or remove some that are redundant, in other words, make changes. The "correct" choice would be to use Word's inherent functions to generate a table of contents. To do so, you need to select the main headings one by one and assign each heading a style. Word's interface looks different depending on the version, but the *Style* menu is basically the same.

If you are largely unfamiliar with styles in Microsoft Word, first locate the style gallery with a selection of style choices. It will probably be a group of styles on the *Home* tab:

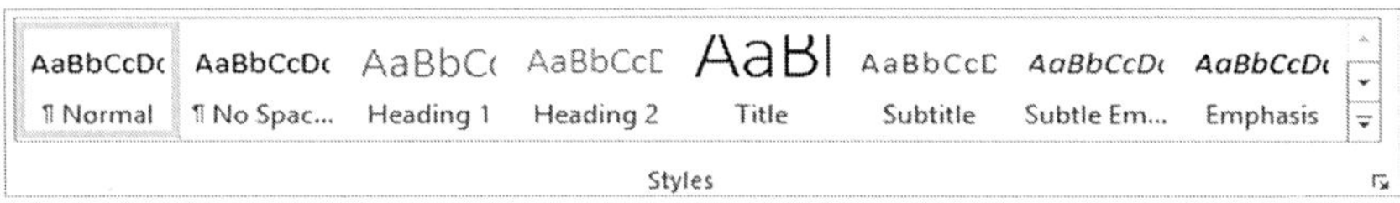

You can click the *Options* link in the lower-right corner to customise your *Quick Style* list, but to generate a table of contents, you will need to locate the in-built *Heading 1* and *Heading 2* styles among the available choices. These are styles to format your headings and subheadings. Going through the document, select headings and subheadings in the text[34] and assign the relevant styles. You can modify the set of attributes that comprise a specific style by choosing *Modify...* – select another font, change its size, colour, emphasis (bold or italics). You can also assign shortcut keys to styles, for instance Ctrl+Alt+1 for *Heading 1* and Ctrl+Alt+2 for *Heading 2*.

Once you have formatted your headings in this manner, you are ready to create a table of contents. Navigate to where you'd like it to appear, place the cursor at the top of the page and go to *Table of Contents* (depending on your version of Word, either in the *References* tab or by clicking *Insert → Index and Tables...*):

34 Since *Heading 1* is a paragraph style, you don't have to select the entire heading: it is enough to place the cursor somewhere on the line (in the paragraph) to apply the style and instantly reformat the whole paragraph of text. Besides paragraph styles, Word also has character styles as well as table and list styles. In the list of styles, they are identified with symbols – ¶ for paragraph styles and *u* for character styles. Paragraph styles are used more often than character styles.

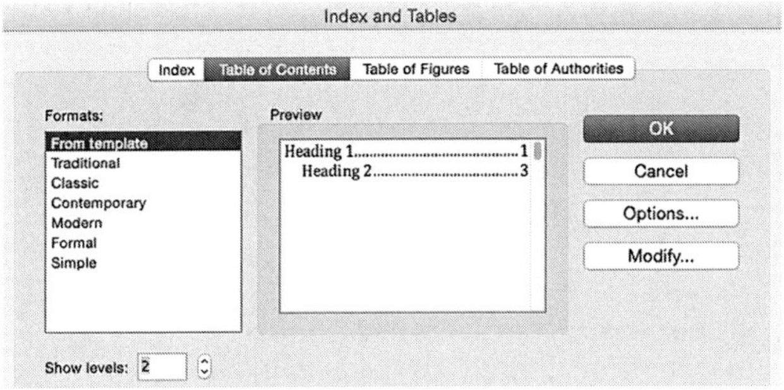

Once you have clicked *OK*, Word will automatically generate a table of contents and insert it where the cursor is placed. You may find that you missed a few headings when assigning the heading styles to your chapter or section headings, or applied a heading style to a blank line after the actual title, so you may make a few adjustments.

To update an automatically created table of contents, select the *References* tab and click the *Update Table* button. Or right-click with your mouse on the table of contents area in your document and choose *Update*.

When faced with a complex, multiple-chapter source document, the choice to apply styles consistently and create an automated table of contents will save you time and simplify your work process in the long run. You won't have to check and update page numbers in the table of contents manually after editing your translation and you won't have to reformat each paragraph separately if a change in style is needed. Instead, you modify the *Body Text* style or the *Heading* style to automatically apply your changes to all corresponding paragraphs throughout the entire document.

As well as benefitting you, this brings obvious benefits to your client. A manual with an automatically updatable table of contents will be more useful in view of potential changes and follow-up modifications. Using styles does not only help to generate a table of contents, but ensures consistency that is tantamount to quality. Consistency has been a magic word in marketing pitches, especially for promoting quality legal and technical translation. I would like to encourage us to start using the concept of consistency with regard to our product as a whole, as something that holistically embraces both verbal content and its visual implementation. A properly formatted document can be a valuable asset for the translator herself. It reflects positively on the value of the entire package of services provided by a quality-focused professional. In fact, a visually convincing deliverable is a more credible argument than any marketing promise.

There is a certain challenge to refining and improving the initial "raw material", but I regard this as an opportunity to deliver a better product. This is a step to eventually becoming a go-to expert for the client, a provider of high-quality, added-value services.

I do believe that when the purpose of translation is not purely academic, there is no point in limiting the transformation to language only, while replicating the flaws and imperfections of the source. For me, professional excellence in translation goes beyond formal accuracy. In fact, I would go as far as saying that translation excellence, or perhaps even the future of translation, lies beyond translation itself (I'll get back to this subject in the last chapter, p. 274).

Of course, translation is and will remain focused on the verbal content rather than its graphic presentation. For high-end translation, though, there might be more opportunity not in ever faster transformation of ever more verbal data, but in curating the enormous information flow to distil more sense and meaning and to better assist our clients' communication needs. Graphic presentation aims at making more sense rather than merely multiplying information. Incorporating principles of good design helps produce a more clearly structured, crisp and understandable result. For me, the nonverbal part that creates added value is an integral part of the curating process, a fun part of the job.

■ ■ ■

In the case examples discussed in this chapter, the suggested "change management" approach seams the obvious and reasonable choice. Having said this, I don't advocate any injudicious alterations. As always, it depends. The competence of a professional translator – and a sign of professional excellence – is the capacity to make choices depending on the purpose of the job and after thoughtful consideration of the client's needs.

2.6 Make typography rules work for you

> You've been fooled into seeing design as art, but these disciplines are different. [...] Whether a designed object is innovative, unexpected, or interesting may bear little consequence. It just needs to work.[35]

I believe that the question of how typography and design relate to a translator can be answered accordingly: typography and design need to work. And to make them work for us, I have a simple suggestion: compile your set of rules and translate them into processes.

Rules are part and parcel of our daily job. We perform our translations according to an existing set of rules, whether those that came with the job, or practices that seem innate: they barely count as rules. Many more don't need to be stated explicitly either, since they are part of a translator's essential toolkit. Then again, a list of specific requirements that accompanies the source text may turn out longer and more comprehensive than the text itself. It may also be limited to a polite rule for finishing off the translation job: "Please don't forget to run a spellcheck before you email your translation".

Rules and tools not only rhyme but are similar in many regards. Both are useless if you don't know what to do with them or where to find them. Since there are simply too many rules, it may be a good idea to apply principles of design to sort them out first. A good place to start may be taking a careful look at what is considered as authoritative sources for your working language. Small wonder that translators have a soft spot for dictionaries, glossaries and term bases. But monolingual references should also find their way to our lists of work tools. Subject-specific references, especially those that are available online, are a must when researching the topic under translation and they can obviously stand us in good stead. Standing on the sidelines is another genre of useful resources for your queries – editor's or writer's resources.

Apart from the fact that these resources can help improve your copy-editing skills and habits, they set the pattern for a value-added, comprehensive approach. It does not matter particularly which well-established style guide

35 Karjaluoto, *The Design Method*.

you follow – for English, see the *Chicago Manual of Style*[36] and *The Elements of Style* by William Strunk and E.B. White,[37] or take the BBC News style guide (*Grammar, Spelling and Punctuation*)[38] or the *D.C. Manual of Style and Usage* by The Washington Post.[39] You may need to complement these general resources with more translator-oriented references, such as the style guide of Directorate-Generale for Translation (DGT) of the European Commission.[40] If you work in German, then try to come to grips with an industrial standard, like the German DIN 5008 norm (the standard spells out "text processing" but, in fact, specifies time-tested rules of typography and graphic design). The sheer scope of information contained in these guidelines may be overwhelming. There are rules for grammar and spelling, stylistic tips, but also advice on typography and punctuation. Most existing style manuals cover too much ground but they can be made more manageable to fit to our practical translation work. A translator has to pick and choose rules that are relevant for her field of work and type of documents she translates and complement them with language-specific ones.

Punctuation rules may be different for the source and target languages, so an appropriate language-specific rule of conversion could help to achieve coherence. There are borderline cases where the verbal and the visual intermingle. Regular (Arabic) numbers, for instance, are usually replaced with Roman numerals for periods of time in Russian and French: 20th century – XX век / XXe siècle. It's a small but conspicuous enough difference that adds to the impression of a quality translation. Other borderline cases can be rather complex and relate more to the verbal style, but they comprise conspicuous elements that become all the more meaningful when taken in by a client looking at the translated text with the source text in mind. For example, the colons that are used in many German headings and titles for emphasis (like "Yummy: our oxtail stew") may need to be replaced by other punctuation marks in other languages, or the headline may need to be reworded. It is those minuscule details that jump out at the reader – or client – looking for signs of quality in a translation.

---

36 *The Chicago Manual of Style*, 17th Edition (University of Chicago Press, 2017).

37 William Strunk Jr and E.B. White. *The Elements of Style*, 4th Edition (Pearson, 1999).

38 "Grammar, spelling and punctuation". *BBC Adacemy* <https://www.bbc.co.uk/academy/en/articles/art20130702112133530 accessed 21 August 2018.

39 Thomas W. Lippman. *The Washington Post Deskbook on Style* (McGraw-Hill. 1989).

40 *English Style Guide: A Handbook for Authors and Translators in the European Commission*, 8th Edition. European Commission, 2016 <https://ec.europa.eu/info/sites/info/files/styleguide_english_dgt_en.pdf> accessed 21 August 2018.

Ideally, picking and choosing rules would produce a streamlined and customised mix that can be consistently put to use to serve both the content needs and the content presentation. The result is a **personal style guide** as a valuable asset for the routine work of a translator and for communicating professional excellence to the client.

Some translators set up their rules in the form of a checklist. Most look like a guide or a shortlisted collection of reminder notes for quality control once the translation is done. Sample checklists of this kind can be found on the Internet and adapted to your needs to automate the final checking of your document, in a way similar to what an editor or a proofreader would do (we will get back to this example in the next chapter, p. 109):[41]

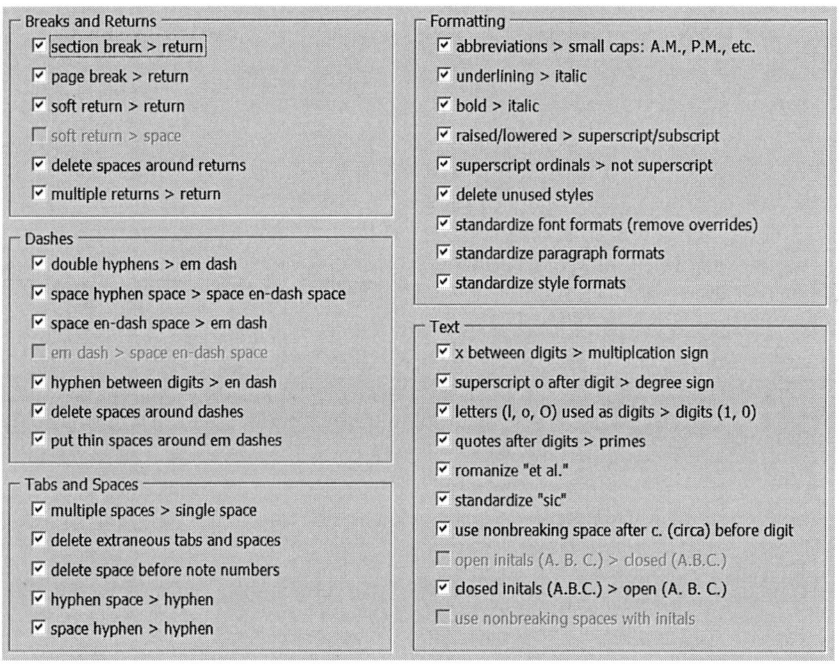

Whether using a more conventional, descriptive style guide or an automated checklist, a translator is free to settle for whatever works best for them (meaning whatever is more likely to be used routinely instead of being kept

41 For instance, see FileCleaner from Editor's ToolKit PLUS 2014 <http://www.editorium.com/ETK-Plus2014.htm> accessed 21 August 2018.

in a drawer for emergencies). The checklist shown above translates rules into actions. Of course, some translators might have a point saying that consistency of processes is no guarantee for consistent quality. However, I believe that there is a closer relation between a rule-based, somewhat technocratic workflow and professional excellence.

Checks like in the example above fall under quality assurance (QA), a concept that has taken a prominent place in tools and practices for translators. Whether or not they are appropriate for quality improvement depends on the kind and context of the translation project. Among issues and concerns raised in relation to QA tools (such as false positives or questionable improvement in productivity), I would like to look not at QA checks as such but rather their area of application.

As a rule, QA checks are based on comparing the translation with the source text and detecting obvious divergences in the translation. The essential shortcoming of such tests is that they take source documents at face value. However, to prevent replication of faults and shortcomings in the target text, QA checks should **start with the original document** prior to translation, particularly in regard to the format, layout and typography. I believe that the steps to prepare the source text for translation need to go beyond the usual clean-ups, such as correcting spacing in a rewritable Word document exported from a PDF. A more thorough review of the source text is appropriate, including, where necessary, adjustments to achieve a well-structured, consistent and logical design. This step will prevent issues that may arise during translation.

Not taking source documents at face value means that a translator has to override the client's – mostly unintended – settings and, as the case may be, prepare an improved version of the document for translation. Such actions can be really simple, like fixing unnecessary paragraph breaks in the example below:

▪ ***Chauffage·autonome¶***
¶
Le·chauffage·autonome·se·commande·au·moyen·du¶
bouton·rotatif·situé·dans·le·show-room.·Toute¶
modification·des·réglages·est·exécutée¶
après·une·certaine·temporisation.·Vous·trouverez¶
des·informations·plus·détaillées¶
dans·la·notice·d'utilisation·fournie·avec¶

As a rule of thumb, it is better to deal with problems before they arise and preparation is key to assure quality.

Pre-processing could include standardising styles, correcting bulleted and numbered lists, ensuring that pictures and captions keep together, deleting multiple spaces, inserting non-breaking spaces between numbers and units of measurement, preventing widows and orphans, reformatting paragraphs, adjusting tabs or setting up tables for better alignment. Again, a checklist can be of help.

Do unto the client's text what a demanding reviewer would do unto your translation. Poor quality of the input does not necessitate poor quality of the result.

In the grand scheme of things, though, both checklists and style guides are part of a more comprehensive approach to the process. The ultimate step would be to set up a quality management manual, not unlike those that are drawn up when an organisation seeks to certify its management system as compliant with international quality standards (such as ISO 9001 and others). Identifying all the steps and activities that you take to complete your translations may turn into an improvement to your whole translation business. It will also help you to become more aware of the effort that you put into the process of creating and adding value for the customer.[42]

To use management speak, your set of rules spells out a systematic approach as a kind of TQM (total quality management) programme. It should start with assessing your client's needs ("a simple translation" that a client wants to hire you for usually goes beyond "replacing words of one language with those of another") to tailor your service to meet or exceed these. When the work is done, TQM requires a feedback mechanism as a means to continually improve your performance. Individual translators tend to bracket out and treat lightly all preparatory or administrative tasks needed both to perform translations and, in the long run, have a successful translation business. A clearly defined set of rules or, better yet, a process-based approach could help you to develop a ho-

42 You may ask whether clients will be willing to pay for all these steps and "extras" that it takes to perform a translation. But in a good many cases they are not "extras", but rather indispensable parts of delivering quality in translation. Whenever you have to convince your client that this is the way to produce a better translation, make the benefits visible. Remember the classic rule of copywriting – "show, don't tell". Perhaps it would make business sense to graphically explain how your translation would look if you didn't do anything about the layout.

Whether listing all the steps in an invoice or a quote is appropriate depends on the specifics of the job and your circumstances. A long list of features and steps may scare off a client who came for "translation only". But defining too narrow terms of reference for the job ("just translate, don't change anything") or interpreting the client's wishes and needs too literally, without taking into consideration the purpose of translation, may also backfire. Whenever a translator takes her task too literally, the result risks turning out inferior to the source.

listic, entrepreneurial mindset. Your set of rules should embrace not only the immediate translation tasks, but also such steps as confirming a client's order, entering the order details into your project management system (whether a journal, an Excel spreadsheet or an online tool), making a copy of the source file for translation, and so forth, up to delivering the translation, producing an invoice and responding to client feedback. You may consider all this to be tedious housekeeping chores (I do), but since those steps are unavoidable regardless of how you feel about them, I prefer to have a system to deal with the "inevitable evil" rather than perpetuating the mess.

While setting up a process-based quality management system (QMS) is beneficial to achieving consistent quality of service and improving your productivity, in the context of this book it is the style guide that matters most. The advantage is not only having a useful reference at hand, but also the essential rules and elements that constitute your style.

In the narrow sense, the style of your translation will largely depend on that of the source document. Ideally, it will factor in the purpose of the translation, the needs and preferences of your client and the client's target audience. Still, the mark of your own linguistic, professional and individual preferences will remain. This can be turned into a powerful asset that makes you noticeable and unique. A part of this individual mark in terms of design is a distinctive, recognisable appearance. To make typography and design work, they should become an integral part of your organic branding, not in the sense of a logo or a footer in your email template, but as something that is inherent to your product itself.

For the brand to be perceived as authentic, its elements should take shape in your translation, not just in your communication with the client. The key to making your style work and making it noticeable is a consistent approach, with consistency guaranteed by a style guide.

So what is to be done?

The takeaway from this chapter is as follows:

- Pick a standard reference work for your working languages.
- Identify the rules that you can apply on a regular basis.
- Shortlist them and complement them with your own rules and preferences – bringing your own linguistic, professional and individual experience into the mix.

- Think of consistency and how to make it visible in your communication, your services and products.
- Take a process approach and draw up a style sheet.

When outsourcing, I prefer working with colleagues who need no hand-holding. Exhaustive rules that go along with the text to be translated can be unnecessary and a burden. I rather like the minimalist, don't-forget-to-spell-check-your-translation request as one tiny piece of advice at the end of a purchase order. Only I would replace it with "don't forget to click on the *Paragraph* button when revising your Word document":

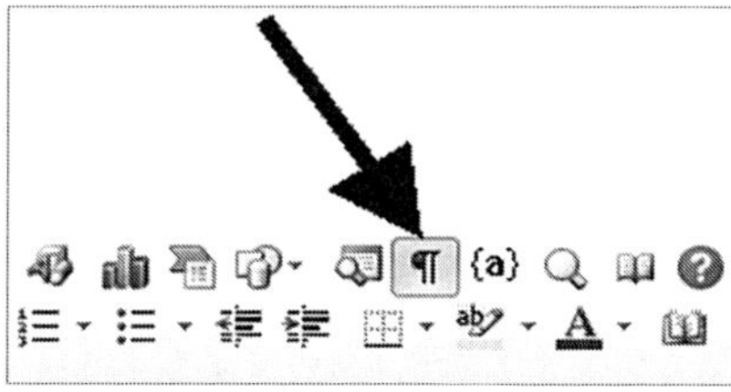

2.7 Make or buy

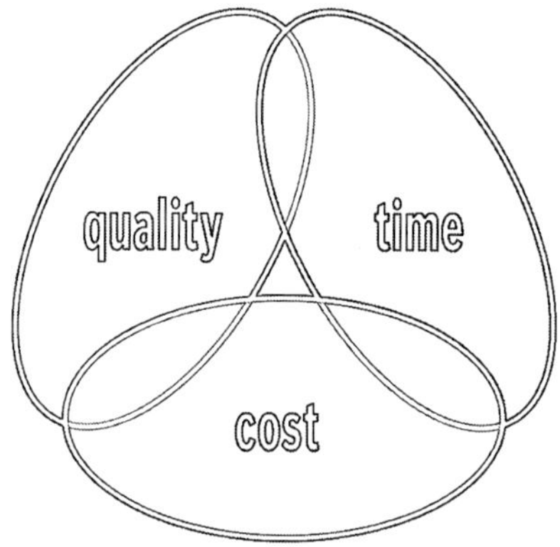

If you have a QA system (one that hopefully addresses the target *and* source texts) and a style guide in place (a style guide that can hopefully be put to use for consistency *and* differentiation purposes), you have tweaked the first of the three variables that define your product (quality – time – cost). In theory, at least. Improvements in process quality are not in themselves a guarantee for improved quality of products and/or services (professional translation means both a product *and* service), but they are likely to have a negative impact on the second variable – time.

Whenever you want to save time and increase productivity, there is always a temptation to take shortcuts. Whichever rules, checks and processes can be safely spared depends on the specifics of the project. However, the eventual cost of taking a shortcut may exceed its benefit. Instead of cutting corners by leaving out checks and processes completely, you can try to save time by performing them in a smarter way, by batch-automating the repetitive parts of your workflow. Probably the most popular way of doing this is cleaning up a file before importing it into a CAT tool.

In Word, if you want to sort out a mess of styles and regain order with the default *Normal* style, you can select the messy part or the whole document (by pressing CTRL+A) and use the shortcut CTRL+SHIFT+N. Or press the *Clear Formatting* button:

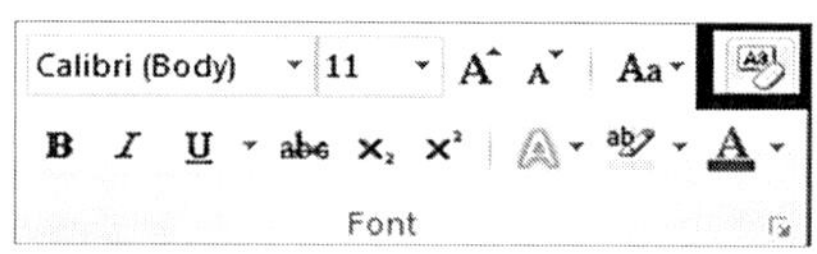

This command does not remove highlighting, so if your document contains any, you have to choose *No Colour* or *None* after clicking the arrow to the right of the *Text Highlight Colour* button:

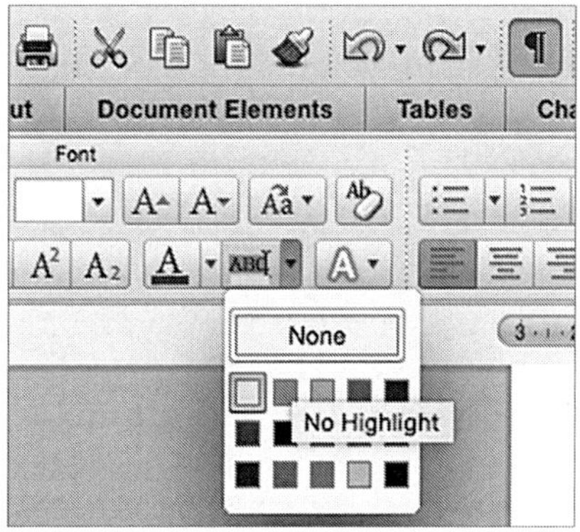

If you would rather remove the unwanted style changes only and recover the standard style formatting (which would keep multiple styles with their default settings instead of replacing all of them with the default *Normal* style), use CTRL+SPACE. This shortcut comes in very handy (it also works in PowerPoint), but the result will depend on whether the source text was consistently formatted with styles or not.

Another alternative is to use **macros**. Here you have a choice – make your own or buy commercially available ones. Setting up your own macros in Word is actually quite easy. A macro contains a series of tasks that run automatically once you start the macro. It is a smart workflow that will save you time on tasks that you repeat on every new file. What you need to do is program or record those actions. Use Word's macro editor[43] or simply manually record a series of actions and save it as a macro. Whereas dealing with Word's Visual Basic Editor (VBE) certainly looks like coding, by using the recorder you can create macros with no programming skills at all. You can always start with the recorder and move on to VBE later, in case you need to edit your recorded macros (though it may be easier to re-record them if you don't have programming experience) or customise the in-built ones. To give you an example of what a macro can do, let's create a macro to remove all accidental double spaces in your Word document (before or after translation). To begin with, you need to plan how to weed out the unwanted spaces manually. You can then rehearse the planned actions, one after another, for instance: select all text (CTRL+A), activate the *Find and Replace* window (click *Edit* → *Replace* or use the shortcut CTRL+H), place your

43 Word's macro editor is an in-built tool called VBE (Visual Basic Editor), while Visual Basic for Applications (VBA) is the programming language. To open VBE, use the shortcut ALT+F11 or enable the Developer mode and click the Visual Basic button on the Developer tab.

cursor in the upper field (*Find What* or *Search Document*) and enter two spaces, place your cursor in the *Replace With* field below and enter one space, click on the *Replace All* button. You might need to write down the steps to be on the safe side when recording your macro. If the rehearsal runs smoothly, you can start recording your *Replace All Double Spaces* macro. Bring up the *Record Macro* dialogue box (usually found in the *Tools* menu), give your new macro an easy-to-remember name, choose a button, assign it a shortcut, add a description if you want, and click *OK*:

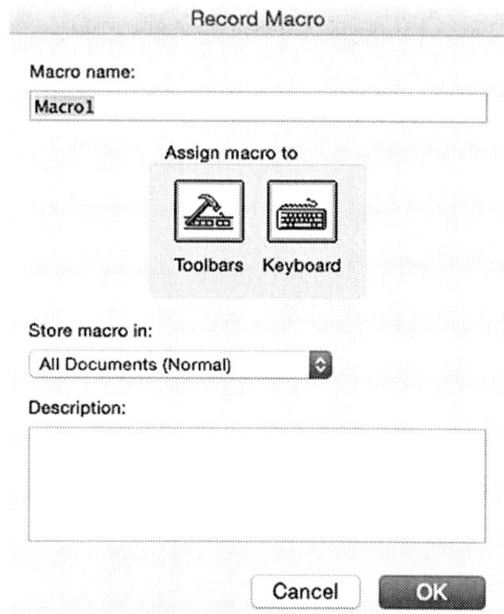

Now repeat the procedure that you have just rehearsed; remember that you are recording live. When you're done, click *Macro → Stop Recording*:

From now on, whenever you play back your macro (use the button, the shortcut or run the macro from the *Macros* list), it will automatically remove double spaces from any file.

However, you may notice that there is more to eliminating multiple spaces than you initially thought when planning, rehearsing and recording your procedure. For instance, you might notice that the *Find and Replace* action has no effect on multiple spaces before numbers or after punctuation marks. Or you will still have two spaces left where there have been three (the *Find and Replace* removed only the first pair and left the following space intact), so you will have to run the macro more than once to clean up the document completely.

More sophisticated find-and-replace tasks require wildcard characters and regular expressions (Regex). Even though this may look like advanced programming, it's not beyond the grasp of a translator. Both translators and editors perform certain programming tasks in order to create macros that suit their needs, and a few have produced more widely used macros. David Turner, a French-Spanish-English translator, was first to compile a set of macros that became known as CodeZapper some years ago. The foremost purpose was to clean up Word documents full of superfluous codes and junk tags, especially Word documents created by OCR-ing PDF files.[44] The tool consists of some 20 macros, for instance for removing redundant tags and bookmarks, eliminating random spacing variations, converting text boxes into convenient tables. CodeZapper is still a highly recommended tool to prepare your "rogue" Word documents for importing into a CAT program. However, there are also more efficient and usable options available today. A tool which offers integrated, comprehensive functionality as well as ease of use is the TransTools© software suite by Russian translator Stanislav Okhvat. TransTools deliver a wide range of benefits at all stages of the workflow – when preparing files for translation and cleaning up documents to be imported into a CAT program, during translation and in quality assurance processes. For instance, one of the TransTools macros removes double spaces:

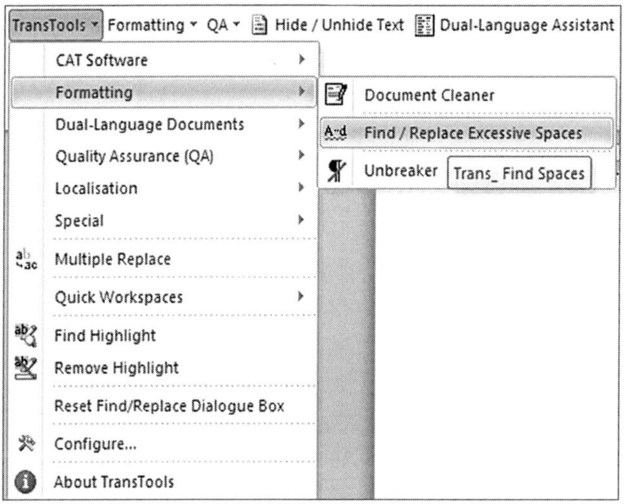

44 OCR stands for optical character recognition.

But it also offers a variety of additional options:

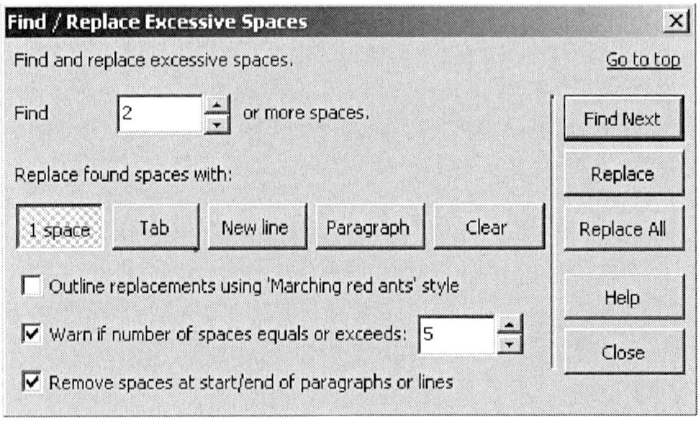

With TransTools, you can set up your own lists of elements to be batch-processed by the *Multiple Replace* macro and the *Correctomatic* feature. If you can make your style guide (or at least a considerable part of it) look like a checklist, the functionality of TransTools macros will allow you to run your checklist for each new document, thus ensuring that your style guide is applied consistently and saving you precious time:

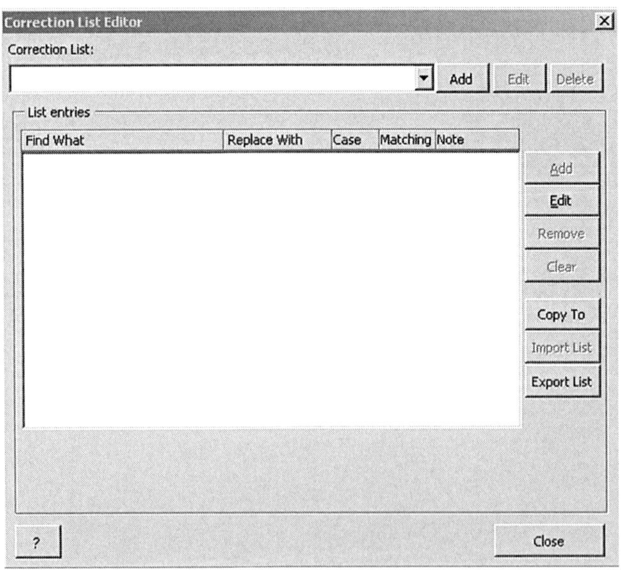

What TransTools is good at is that instead of a collection of macros set up to perform one function each, it provides you with a flexible, customisable, easy-to-use solution to simultaneously handle various repetitive tasks in your workflow.

Looking across related industries, it might be worth considering macros, tools and add-ins for writers, publishers, editors and proofreaders. Paul Beverley, a technical writer and editor, put together a comprehensive set of macros, many of which can be downloaded for free, together with his free book, *Computer Tools for Editors*. The Editorium website (www.editorium.com) offers other useful tools, such as the Editor's ToolKit, PerfectIt from Intelligent Editing and EditTools from WordnSync. The screenshot on p. 99 in the previous chapter was taken from FileCleaner, a Word plug-in by Jack Lyon (Editorium).[45] Similar clean up and copyediting tools (for Windows as well as for MacOS) can be found on the Wiley website (Proofreading Toolkit).[46] You can think of such editor's tools as a compilation of rules and conventions transformed into actions: if you find this, replace it with that. As long as no preferential changes are allowed, these small tools bring order to chaos.

Many of these tools can help you to build up your style guide or are useful for reverse engineering: you can model your own macros based on the existing ones. However, it is worth remembering that though useful, no tool is a one-size-fits-all solution. In fact, they offer so many options that to identify what will fit your workflow, your language combinations and your specialisms, you will have to do your own math before making any decisions. When deciding which tools and rules are applicable to your workflow, you may realise what differentiates you from other translators and become more aware of your professional strengths. Differentiation and control over what is essential and specific for your business is more than what can be expected from a technical tool, but with the right methodology, advantages are not limited to an increase in productivity only.

The next chapter presents a case example and workflow for using macros when dealing with legal documents, such as contracts. In this scenario, macros do not only help to save time and enhance productivity, but they can add value for your client and even improve your marketing strategy. Macros can be small tools, but they can help you reap big rewards.

---

45 <http://www.editorium.com/ETKPlus2014.htm> accessed 21 August 2018.

46 <https://authorservices.wiley.com/author-resources/book-authors/production/proofreading-toolkit.html> accessed 21 August 2018.

2.8 Going bilingual

In my field of work, translations are not ordered for academic purposes, but rather for clients' communication needs. That is why source documents often serve as raw material or drafts for producing final versions in the target language. Of course, clients also need to comply with existing plans and regulations, which sometimes has the consequence of producing content for bureaucratic conformity. It is unlikely that such content will be used by a human reader much, but it must be made available nevertheless.

The degree of accuracy or, by implication, a translator's freedom varies substantially depending on the purpose of translation. In the first case, especially if the client's intent is to convincingly convey the message to the target audience (or decipher the true meaning of the message they themselves received), a translator virtually rewrites the source text or casts the client's ideas in a new form. I started this book by showing how a client might be inclined to compare the translation to the source text based on the visual differences and commonalities between the two. However, when a translator serves as a facilitator in communication and provides added value through service excellence and expertise, a comparison becomes irrelevant – translation then becomes a standalone product that is judged on its own merits, depending on whether the message brings about the desired communication effect. Here, the functions of a translator and a copywriter (or a technical writer who creates a presentation or a business document) actually merge.

From the range of a translator's liberties and choices, formal accuracy is the opposite pole of clarity and facilitation. This chapter is about such a case – there are conditions that make it appropriate to precisely align the translation with the source text. In such circumstances, accuracy in terms of verbal content goes hand in hand with its visual presentation. Multi-language technical manuals come to mind, but a more compelling example can be legal documents, such as contracts and agreements. A draft contract is translated into the language of the other party; it will be perused and agreed, often in the course of negotiations and with inevitable multiple revisions as a result. Careful comparison of chapters, articles and paragraphs will take place in both languages. A bilingual document is a welcome solution for navigating through convoluted sentences and meandering from one language version to another.

I have realised that a bilingual solution is genuinely welcomed by legal translation clients. When I respond to a request for quotation for the translation of a legal document, I often offer a bilingual document as an option and briefly describe the format, with two versions in aligned, parallel columns. In my experience, most clients opt for this alternative instead of ordering a "regular" target-language translation of their contracts. As a marketing case, this could be called "How to Land a Translation Deal by Offering an Alternative Translation Format". Needless to say, your proposed alternative should deliver an added value to the client and needs to be communicated as such.

A marketing benefit for the translator lies in **proactively offering** a product or service that the client might be unaware of. In a competitive market, especially where clients' decisions are based on time and cost constraints, this is a useful way to make the client consider the third element of a project's triangle – the product and/or service itself. Differentiation **on products and services** as manifested in the translator's job specification helps the translator achieve a competitive edge.

■ ■ ■

If I have managed to convince you that competitive differentiation is worth investing in, let's see how we can deliver the goods. Let's say that you received a purchase and sales agreement (a Word document) for translation.

SALES AND PURCHASE AGREEMENT

between

…………………, whose registered office is at ……………………,
[company legal name] [address]

represented by ……………………………………………………,
[surname and name, position]

hereinafter referred to as "the Supplier",

and

…………………, whose registered office is at ……………………,
[company legal name] [address]

represented by ……………………………………………………,
[surname and name, position]

hereinafter referred to as "the Purchaser".

It is agreed as follows:

1.1 The Supplier will sell and deliver and the Purchaser will buy the products specified in Annex 1.

Your task is twofold: to translate it into your target language and to deliver your translation as a bilingual document, with source and target texts running parallel. If your contract consists of only a few paragraphs and, ideally, covers half a page, you can put your translation right under the source text and insert a column break:

SALES AND PURCHASE AGREEMENT	CONTRATO DE COMPRA E VENDA
between	de una parte,
...................., whose registered office is at ...., [company legal name] [address]	.... con domicilio en ...., [denominación social de la empresa] [dirección, ciudad y país]
represented by ...., [surname and name, position]	representada por ...., [nombre y apellidos, cargo]
hereinafter referred to as "the Supplier",	en adelante, "el Suministrador",
and	y de otra,
...................., whose registered office is at ...., [company legal name] [address]	.... con domicilio en ...., [denominación social de la empresa] [dirección, ciudad y país]
represented by ...., [surname and name, position]	representada por ...., [nombre y apellidos, cargo]
hereinafter referred to as "the Purchaser".	en adelante, "el Comprador".
It is agreed as follows:	Ambas partes acuerdan lo siguiente:
1.1 The Supplier will sell and deliver and the Purchaser will buy the products specified in Annex 1.	1.1 El Suministrador venderá y entregará, y el Comprador comprará, los Productos descritos en el Anexo 1.
——————Column Break——————	

However, your contract is likely to consist of a dozen or more pages, therefore a column break won't work. To set up multiple column breaks would be too time-consuming and wouldn't work in practice either, since you would have to place your translation after each article, point or paragraph before you insert your column break before and after each translated piece. A similarly impractical idea would be to use text boxes. Text boxes can be linked for the text to automatically flow from one to another, however, misalignment of the source and target texts may be a major problem.[47] Source and target texts vary in length. You can try to adjust your translations with line and paragraph breaks, but it means that you will have to insert empty lines in the source document, too. However, you will never reach a perfect match visually

47 The same will happen if you use a two-column table with a couple of rows and paste your source text into the left column and the translation into the right column. This may be problematic with complex documents, but once or twice, I did receive such tables for bilingual documents from my clients. Once, many pages of the source document were squeezed together into a single table cell on the left side with the corresponding right-side cell left empty for me to insert the translation. The client wanted a bilingual document with two language versions running parallel but this kind of table wasn't going to work. You either have to split the table into cells (and the body of the text into paragraphs) or, better yet, delete the table and use the TransTools to do a proper job.

and the parallelism will be broken again, whenever the text format or the text itself is changed.

The only logical approach is to prepare the source text **prior to translating** instead of trying to remedy the format afterwards. The table functionality in Word enables creating a framework, not unlike a **grid structure** in graphic design software. Whereas a grid helps the designer to arrange various elements on a page in an orderly fashion, we will also produce order with text, separating the source and target text vertically and aligning first lines of each pair of corresponding passages horizontally.

To begin with, you need to convert your text to a table (CTRL+A or *Select All*):

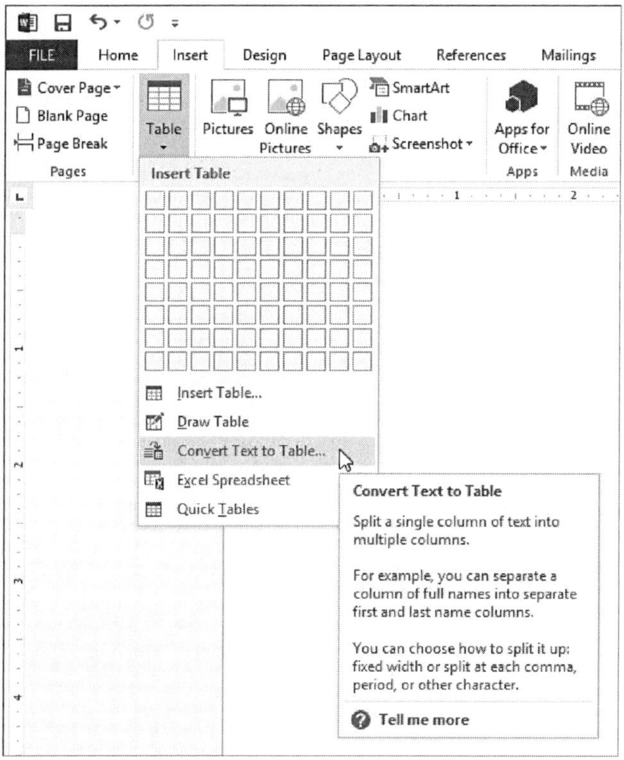

In most cases, you should set the number of columns to 1 and use paragraphs to separate text.[48]

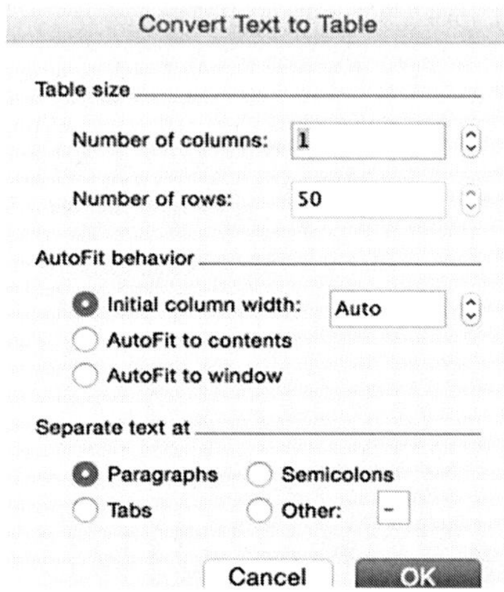

Only once your source document has been re-formatted, and each article, clause and provision is consistently numbered and separated from the relevant numbers by tabs (or indented with tabs wherever numbers are missing), can you produce a two-column table with numbers and text segments in two separate columns:

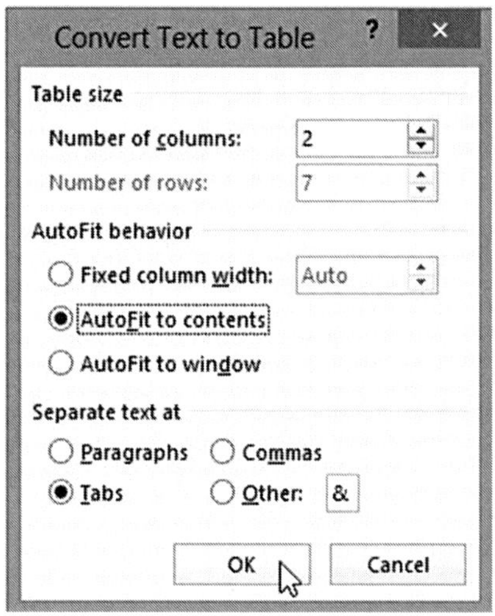

This, in theory, should take care of numbering in your translation, but in practice, you never get perfectly formatted and numbered Word documents and

48 It is always a good idea to check the source document before converting it to a table in case any tidying up is needed. If a paragraph return was used merely to start a new line within a cohesive paragraph, it is better to replace it with a manual line break; then, delete all the superfluous paragraph returns that might be used to start new pages, and continue until you have a clean document.

will probably have to deal with a second or third level of numbered lists manually afterwards:

2.2.3.		**A partner adatbiztonságra vonatkozó jogosultsága**		**The counterparty's rights with regard to data protection**
2.2.3.1.		Az érintett személy jogosult:		The person concerned is entitled to
	a)	tájékoztatást kérni személyes adatainak kezeléséről, valamint adataiba betekinteni, valamint	a)	request information about the processing of its personal data and to have an insight into its data,
	b)	adatai helyesbítését kérni.	b)	request the rectification of its data.

After converting your text to a one-column, multiple-row table with numbered articles, clauses and provisions, you can now copy the entire column and paste it to the right side to produce a two-column table. Now you only have to overwrite one column with the text of your translation to create a bilingual document.

If you use a CAT tool, it would be a good idea to hide the column with the source text, so you don't have both to copy and translate identical segments in your tool. Select one of the columns and choose *Hidden* in the *Effects* section:

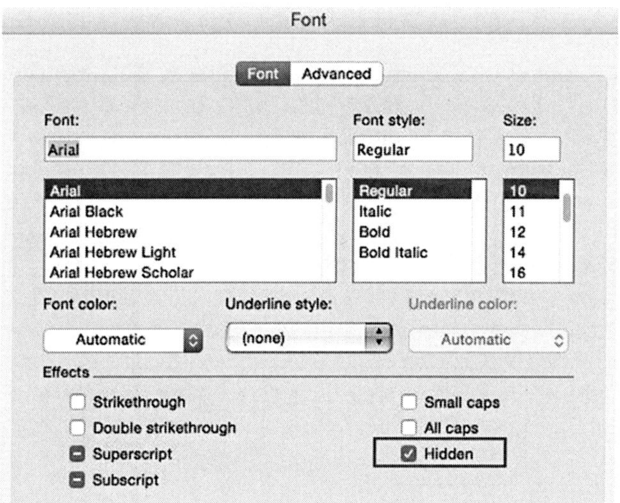

After exporting the translation from your CAT tool, you will have to go back to this menu again to un-hide the invisible column.

All this is perfectly easy, but so is the whole first part of the job itself – ensuring a perfect alignment of the source and target texts in two parallel columns. The other task is more difficult, namely to ensure proper numbering in both documents. Your Word document was most likely created with automatic numbering and outline styles. The problem of numbering in Word tables is the direction: the next ascending number is assigned to the table field to the right instead of the one below. So, while you'll expect your perfectly aligned two-column bilingual document to look like this:

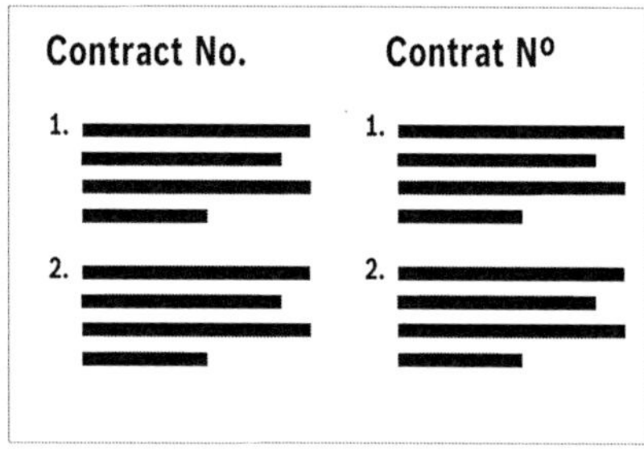

It will most likely look like this:

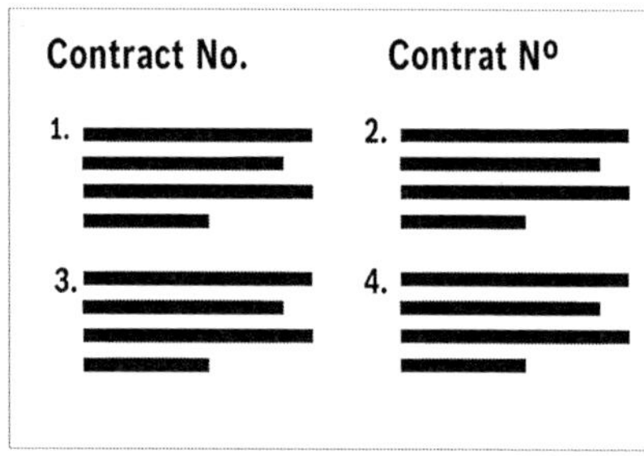

If you have a fairly complex contract with a great number of articles, subarticles and sub-subarticles, then automatic numbering will leave you with a mess. You will have a hard time trying to clean it up, so the best solution is preparation. We cannot change the way Word automatically numbers rows and columns in a table, so we'll have to disable the automatic numbering either in the source or in the target column. To do so, copy the entire one-column table and paste it into a new document. Now you can replace the automatically generated numbers (which are bound to change whenever a new numbered field is added) with identical fixed, unchangeable, plain text numbering. You don't have to waste time trying to replace all list numbers and letters manually, we can do this much more efficiently.

Press the keyboard shortcut ALT+ F11 to open the Visual Basic Editor. Open the View menu and click *Immediate Window* (or use another keyboard shortcut, CTRL+G). In the *Immediate Window* below, type "ActiveDocument.ConvertNumbersToText" and press *Enter*:

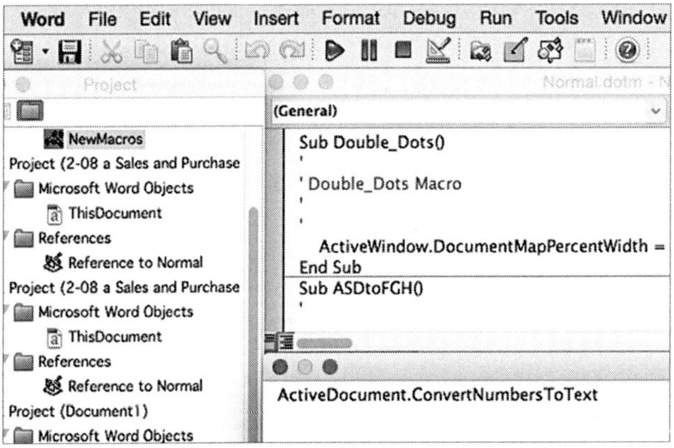

Close the Visual Basic Editor window. At first glance, nothing has changed – the numbers are the same. However, now they have become plain text, as if you entered each of them manually instead of using the auto numbering function. Now you can copy the translation column that you saved in a new document and paste it back into your document: the numbering will be intact and remain automatic. Or you can turn off automating numbering in your translation – it may be more practical for draft contracts, when new versions and modifications are expected, so you will only have to update the numbers in new or altered sections.

If you prefer a ready-made option to this workflow, you can use the *Dual-Language Document Assistant*, a set of macros from the TransTools software suite introduced in the previous chapter (see p. 106). The range of options available may seem a bit complicated, but they are all there for a reason.

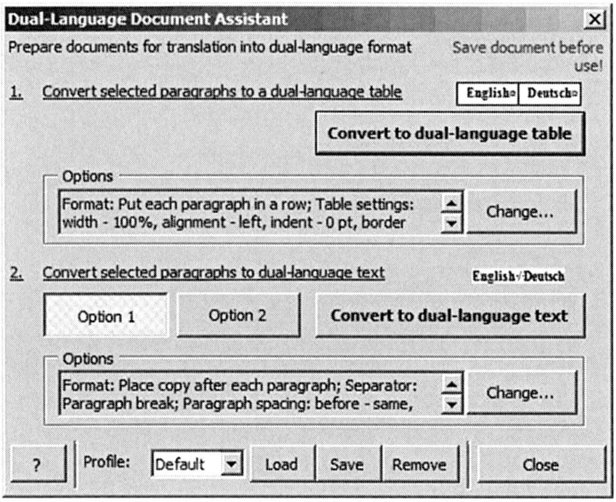

Whereas "Convert to dual-language table" means duplicating your text in a second table column, with the second option, "Convert to dual-language text", you can place the duplicate paragraphs below the original ones:

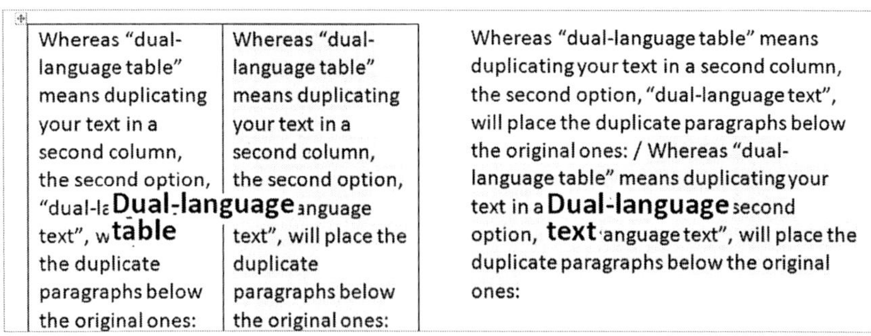

Even if you are dealing with an unambiguous job of setting up a bilingual table only, there are at least two cases when the "dual-language text" will come in very handy. First, whether you do it manually or use TransTools, some parts of the source document may already contain columns or tables. In this case TransTools will fail:

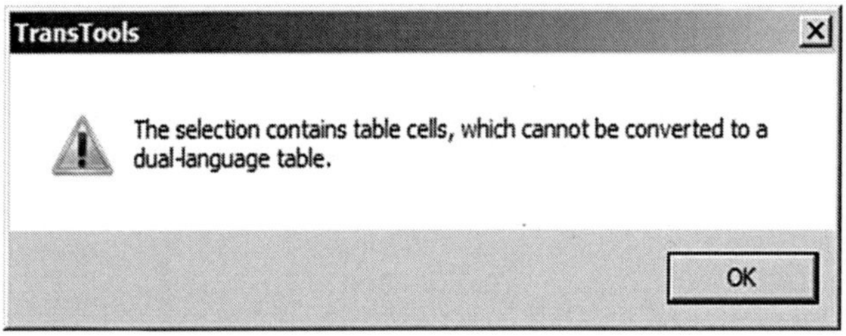

Table cells in the source document are easy to overlook. They may be not so obvious at first sight, especially if there are no tab indents and no numbers. A typical example of unnumbered columns or tables is a "Definitions" section:

Purchaser's Warranties	means the warranties of the Purchaser contained or referred to in clause 4.2 of the Agreement.
Relevant Claim	means claims made by one Party to another Party pursuant to clause 7.1 of the Agreement.
Seller's Warranties	means the warranties of the Seller contained or referred to in clause 4.1 of the Agreement.

The best way to cope would be to keep the two-column structure of the source text and replicate it in the right side of your bilingual table manually, limiting the number of paragraphs to which you apply the *Dual-Language Document Assistant* within the TransTools plug-in.

Another section of a contract document where the dual-language text option can be very useful is at the end. In my experience of working with legal documents, names and functions of the signatories are carefully accommodated on the left and right sides of the page using a mixture of tabs, spaces, columns and tables:

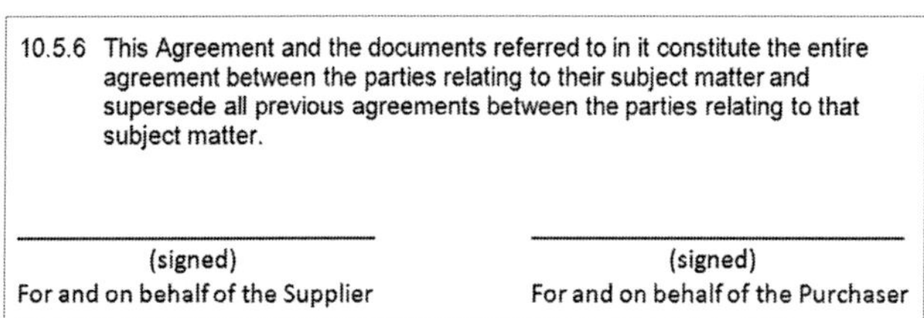

10.5.6 This Agreement and the documents referred to in it constitute the entire agreement between the parties relating to their subject matter and supersede all previous agreements between the parties relating to that subject matter.

(signed)	(signed)
For and on behalf of the Supplier	For and on behalf of the Purchaser

It is this symmetrical two-column section where the dual-language text function suggests itself.

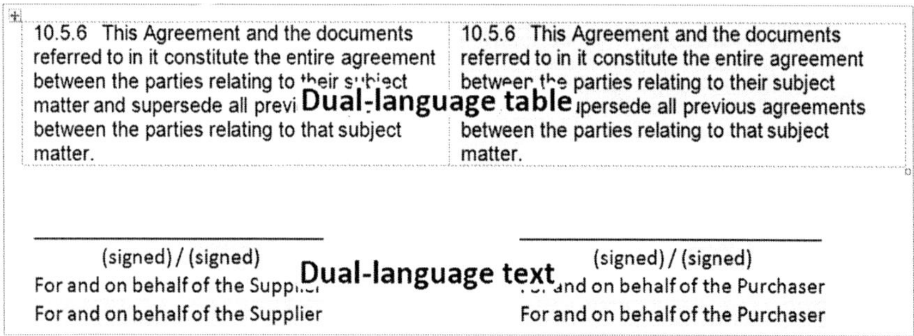

Dual-language table

10.5.6 This Agreement and the documents referred to in it constitute the entire agreement between the parties relating to their subject matter and supersede all previous agreements between the parties relating to that subject matter.	10.5.6 This Agreement and the documents referred to in it constitute the entire agreement between the parties relating to their subject matter and supersede all previous agreements between the parties relating to that subject matter.

Dual-language text

(signed) / (signed)
For and on behalf of the Supplier
For and on behalf of the Supplier

(signed) / (signed)
For and on behalf of the Purchaser
For and on behalf of the Purchaser

After having set your translation in a two-column table, it is a good idea to adjust the column width. A difference between interpreters and translators consists not only in the fact that interpreters translate orally, whereas translators work with text. Translators tend to be more *like* interpreters than interpreters in the true sense of the word: while interpreters, especially conference interpreters, simply have no time but to compress or even only give the gist of the content, translators can be painstakingly over-excessive with rendering (and explaining) every detail of the source text. As a result, written translation almost always takes up more space than the original document. It is particularly noticeable in my language combinations,[49] but it might apply to any aligned pair of the source and target texts, notwithstanding the language.

49 The example on the opposite page is taken from an exercise book for English-Russian interpreters by Andrei Falaleyev and Elena Malofeeva (*Uprazhneniya dlya sinkhronista. Vertolyot beregovoy okhrany.* Perspektiva, 2014).

The National Security Agency of the United States is a spy outfit so **sensitive** that its very existence was once secret.	Агентство национальной безопасности США — настолько засекреченная шпионская структура, что одно время даже ее существование держали в тайне.
He spent years learning tiny languages in **forbidding** jungle villages.	Он годами изучал наречия жителей крохотных поселений в непроходимых джунглях.
Writing on Nigeria, it is always tempting to focus on the colorful **insanity** that is Africa's most populous nation.	Когда пишешь о Нигерии, всегда тянет сосредоточиться на пестром бедламе, который царит в этой самой густонаселенной стране Африки.
The state-owned Coal India company is hardly an **advertisement** for efficiency.	Государственная угольная компания «Coal India» никак не может считаться образцом /эталоном высокой производительности.

Now that you've done your "checks and balances" (see p. 23) and, if necessary, made the translation column a bit wider to match the source text, there are only a few things to do to reach your final bilingual outcome.

If the source document didn't have any extra lines between paragraphs, you should remove borders from the table. However, it's best to keep the vertical line separating the translation from the source text:

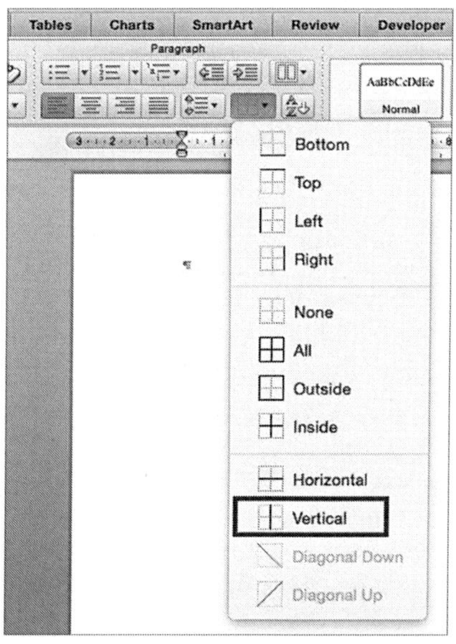

You can also consider changing the page orientation from *Portrait* to *Landscape*. Especially if your document is meant to be used in discussions and negotiations, the landscape format will make it more readable on a notebook display. Text lines in a two-column table on a portrait-type page are usually too short. Extending the column width might not help to achieve exactly Emil Ruder's "sweet spot" of 50 to 60 characters per line (see p. 67), but it will still make the text visually more coherent and easier to read.

As a final step, I would add or adjust page numbers. Given that your page already looks quite symmetrical, a page number in the centre of the header or footer (or lightly shifted to the separating line between the table columns, if you adjusted their width) would fit in very well. You may also choose to use the more traditional, language-specific "Page ... of ..." both on the left and the right hand-side of the page in the corresponding languages.

If the footer looks like the example below, it definitely requires a bit of tuning, from:

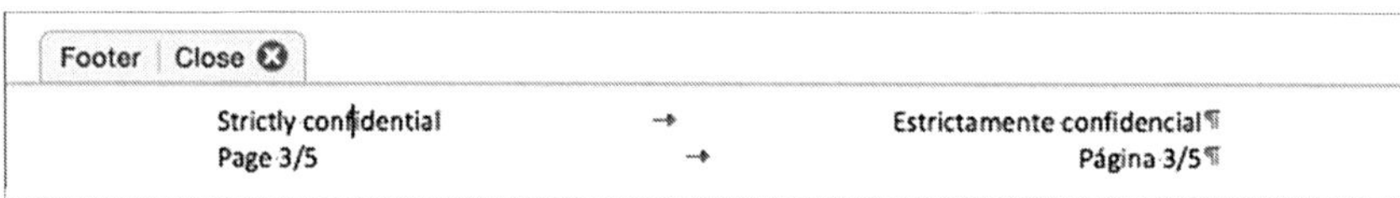

to:

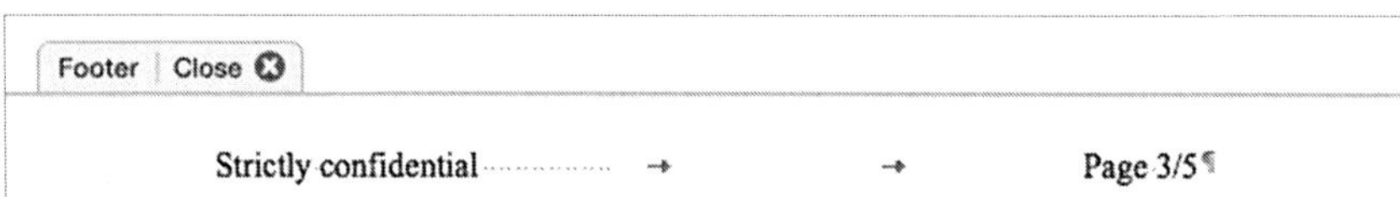

That's it. Your bilingual document is ready to go to your client.

Of course, there are other methods to create bilingual documents that have their benefits and drawbacks. CAT tools may seem the obvious choices, but the benefits are rather nominal. Though SDL Studio and MemoQ are capable of exporting bilingual documents, they generate a format for external review, for instance with an extra column for comments or colour codes to indicate matches from translation memories. The result of using the convert-to-bilingual functions is still a semi-finished product for further processing within the same CAT tool or another application. As an example, the SDL LegIt! plug-in creates bilingual files to be handled with the legacy Trados Workbench software. These files, however, are called "unclean" – they are still-to-be-processed documents in an intermediary stage. Standalone aligners like ABBYY Aligner are capable of producing bilingual files in a regular Word format (e.g. .rtf), but the purpose is to prepare a document for revision, not for the end client. Also, aligners usually strip both the source and target texts of all formats and impose their own segmentation, thus playing havoc with the original document structure.

But at the end of the day, it is of minor importance which tools and methods you choose to create a perfectly aligned bilingual document, as long as you find your tools and methods comfortable to work with and efficient. The workflow described here offers just an example of how I usually approach the task. As with all design tasks and approaches, the focus should be on the client and the purpose of your translation. When seen through your client's eyes, a bilingual legal document is a better, more convenient option for revising or negotiating a contract. Whether you call it "enhanced usability" or "value-added translation", it is up to the client to choose the most appropriate format (but up to you to communicate the possible benefits). Coming back to the question raised at the beginning of this book – why bother about the nonverbal aspects of content – the answer is that, as with the other adjustments we have discussed, to volunteer a bilingual solution may help you make a difference in a competitive market and make a case for the **value of your product** as a crucial selection criterion. To think outside the box means to think of alternatives while keeping an eye on the bigger picture (what does the client need the translation for?). Don't be afraid to visually prove that you can deliver more than just another copy of your client's document in just another language.

2.9 If you start throwing stones at CATs, you may end up with ISO standards

The title of this chapter derives from Douglas Rushkoff's book *Throwing Rocks at the Google Bus*.[50] In revealing how the digital economy has gone wrong, Douglas Rushkoff tracks our current grievances back to the first days of the industrial age; I'd like to quote him at some length:

> The object of industrialism wasn't to make more stuff better and faster, it was to disconnect labor from the value [it] created. [...] Today when we implement digital technologies we try to do them in ways that get rid of people. We don't want employees. If you need human beings, well then how are you going to scale up? It has to be able to be an algorithm. [But] when we implement digital technologies, in order to get people out of the way, in order to get them out of the company we end up really killing the only expertise we have. If you're using algorithms and big data..., what's your competitive advantage? The other company is using that same data and probably hiring the same big data analytics company... So now you've been turned into a commodity.[51]

CAT tools have been more than a translation technology: they have served essentially as a tool to industrialise and corporatise the traditional translation business model and translation services as a profession. Their proliferation, paving the way to and converging with machine translation, can be regarded as an industrialism case study much in line with Rushkoff's critique,[52] including

50 Douglas Rushkoff. *Throwing Rocks at the Google Bus: How Growth Became the Enemy of Prosperity* (Penguin, 2016).

51 Sheeraz Raza. "Algorithms: killing jobs, narrowing our personalities, says Douglas Rushkoff" [blog]. Value Walk, published 25 April 2016 <http://www.valuewalk.com/2016/04/algorithms-killing-jobs> accessed 22 August 2018.

52 "What we now call industrialization was actually an extension of the aristocracy's effort to usurp the growth it witnessed in the peasants' marketplace and to imitate it by other means. Industry was really just the development of manufacturing processes that required less skill from human laborers. Instead of having to learn how to make shoes, each worker could be trained in minutes to do one tiny part of the job. In the long run, many industrial processes have ended up more efficient than production by individual craftspeople, but that's most often because their total costs are hidden or externalised to others. (The government pays for wars to procure cheap oil and roads to convey mass-produced products, while we all pay for the environmental stresses caused by corporate agriculture, and so on.) Prices may be low, but

digital industrialism in its current form. Like the other tools that "are getting smarter while we humans are getting relatively, or perhaps absolutely, dumber", they weren't "sold to us as the disempowerment of workers, but as the triumph of technology". In the case of CAT tools, this technology has benefited translation companies, most of which acted as trading middlemen between the consumers and the producers of translation (translators), more than it has helped working translators. Technology has alienated translators from the end users of their products. It has fostered a forced, unnatural and uncalled-for division of labour that disenfranchised language professionals from producing and delivering finished products directly to their clients. Instead, a translator's role has been reduced to that of a replaceable contributor to the mass production of intermediate goods, with the finished value extracted and owned by middlemen, wholesalers and retailers instead of producers.

With this out of the way, let's get the book back on track. CAT tools are here to stay (and to transition to even more powerful, more dehumanising, more algorithm-driven rather than operator-driven tools), so the best thing a working translator can do is to try to figure out how to use them to their own advantage. In the words of Douglas Rushkoff, "if you don't know what a piece of software is for, the chances are you are being used by it".[53]

■ ■ ■

What is the upside of CAT tools? How do they level out the disadvantages of losing control over the final product? How does technology compensate and reward an individual translator – user of CAT tools?

Initially, the promise of a bright future for translators that was supposed to arrive with CAT technology came down to two things: higher efficiency and increased quality through consistency. CAT tools were praised as productivity boosters that remove a lot of the drudgery, especially in the case of repetitive, monotonous texts. When applied to texts or corpora with consistent and straightforward terminology, CAT tools were expected to reduce variability in translation and ensure an accurate reproduction of identical or similar fragments of the source text, efficiently and fast.

---

the costs are high. It was never really about efficiency anyway; industrialization was about restoring the power of those at the top by minimizing the value and price of human laborers. This became the embedded value system of industrialism, and we see it in every aspect of the commercial landscape, then and now" (Rushkoff, Throwing Rocks).

53 Douglas Rushkoff. *Program or Be Programmed: Ten Commands for a Digital Age* (Soft Skull Press, 2011).

It's not that CAT tools have not lived up to this promise. Although there is a plethora of issues cited by users of CAT tools in the discussion forums,[54] translators usually don't question the fact that they manage to increase their output and adequately recover all the repetitive instances of the source-language text in their translation when working with CAT tools. Yet while translation memories allow translators to leverage the translations done in the past, recycling the previous, "used" stuff may be detrimental rather than beneficial for the quality of translated text. Repeating and paraphrasing what has once been said and what now constitutes part of the verbal stock in a translation memory can become counterproductive for translating – and hence creating – new, fresh content. In terms of its effect on quality, consistency as a principle is no less controversial. Basically, the concept of consistency in translation is characterised by the idea that the same words and phrases in the source-language text should be conveyed with the same words and phrases in the translation – always the same.[55] The opposite of consistency in that sense would be synonymity, that is allowing for diversity when translating identical terms and phrases of the source text. Are synonyms bad? Should the translator stick to the choice of words previously used when rendering repetitive ideas? The concept of consistency seems to imply precisely that, while it places constraints on a translator's freedom to choose their means of expression as a driver for "higher quality".

Translating is writing. This fact is often forgotten when the quality of translation is judged primarily on whether it is true to the source text. It is easier to compare words than meanings. It is even more difficult to put the purpose – to what purpose the source was written and why it needed translation – into equation. Admittedly, it is just as difficult to judge the quality of writing. In terms of diversity vs. consistency, one doesn't have to go too deep into what constitutes good and bad writing.[56] The answer lies in the source text itself.

The Associated Press Stylebook lays down the following rule for its broadcast writers: "Don't strain for synonyms. 'Arizona,' not 'the state.' Someone who

---

54 See, for example, "Cats 'Я' us, but we like dogs too!" on my blog, *Translator's Notes*, published 2 September 2013 <https://anmerkungen-des-uebersetzers.com/2013/09/02/cats-я-us-but-we-like-dogs-too> accessed 21 August 2018.

55 SDL in its brochure on SDL Studio, the CAT tool par excellence, speaks of "defining a concept and assigning one allowed term per language to it" (Nigel Watson. "Are you speaking the right export language? Ask the expert – SDL" [blog]. *ITM (In Trade Magazine)*, published 14 January 2016 <http://www.intrademagazine.com/ask-the-expert-sdl/?lang=es accessed> 21 August 2018).

56 Gary Provost. *100 Ways to Improve Your Writing: Proven Professional Techniques for Writing with Style and Power* (Berkley, 1985).

hears '...in the state's history' might not have heard the rest of the story."[57] The opposite is valid for authors of what will be received in writing, whether on paper or on screen. In fact, the advice "don't strain for synonyms" is targeted specifically at **broadcast** writers to remind them that theirs is a large **live listening** audience who cannot go back or forth in time, unlike individual readers, who can move across their text, on paper or screen. When I try to look at the source-language text through the eyes of its author, I often discover a search for synonyms that the author had hoped would yield fresh and more convincing ways of expressing their message. And it is not in creative writing, but in the mainstay of my work – business and corporate documentation. It is perhaps surprising how many synonyms are used in financial reports, for example. If you read about developments in financial markets, you may notice a massive number of terms and idioms to describe key figures, typical movements, events and trends. A downturn in the stock market may qualify as a concept that could do with only "one allowed term per language to it", as SDL Studio would put it, but in reality, financial reports abound in such terms as fall, drop, decrease, decline, plummet, plunge, sink, dive, dip, tank, tumble, go soft or go South.[58] These terms may be regarded as synonyms in a relevant context but they can occur within a few paragraphs describing a single concept.

Shouldn't the translator take the same approach and vary their wording accordingly? Wouldn't variety contribute to a more readable text and more appealing content?

In technical writing, it's crucial to prevent ambiguities that may arise when a "tool" is variably called "device" or "equipment". People should be given clear instructions so that they could follow every step. But obviously, clear instructions are not meant to sedate the audience! Yet this is what happens when the reader is fed with monotonous repetitions of the same sets of words. This happens when each piece of equipment or each operation is referred to using only one, invariable, "allowed" term. To make the ban on synonyms even more extreme, all for the sake of so-called consistency, we could do away with **pronouns** as **substitutes** for unambiguous terms as well. Doesn't consistency require that pronouns such as "it" for "tool" be put on a list of

---

57 *The Associated Press Stylebook 2015 and Briefing on Media Law*, 46th Edition (Basic Books, 2015).

58 It is a good idea to maintain your own thesaurus of synonyms, turns of phrase, catchy and interesting alternatives to express ideas in your target language – in addition to your TMs and termbases. Treating your original text with respect doesn't mean you shouldn't view it with a critical eye, bearing in mind the author's intentions, articulation and writing skills.

banned synonyms together with "equipment", "device", "appliance", "unit", "aid" and whatnot?

As a technical translator, I come across a good many manuals with unavoidable warnings and alerts scattered on every page – always the same symbols that look like triangles with exclamation marks (I'm a strong believer in visual consistency, therefore no objections on my part) and the same wording (verbal consistency is different – repetitions cease to arouse attention and are easily skipped over). Perhaps, for warnings to be paid more attention to and be taken more seriously, it would be good to vary the phraseology and use occasional synonyms instead?

Technical documentation authors are not averse to violating the tenets of consistency themselves. I'm not certain why they do casually refer to their "tools" as "devices" or "equipment" instead of opting for a general term. Sometimes I think that it simply happens whenever authors have their audience in mind. It happens when humans write for other humans instead of algorithms or machines. And as humans, they are naturally biased against monotony that lulls them to sleep. Sometimes, to draw the user's attention to something important, a discerning author of a user's manual has no better choice than to do away with "consistency" and break the routine.[59]

For the sake of readability, it is better if technical writers are left with a certain degree of freedom and can decide for themselves when they stick to the rules and when the rules are fine to break. A similar choice should be the prerogative of a discerning and competent translator. In stating this, I certainly don't call for any revolutionary approach either to technical writing or to technical translation. Neither is this an appeal against monosemantic terms or anything subversive in terms of precision and clarity in technical content. The only thing that I wish to emphasise again and I think that it is worth repeating: **translation is writing, too**. Competent translators, be it technical, financial or legal translators, are above all competent specialist writers. And here lies the crux of the problem that competent, reader-centred translators face when writing in a CAT environment. Perhaps the biggest stone to throw at CATs is that this technology **takes the source text for granted**.

One may argue that SDL Studio provides the "edit source" function, which is meant "to correct small typos, such as a spelling mistake" (SDL Studio web-

59 This is also why repetitions are often considered poor writing style and editorial apps are offered to help authors spot and weed out too frequent instances of repetition.

site, "How to Edit Source Segments"). Similar functions are provided by Wordfast and memoQ. Characteristically, memoQ defines the purpose of the "edit source" function as if taking its cue from SDL:

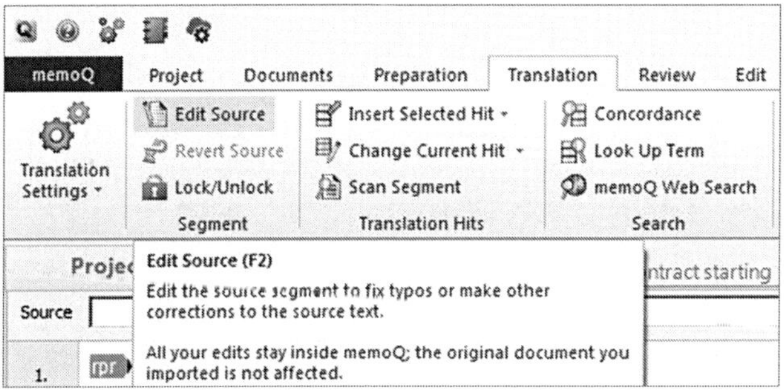

In conjunction with other features, such as split or merge segments, original content to be translated in a CAT environment may seem far from being immune to modification. However, the default condition is that the source text is a given. CAT tools make the translator's dependence on the source-language text more pronounced, sometimes to the point of slavishness. The rather limited options of adapting the original in a CAT tool are of little consequence given how a CAT tool presents and structures the original document for translation. That is another aspect of the issue with CAT tools mentioned above: the fact that the source text is not untouchable does not change one of the most basic properties of a CAT tool, that of **segmentation**. Original texts are divided into segments, each segment usually presented in a table cell. No matter how your client's information was structured and arranged visually in the original context, the translator is provided with an extract, split into visually uniform chunks in a tabular form. Formats are reduced to tags that serve as a reminder that the verbal content is structured or marked in some way or may contain links, graphics etc. Most translators find these placeholders rather distracting or downright annoying and would prefer tag-clean texts. The WYSIWIG preview features, i.e. displaying the document in the same visual format as the original, usually below the work area, are secondary to the tabular form and in no way precise, especially when the original is a combination of text and graphics, such as a PowerPoint document. The fact that images are removed and texts cleaned of any formats might be considered no serious stones, rather small potatoes to be thrown at CATs. Also, it may seem an odd objection from the standpoint of someone whose task is to convert purely verbal content. However, the importance of visual presentation in a CAT environment is largely overlooked.

Extracting individual text elements obstructs the perception of a larger whole. Similar to how CAT tools alienate translators from direct clients and end users of translations, they also alienate them from the clients' documents that they get to translate. The absence of clear visual cues carries a risk that the translator will not recognise the relationship between text components and meanings. This is not a cerebral speculation but a real-life challenge, for instance when translating PowerPoint presentations in CAT tools. Those who translate from English often come across typical noun chains. Whereas Germans cram separate words into huge compounds, English speakers usually don't realise that the notorious German long words occur in their language too: *Donaudampfschiffahrtsgesellschaftskapitän* vs. Danube steamship company captain.

Bearing in mind that PowerPoint presentations usually contain a lot of key words and cue statements with little or no context, let us see how this most often cited and easily recognisable German compound might be handled in a CAT tool. Imagine how the compound would be presented if our notorious steamship company had an English organisation chart. Add a paragraph break after each word and you will come up with a typical building block:

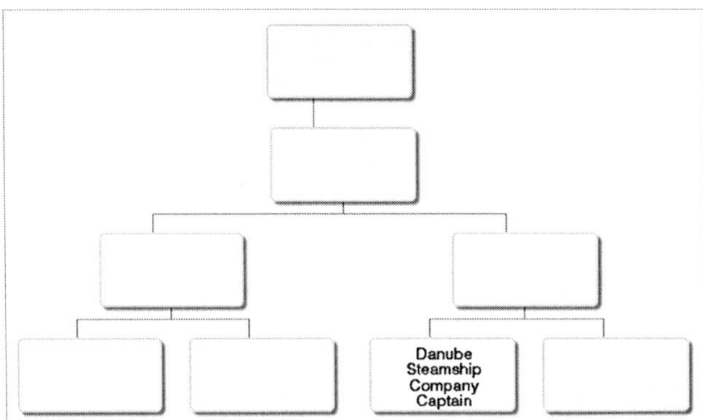

For CAT tools, a paragraph break is a default rule of segmentation, so you would probably end up with four separate segments to reconstruct the original meaning from. The example is fictional, but the segmenting of Application Documents Approval Authority below is taken from a real presentation that I was asked to translate. It is here that I found how visual alienation of the source document can affect the semantics:

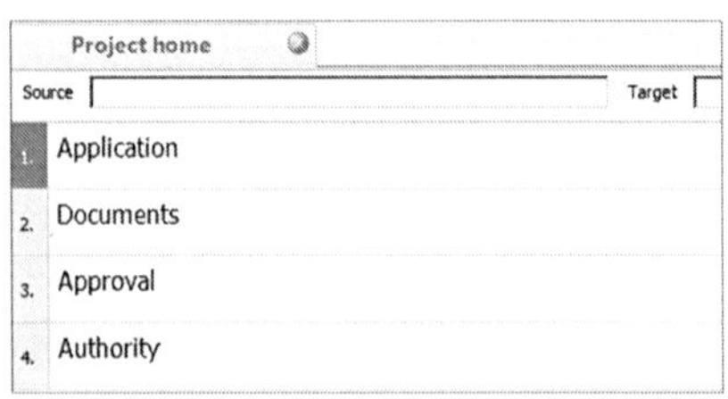

As is well known, it is not advisable to translate captions without seeing the pictures they refer to. For quality translation output, the same goes for anything beyond plain running text: when you translate verbal content that was initially arranged in a graphically meaningful way, you should be able to see the bigger picture. The absence of clear visual cues is a case of double trouble. Not only does it hinder the translator's understanding of the relationship between text parts presented as standalone segments, it also has adverse effects on text **presentation in the translated document**.

■ ■ ■

Meaningful ties between chunks of text that are obvious from their arrangement relative to each other may become disrupted. This happens all too often when the translation doesn't quite fit into the original space. In a German to Russian translation of safety instructions below the corresponding parts in two columns were upset, as the Russian words turned out to be way too long for the available space:

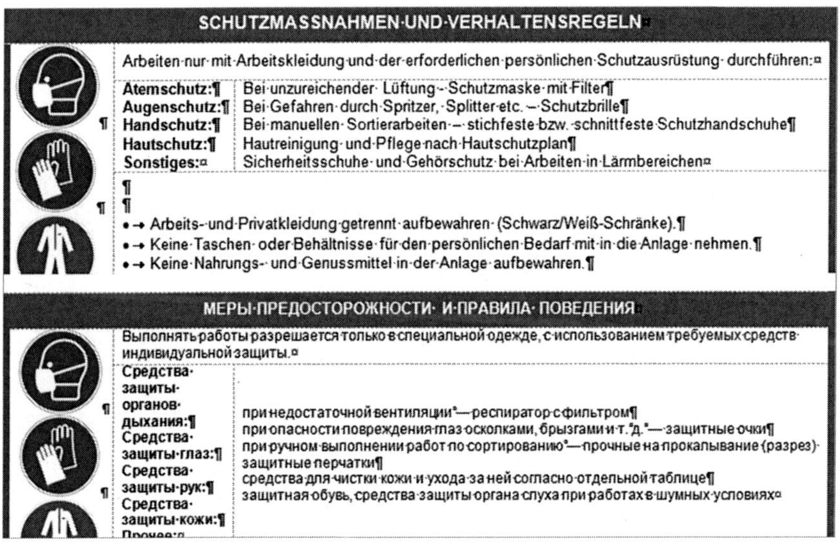

SCHUTZMASSNAHMEN UND VERHALTENSREGELN

Arbeiten nur mit Arbeitskleidung und der erforderlichen persönlichen Schutzausrüstung durchführen:

Atemschutz: **Augenschutz:** **Handschutz:** **Hautschutz:** **Sonstiges:**	Bei unzureichender Lüftung - Schutzmaske mit Filter Bei Gefahren durch Spritzer, Splitter etc. – Schutzbrille Bei manuellen Sortierarbeiten – stichfeste bzw. schnittfeste Schutzhandschuhe Hautreinigung und Pflege nach Hautschutzplan Sicherheitsschuhe und Gehörschutz bei Arbeiten in Lärmbereichen

- Arbeits- und Privatkleidung getrennt aufbewahren (Schwarz/Weiß-Schränke).
- Keine Taschen oder Behältnisse für den persönlichen Bedarf mit in die Anlage nehmen.
- Keine Nahrungs- und Genussmittel in der Anlage aufbewahren.

МЕРЫ ПРЕДОСТОРОЖНОСТИ И ПРАВИЛА ПОВЕДЕНИЯ

Выполнять работы разрешается только в специальной одежде, с использованием требуемых средств индивидуальной защиты.

Средства защиты органов дыхания: **Средства защиты глаз:** **Средства защиты рук:** **Средства защиты кожи:** **Прочее:**	при недостаточной вентиляции — респиратор с фильтром при опасности повреждения глаз осколками, брызгами и т. д. — защитные очки при ручном выполнении работ по сортированию — прочные на прокалывание (разрез) защитные перчатки средства для чистки кожи и ухода за ней согласно отдельной таблице защитная обувь, средства защиты органа слуха при работах в шумных условиях

This wouldn't have happened if the creator of the original document had properly formatted all the corresponding parts by placing them into table cells:

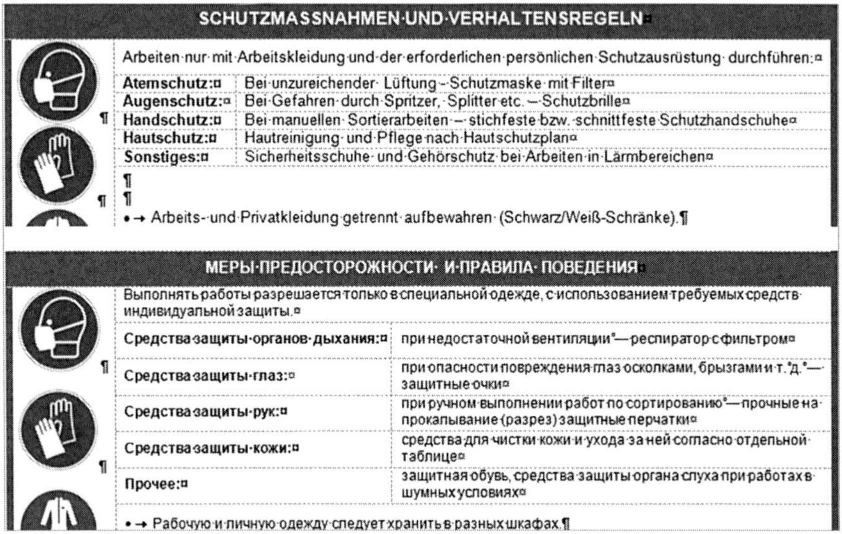

SCHUTZMASSNAHMEN UND VERHALTENSREGELN

Arbeiten nur mit Arbeitskleidung und der erforderlichen persönlichen Schutzausrüstung durchführen:

Atemschutz:	Bei unzureichender Lüftung – Schutzmaske mit Filter
Augenschutz:	Bei Gefahren durch Spritzer, Splitter etc. – Schutzbrille
Handschutz:	Bei manuellen Sortierarbeiten – stichfeste bzw. schnittfeste Schutzhandschuhe
Hautschutz:	Hautreinigung und Pflege nach Hautschutzplan
Sonstiges:	Sicherheitsschuhe und Gehörschutz bei Arbeiten in Lärmbereichen

• Arbeits- und Privatkleidung getrennt aufbewahren (Schwarz/Weiß-Schränke).

МЕРЫ ПРЕДОСТОРОЖНОСТИ И ПРАВИЛА ПОВЕДЕНИЯ

Выполнять работы разрешается только в специальной одежде, с использованием требуемых средств индивидуальной защиты.

Средства защиты органов дыхания:	при недостаточной вентиляции — респиратор с фильтром
Средства защиты глаз:	при опасности повреждения глаз осколками, брызгами и т.д. — защитные очки
Средства защиты рук:	при ручном выполнении работ по сортированию — прочные на прокалывание (разрез) защитные перчатки
Средства защиты кожи:	средства для чистки кожи и ухода за ней согласно отдельной таблице
Прочее:	защитная обувь, средства защиты органа слуха при работах в шумных условиях

• Рабочую и личную одежду следует хранить в разных шкафах.

However, it wouldn't have happened either if the translator hadn't been visually impaired about the document structure due to the segmentation of this document in her CAT tool.

Segmentation is one of the key features of any CAT tool. It is the fundamental way a CAT tool displays a document to be translated – segment by segment, as if dictated by a machine. The resulting granularity gets in the way of cohesion, fractioning leads to the development of divisive lines – borders between separate pieces of an otherwise cohesive text. Focusing on a segment as if it were a self-contained unit, the translator easily overlooks the connections between segments. This may cause all kinds of disturbance to a natural, smooth text flow – from lexical (a chosen word or phrase fits perfectly in one segment, but seems out of place when it repeatedly appears in a number of consecutive sentences) to phonetic (the ending of the preceding segment and the beginning of the next one don't sit together well). Similarly, logical transitions might be disrupted – starting with the accidental use of wrong pronouns and ending with misleading interpretations of larger chunks of text that overarch two or more segments.[60]

Drawbacks of working in a CAT environment become increasingly noticeable when a translator is assigned a job exclusively in a CAT tool, as is often the case in the corporatised translation industry. With no original document in its initial format available to the translator, all the shortcomings of working blindly come out: the translator may have to recycle the old wording all over again and hasn't much of a chance to at least look at how her output fits in within the real document setting. Promoting dependence on source-language text or, more accurately, on automatically **segmented parts** of source-language text, CAT tools undermine the translator's editing skills. Yet it is these skills that become increasingly more valuable for delivering quality work that goes far beyond accurate rendering of the source segments.

Taking into account the space allowed by document layout or considering hard page breaks can be important not only when working on product brochures or company magazines. I learned the value of considering layout constraints when working as a translator of marketing materials and technical documentation, such as user's manuals. A translator may need to extend or shorten copy depending on the available space on a page and adapt it to the layout of a specific template or web page. To deliver quality translation, a translator has to be in control of the finished product. Comprehensive service pays off: in my experience, an end-to-end solution is preferable to the alternative of dealing with a translator who is blind to the layout, while also dealing with a layouter (or typesetter) who has to consult the translator each time layout considerations demand changes in the text.[61] Besides, translating with final layout in mind is enjoyable work. I can only second long-time magazine editor Hanya Yanagihara, who said of his job: "I found it relaxing, as well

60 One might argue that, provided the original document is available, the translator can open the source text in the native program and use it parallel to working in her CAT tool. That is true, but switching from one open window to another on the screen would reduce rather than enhance your productivity and make the entire point of using a CAT tool to speed up translation irrelevant. The same is true of using SDL's Preview feature "to generate an initial preview" or "open the document in its native application" (*File → Print and View → View in*).

61 This is an odd coincidence, but five minutes after I wrote this I read the following post on Facebook, in the group Things Translators Never Say: "Dear client, today I visited your website to see how you implemented my translation on it. Well, it's absolutely normal that the translated text is sometimes longer than the original and does not always fit in the layout. But believe me, it's not the best idea to randomly leave out 30–50% of the words to shorten the text. I know, you don't speak this language and everything looks fine for you, but please let me help you eliminate this nonsense. I dare say nobody will buy your luxury goods after s/he have seen this nightmare of localization."

as satisfying: so much of this type of magazine work is fitting words to space, not the other way around, and is thus a largely visual exercise."[62]

■ ■ ■

Having thrown these stones at CATs (I have intentionally left out the usual complaints of a more technical or program-specific nature), it is time to ask the crucial question: what good will it do to know that CAT tools have disadvantages for me as a translator? How can I cope with all these and how should I deal with CAT tools if I am still going to use them, notwithstanding the critique?

My first suggestion is to be aware that the output from a CAT tool is **a semi-finished product**. Or rather, it should be treated as such if the translator is to take full control and responsibility for her work and is committed to the comprehensive quality of her service. CAT tools' modus operandi is based on splitting integral texts into translation segments. Likewise, CAT tools split the entire translation process. In a corporatised and technologised translation industry, this inherent property of CAT tools is used to marginalise translators, who become one of several replaceable "resources" in a departmentalised, multistage process. The latter implies setting up projects, creating packages, pre-translating documents with matches from existing translation memories (TMs), splitting documents and tasks among translators, proofreaders, reviewers, revisers and so on to extract value – less for direct clients and translators, but more for the process owner.[63]

Becoming aware that the output of a CAT tool is **a semi-finished product** helps maintain a holistic work approach and ensure that the ownership of the process remains with the translator. The translator decides on the application of technology and tools to obtain the best results. The more selectively CAT tools are employed, the more effective their use.

62 Ilana Masad. "'I Wouldn'tve Had a Biography at All': The Millions Interviews Hanya Yanagihara, 2015". *The Millions*, published 5 August 2015 <http://www.themillions.com/2015/08/i-wouldntve-had-a-biography-at-all-the-millions-interviews-hanya-yanagihara.html> accessed 21 August 2018.

63 As Kirti Vashee states in his observations on the translation market (June 2016), "[p]roject management is the core business function [of the LSP Translation industry] and the most important tools are TMS systems and TM" ("[The larger context translation market" [blog]. *eMpTy Pages*, published 20 June 2016 <http://kv-emptypages.blogspot.de/2016/06/the-larger-context-translation-market.html> accessed 21 August 2018).

CAT tools are best suited for plain running text and least suited for documents containing graphics and text or presenting a complex arrangement of graphic components and text parts. Such content is worth at least a second look before importing it in a CAT tool for translation. Bearing in mind the inevitable segmentation, poor or inconsistent formatting of the original document may present an obstacle for the translation process or wreak havoc on the layout in the finished translation.

The most universal piece of advice is to **fix any layout and format issues** in the native format **prior to importing** the document into a CAT tool. This is where the adage "Fail to prepare and you prepare to fail" really comes into its own. Having a second look at the document before starting to translate it in a CAT tool means checking it for hidden or barely visible details that could grow into issues once the content is changed. Are blank spaces and tabs used as a shortcut for columns or table cells? Would it help to create a table where the structure needs to be strictly controlled, no matter how long or short the translation will eventually turn out in comparison to the source text? Did the author of the document use styles for headings? Are there any inconsistencies with paragraph alignment, line spacing, indentation, numbering, page breaks, and so on? This may seem a hassle at first, but in the long run, **proper preparation** can save you headaches further down the line and make the finishing stage of your translation a breeze. The focus is on **making things right**. Neither should preparation serve as an end in itself, as a process that is unreasonably perfectionist or demanding. The rationale behind it is that taking care of nonverbal elements, such as layout and formatting, at the outset makes the actual translation process easier and the final product crisp, readable and usable for the client. The product will also bear the mark of its creator – of someone who cares.

If you think "why bother", it is probably how 90 percent of your colleagues think, too. I have seen countless examples of translations with unworkable format identical to that of the original, with every blank space and every tab kept fastidiously intact. Sometimes such translations look as if the translator took the extra trouble to expose the poor formatting of the source text, but wasn't fussed to go against the rule of "faithfulness to the original", down to the last meaningless detail. Making improvements that facilitate the workflow and produce a better result is a straightforward and economical way to **make a difference**. The ideal way to this is to define the single steps. In the end, you will have described a process that ensures consistency and saves time.

It may seem counterintuitive and much in line with the technocratic standards and attitudes that are characteristic of the corporatised translation industry. In terms of achieving quality, however, the effectiveness of such standards and processes depends on who they serve – "productive forces" or trade intermediaries.

■ ■ ■

If we list the steps that we think are reasonable in order to produce a quality translation and meet the requirements of our translation project, the resulting description will be "a set of interrelated or interacting activities that transforms inputs into outputs", according to an ISO definition of a process (ISO 9000:2015).[64] The important thing is to make clear that in practice this list is to be applied selectively: steps and actions need to be grouped together and prioritised. Steps and actions that are performed in a CAT environment are best suited to producing **an intermediate product**. Therefore, the output of a CAT tool should be checked in the native application before delivering the translation to the client. Even more importantly, the **initial document should be checked**, too, before importing it into the CAT tool. To optimally use the software, rather than be "used by it" (remember "program or be programmed" by Douglas Rushkoff), we need to consider adjusting and "programming" the native document as the first stage. Having done that, we will arrive at a very general description of the translation workflow:

- **Step 1:** Check and adjust the original document in the native application.
- **Step 2:** Translate the document in your CAT tool.
- **Step 3:** Revise the translation in the native application.

Each of these steps is similar to an item in a dropdown menu. In the ideal description of a workflow we should be able to "click" on each point to open up a sublist of more specific, actionable items. ISO differentiates between processes (what is to be done), procedures (general rules of how it's to be done) and work instructions (detailed descriptions of tasks). Whatever hierarchy you apply to the description of your workflow, the highest level will be composed of a sequence of very general, self-evident steps, like in the above list. When zooming in on it, we will end up with a detailed checklist of actions for each step. The checklist shown in the chapter "Make typography rules work for you" (p. 99) is a good example of an action list. Given the variety of translation projects, subject matters, specialties and document formats, any standard would work best only if it would logically describe your personal, customised approach. But to work effectively, it must be consistently used.

64 <https://www.iso.org/obp/ui/#iso:std:iso:9000:ed-3:v1:en> accessed 22 August 2018.

I believe that many actions listed in the example taken from the Editor's ToolKit should be performed at Step 1 above rather than after the translation. This goes for *Breaks and Returns*, *Tabs and Spaces* or a number of *Formatting* actions:

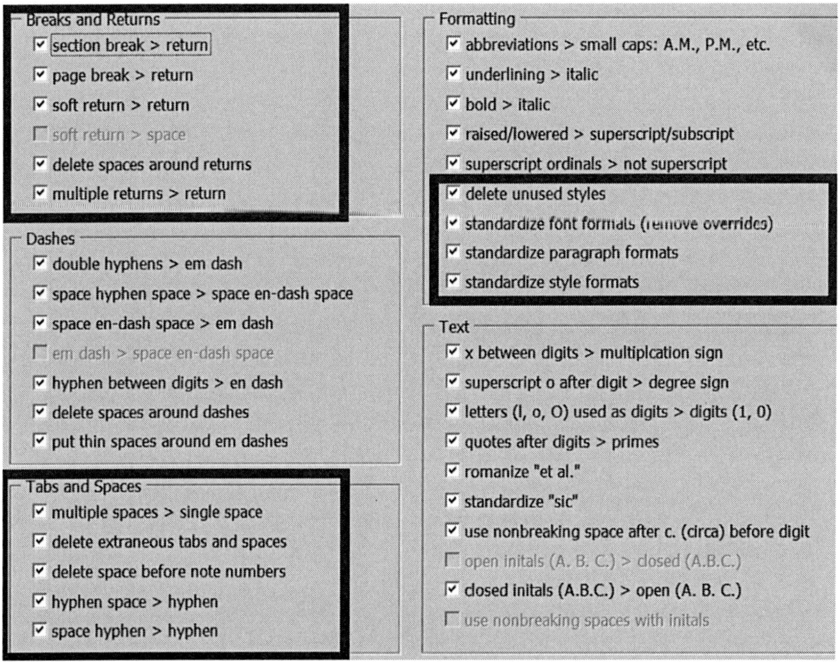

On the other hand, Step 3 could include far more actions that belong to the repertoire of editors and proofreaders. Well-known editing techniques can be useful, too. For example, if you work on marketing copy, you can read your text out loud to smooth out the edges and make sure that neighbouring segments don't butt heads, as may be the case after translating segments in a CAT tool. Editing for structure and content and, above all, taking a fresh look at your translation "through the client's eyes" is essential for the final stage. There is more to it than simply correcting mistakes or running your work through a spell-checker. There may be inconsistencies, irregularities and imperfections in the final translation **inherited** from the original. However, there is chance of discovering them at this stage, when finalising your translation, rather than when looking through the source document before starting to work on it. This is where it makes sense to make improvements **despite**

the original and perhaps, if you consider your service an added value, advise or help the client to apply similar corrective measures to the initial text.[65]

■ ■ ■

They say that standards do not guarantee quality. A **consistent, standardised workflow** can still produce a consistently poor-quality outcome or a consistently erratic service. However, in regard to processes I propose a pragmatic approach. At this point let's recall my four P concept (p. 19) – and perhaps even bring in a few more P-words. Defined **processes** and **procedures** don't automatically stipulate the quality of products and performance. However, I believe that processes predicate **professionalism**, the first P in my acronym.

A pragmatic approach means that processes do not need to be promoted solely as something that helps you stay more organised and be more professional about your business. "Sell the outcome, not the process" is one of the most common marketing axioms. If we look at our products through the client's eyes, it is mostly translation agencies that order and purchase translations in the form of semi-finished products, such as the outputs from a CAT tool. Direct clients prefer complete solutions. Notwithstanding this difference, having **processes in place**, whether to produce translations for resale with or without further processing by agencies or for end use by direct clients, is **perceived** as a sign of being more professional, more efficient and productive, by both groups. Processes might be unsexy, but they are **regarded** as adding value and a competitive edge. That is exactly how translation companies use their standards and workflows – not only to manage the work (which is project management at large), but to attract business through instilling trust – persuading potential clients and pledging quality through processes, tools and resources.

ISO standards describe operations management processes. Yet for many translation companies, the point of ISO certification might be marketing rather than operations: an implemented standard serves as a value proposition and an ISO mark can be used in marketing materials. The ISO 17100 standard describes "Requirements for translation services". One of its central definitions, that of language service provider or LSP, equalises the rights of

65 Of course, this advice assumes that it's not important to retain any inconsistencies or imperfections of the original language text (being faithful to the original is crucial in areas such as Bible studies, forensics and various types of academic translations). In most other cases, however, I don't see any reason not to correct inconsistencies that might be present in the original.

translation companies and individual translators.[66] The standard determines the translation process steps that an LSP must follow to achieve quality in compliance with the standard: translation, check, revision, review, proofreading, final verification and release. While "check" is defined as "self-revision" by the translator and "review" and "proofreading" are optional (they depend on whether "project specifications" include those steps), revision is a mandatory step to be done by "the reviser, who shall be a person other than translator". No logical explanation is provided why this step, unlike the others, is not declared to be dependent on "project specifications". The only reason to make it compulsory was to compromise the position of individual translators as "non-compliant" providers (though formally defined as LSP) unless they employ services of a "person other than translator".

ISO 17100 and its predecessor, EN 15038, were designed to serve the interests of the corporatised translation industry. Like CAT tools, the standards were used to force the division of labour and create a competitive edge for translation agencies, whereas individual translators were being demoted to serving as producers of **semi-finished** goods, requiring control and refinement by other parties. CAT tools started with segmenting source-language content and evolved to help the translation industry to fragment the entire translation process. The industry validates the disintegrated translation process "to disconnect labor from the value they created" (Douglas Rushkoff) and equates it to quality assurance as a competitive edge. A pragmatic approach to this is to be aware of the disconnect between the claim and the reality: standards set to describe production processes are used as marketing tools. We can go on and on to disprove the claim of quality on the basis of standardised processes, but apparently, process thinking is seen as a sign of professional competence if it is successfully used to such effect.

A pragmatic approach is another way of looking at things through the client's eyes. For a translator, not "a person other than translator", to extract and **own the value** requires **communicating value to the client**. "Sell the outcome, not the process" is only partially true. There is no guarantee for the outcome, we can only guarantee that we'll employ the best skills, experience, tools and processes in order to deliver a product to attain the desired outcome. This is not what a **semi-finished** product can attain. To sell the outcome, we must take the responsibility for the final product. This book was

66 LSP: "person or organization who provides language-related services"; TSP: "language service provider that provides professional translation services, examples: translation companies, individual translators, or in-house translation departments" (ISO 17100:2015, Art. 2.4).

conceived as a means to help professional translators take back control over the translation process, visualise its results and communicate value to the customer. Throwing stones at CATs (or standards) is in no way an appeal to dispense with technology (or standards). The point is only to become aware of what role these tools and processes play.

In the next chapters we will look into how to take credit for your translation in order to make its quality more visible within the software applications used by direct clients and end users. Technology for translators isn't limited to the so-called translation technology. There is no reason why translators should focus on CAT tools, whereas regular Office applications, such as Microsoft Word or PowerPoint, fall by the wayside.

2.10 What I think about when I think about signing

"Acknowledging the translator" is a subject that occasionally comes up in the media or on the internet, but mostly with regard to literary translation. Non-literary colleagues remain largely invisible. For years, probably the most vocal translator's voice for standing by one's work and signing it was Chris Durban's. Her 2011 interview, titled "To sign or not to sign",[67] is still relevant.

If you read the interview and the comments, you'll see that the arguments in favour of signing can be roughly split into two groups. On one hand, there are those that relate to **quality**. The most relevant keyword is **responsibility**. Signing your product to take the responsibility for it is seen as a commitment to quality, whereas being anonymous is likened to a no-risk attitude that exempts from the quality guarantee. Apparently, taking responsibility for the translation is only possible when the translator has the ultimate control over the product. I re-read "To sign or not to sign" after I completed the previous chapter of this book. It struck me how the idea of responsibility for the final product reflects my own train of thought when I was writing about the output of a CAT tool as an intermediate, semi-finished product.[68]

Segmentation or rather, in a broader sense, fragmentation of the translation process runs contrary to the idea of responsibility. Distribution of risks and responsibilities doesn't promote quality, especially in view of "too many cooks in the kitchen" and despite all attempts to prove otherwise with industrial standards and tools. Signing in terms of acknowledging the translator and a sign-off function in a CAT tool are two different pairs of shoes. Both industrial standards and CAT tools open the way for intermediaries to take credit for the translator's work.

---

67 Catherine Jan. "To sign or not to sign? Chris Durban answers the question by Catherine Jan". *ATA Chronicle*, June 2011 <https://www.atanet.org/chronicle/feature_article_june2011.php> accessed 21 August 2018.

68 There are two aspects of risk: to be made accountable for poor quality or for one's own faults, or to become associated with content that is subject to changes and, potentially, subsequent tampering outside the translator's control (this is a reputational risk). Again, this shows the importance of a translator having a final say, as opposed to taking care of an intermediate, error-prone stage in a fragmented translation process.

Besides the aspect of ensuring high quality through accountability, other arguments in favour of signing your work invoke **marketing** and **self-promotion**. Having a signed product at hand or in your portfolio gives you better exposure, which means an increase in visibility both for the current client and for potential future clients. My favourite adage is "anonymity kills": you have less of a chance to build a name and succeed in your business if you don't brand your work. Of course, the reverse is also true: anonymity can be your saviour if you deliver only sub-par, mediocre service.

Those who don't feel comfortable about signing have one more typical argument up their sleeve – their work doesn't bear a mark of "creativity". Indeed, translation of a technical manual is not something that you can take credit for as creative work, as a colleague once put it. From my experience, documents usually handled by certified translators, such as sworn translators, are perhaps the least creative translation genre, though this kind of translation is inconceivable without the signature and seal of a translator. Also, a typical official statement of ownership or authorship such as a German *impressum* or a UK *imprint* (as under the UK Printer's Imprint Act 1961) requires that persons responsible for the publication are listed, no matter how uncreative their part may have been. And I think it odd when a translated publication's masthead or colophon withholds the names of translators, while providing such details as lithography, type of paper or the printing house. True, a translator's signature would look presumptuous under many kinds of documents, but a more valid reason (or excuse) for a translator's reluctance to include her signature is her notion of **faithfulness to the original** text. A statement such as "Translated by ..." is simply missing in a document that we get to translate. Perhaps, to add something to the translation that was not there in the original may feel like an offence against the principle of faithfulness, one of the gravest transgressions for a translator. But when you are used to looking at your translation (and the original) through the client's eyes, you see things differently. You may look at the idea of faithfulness from another perspective. If following instructions to the letter is the most subtle form of sabotage, then refusing to sign your translation on the ground of protecting its accuracy to the original can be a similarly subtle form of **self**-sabotage.

That said, I don't advocate taking liberties with the original text or adding your signature wherever possible, indiscriminately. A credits note always depends on the type of document, context, your relationship with the client and, ultimately, common sense.[69] But for those of us who are committed to excellence and are looking to progress and taking ownership of their business, the answer to the question "to sign or not to sign" is an unequivocal yes. For the purpose of this book, let me assume that to pursue the merits of signing your translations any further is preaching to the choir. The big question is not **why** sign, but **how**.

■ ■ ■

69 The issue of signing is heavily debated among web designers, but causes almost no controversy among illustrators and photographers. For example, strong opinions have been expressed against setting the so-called footer links ("Design by") on the client's web sites. While many website designers and developers regard footer links as "piggybacking" and unprofessionally cheap, others claim their right of attribution or simply default to this practice, provided the signing is done unobtrusively and discussed with the client upfront.

Obviously, not every translation can and should be signed. As a rule of thumb, the more explicit the degree of authorship in the original document, the more appropriate it is for a translator to sign it. However, on the scale between authorship and anonymity, the majority of business communication documents will fall somewhere near the anonymous end of the range: authorship of many generic documents is blurred due to multiple revisions or is irrelevant. This is the case where signing a translation could be anything but unnecessary and intrusive.

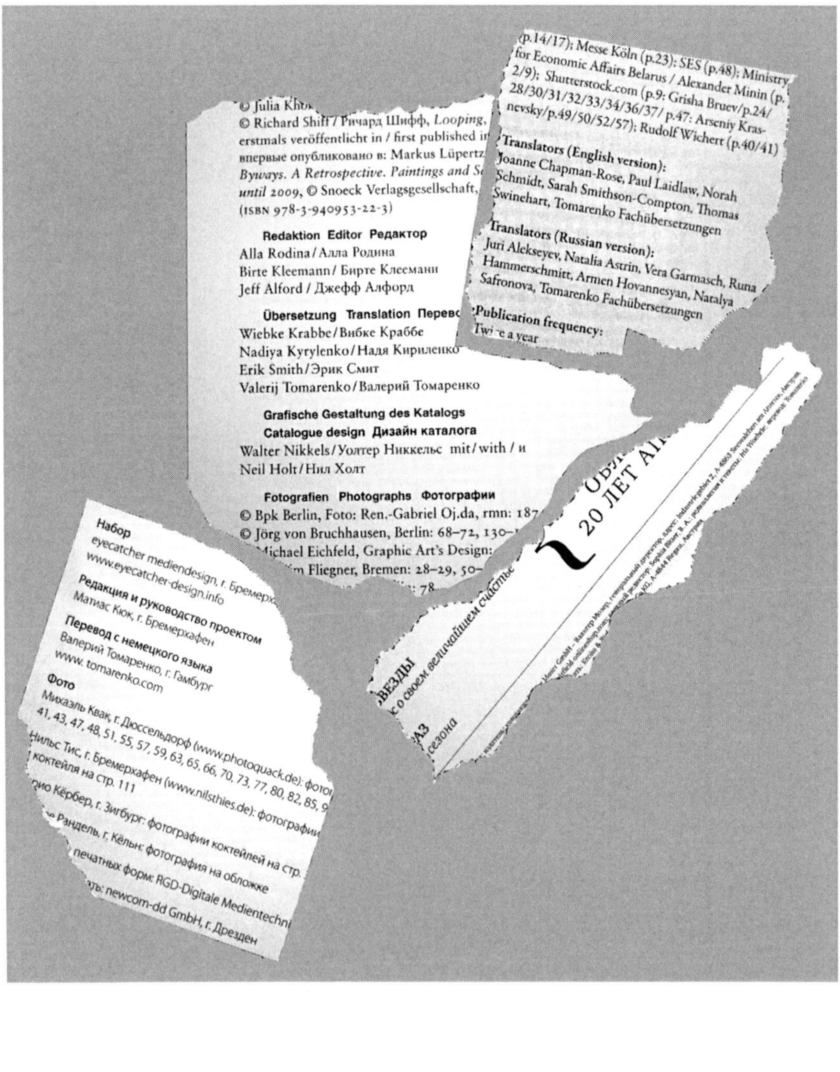

On the other end of the scale, whenever a document to be translated reveals a statement of its authorship, such as in a colophon, it is a good idea to consider adding the name of the translator. Once a formal impressum is available, it is only a matter of complementing it with the credits for translation.

Acknowledging the translator in a formal credits note is the least controversial form of signing their work. However, as is the case with many publications, a formal impressum may not necessarily be part of the document to be translated and hence outside the translator's remit. This is most likely the case when adding credits for the translation could be suggested to the client. If it sounds complicated or something that can put them off, well, it isn't. Giving credits for the translation can be stipulated in your quotation, along with the date of delivery and other terms. In my experience of working with direct clients, this is not a point that your client will ever question. More often than not, the suggestion to include credits for the translation comes from the client, not the translator. However, if you ever need an argument to support your point for an acknowledgement in a translated publication, there are many. Copyright and authorship issues are generally decided beforehand and outside of the translator's remit, but referring to a precedent usually helps. I remember only one case when the client seemed to vaguely object to including the credits for translation on the publication's information page. In this case, I referred to the available information in the impressum as a sort of precedent: those in charge of the publication were specifically named, including the layouter, photographers and illustrators. The client could not logically explain why someone in charge of the translation would be made an exception of.

In the ubiquitous meme "I'm a translator, not a graphic designer" (p. 36), you can substitute "graphic designer" with "a ghostwriter". In practice, I will probably never have to resort to this memeworthy argument to convince a reluctant client to give credits for the translation, though the comparison of a translator vs. a ghostwriter deserves an essay in itself.

■ ■ ■

So the question is not why, but how, and in case of an available impressum format this question has already been dealt with. Yet the majority of documents that we translate have no dedicated space or format to put our translation credits into. What should we do?

Since we usually deal with documents in a digital format rather than on paper, there are two options: add our data to the file's metadata or incorporate them into the visible content. The easiest way to add your "signature" to a Word file's metadata is to open *Document Properties* (*File* → *Info*, then click the *Properties* button on the right-hand side of the *Info* screen and select *Advanced Properties*) and enter your credits, for instance in the *Comments* field:

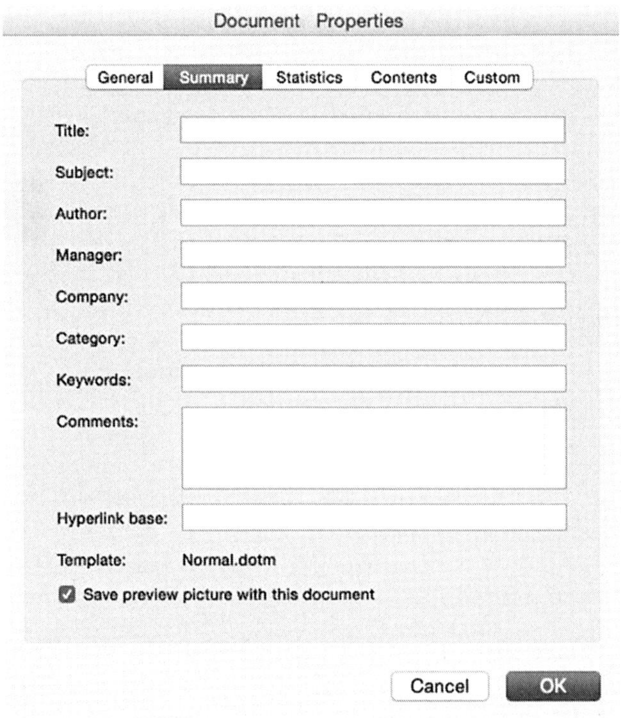

You can make your metadata signature even more sophisticated. After you click on the *Custom* tab, you can add a new document property, such as "Translator", and enter the translator's name in the *Value* field:

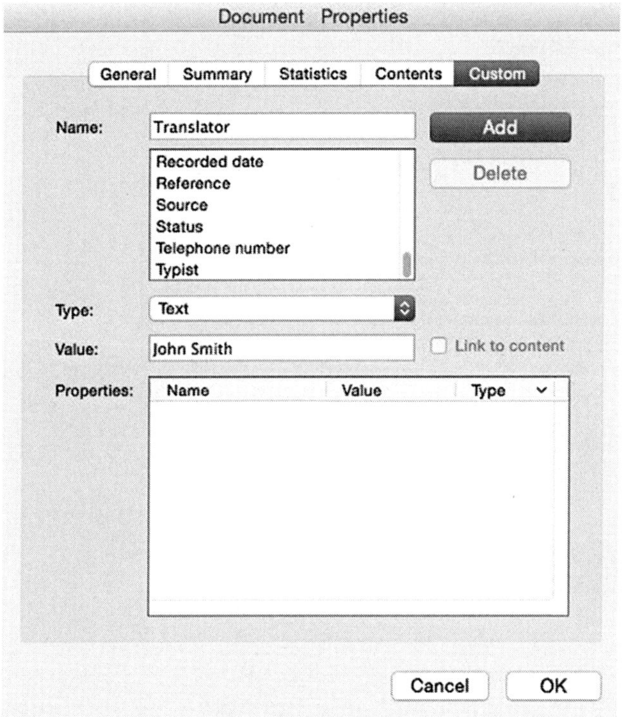

In complex documentation, fields may serve as useful placeholders for common elements of content that can be updated by changing the value throughout the document instead of having to edit every place where the element occurs. This most likely won't be the case with the custom property *Translator* – no multiple references are to be expected. Adding a new custom property with the translator's signature as the property value doesn't serve any purpose other than adding an invisible tag to the document.

More recent versions of Microsoft Office make it possible to detect metadata and other hidden data in Word, Excel or PowerPoint files. The *Document Inspector* (*File → Info → Check for Issues → Inspect Document*) is intended primarily to find and remove personal information before publishing or publicly sharing documents. It opens a convenient list of options, including *Headers, Footers, and Watermarks*, to add any hidden information to the file:

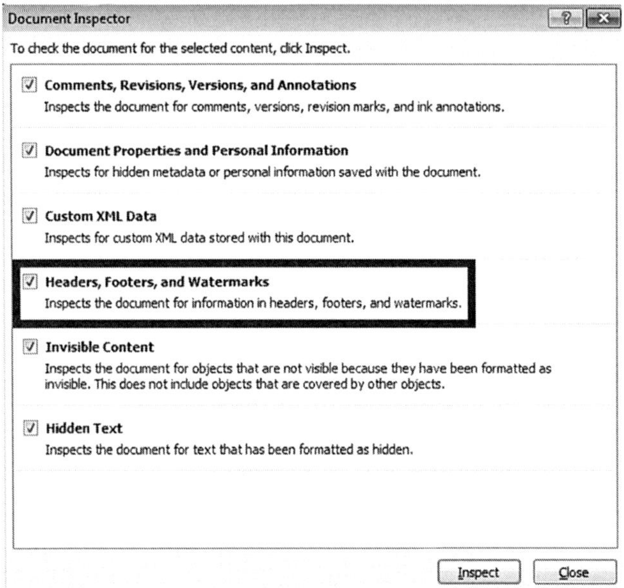

This is one way to sign your work which may be reasonable when you want to leave your mark, but still remain in the background. However, anonymity kills and metadata that doesn't provide immediate visual proof of the authorship of your translation won't make you or your content recognisable.

A more visible way of using the file metadata for your signature is provided by the file name. In keeping with the usual naming conventions, the original file name may be expanded: the translator can add her full name or initials along with the shorthand symbol for the language. I consider this type of signing an "in-between" kind of thing. It's more straightforward and clearly serves to identify the translator, but a file name is only an external identification tag attached to the document. Nothing is incorporated into the document itself. On the upside though, this kind of signature is the least intrusive way to mark your work: the translator doesn't add anything to the source document that initially wasn't there. An additional benefit is that you don't have to discuss the matter of signing with the client in advance, though this only confirms that changing the file name feels more like a way to track changes to the original document than asserting your role in the communication process.

A great way of signing is the simplest one: a plain byline at the end. To distance it from the proper text, use brackets. In keeping with the citation etiquette, use square brackets. Square brackets usually indicate that the information was added by someone other than the original author. They have more of a signal character, which is just as well: it doesn't leave a good impression if your clients think that you are trying to promote yourself to their partners and clients in an underhand way.

A more sophisticated way to place your signature at the end of the translation is to offset it visually by putting it at the bottom of the last page. If Word is still the preferred format, the possibilities are scarce. An absolute no-go is, of course, using carriage returns to move your signature to the bottom of the page, as the signature may shift if any changes are made to the body text. The idea is to make your signature sit at the bottom of the last page irrespective of the number of changes to the text. A more elegant way of doing this would be to use a footer. However, for a multi-page document that would also mean inserting a section break for the last page to prevent your signature from appearing on every page. This may not be a justifiable interference in the layout and it can seriously affect the layout if the amount of text were to change.

If a footer isn't worth the trouble, the idea of a footnote or an endnote may present itself. On a closer look, though, it is just as unfortunate: footnotes are used for providing additional information or clarifying a particular statement in the text. They are either explanatory or refer to additional sources of information. Of course, to sign your translation, you could put the footnote at the end of the last sentence, but to my mind it would still appear rather awkward, as if it were a reference to the last paragraph only. So what's next?

Microsoft Word has a little-known feature that lets you define the position of characters or text parts on the page. This feature is called the *Advance* field and can be accessed in *Insert → Quick Parts → Field*:

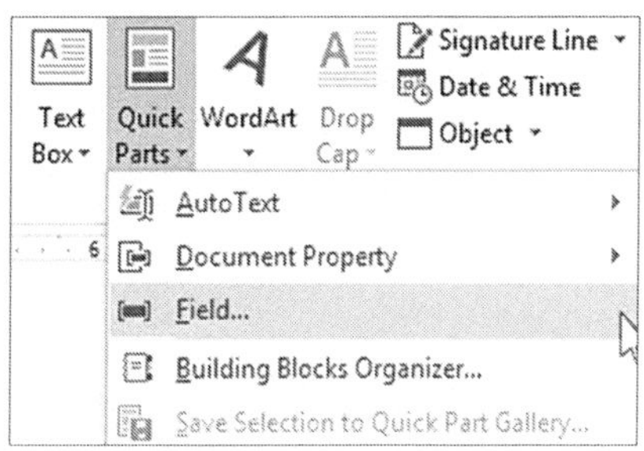

The *Advance* field has four main commands, \L, \R, \U and \D – to offset the following text to the left, right, up or down, and two more commands, \X and \Y – to shift it horizontally from the left or vertically from the top by a specified number of points:

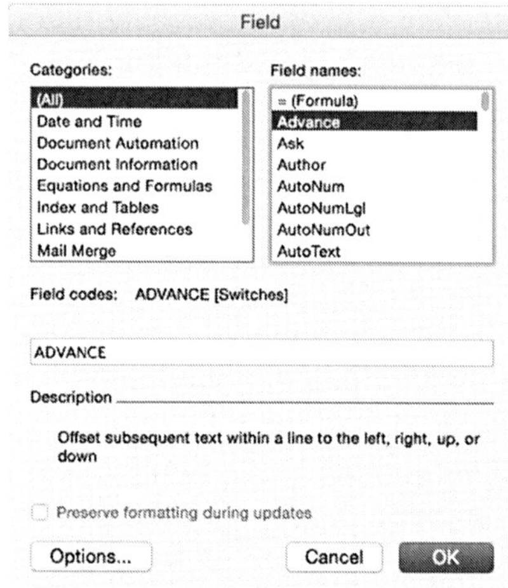

This generally remains impractical, since the offset is relational and the signature position on the page would change were the document to be edited. Apart from that, the *Advance* field feature of earlier Word versions is not supported in more recent versions, starting from Word 2013. Instead, for absolute vertical positioning in a Word document, you can put your signature into a text box. Go to the *Insert* tab and click the *Text Box* button. Instead of choosing one of the preformatted text boxes from the list, draw your own:

Type and format your signature (e.g. "Translated by...") in the box and right-click on the text box border. It's best to choose *Bottom* as *Vertical alignment* (*Format shape → Text box...*):

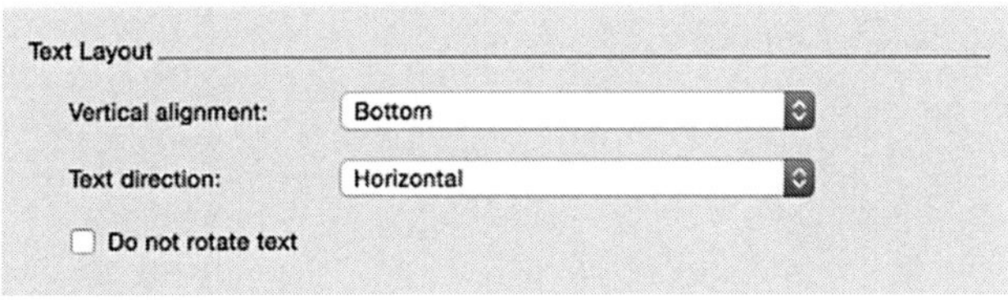

You need to anchor the text box to the bottom of the page. Click on *Layout* instead of *Text Box* and choose any option other than *In line with text* as *Wrapping style*. The options *Square*, *Tight*, *Behind text* and *In front of text* make your text box a floating object. The text box will be anchored to a paragraph, but its position can be controlled through the *Advanced* options. Click *Advanced* in the bottom right of the screen:

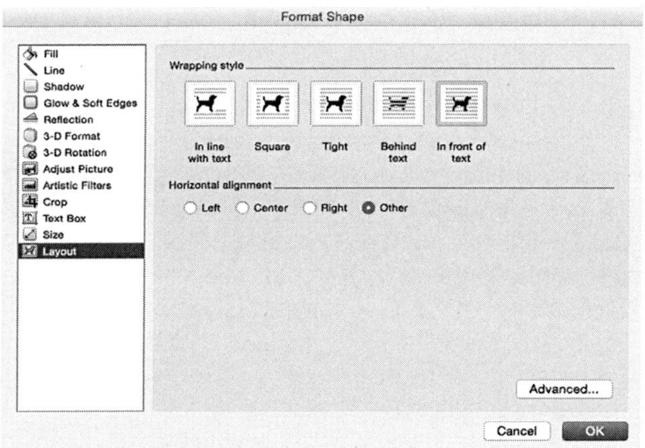

Now you can choose the vertical alignment (*Bottom*) relative to *Margin* or *Page*:

Note that the absolute positioning on the page refers to the page with the paragraph to which the text box is locked. If the paragraph is moved to a different page, the text box with your signature will move with it. This is the function of a small check box *Lock anchor*: it ensures that the object is always on the same page as the object anchor. Word was developed as a text editor, not a graphic design program. To call these options *Advanced Layout* is a bit of an overstatement, but they get you as close to a perfect page layout as a text editor can.

Using a text box feature is easier and more natural in PowerPoint. The most appropriate place for the translator's signature is likely to be the last slide, under the contact data of the presenter or the usual "Thank you" note, as a small byline at the bottom of the slide. I don't recommend making use of the more sophisticated options that Word offers (e.g. custom watermarks, digital signatures or handwritten signatures inserted as graphics), but they are nonetheless worth mentioning for the sake of completeness. For example, digital signatures may be useful for documents certified by sworn translators.[70] However, I don't see any application possibilities for signature lines or invisible digital signatures

70 Signatures and custom digital stamps, including dynamic stamps, are worth looking into for translators whose deliverables are digital printouts such as PDFs.

in commercial translation practice. The same goes for handwritten signatures or stamps. They are fine as long as you have to officially certify your translation or use them for printouts. If you have a scan or saved your signature, logo, boilerplate, note in one of the common image file formats (.bmp, .gif, .jpg, .png), you can add it to your Microsoft Office Clipart library. Depending on your software version, you can use Microsoft Clip Organizer in the Office tools or go to the Clipart gallery directly (*Insert → Clipart → Clip Gallery*):

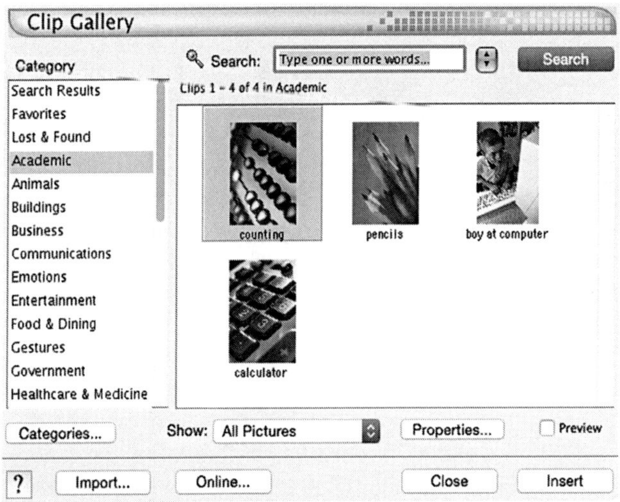

It is important to type in a few keywords (e.g. *Translated*, *Signature*) that describe your image so that you can easily locate it later. Now, whenever you open your Clipart browser, you can locate your signature and drag and drop it into your open document. For precise positioning on the page, use the procedure described above for positioning a text box.

That said, using images such as a handwritten signature, logo or a text line in special typeface on a client's document may look pretentious or too conspicuous. What is fitting for your own corporate style template, such as when generating a quote or an invoice, is not necessarily a welcome input to a document meant for your client's audience. In my opinion, an unassuming, matter-of-fact byline such as "Translated by..." is still the best option in the right circumstances. Your byline may be placed into a pre-formatted text box at the bottom of the page (save the text box for future use) or you can save it as an AutoText building block. Depending on your Word version, select your byline and go *to Insert → AutoText → New* or go to *Quick Parts* in the *Text* group on the *Insert* tab, click *Save Selection to Quick Part Gallery*, and assign it a name in the pop-up box. So long as you deliver products that are editable files, your playfield is limited, but it might be for the best.

■ ■ ■

And here lies the crux of the matter of signing. In former days, when the work was done on paper, you could overcome the problem of signing by using personalised stationery. I can imagine that my letterhead of choice for translation printouts or the first page of a translated document would have been a regular white sheet of paper with an embossed logo in lieu of a signature. Physical objects – in contrast to digital ones – are essentially three dimensional, even if they are paper-thin. Embossed logos or symbols used as signature lines would have made all the difference, a small embossing press would have been of help. Three-dimensionality can provide a natural partition between your content and your metadata, such as the credits for your work. However, I'm not sure if 20 or 30 years ago there was a single translator who considered embossed paper as an unobtrusive, non-invasive way to put her mark on her translations. Perhaps it is just a belated idea that comes to mind when thinking about signing.

Today, our work is digital in nature. It makes it infinitely subtler than what was possible at the age of rubber stamps and embossing presses, but on the other hand, less robust against destruction and manipulation.[71] At the moment, the concept of **digital stationery** seems to be a contradiction per se.

■ ■ ■

Since digital stationery is a seductive, but unrealistic concept, another term that I introduced in the chapter on my four Ps (p. 19) would serve us better at this point. It takes two mouse clicks to remove the "Translated by" byline from the translation (similarly, the embossed symbol would disappear once the page was copied or faxed), but that doesn't mean we shouldn't look to other ways of putting our stamp on our work. Especially if that means shaping our work to make it more helpful and accommodating for our clients. I consider it more important to leave a consistent, visually recognisable "footprint" on your translation than simply sign it and leave everything else in your client's document as is, layout-wise or format-wise. There is no law prohibit-

71 Aesthetics and tangibility – both in the sense of being discernible by touch and in the sense of having some substantial, physical existence – are two reasons, somewhat overlooked, why many consider direct paper mail to be preferable to email in marketing campaigns.

ing improving your translation over your client's original as far as the visual presentation is concerned, provided the improvement serves communication and helps your client reach their goals.

Most translators I know see their clients' original layout as something not to be interfered with at any cost. Yet, the visual identity of the initial document is not always ironclad. Often, clients are unaware of the visual identity of their documents at all, or treat it lightly and don't realise how better design can help facilitate the reception of their message. It doesn't only apply to presentation-type documents: not only in marketing, but also in financial, legal, business and corporate communications, we get to translate what our clients intend to "sell" – their message, idea or plan. That is exactly what good design can help you achieve. "Design is intelligence made visible", to quote the American graphic designer and educator, Lou Danziger.[72]

In my experience of dealing with corporate clients' paperwork, clients tend not to realise the impact that visual presentation can have on verbal content. As a rule, layout and formatting issues are **low down** on the **list of their priorities when dealing with corporate paperwork**. Clients are consistently surprised and appreciative when they find that the translation can do more than be an exact double of the original document, namely be a better vehicle for their message, and can even be used to adjust and improve – in retrospect – the source (if at all needed, since sometimes the originals are created only as drafts for the final document in another language).

"Most human beings have an almost infinite capacity for taking things for granted," wrote Aldous Huxley in *Brave New World*. That certainly applies to the overwhelming majority of translators in regard to how they treat their clients' documents, in particular everything besides the verbal content. Like most clients, they don't realise how the visual presentation helps make the content more intelligible or don't consider it part of their job to take care of anything beyond pure text. That may seem to contradict the idea of "checks and balances" – the visual comparison of the source and translated documents that I wrote about in the chapter on asymmetry and alignment (see p. 30). However, as soon as visual discrepancies take on meaning as part of a systematic, well-thought-out approach, the impression of a possible mismatch disappears. It is critical that if something is to be changed, all changes are always warranted and consistent.

72 In: "Designer interview with Alina Wheeler". *The Logo Creative*, published 23 May 2018 <https://www.thelogocreative.co.uk/designer-interview-with-alina-wheeler> accessed 22 August 2018.

The idea of packaging is to apply the basic principle of design, that is making order out of chaos, for more effective and convincing communication. Packaging is not about style, but about function: putting your client's message into shape and adjusting and improving what the client has chosen for the translation. That applies both to the verbal content and to its visual appeal. You can think about it this way: if you feel uncomfortable about signing your work or are somewhat clueless about where to place your signature, consider **a signature style** instead. Think about it both in terms of content and form, that is both verbal and visual representation. Sometimes this may involve only minimal changes, like merging or splitting paragraphs, adding bulleted or numbered lists (see "Design in practice: real-life lessons", p. 90) or subheadings, to mark the logical structure of the argumentation. If more invasive changes are needed, consistency remains key. In no circumstances may such changes appear random or arbitrary. Anything that stands out against the initial visual presentation should fall into a clear, distinctive, reproducible pattern.

In rare cases, your client's text could benefit from a more significant layout change. For example, a press release for print could be made more readable and attractive in a two-column layout instead of the standard single-column format. If that is the case, if you are uncertain of the possible reaction or even fear that your "high handedness" can backfire if the client views it as an abuse of your remit, you can provide them with both alternatives: staying faithful to the original and a new version with changes. In "Going bilingual" (p. 110), I referred to the proposal of an alternative format when responding to the client's request for a quote. However, sometimes it is not helpful to explain everything beforehand: "show not tell" may be a better option. Sometimes it becomes a clear case of "under-promise and overdeliver".

An attempt to produce a more intelligible translation against the client's original is not without risk. It is always wise to access if the risk is work taking. However, you can be doubly rewarded: with a better product for your client and a visual identity (that can function like a signature or an imprint) for yourself. Again, it all depends on how **consistently** your formatting and layout changes are applied. You can make your translations visually recognisable and perceived as a sign of added value only if you strive for visual cohesion. It is not dissimilar to consistency in branding: in fact, the advice about branding can serve as a valuable guideline for packaging your translations. That is why packaging – the way I define it in this book – anticlimactically boils down to developing a series of templates to apply to your translations and your communication with the clients. In the next chapter I will try to show how a style template can be imposed on Word documents which can do with some improvement. The general approach is to start with your style guides.

Some can be distilled from your clients' source documents. I also consider it extremely helpful to develop a basic, universal style guide to apply to translations for those occasions when your client's documents do not come with a style guide. Beside this, it is helpful to have a custom style guide for your own client communications, and stick to it!

Press releases may serve as a starting point, but generally, any more or less formalised type of "branded" documents offers inspiration, provided it is in line with your field of work and your type of client. I prefer a minimalist, stylistically neutral choice, though to insist too much on neutrality is at odds with another P in the four Ps recipe, that is personality.

If you mostly work with Word documents, the next step is to transform your style guides into templates that may include signatures (or a boilerplate for your own "communications" template) for your clients' and your own use. This is most useful for your regular clients and for documents of a repetitive kind. Today, it is common to set up multiple translation memories specially tailored for different clients. The idea to have purpose-built style guides and templates for different clients complements this approach in terms of presentation.

■ ■ ■

Thinking about signing brings to mind how difficult it is to make an imprint in order to differentiate your products and services. Clients' documents fly into our inboxes already "prepackaged". However, you don't "re-brand" your client's work. The challenge is to make your part in its creation obvious – in a subtle and well-intended way. That is nothing else than taking responsibility and showing your commitment to quality, be it a plain Jane signature or an overall better product.

2.11 Templatise your Word: to each their own

For those who translate mostly Word documents, the purpose of this chapter is to show how to **templatise** your style guides. After all this "theory" about signing and packaging in the previous chapter, this one may appear anticlimactic. But if formatting or graphic design won't work for the type of documents you translate, and you still have some serious thoughts about marking your work as your own, this may be the chapter for you.

You can apply your style templates in a number of ways. First of all, style templates are an easy way to consistently apply custom style guides for each client. This helps to make your clients' documents visually recognisable and highlight their corporate identity. At the same time, as the British graphic designer David Airey says, showing that you care about appearance immediately sends out a professional vibe.

Another area of application are all kinds of clients' documents which could benefit with some order and visual control. Appearance is not an end in itself, the actual purpose is to add structure. A templatised style guide is used to create order out of chaos – and your clients' documents will benefit from more clarity. Whether your clients don't think about appearance or simply have no time to be meticulous in their source documents, a consistent style guide approach can help to make their content more usable and effective. A template emphasises logical structure and may set you aside from your competition.

Third, a clean template with a clear hierarchy of styles can be useful when working on Word files which have been converted from a PDF (more about it in "The burden of PDF", p. 201). Of course, you can just use the *Normal* template with the default styles, but by customising your styles and saving them as your signature template, you create your own personal business identity that makes the packaging and the product recognisably yours.

The idea is really simple. When you receive a Word document to translate, take a look at the *Style* group on the *Home* tab:

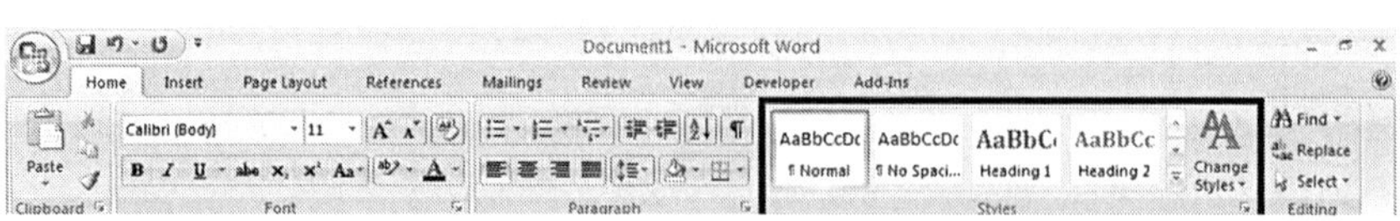

Documents with a certain complexity and structure are usually constructed with a set of styles. Headings, subheadings and lists help to break up content, while emphasis styles – on the character or paragraph level, with or without graphical elements such as rules or frames – are there to draw attention, for instance to warnings:

Manual de instrucciones

CUICADO

Leer cuidadosamente y cumplir con las instrucciones contenidas
en este manual y con las que se encuentran sobre la máquina.

Guarde estas instrucciones.
Para su seguridad, es preciso que Ud. lea y entienda las informaciones contenidas en este manual. Si tuviera alguna duda sobre el uso correcto y seguro de este producto, según lo descrito por el manual autorizado por el fabricante, deje inmediatamente de utilizar el equipo.

Controle el dispositivo antes de utilizarlo.
Aconsejamos que el mismo sea controlado por personal cualificado antes y que todas las partes dañadas o faltantes, adhesivos, etiquetas de seguridad o de advertencia o señalizaciones se sustituyan sólo con repuestos autorizados por el fabricante.

NOTA

Controlar siempre las conexiones antes de utilizar el producto.

ANTES DE UTILIZAR EL PRODUCTO

- Antes de utilizar el producto, leer el manual de instrucciones para conocer el producto, sus componentes y reconocer los peligros relacionados con su uso.
- Cuando se utiliza el dispositivo, llevar siempre prendas de seguridad y protecciones para los ojos.

Headings, bulleted items, italicised phrases or centred paragraphs such as in the image above may be created by direct formatting or by applying Quick Styles. Direct formatting means applying character and paragraph attributes (italics, centred) to selected pieces of text. Quick Styles are in-built combinations of character and paragraph formatting that come as standard with Word; they are called *Normal*, *No Spacing*, *Heading 1*, *Heading 2* etc. and can be found in the *Styles* panel. They may also be custom styles defined by your client.

You can see whether direct formatting or a Quick Style was applied by selecting a formatted text (heading, bulleted paragraph or italicised word); if a style was used, it will be highlighted with a frame:

Direct formatting overrides Quick Styles. This means that character or paragraph attributes will modify the appearance of text whether or not it was formatted with a Quick Style.

To ensure a clear, consistent visual packaging of your translation, **direct formatting** should be avoided or limited to the absolute minimum and, wherever possible, replaced with styles. The most straightforward way to do so is to keep any existing styles in your client's document. Whether or not it is worth the time and effort to reformat the client's document with styles is always a conundrum. It largely depends on whether your translation is a one-off job or something that promises to grow into an ongoing relationship. A rule of thumb is that if you're likely to use something regularly or at least more than once, it may save you time to create a template. Personally, I tend to think that **packaging** your translation is a powerful enough argument in favour of going the extra mile. However, a **project approach** works as a counterbalance – time is often of higher priority.

If there is one thing I would hope you'd remember about formatting after you close this book, it's that it is always preferable to adjust the format of the original document while preparing it for translation rather than translating it as is and adjusting your translation post-facto. So, if you decide that reformatting your client's document is worth the effort, it is better to do it **before you begin translating**.

Do formatting styles need adjusting? This depends on the purpose of your translation, the genre and a dozen other factors. Looking at the document through your client's eyes is always a boon, but this time, to answer the question, I believe you should also try to look at it through the eyes of the translation reader. To find the answer, you have to decide whether an adjustment would add to the clarity and purpose of the content, not whether the target audience for your translation might prefer your personal choice of formats and styles. For example, I often work on Russian legal and financial documents that are formatted according to classic book layout conventions – right edge justification, no extra line space between paragraphs. This kind of layout and typography is fine in a book of fiction, but not in a legal contract with countless numbered paragraphs formatted as lists. Not only does content look cluttered and broken down, the real problem is readability rather than aesthetics.

6.3.3.2 При погашении кредита (полностью или частично) ранее установленных в п. 6.2.3.5 Договора дат Заемщик уплачивает плату за досрочный возврат кредита.

- Плата за досрочный возврат кредита не взимается:
- при поступлении средств в погашение кредита в соответствии с пунктами 9.3.1, 9.3.2 Договора,
- в случае осуществления досрочного погашения сумм кредита, если период с даты фактического погашения (не включая эту дату), а при погашении в соответствии с п. 3.11 Договора с даты получения Кредитором письменного заявления Заемщика (не включая эту дату), по ближайшую к ней дату, указанную в п. 6.1 Договора (включительно), по которой имеется непогашенная ссудная задолженность по кредиту в соответствующем размере, не превышает 10 (десять) календарных дней.

6.4. Дата полного погашения выданного кредита: 10 июня 2019 года.

Погашение кредита производится по следующему графику:

6.4.1. 30 процентов не позднее 10.07.2017 г. (включительно),

6.4.2. начиная с 10.07.2018 г. в соответствии с таблицей.

Although I don't advocate indented, justified paragraphs that tend to produce irregular word spaces for aesthetic reasons, the real disadvantage in the example above is that in a long and complex contract formatted in this way, it is hard to navigate through all the sections, subsections and pages. That is why I would usually reformat such paragraphs – change alignment from justification to flush left, add space between paragraphs, use hanging indents in listed and numbered paragraphs. My bottom line is that if I'm to produce a German translation of a Russian contract, I'll try to make it more reader-friendly and adjust the formatting to the layout preferences of a typical German reader.

6.3.3.2 Der Kreditnehmer bezahlt im Falle der Rückzahlung des Darlehens (vollständig oder partiell) vor dem jeweiligen in Vertragspunkt 6.2.3.5 festgehaltenen Stichtag eine Gebühr für die vor Fälligkeit erfolgte Rückzahlung des Darlehens.

Vorfälligkeitsgebühren fallen nicht an:

- wenn Beträge zur Verwendung als Rückzahlung des Darlehens gemäß Bestimmungen der Vertragspunkten 9.3.1, 9.3.2 einbezahlt werden,

- im Falle einer vorzeitigen Rückzahlung der geschuldeten Darlehenssummen, wenn der Zeitraum beginnend mit dem Tag der tatsächlichen Rückzahlung (dieser Tag nicht mitgerechnet), und bei der Rückzahlung gemäß Bestimmungen des Vertragspunktes 3.11 – beginnend mit dem Tag des Eingangs beim Kreditgeber eines schriftlichen Antrags des Kreditnehmers (dieser Tag nicht mitgerechnet), bis zum diesem Stichtag am nächsten liegenden in Vertragspunkt 6.1 festgehaltenen Datum (einschließlich), an dem eine nicht zurückgezahlte Darlehensschuld in entsprechender Höhe besteht, die Dauer von 10 (zehn) Kalendertagen nicht übersteigt.

6.4. Der Stichtag für die vollständige Rückzahlung des gewährten Darlehens ist der 10. Juni 2019. Rückzahlung des Darlehens erfolgt nach dem folgenden Zeitplan:

6.4.1. spätestens am 10.07.2017 r. (einschließlich) – 30 %,

6.4.2. beginnend mit dem 10.07.2018 r. – gemäß der folgenden Tabelle:

I'd like to emphasise that it is the perspective of the audience, not my personal preferences, that answers the question whether my document needs a layout change. In your own work, focus on your client and your client's audience and try to see things - both with regard to content and layout - through their eyes.

Now let's go back to the method. The best way to alter the look of your document using styles is to make sure that any formatting applied is captured by styles listed in the *Styles* panel. Once you have identified which style has been applied, right-click on it and choose *Modify*:

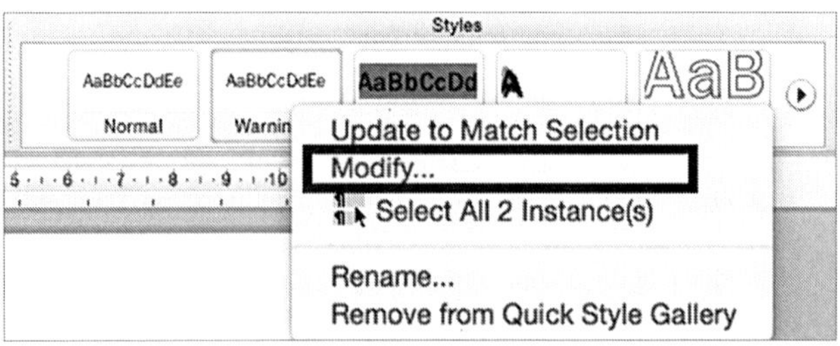

You can modify the properties of a style such as paragraph or font attributes:

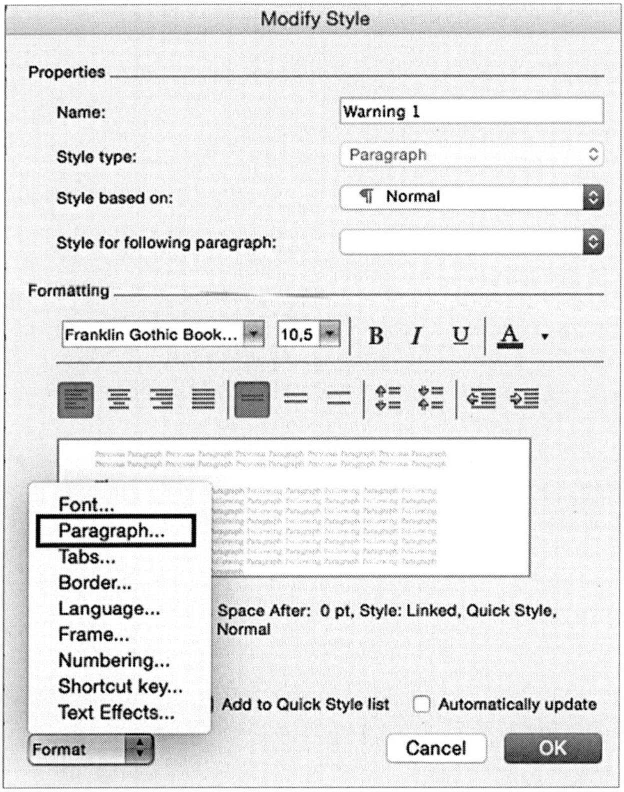

Alternatively, you can first change the character and paragraph attributes in the document directly and then click on *Update to Match Selection*. This command is also useful when attempting consistency throughout an entire document. For every style to be used consistently (e.g. by removing all random font modifications), right-click on the paragraph where one of the Quick Styles has been applied and select *Styles → Update to Match Selection.* The selected, updated style will be applied to all the other instances in your document.

When modifying the content styles in the document, two shortcuts may come in handy. First, to retain the selected style and remove any additional character and paragraph formats, press CTRL+ SPACEBAR. You can also change the style to *Normal*, while preserving individual character and paragraph modifications. To do this, use another shortcut: CTRL+SHIFT+N.

When you have finished formatting, reformatting and adjusting styles in your source document or found it fine as it is (just make sure it is styles, not direct formatting that has made the document look like it does!), it is essential to save your template. This is when you'll templatise your styles. If you are going to use a specific configuration of styles repeatedly, for all or the majority of documents for a specific client, setting up a dedicated template is one way of establishing the client's corporate identity in your translations.

You can set up a master document and save it as a template for future jobs. Think of a template as a group of styles that can be conveniently imposed on any new document as your reusable signature packaging. All Word templates, including templates for your clients, are saved in a dedicated folder on your computer. The path depends on the operating system: in earlier versions of Windows, click *Start → Run* and type *%appdata%\Microsoft\Templates* in the *Open* box; in Windows 10, use Cortana's *Ask me anything* option instead.

Now to the practical part. My advice is to start with having a closer look at the translation (or your source document) rather than creating styles and templates from scratch. Let's say you've noticed that your document has a few captions that would benefit from a special style, for instance italics and centred. Select a caption, apply italics and centre the text. Right-click the formatted text and choose *Styles* from the context menu (or identify the same function in the *Styles* group). Select *Save Selection as a New Quick Style*.

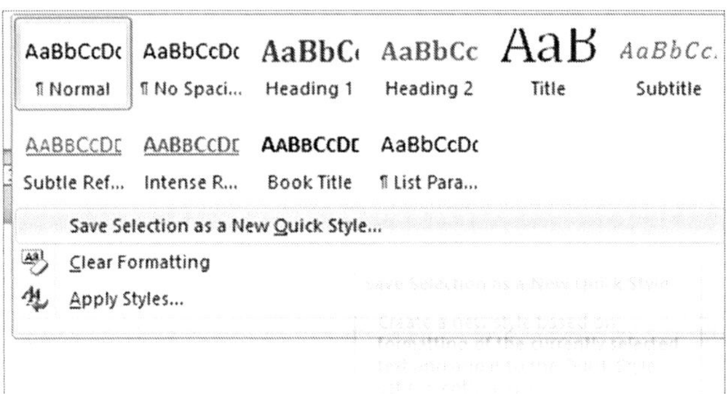

After you've entered a name for your new captions style and clicked *OK*, the style will be highlighted with a frame in the *Styles* group. Right-click on the new style to open a menu similar to the one shown above (*Modify Style*). You can tick the *Automatically update* box. This means that all subsequent changes of the style's properties will be automatically applied to all text elements formatted with this style. This really helps to achieve consistency and saves time. Repeat this procedure for all styles used in the document. If you are both of the perfectionist and the minimalist disposition, you may also want to remove all styles that are not in use. However, at this point all your new styles will disappear as soon as you open any other document. The solution is to save these styles in a template.

My advice is not to create any abstract templates for future use, but to take your current translation and apply your styles throughout. Remember that the goal is consistency, clarity and a reduction to the most essential styles. The appearance of any individual style is not your priority; the relationship between various styles is. It is this relationship that defines the logical structure of your document and, therefore, makes it all worthwhile. When you're happy with your document in terms of order, logic and consistency, save it as a template.

To do so, go to *File* → *Save as* and then choose Word Template (.dotx) from the *Format* drop-down menu:

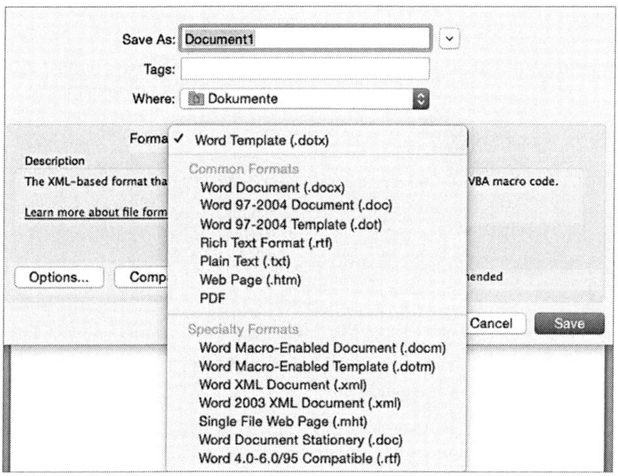

It is a good idea to set up a dedicated folder for your custom templates.

Now that you've saved your template, the next step is to learn to apply it to new documents. Open the *Templates and Add-Ins* dialogue box and identify your custom template. (In older versions of Word, this was hidden in *Tools*, in more recent versions you have to navigate to *File* → *Options* → *Add-Ins* and select *Templates* next to *Manage*. You may also choose to activate the *Developer* tab: *File* → *Options* → *Customize Ribbon* and check the *Developer* box; or click the *Microsoft Office* button, then *Word Options* → *Popular* and select the *Show Developer* tab in the *Ribbon* check box).

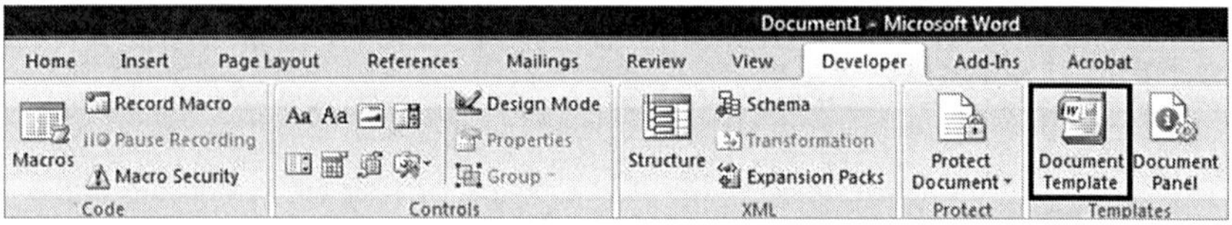

Click on *Attach*, select your template and – this step is crucial – tick the box *Automatically update document styles*:

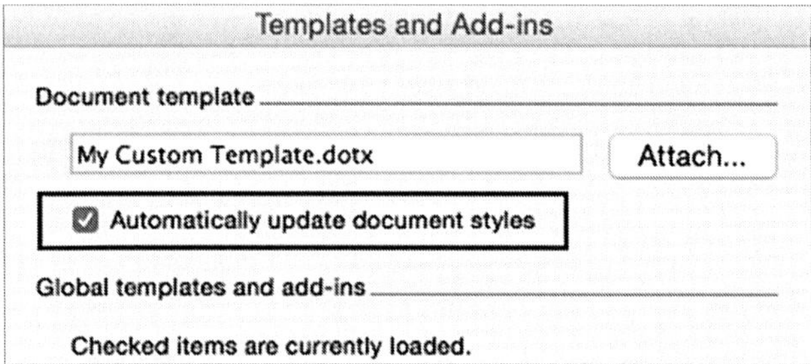

Click *OK* and the styles in your document will be instantly updated to match your chosen template.

Another way to apply templates is to open a new document based on the template you chose to apply. Then you simply copy the contents of your client's document into your new one (CTRL+A → CTRL+C → CTRL+N → CTRL+V or *Insert* tab → *Object* → *Text from File*). The result will be the same, while the workflow might be more comfortable and efficient for you.

It is a good safety rule not to leave the box *Automatically update document styles* ticked when sending your translation to your client, to prevent the style definitions in your client's template overriding your chosen definitions. Unticking the box means that Word on your client's computer won't try to adjust your styles to their templates.

Regardless of the method, there is no guarantee that your carefully designed translation will have exactly the same look on your client's computer. Your fonts may be replaced by whatever defaults your client's software sees as appropriate (or has available). The same, of course, is true for your client's documents formatted with fonts that are missing on your computer. But we shouldn't worry about that. The point of templates and styles is order, meaning a clear hierarchy of styles to help navigate across your document and make it more readable for the user. The priority is logic and consistency rather than any specific visual appearance. The value of templates lies in that they can be reused over and over again. This, in turn, ensures that consistency – which stands for quality in your work – becomes visible.

Elements that can be reused are not just styles. Templates include reusable pieces of content that are called building blocks. For instance, if you created a signature ("Translated by..."), you can save it in your custom template for future use. The practicalities may differ, depending on your operating system and your version of Word. In recent versions this function is referred to as *Building Blocks*, while earlier versions, particularly for Macs, used the term *AutoText*. The easiest way is to create your signature, select it and then save it as a *Building Block* that you will probably find on the *Insert* tab in the *Quick Parts* drop-down menu:

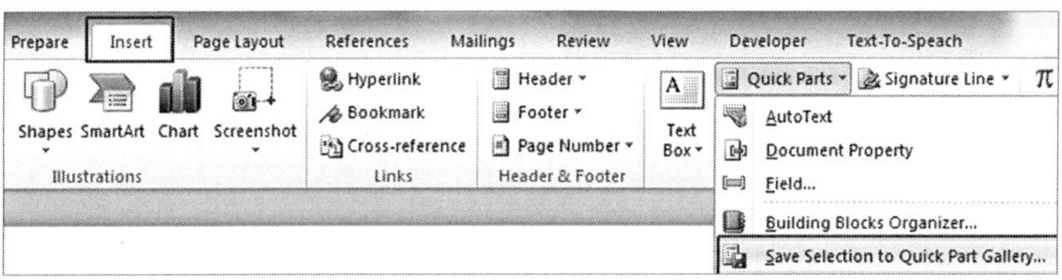

There is more to be done with templates, we just covered the most important points. Templates help increase efficiency, but in the context of this book they are just one method of packaging your translated content and building your visual brand while making your translations noticeably more useful for your client.

3 Working with images

3.1 What this section is about

I believe that today's how-to tutorials on office software or translation-related applications are extremely short-lived. Software versions change quickly and manuals can become obsolete almost as soon as they are printed. Google is a better instructor. All it takes to find an answer to a technical problem is to formulate a search query (and have patience looking through the many results, often in subject-specific discussions or forums, seldom in all-inclusive manuals and repetitive product and user guides). However, this doesn't make any advice committed to paper impractical and pointless. The more options you have, the bigger the differences between various programs, versions, builds and updates, the more valuable is your ability to see the forest for the trees.

I believe that the ability to keep the big picture in mind is a crucial element of a translator's professional competence. I usually refer to this ability as "methodical competence" or "methodical intelligence", though I'm not sure if that's the best term in English. Professionalism, one of my four Ps, comprises not only language and subject-matter skills along with some business acumen, but also a certain emotional intelligence (looking at your work through your client's eyes presupposes a degree of empathy) **and** methodical competence. In this book, methodical competence, even though it has little to do with teachers, educators or psychologists (that is the area where the concept usually comes up), can be best illustrated by the old adage about giving a man a fish versus teaching him how to fish. You can rely on detailed, step-by-step instructions on how to achieve a desired result when using particular software (which may become outdated as soon as the next version is released) or you can try to identify basic functions, principles and approaches that could help you find a solution with (or perhaps even without) any program at hand. And of course, methodical competence is not limited to dealing with software or technology in general. It is of analytical nature, since you need to think rather than memorise or mimic past actions.

Another point I'd like to stress is that we shouldn't get too attached to any specific program, operating system, software or hardware. As translators, we are information workers. Any technology is only as good as it is useful to convey information – both content and form (which, in the majority of cases, is set by our clients). As someone who has been working with both PC (Windows) and Apple (MacOS) programs since the 1990s, I cannot say the development was always in the best interest of users. Many typically "enhanced" and "upgraded" versions deserve to be called disimprovements (German *Verschlimmbesserung* is one of my favourite expressions for "improvement for the worse"). The general trend in software development doesn't necessarily follow the KISS principle ("keep it simple, stupid"). As a result, there might be an abundance of new features and options, but a regular user rarely taps into all the resources that a program is supposed to empower them with.

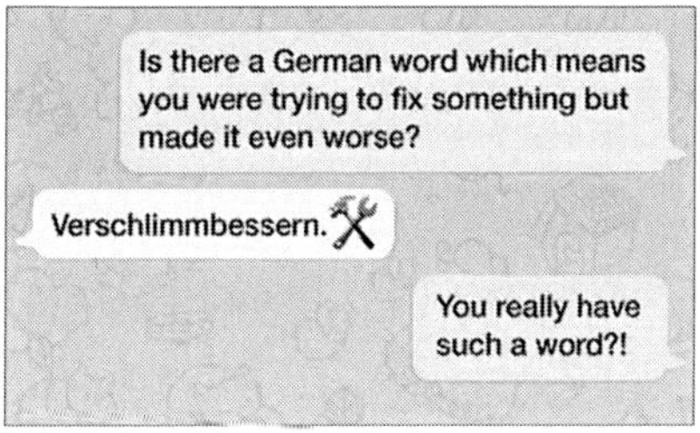

Our clients' documents provide a good example. "Better done than perfect" is the reality against which the well-meant advice of how-to tutorials often appears helpless. So when I say that we shouldn't obsess over technology, it shouldn't be mistaken for technophobia on my part. Rather, it is how "technology", such as software used to produce documents for translation, is actually applied by users, our clients. Methodical competence is more about general approaches than specific techniques. Software users' manuals tend to cover an entire range of technical possibilities in a regular, systematised way. I find that comprehensive descriptions with too much focus on the detail can be overwhelming and sometimes distract from the purpose of a task.

It may seem contradictory after the previous chapters, where the ultimate goal of a methodical approach to design was proclaimed to be "creating order out of chaos", but the practical know-how of dealing with graphics in translations resists an imposition of tutorial-like order. In my opinion, it is better to "**show not tell**" and focus on translation-specific problems. We will start with a case study.

3.2 Translating charts

In this chapter we will follow up on translating Word documents, the bread and butter of many translators.

As long as you only stick to contracts and legal agreements, you'll seldom come across it, but those who specialise in corporate communications often deal with documents that **contain images**. Business letters, proposals, reports, surveys, marketing plans, feasibility studies, organisational charts, financial documents and press releases include tables, diagrams and charts, whereas technical manuals almost never come out without pictures, drawings, photos and text boxes. How do you "translate" images that contain non-editable text? There are several ways of going about it. The most common perhaps is writing down all text **under** the picture, typically in a two-column format, with the original text on the left and the translation on the right. This may be in a plain two-column table (with or without specifying the relevant languages in the header) or using colons, dashes or tabs as separators. Another way is to add a similar list at the end of the translated document, though using footnotes for this purpose isn't common. Some translators like to create a separate Word document for the list or include the source and translated image text in an email to the client. Others provide a target-language list only, especially if the words and phrases are few and can be matched with the source language in the picture quite easily. Word's *Comments* feature can also be used. Lastly, some translators prefer to just leave the graphics intact.

I believe there is a better way to deal with images. To begin with, it is almost always worth asking your client about the **source** document that may have been used, for example, to generate a chart in your Word translation. When, on attempting to edit the chart (either on the *Charts* tab, under *Data*, or by right-clicking the chart and choosing *Select Data*), you get a pop-up message that *The linked file is not available*, it means that the chart was generated elsewhere (e.g. in Excel). It was then pasted as a picture rather than being embedded into the file or instead of linking the spreadsheet as an Excel object. This can be easily fixed if the client has retained the original (linked) file, so that you can translate and update the text in the original format and, without much ado, recreate the chart in your target language.[73] If this is not the case

73 A copied Excel chart can be inserted into a Word document in a number of ways: *Paste Special* options that embed workbook or link data allow editing the original spreadsheet. On the other hand, if you paste the chart as a *Picture*, you effectively prevent it from being edited. Ask the

and there is no source document, you are left with an image with non-editable text, like this example of a Maslow's pyramid of psychological needs:

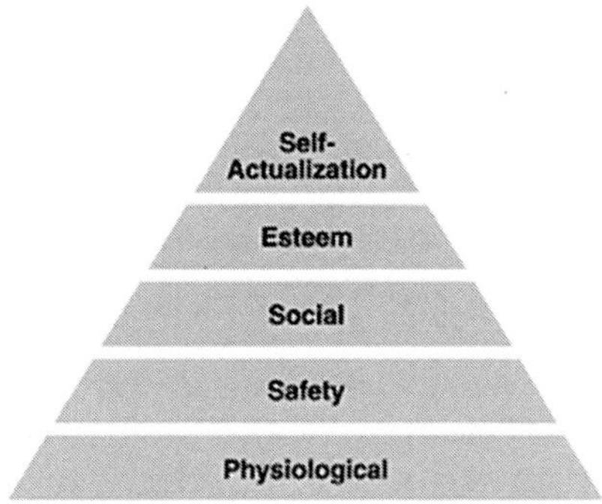

Aside from using a ready-made, easy-to-find picture in the target language,[74] a translator can get away with nearly any, however unsophisticated, legend to this picture. A straightforward list of five items would do, possibly with a note "from top to bottom" or something similar. It would be just as easy to create a small, two-column, bilingual table (e.g. English to Danish, as in the example below; I would recommend using the TransTools' *Dual-Language Document Assistant*, p. 118):

Self-actualisation	Selfrealiseringsbehov
Esteem	Egobehov
Social	Sociale behov
Safety	Tryghedsbehov
Physiological	Fysiske behov

What would you do, however, if the layout of text in your image was far more complex and intricate, and it was difficult to decide the direction and order in which to list the words (e.g. left to right, row by row or clockwise starting from the top left corner)? Think about multilevel flowcharts, thoughtfully designed and compelling infographics, or thought-tree diagrams. Again, a table might be sufficient, but my major peeve with tabular legends is that those on the

client to update the Word document with an embedded chart or request the source Excel file and reinsert the chart into your document with an appropriate *Paste Special* option.

74 Using another version of a graphic in the target language is not such an outlandish idea. Marketing reports and all kinds of business papers sometimes contain references to official sources that may be found on the Internet in several languages. If you find a relevant graphic online, you can insert it into your translation, providing the reference or a note to your client. I consider it a translator's due diligence to check the references in your client's document, images being no exception, because this delivers an added value to the client.

receiving end will get an ad hoc **glossary** rather than a bona fide translation. In terms of readability, it will make your work more difficult to handle, as the user will have to map your table to the image themselves. Whereas a picture is processed as a whole, a picture with a complicated legend loses this immediacy.

There might be an exception in rare cases when the first intermediate user of your translation is a layouter tasked with copying and pasting the translated items from your list into the original picture using graphics software. However, the user experience when dealing with a glossary-type table is still underwhelming, particularly if the layouter isn't familiar with one or either of the languages. The latter is exacerbated when the layouter works in a Latin-alphabet language but one of the document languages is based on a non-Latin alphabet. The same goes for the actual reader of your translation: not only does a bilingual legend under a complex picture require more eye movements, but your reader's effort to identify the proper string of words written with unfamiliar characters makes your translation dramatically less user friendly. In the same way that a typical European will struggle through Cyrillic inscriptions, it may be difficult to deal with text-heavy graphics where the translator's comments refer to Arabic or Chinese text.

So are there any better, less cumbersome ways of improving the reader's experience while basically **explaining** the image in your translation? Of course!

My suggestion would be to provide an **enhanced** bilingual table or an enhanced monolingual legend under the picture. The enhancement is done by adding numbers to words in the picture that will correspond to an explanatory legend.

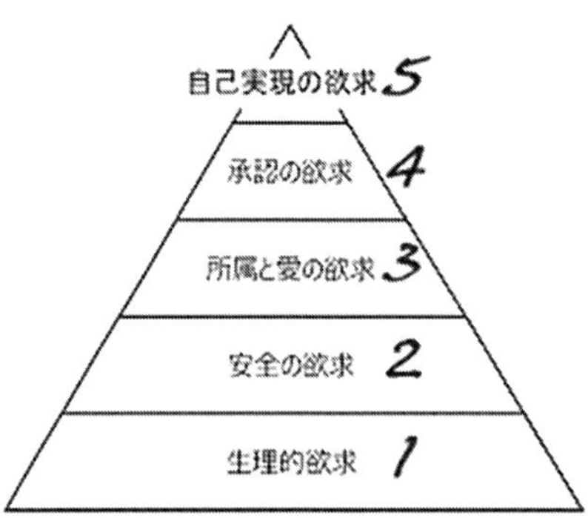

Maslow's hierarchy of needs: physiological (1), safety (2), social (3), self-esteem (4), self-actualisation (5)

This still draws the reader's attention to the fact that it is a translation, but unlike a bilingual table, the caption appears smoother and more appealing.

To put numbers over pictures you can use any tools available, many of which are free: Microsoft Paint (Windows) or Preview (MacOS, which has a simple *Annotate* → *Text* tool). Whatever application you use, the next step is adding your translations to the image. Depending on the layout of your picture, there may also be convenient options for shape annotations, including text boxes of various shapes, callouts or arrows. As with all matters of design, readability and consistency take precedence over other preferences, so the basic principle still holds true: the less, the better. However, the risk of making a mess isn't the only downside of using an app to dress up your picture. A more serious problem is that the result will be another picture with **non-editable** text. Once you have placed your annotations over the original graphic and saved it as an image, your text becomes inaccessible for future edits or revisions, whether by yourself, your client or the layouter.[75]

Adding editable texts to the image is definitely a less intrusive and less destructive way. There are several methods of doing that, of which I will outline three.

75 You can try to use OCR that works not only for PDFs, but also for the most common image formats such as JPG, GIF or PNG. However, my experience shows that OCR produces rather poor results and is prone to destroying graphics, particularly those with superimposed text.

First, you can use **text boxes in Word**. They allow you to position your text wherever you want, including over graphics. Click *Text box* in the *Text* group on the *Insert* tab or, alternatively, on the same tab, *Text box* among *Shapes* in *Illustrations*:

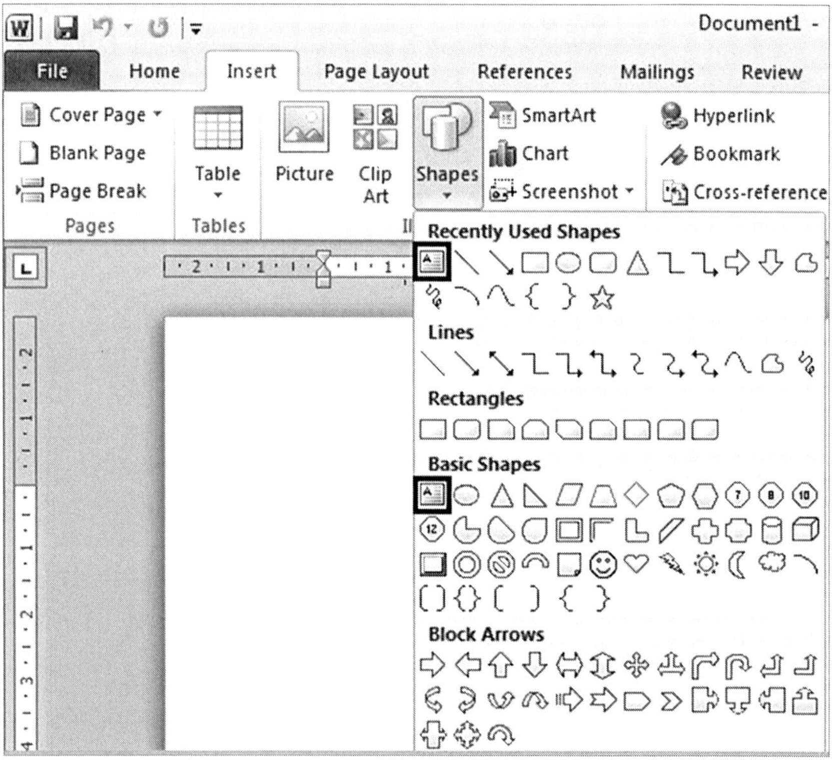

With a box chosen, your mouse pointer becomes a cross. Position it where you want to add your translation and draw a rectangle. The insertion point for your text will appear inside the rectangle together with a paragraph mark (¶). Type in your translation in the box. Before you proceed to the next text element in your picture, I'd recommend adjusting this text box, so that, once tweaked to your liking, you can use it as default for all the inscriptions remaining in your file. Right-click the border of the text box and select *Format Text Box* to make a few changes. More often than not you need no frames for any inscriptions in your picture, so start with the *Colours and Lines* tab.

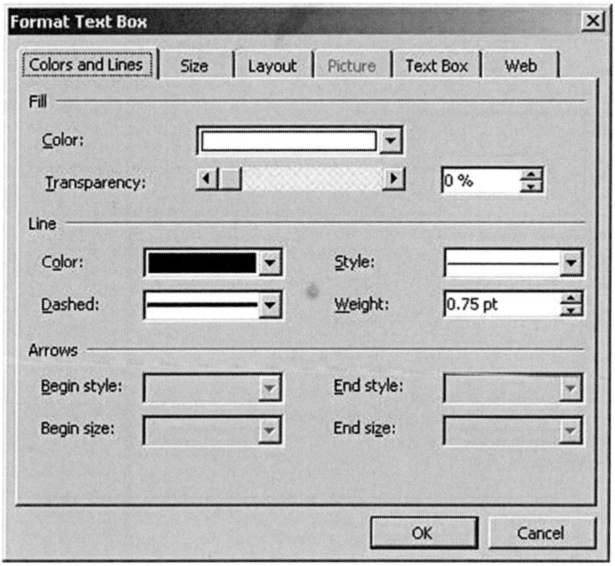

Depending on your software version, choose *No fill* or *No Colour* both for *Fill* and *Line* to make your text box transparent. That will make your translation easier to position, as nothing that sits underneath will be accidentally obstructed.

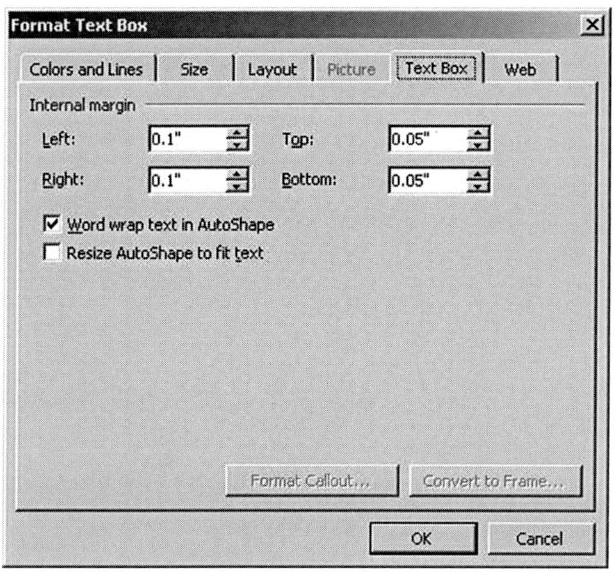

On the *Text Box* tab, I prefer to set internal margins to zero (though it doesn't really matter if the frame is invisible) and to unselect *Resize AutoShape* to fit text. Click *OK* once you've specified all parameters. You'll have to do it just once. For any further translations of image text, you can copy and paste this text box, modifying the text.

Working with graphics in Word doesn't have to be tedious, and there are ways of making things easier. One trick is to select your formatted text box and press the ALT+F3 keys to create a new building block.[76] Assign it a custom name (a single character or symbol such as an asterisk will work best) and save it for future use:

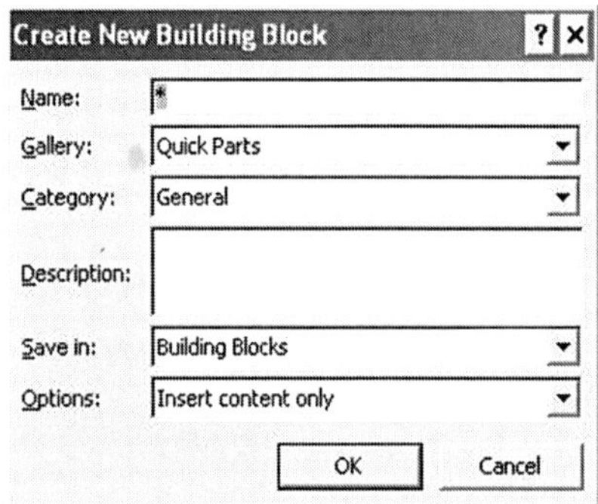

To reuse your text box, simply type its name (an asterisk in our case) and press F3.

You don't have to use a standard text box or limit yourself to one custom frame for all picture legends. In fact, you can use any shape to add text to. For example, to create a neat, consistent look for all picture annotations in your translation, you can choose a shape with rounded corners and use it as part of your style guide/template/packaging.

76 In a MacOS, you may have to use AutoText instead of Quick Parts. The default shortcut to create a new auto text is OPTION+F3. If you use a MacBook, you may need to assign your own shortcut or you can use AutoHotKey, a third-party utility (https://AutoHotkey.com), to manage scripts that can remap keys on your keyboard.

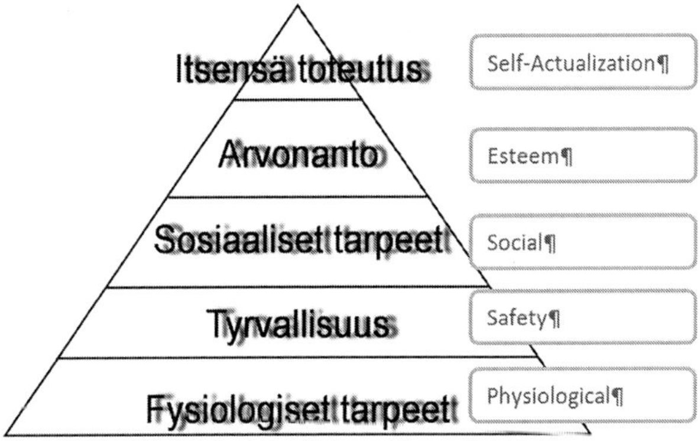

Templatising your style guide, as shown in the previous chapter, is a true side benefit to building blocks. Your signature way of placing translations over images is a seemingly small detail. However, I find that paying a little extra attention to such details along with their consistent use is how you create your brand identity. It is worth discovering such details, because they are what make your translations – your products – visually recognisable (and probably more likable and "human" in the long run).

To align your text boxes and give them a uniform look, select all text boxes holding down the SHIFT/COMMAND key and specify their parameters. It is also a good idea to group the text boxes together with the annotated picture (select the picture and the text boxes, right-click and choose *Group* or click *Group → Group* on the *Drawing Tools Format* tab).[77]

Most of what you can achieve with editable text boxes over non-editable images in Word can also be done in **PowerPoint**. In fact, PowerPoint is often used to create graphics and diagrams for Word documents, as it allows more freedom and ease of use with images. When working with images, you can use PowerPoint much like you can Word. You'll find that text boxes, for example, are already tailored for picture comments: they are transparent and have no borders as a default. The CTRL+D (COMMAND+D or COMMAND+D on a Mac) shortcut is very useful for duplicating items, but you can also select your text box, press the CTRL key (the cursor will change to an arrow with a plus sign) and drag the text box elsewhere on the picture to create a copy. If you press

77 If you find that you cannot group the picture and the text box, right-click the picture, select *Wrap Text* and change the layout options to anything but *In line with* Text. You may have to reposition the picture afterwards, but the *Group* function shouldn't be greyed out any longer.

the CTRL+SHIFT keys, you can move the duplicated text box along a vertical or horizontal axis, so that both (or multiple) frames will be perfectly aligned.

Another trick that works particularly well with PowerPoint, though you can achieve the same result in Word, is to add an "augmented reality" look to your picture. If the image is full of text in the source language, superimposing your translation may cram the image and obstruct some of the detail. Some over-crowded diagrams make it extremely hard to find enough empty space to fit your translations and link them clearly to the originals. If you're faced with such a diagram, what you can do is push the original image to the background, making it semi-transparent; it then won't interfere with your translation. For instance, the wordiness of Maslow's pyramid below leaves little room for your translation:

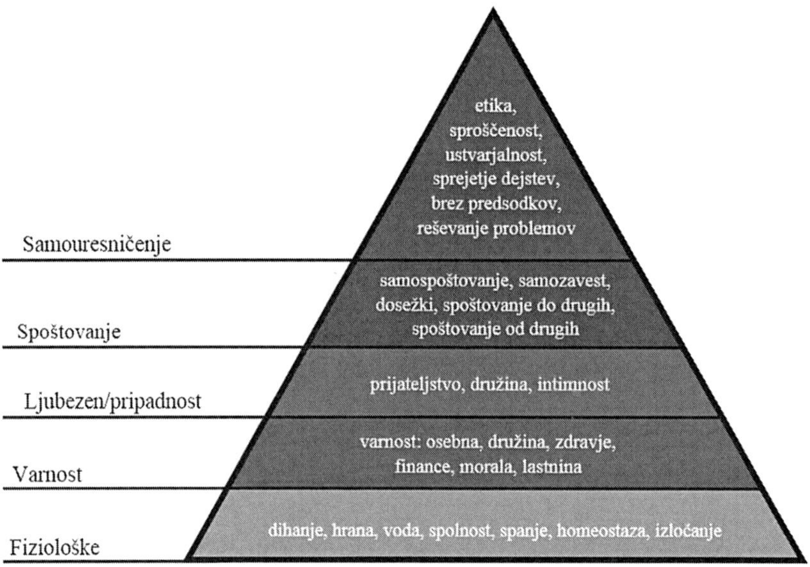

We can format it using the background method and see whether that would help. First, copy your picture from the Word document and paste it into a new PowerPoint slide. Select a rectangle tool and draw a shape over the picture. Ideally, just cover the picture, so that the rectangle is roughly the same size. Now, move the rectangle off to the side of the picture. It can partially or completely go off the slide, it doesn't matter. Select and cut the picture to the clipboard (CTRL+X). Now go back to your rectangle. Depending on your PowerPoint version, right-click the rectangle to access *Format Shape* or go to the *Format* tab. Remove the border: click *Shape Outline* and then *No Shape*. In the *Fill* menu, choose *Picture or texture fill* and then *Clipboard*:

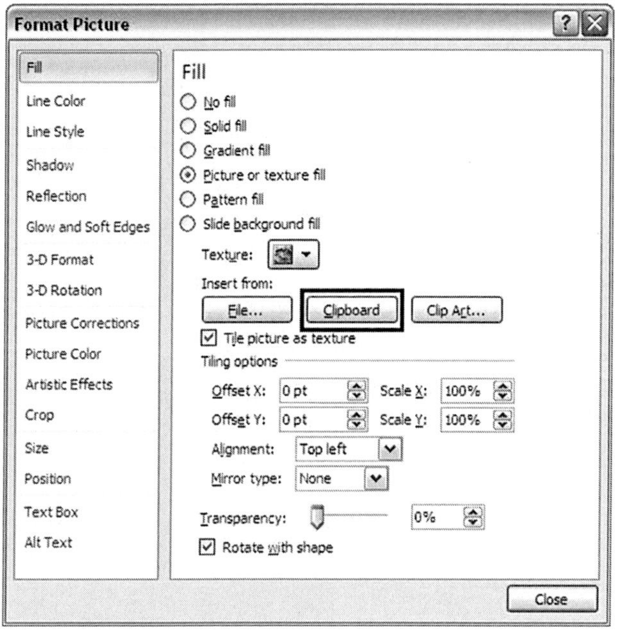

The rectangle will fill with the image that you placed in the clipboard a few seconds earlier. If the rectangle had the right dimensions, the picture will appear unchanged. Now move the transparency slider or type in a percentage figure to make the picture look lighter (50% may be enough, but play around with it and see what works for you).

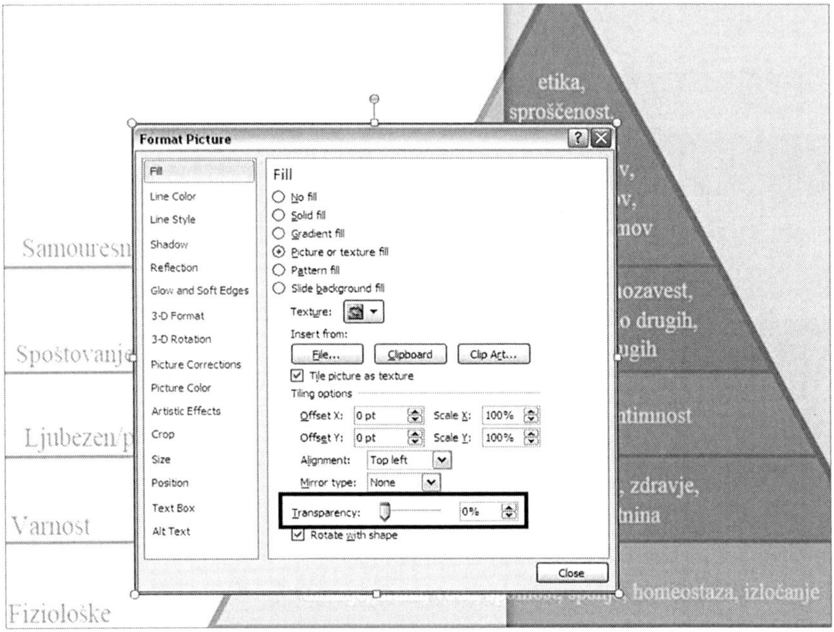

The next step is to use your text boxes to build up a translation layer. The dimmed picture underneath remains visible, but doesn't affect the readability of your translation: it is perfectly clear what belongs where.

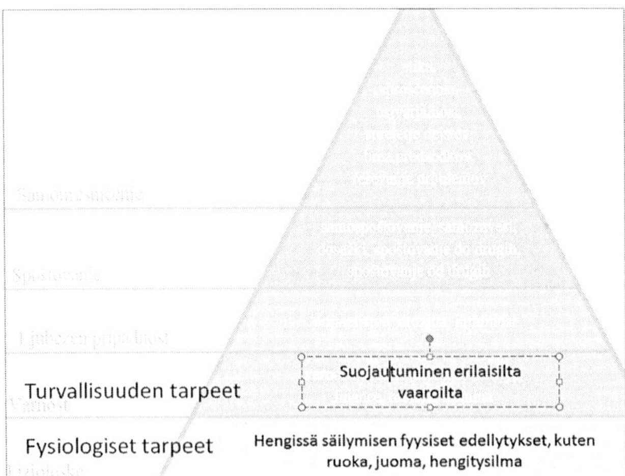

The description of this workflow may seem complicated, but the process is remarkably simple in practice. The crux lies in using the picture as the background of a regular PowerPoint slide, which offers all the convenience you need to position your text boxes and type your translation inside. When you're done, select all (Ctrl+A / Command+A), group everything together to prevent accidental shifting, and then copy and paste everything back to your Word document. If the image is too complex, you can keep the original and place your translated copy underneath: in many cases the result will still be less time-consuming than creating a bilingual glossary-type table, as you're not having to retype both the source text and your translation. In most cases, it will also be far more satisfactory for the reader while remaining editable for any future revisions.

Another big advantage of using PowerPoint to work with images is its collection of SmartArt graphics. Perhaps the simplest and most effective way of dealing with our pyramid is to create a fresh PowerPoint slide: go to the *SmartArt* tab and choose a template that fits best; this is probably how the pyramid was created in the first place. You will find that many non-editable graphics that you come across in your Word documents can be easily replicated and translated in this way.

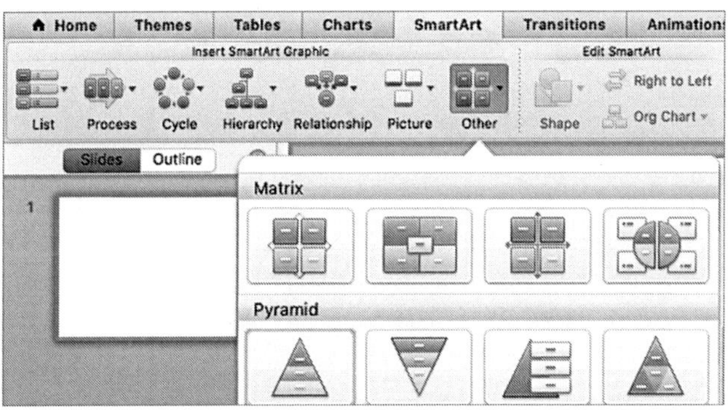

The next thing that you need to know – and take care of – when dealing with pictures in your client's documents is **text wrapping**. The two pictures below may look the same as long as the *Show Formatting* option isn't activated. However, when you click on *Show all nonprinting characters*, the difference will become obvious:

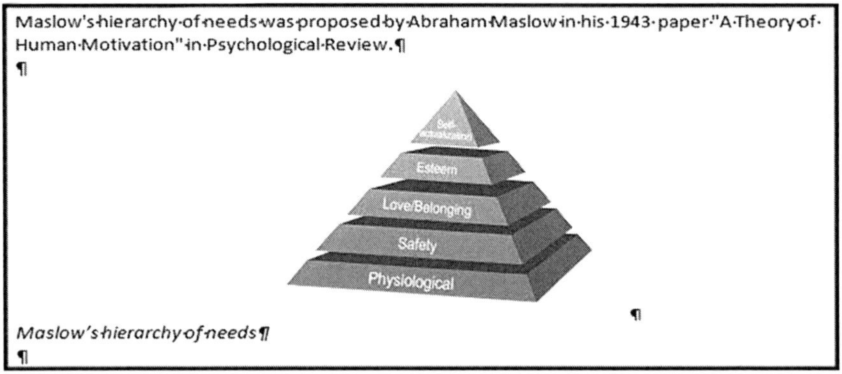

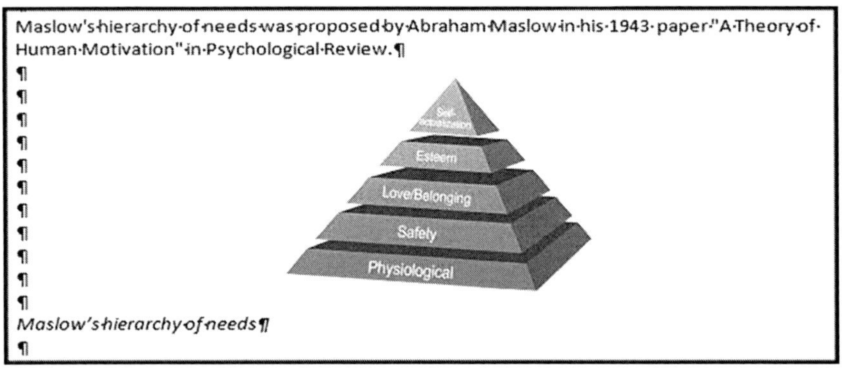

A vertical row of pilcrows running through your picture is a sign of trouble. In Word, you have two layout options for objects (images and other): *Move with text* or *Fix position on page*. If an object is fixed, Word generates an "anchor" in one of the paragraphs. This anchor becomes visible once you select the object, for example to adjust its position relative to the text.

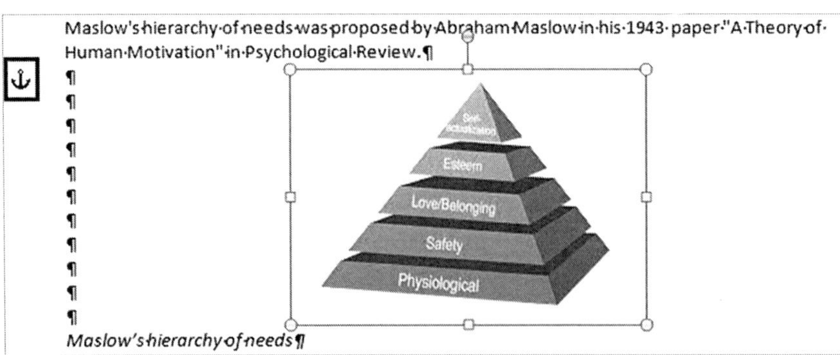

When the translated text expands, it can overlap with your object. Also, if you move or delete a paragraph that contains the anchor, the anchored object will move or will be deleted, too. Another typical nuisance is that fixed objects tend to "jump", because they need to be on the same page as their anchor. All this might leave you with a bit of a mess to clean up when proofreading and revising your translation.

This mess is avoidable, if you check your client's file before you start working on it. It is always good to make sure that images are placed *in line* with the text and, whenever possible, replace the *Fix position on page* option with *In Line with Text* (to access it, right-click the picture or go to the *Format* tab → *Wrap Text*):

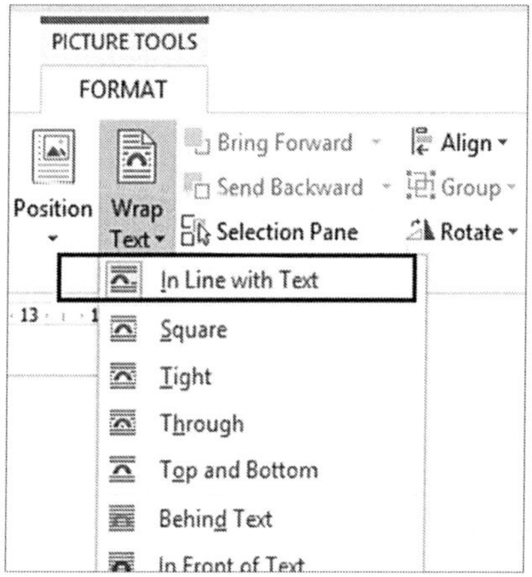

Stanislav Okhvat's TransTools can help achieve consistency with object anchors. One of the tools in the plugin, *Document Cleaner*, whose main purpose is to fix issues in documents created by OCR/PDF conversion, is useful when a "regular" but poorly formatted Word document needs a quick fix:

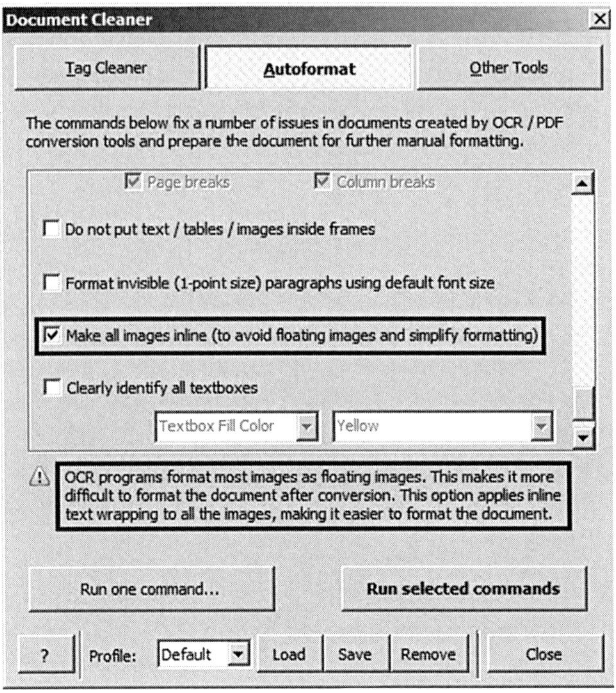

If it is critical to ensure that specific paragraphs flow around certain images, you can use a transparent table instead of such wrapping options as *Square* and *Tight*. Place your image inside one table cell and fill the other cell with your text; format the table to remove any automatic strokes and fills. The text won't wrap tightly around the image and neither will it flow in and out of the table freely, but at least you'll make sure the image is linked to the right portion of the text and the document structure will remain intact.

The next thing to think about is **captions**. We already know that an isolated heading straggling at the bottom of the page (or single lines of text – widows and orphans) doesn't show care in your product. Neither does a page break between an image and its caption, especially if your images are cross-referenced, which can cause navigation problems. In Word, it is never a good idea to keep two elements together by punching the return key or inserting a page break above. Instead of hard page breaks, it's better to specify where you **don't** want any page breaks, for example between a picture and its caption. For this, use the paragraph setting *Keep with next*. Select your object, go to the *Paragraph* tab, click *Line and Page Breaks* and make sure *Keep with next* is checked. This will glue your picture to the next paragraph, which you can format as a caption.

Also, you can create a custom style with only two attributes: line spacing set to single (tab *Indents and Spacing*) and pagination set to *Keep with next* (tab *Line and Page Breaks*). This style can be part of your templatised style guide for a consistent positioning of every picture with a caption underneath.

Similarly, for the sake of consistency, consider applying your *Caption* style to all captions in your documents. If they sit above images, check the attributes of the style to make sure that the caption will stay on the same page as the picture: open the *Modify style* dialog box, go to *Format* and *Paragraph*. Tick *Keep with next* on the *Line and Page Breaks* tab. You've just taken another step towards creating your brand packaging.

There may be all kinds of images in the documents you will translate. It is tempting to opt for one standard method, whether a bilingual table below the object or a series of superimposed text boxes over it. However, I believe the focus should be placed on the user's perspective. A recent example from my own practice shows that sometimes you can achieve more (and save time and effort) with a simple comment – regardless the missing description or reference in the source text. The photograph below is adapted from a property developer's prospectus. It was rather self-explanatory and didn't need any legend or additional comments. Still, in the context of the presentation in the prospectus, it seemed appropriate to add a few words to help identify the sites:

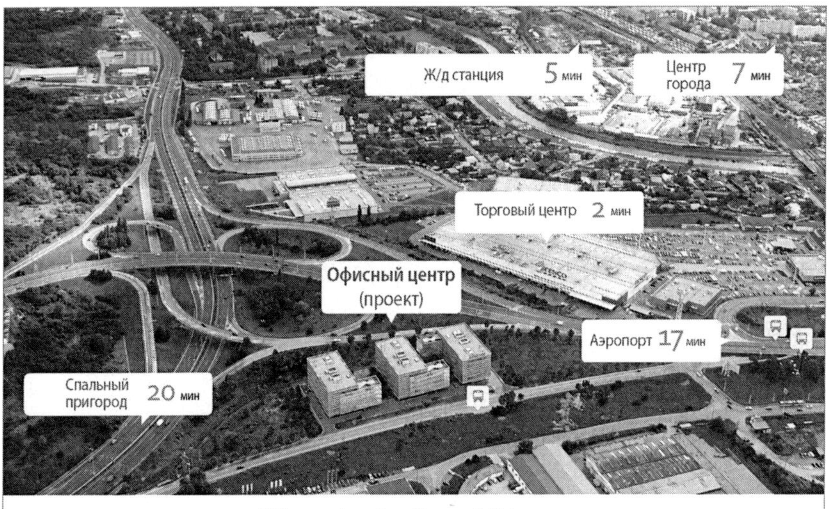

Office centre: location and distances
5 minutes from the railway station, 7 minutes to downtown,
2 minutes to the mall, 17 minutes to the airport, 20 minutes to the bedroom suburb

Graphics in a Word document are not limited to images. I'm always surprised how little attention is paid to tables, although they are usually just as prominent and important as images, especially in business documents. Table layout bears on clarity and legibility of presentation, and can make your documents look crisp and professional. A distinct table layout can also be part of your own visual brand.

Microsoft Word has an in-built gallery of table styles. In my experience, however, most clients' documents contain plain grids of black lines with unformatted cells. To begin with, you can start with in-built table styles, choose whatever you consider most appropriate for the document, and perhaps make it your signature choice for future tables in other documents. The procedure is very simple:

1. Select the table (click the move handle at the upper left corner)
2. Click *Design* under Table Tools
3. Try some of the styles.

If you don't feel comfortable with introducing conspicuous design changes to tables preformatted by the author, you might still like to slightly brush up the table in order to make it more readable and appealing to the translation user. If you feel the text doesn't fit properly in a table, you need to check table row height and column width. To do that, go to *Table Tools → Layout → Properties* or right-click your table and choose *Table Properties* from the context menu. If the table cells are frozen (see *Row → Size → Specify height*), part of your translation may disappear. To prevent it from happening, select the option *Automatically resize to fit contents.*

Banding is highly preferential and soft, low-key shades of grey may considerably improve readability. You can tick *Banded Rows* to display the predefined stripe colour schemes:

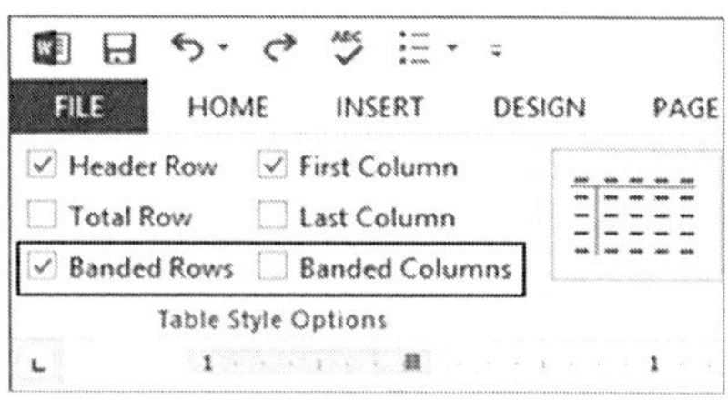

After selecting the style that suits you, go to *New Table Style* or *Modify Table Style* to adjust the colour (note that the *Banded Rows* and *Banded Columns* are always greyed out and cannot be accessed if your document is saved in a .doc format, so consider saving it as .docx).

Banded rows are optional, but a table style feature that can really improve the look of your tables is vertical centring. It is also largely overlooked or little known, since every now and then I come across tables in Word documents where the author used multiple paragraph marks to move the text down to the centre. To properly centre the content of a table cell, select the cell (or column, row or entire table), right-click and choose the vertical alignment option from the context menu. Alternatively, use one of the buttons on the *Table Tools → Layout* tab:

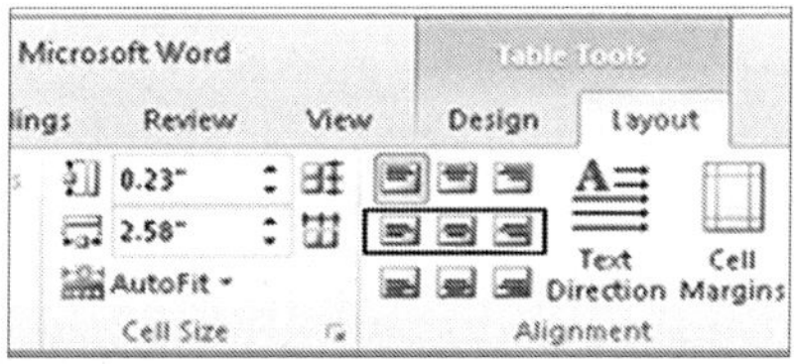

You may argue that these are all unimportant details that have little, if at all, to do with our language-focused role as translators. However, I know from my own experience that most of my clients take a very brief look at my translations. Regardless of whether they know the language of the translated document, they don't waste their time to actually **read** it (they trust me), but they still register the language-independent **visuals** it contains. Appearance, including small details of no particular importance, works. It is highly subjective (and yes, it can be deceiving), but the client's judgement is mostly dependent on it.

For more experienced colleagues, "technical" tips from this chapter may appear a given. Yet every now and then I come across translations that show neglect of the most elementary principles of good typography and design, heavily affecting the readability or usability of the translated documents and shedding bad light on their creators. Nowhere is the disregard (or rather an unconscious lack of consideration) so striking as in translations of PowerPoint presentations, as we'll see in the next chapter.

3.3 Charging extra for PowerPoint? Not until you read this

A typical discussion about translating PowerPoint documents in translators' forums inevitably turns to the question of how to charge for them. Just as typically, it appears that those in favour of a surcharge tend to justify the extra fee with the extra effort they have to put into adjusting their .ppt or .pptx documents after the translation. On the other hand, as an outsourcing client myself, I am regularly on the receiving end of a PowerPoint translation. More often than not I wish that those commissioned to provide such a translation would **cut** their rates rather than increase them when translating presentations. From the client's perspective, the quality range of many PowerPoint translations, in various language combinations, on various subjects and provided by quite a few otherwise experienced and skilled colleagues, varies from clearly lacking and inferior to the original to nearly useless unless reworked.

As one extreme in this spectrum, I would mention a translator who used to deliver decent quality work I normally didn't have much to complain about. That is to say until I hired him to translate my client's PowerPoint presentation – a regular set of slides with headers, bullet points, a "Thank you" on the last slide and very few graphics, including a modest company logo on the first page. The translation I received was a Word document, with typed up or copy-and-pasted chunks of text that was then translated. As a value-added service, the translator put the slide number in brackets before the respective texts. Another translator, challenged with text-heavy slides, moved part of her translation to the *Notes* pane, obviously for the lack of space in the slide area:

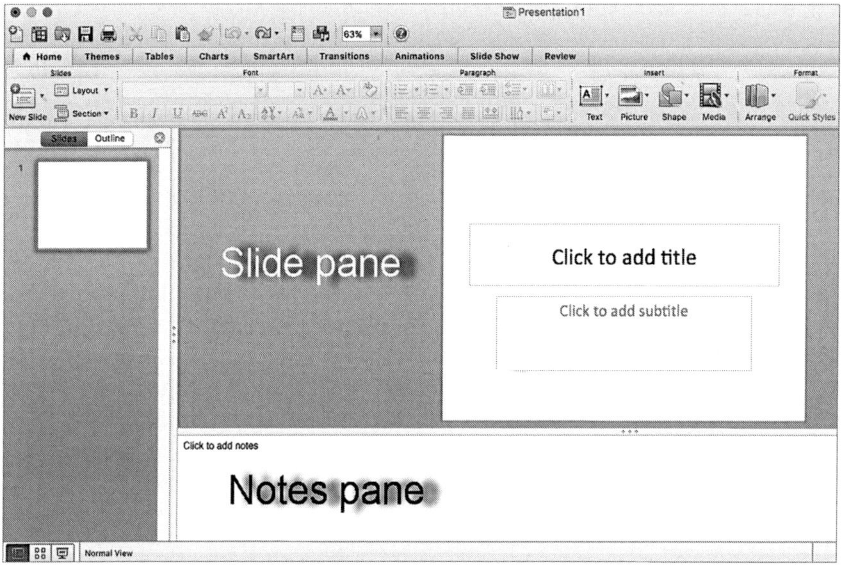

The *Notes* pane can be useful as a clutch for the speaker during the presentation. Occasionally, it is used to prepare handouts, by combining visual (to be shown on screen) and additional (to be distributed on paper) content.[78] However, this was not the case here – shifting a sizable part of the translation to the *Notes* pane made it of no use to the speaker and, more importantly, to the audience, both during the presentation and when studying the handouts. What struck me most was the fact that the translator didn't seem to have the faintest idea of the purpose of the empty area below the slide pane – apparently, she used the *Notes* simply as part of workspace to fit in "too much text".

Less extreme but far more common cases involved numerous layout issues which made the translated slides nonsensical, misleading or, in a few cases, useless. Last but not least, at translators' conferences, I viewed PowerPoint presentations which made me doubt that their authors, themselves translators and interpreters, could be reasonably entrusted with translating anything in this format for direct clients. Characteristically, many of the problems encountered would have been easy to avoid and the tedious fixing afterwards saved.

78 The *Notes* area is used to provide a description or an extended caption to the slide, which appears on a handout page as a fixed image in the upper half. To get it out on paper, you will have to dig out the *Print slides with notes* option, which is concealed deep within the *Print* settings (*File → Print → Settings → Full Page Slides → Notes Pages*).

The approach I present in this chapter can help you avoid layout-related issues from the start. That doesn't mean that the workflow will eliminate all extra effort. Neither do I dismiss the idea of charging extra for translating PowerPoint. The opposite is the case, but my justification is different. My procedure focuses on the formal aspects of PowerPoint presentations, yet I believe that the real difficulty of translating PowerPoint – well worth charging extra for – lies in the content of a typical presentation, not in its format.

An effective – usually synonymous with economical – presentation makes use of the "iceberg principle", also known as the theory of omission. Unlike the audience that learns the underwater portion during presentation, a translator typically has to make do with only the visible part – and try to get the most from the least. On the flipside, the translator often has to contact the client or the presentation author for clarification and more context. To me, rather than being a nuisance, a direct, problem-centred contact is beneficial to the translator as it offers an opportunity to turn the client's attention to the meaningful aspects of our work and to ourselves as forward-thinking solution providers. Think positively – your difficulty in understanding may bring up an opportunity to reach out to your client if you are ready to step out of your comfort zone.

A proactive approach is justified both to deal with a lack of clarity in the content and to address the layout. Layout-related errors are easier to prevent than fix afterwards and with due preparation, PowerPoint translations become easily manageable. The workflow described below consists of just a few steps.

■ ■ ■

We should bear in mind that PowerPoint presentations are largely of two kinds. The majority contain some reference to the occasion of the presentation. This may be the date on the title page, a subtitle or a footer that mentions a specific event, or any other signs that the presentation is scheduled to be delivered to an audience, typically on a tight deadline. In other words, what you are going to work on is meant as a visual aid to be used by the speaker during their presentation. What is less obvious is the fact that PowerPoint software is also used to create **documents**, similar to Word, though more visually persuasive. Garr Reynolds, a communication consultant and author of a popular book *Presentation Zen*, coined a catchy term for content-dense slides – slideuments.[79] Slideuments have some merit if used for information only,

79 Garr Reynolds. *Presentation Zen: Simple Ideas on Presentation Design and Delivery*, 2nd Edition (New Riders, 2011).

containing facts and figures, and circulated and perused like standard business documents. If used for presentations, slideuments – especially those that are jammed with information – don't work so well, as they can overwhelm and annoy the audience, rather than help the speaker connect with it.

Admittedly, not everyone is born to be a great presenter – or use PowerPoint according to its purpose as an effective visual communication tool. In the majority of cases, PowerPoint files that we get to translate are meant to be shown to an audience during an actual presentation, even if occasionally they do look like slideuments. I believe that a translator's approach to the source document should always be in line with the document's purpose. This determines how we need to approach PowerPoint files.

From discussions with my colleagues, my impression is that most are likely to rush into translation. Many skilled and efficient professionals simply import the files into their CAT tools and start to translate on the go, without actually reading or having a closer look at the documents first. While this approach is fine with a Word document, PowerPoint files deserve more attention.

The **first step** I consider imperative when settling down to work on a PowerPoint file is to view it in presentation mode (open the file and press F5 or COMMAND+ENTER). There is a difference between what you see when you open your presentation in *Normal* view mode and what will eventually be displayed to the audience (or printed on paper). Essentially, viewing the slides in presentation mode will help you get a better idea of the visual story that a good presentation should tell. The contrast between the purpose of the presentation (visual communication with the audience) and the isolated text segments that you get to work on in your CAT tool is even sharper. At the time of writing, CAT tools' preview functions are still rather limited, particularly concerning the visuals. Besides the problem of flawed segmentation so typical with PowerPoint, you may miss the logic and flow of information, both on single slides and within the presentation as a whole. You are probably well acquainted with the concepts of front-end and back-end, which are used in the web industry. My recommendation is to first familiarise yourself with and pay attention to the user-facing front-end part of your PowerPoint presentation. With that done, you can return to the back-end – the *Normal* view in your software.

Second, we should bear in mind that text can be added to a presentation in two different ways. Let's assume your presentation has pages or slides where individual words are placed inside a collection of geometric shapes:

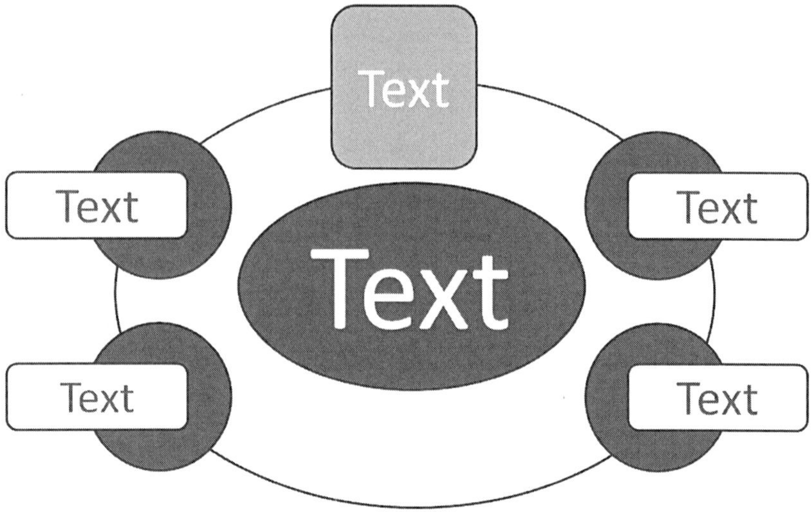

In PowerPoint, you can add text within almost any geometric shape chosen from the menu, except for lines, which aren't text containers.

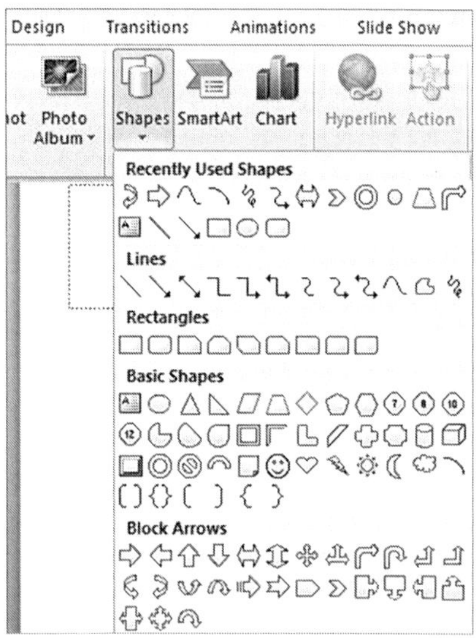

You can start typing as soon as you insert your shape, and then adjust the default settings (use the formatting bar or right-click on the shape and choose *Format Text*). Nevertheless, in many clients' presentations, I often find additional text boxes as overlays over diagrams, images, shapes and the like. In fact, presentations often look very much like the example with text overlays on the Maslow pyramid in the previous chapter.

Typing in a PowerPoint text box is different from typing in Word. One difference is the absence of a button to display formatting, like *Show all nonprinting characters* in Word. This difference becomes apparent when you change the text, as happens in translation. The default settings for the text format in shapes and in text boxes are different, therefore changing the text is likely to bring about different results.

In practice, changing the text length in the first case – **the text was initially typed in the shape directly** – will cause it to overflow, given the default settings are *Do not autofit* and *Wrap text in shape*:

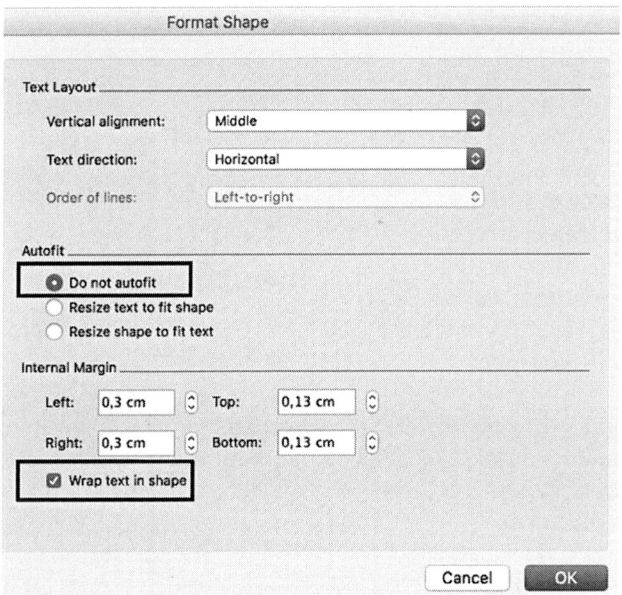

The text may fail to fit into the container:

The *Resize shape to fit text* option will let you keep the longer text visible, but it may change the shape of the container and affect the graphics:

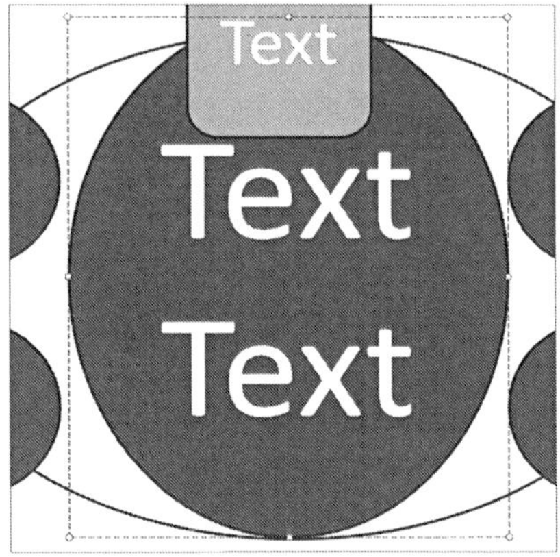

In the second case – **the text is in a separate text box overlapping the shape** – changing the text length will not affect the shapes. However, it may cause part of the text disappear, for instance if it's the same colour as the surrounding area. The risk that something may literally get lost in translation is high with reversed out text:

These two ways of adding text to PowerPoint slides (combined with various autofit options) account for most layout issues that may arise in your translation and make layout adjustments necessary. As always, paying attention and taking a preventive approach is better than fixing problems afterwards.

While at **step 2**, you can check whether the words were added in shapes or in text boxes. We will come to this a bit later and see why the difference is of interest. But to begin with, you need to examine the back-end structure of your presentation to determine what exactly you have to translate – for example, does the presentation contain any notes and do they need translating? You don't want to translate what was never meant to be translated – if the client never mentioned you shouldn't translate anything in the *Notes* area, the reason is they expect you to see the presentation "through their eyes".

Also at step 2, it is essential to examine the slide masters (select the *View* tab → *Slide Master*). This will help you identify the otherwise non-editable elements (those you cannot overwrite while in the *Normal* view) and provide clues about your client's corporate identity design and style guide. Generally, slide masters give you an idea about your client's priorities in terms of communication with their target audience or document management. I find that even the number of customised slide masters may be revealing.

Then you have to take a closer look at the text. How is it formatted? Is it contained in shapes or text boxes? Have any special fonts been used (it may be relevant if the chosen font doesn't have the special symbols for the language of the translation as these might be automatically replaced by your default font)? It is generally easy to use shortcuts in PowerPoint and your client may have done just that. Some shortcuts, particularly hard line breaks, don't make a translator's life easier if the presentation is eventually to be imported into a CAT tool. Lists and numbers are another example. For many, PowerPoint is synonymous with notorious bullet point lists, and in my lifetime as a translator I saw quite a number of presentations where bullet points were actually graphic elements separated from the text – think of all kinds of arrows or ornamental numbers. The consequence? If the amount of text changes, the alignment between the "bullets" and your translated text becomes a mess.

Steps 2 and 3 could partially overlap: while checking the slides at the back-end, you may find it handy to adjust formatting. **Step 3** is about adjusting the original PowerPoint slides (you can rename and save the file first) before getting down to translating them. Of course, you can also adjust and translate simultaneously, but I still think that you will achieve better visual consistency – a crisp, professional look – by performing this step as a separate, necessary preparation.

This is where the difference between shapes and text boxes as text containers turns practical. From the point of view of design, it is preferable to separate graphic and textual layers. This is how the more sophisticated layout applications, such as QuarkXPress and InDesign, work. However, PowerPoint's capacity to use ready-made, customisable shapes to compose graphics and simultaneously use these shapes as text containers is one of its most useful features. When you suspect that a text alteration may result in a change of shape and play havoc with alignment of the other elements in the graphic, it's better to prioritise the shape over the text. This means that you have to check and adjust the *Form Shape* options: to be on the safe side, choose *Resize text to fit shape* and *Wrap text in shape*:

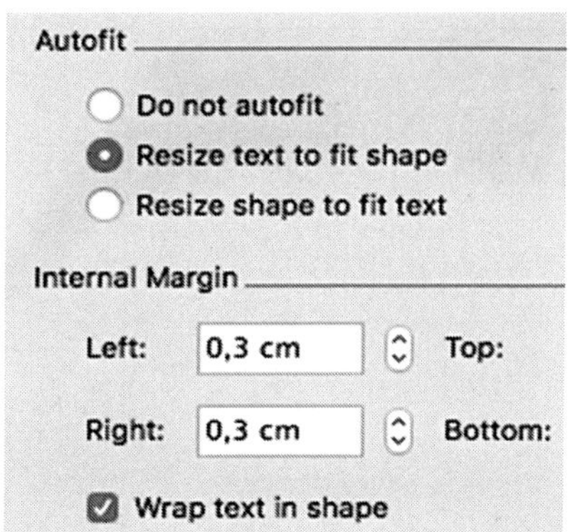

Resize text to fit shape means that your font size will scale automatically if the translation length grows, while *Wrap text in shape* means that your translation won't stretch out in one long line. Instead, the software will automatically insert soft line breaks to evenly distribute your text within the shape. SmartArt graphics (e.g. list, process, matrix) can serve as guides for choosing the proper autofit option.

When adjusting both shapes and text boxes, it is a good idea to use the *Align* function to make sure all the objects are lined up properly. I've seen many presentations where the text was aligned left in text boxes (the default setting on the *Paragraph* tab), while the text boxes themselves were lined up vertically to create an illusion of centred text. Of course, once the amount of text is changed, the order is lost. It's quick and easy to select all text boxes and apply centre alignment.

Similarly, it is better to set proper vertical alignment of text in shapes and text boxes, even though your client may have used paragraph returns to shift text to the centre. For horizontal alignment of text, PowerPoint has the usual keyboard shortcuts: press CTRL+L or CTRL+R to left-align or right-align a paragraph, and CTRL+E to quickly centre it.

Inaccurate alignment not only makes your work as a translator look sloppy, but it may also impair the readability or accuracy of the translated document. The picture below is taken from a presentation that I received for rework after it had been double-checked by the original translator and an additional revisor. This is a small example of how easily things can be overlooked when formatting is considered to go beyond the scope of a translator's tasks:

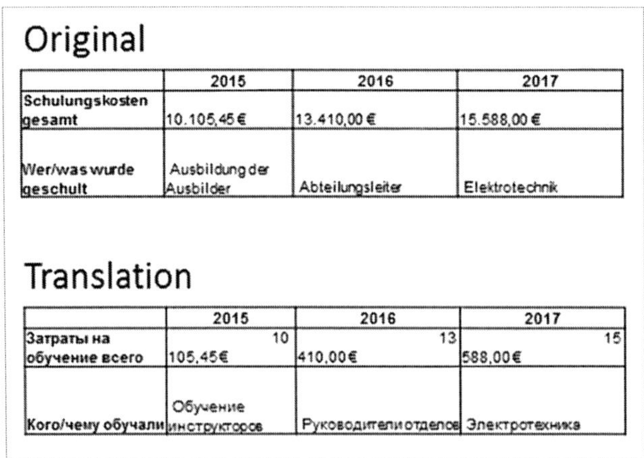

Original

	2015	2016	2017
Schulungskosten gesamt	10.105,45 €	13.410,00 €	15.588,00 €
Wer/was wurde geschult	Ausbildung der Ausbilder	Abteilungsleiter	Elektrotechnik

Translation

	2015	2016	2017
Затраты на обучение всего	10 105,45€	13 410,00€	15 588,00€
Кого/чему обучали	Обучение инструкторов	Руководители отделов	Электротехника

I corrected the displaced numbers by deleting the invisible spaces before them and adjusted the table a bit: I changed the cell margins, using the *Align Center* option.

■ ■ ■

A uniform, professional look results from consistent formatting. To do so efficiently, it's best to select all elements that require uniform formatting and assign the desired format properties (e.g. font size) to all of them at once. I would also recommend making more frequent use of the *Group* function to keep in place the text and shapes that make up more complex graphics. To help achieve consistent formatting, PowerPoint, much like other Microsoft Office applications, has a rather underappreciated feature – *Format Painter*. To copy text formatting from one piece of text to another (in text boxes or slide headers), you don't need to go through all the steps of formatting – font size, bold, colour. A faster and easier way is to use this button:

Select the fragment of text with the formatting you want to copy and click the *Format Painter* button; the cursor will change to a paint brush. Now select the text you want to format and click on it. The same can be achieved with a keyboard shortcut. To copy and paste formatting, use CTRL+SHIFT+C to select the formatting and CTRL+SHIFT+V to transfer it to the next piece of text.

Another useful function is to **double**-click the *Format Painter* button after you selected a fragment of text with the formatting you'd like to copy. The cursor will change to a paint brush and won't change back until you press *Escape*. You can apply the paint brush continuously to all the text on your slides that you want to reformat like the original selection. This can speed up the adjustment enormously and ensure consistent application of styles.

Now that you know your PowerPoint presentation both in terms of content and form, at **step 4** you actually get down to translating. I mentioned before that I prefer to work on PowerPoint files in PowerPoint to have more control and keep in view the visual context. I believe that translation can improve if done with an eye not on isolated segments of text, but on their relationship with one another and with the slide graphics. However, in many cases a CAT tool will make things faster and easier. As usual, this example may seem somewhat extreme, but it is taken from an actual PowerPoint presentation that I translated recently:

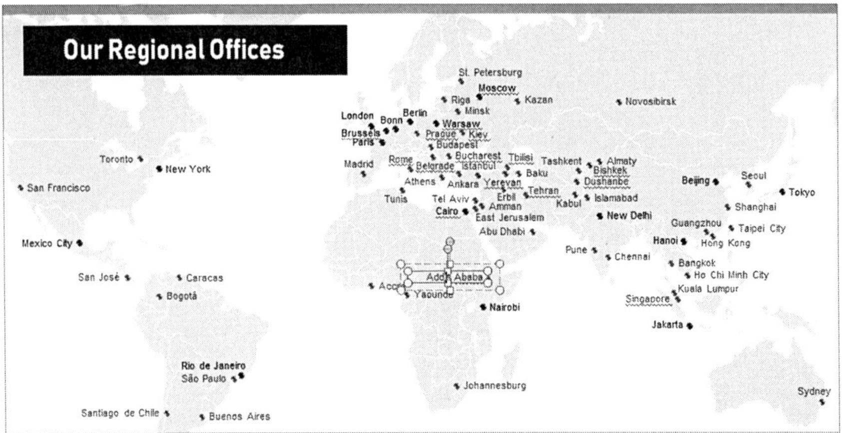

Here, of course, you will save time if you don't have to switch between text boxes manually but use a CAT tool instead.

Step 5 means "back to square one": you check and revise your translation, starting with the *Presentation* view (press F5 to start from the first slide or SHIFT+F5 to resume the slide show from the current slide). There is now little to do if you did all the preparation properly. But again, it is essential to make sure that any adjustments you make are for the benefit of the translated presentation as it will be viewed by the audience.

■ ■ ■

Similar to the question of charging extra, another topic that often sparks discussions among translators is whether they should learn PowerPoint at all. PowerPoint has long ceased to be simply an office software tool to create visual aids for presentations.

> PowerPoint is a critical business skill. PowerPoint has moved beyond just presentation software and is now a critical tool for driving strategy in large companies. Businesses are idea marketplaces and selling ideas requires knowing how to communicate effectively with PowerPoint.[80]

If PowerPoint is a "**language** of business", shouldn't we, as **linguists**, take this metaphor to heart and invest in this new language?

80 Bruce R. Gabrielle. *Speaking PowerPoint: The New Language of Business* (Insights Publishing, 2010).

I believe mastering PowerPoint skills can benefit both our clients' and our own business. PowerPoint is an effective tool for developing and structuring ideas. Whereas the goal of a typical business document may be to inform, PowerPoint is used to persuade. Our clients can benefit from our PowerPoint expertise since it can help them communicate their ideas effectively and convincingly. Similarly, it can help us in our own marketing and business work, for instance when figuring out and structuring our professional strengths, developing successful pitches, designing verbal and visual content that works for us. In my experience, direct clients expect a translator to **help them reach their communication goals**, not simply to provide a textual equivalent of their source documents. This, however, brings us to a third question of translation – whether we can suggest text changes to clients.

There is a rich literature on PowerPoint that falls into two categories: how-to tutorials (mostly online) and books as well as websites that focus on more general aspects of design and communication. Besides Garr Reynolds' and Bruce R. Gabrielle's work, my recommended book list would include *slide:ology: The Art and Science of Creating Great Presentations* by Nancy Duarte and *Presentation Secrets: Do What You Never Thought Possible with Your Presentations* by Alexei Kapterev.[81] All these books are Amazon's bestsellers on the subject. I believe that if we tie the purpose of our business to communication, PowerPoint can teach us to be better and more successful translators.

Coming back to the question of charging extra and suggesting changes to your clients, the answer, as usual, is that it depends. How much you charge depends on the value you deliver to your clients and any changes – suggested and implemented – may be part of this value. Step 2 of the workflow described in this chapter was about adjustments of the original document which *are* changes. I believe such changes have more value if they are aimed not only at making the translation process smoother and less time-consuming, but also when they benefit the resulting presentation. In my experience, tangible improvements don't take much effort to communicate, as they speak for themselves. An extra bonus is that they are the best argument for the value of your service and your expertise. Anecdotally, I once suggested a change to my client's presentation. The PowerPoint document contained a number of black pages, one after every three to five regular slides. The purpose of the black pages was easy to guess, but I still contacted my client. As expected,

81 Nancy Duarte. *slide:ology: The Art and Science of Creating Great Presentations* (O'Reilly Media, 2008); Alexei Kapterev. *Presentation Secrets: Do What You Never Thought Possible with Your Presentations* (Wiley, 2011).

she confirmed that she wanted to make sure the screen would go completely black whenever she was speaking directly to the audience, but didn't want to shut down her laptop. I told her she did not need black slides to do so. PowerPoint has a feature that allows to pause a presentation at any point: if you press *W* (for white) or comma, it'll display a blank white slide; if you press *B* (for black) or period, your audience will see a black slide. The client was really thankful for this small piece of advice and I think it helped my reputation, too. Needless to say, it never occurs to me to charge extra for such advice. In the long run, it still pays off.

3.4 The burden of PDF

After examining why appearances matter (Part 1) and looking into how we can benefit from good typography (Part 2), I wanted this section of the book to be about images that are found in your translations. PDF documents are neither images nor texts. They are, simply put, electronic printouts of documents that may contain both. Yet it is mostly PDF files that **force** us to deal with images if the source text is presented as an image rather than an editable document. In this chapter, I will share tips on how to achieve better results when working with this problematic format.

I suspect that most translator colleagues consider PDF a burden. The perceived problematic nature of a PDF document is at least twofold. The first part of the problem is that the format prevents you from overwriting and replacing the text with your translation. It is obviously the case with scanned, image-only documents. Such documents typically need to be OCR-ed first. Recent versions of CAT tools offer this functionality, however, what they do under the hood is in fact not much different from the conversion methods that translators have been employing for years using third-party OCR software from Nuance (OmniPage), ABBYY (FineReader) or IRIS (Readiris). For example, SDL Studio makes use of a third-party OCR engine by Solid Documents, the developer of Solid Converter, to prepare PDF files for translation. Memsource and memoQ (starting from version 8.1) offer integration with TransPDF by Iceni, the developer of Infix PDF. The purpose of conversion is to separate out an editable text layer in order to produce a workable source document (or workable text segments) that can be exported to a text editor. While this purpose is served, there will still be a huge difference between the document produced by OCR software and your client's original document **printed out** as a PDF in terms of layout, formatting and design.

Here lies the second aspect of the problem: after converting the PDF file it is possible to replace the source text with your translation, but you are still likely to wind up with an inferior – in comparison to the "native" document in terms of text formatting and layout – deliverable. PDFs are printouts of usually well-formatted (or better formatted, to put it cautiously) documents. In fact, saving the original document in a PDF format is aimed at protecting the format from undesirable changes. Unfortunately, there is no reasonable way to overcome the asymmetry between the input and output layout quality other than delivering your translation as a PDF – with all formatting concealed and protected.

PDF as a delivery format is justified when you deal with officially certified documents. If you specialise in such translations, you may want to protect your deliverables from any further edits and changes. In this case, it would also make sense to **lock** your PDF. You probably know how to do it: go to *File → Document properties* and open the *Security* tab. If you choose *Password Security* from the drop-down *Security Method* menu you can restrict editing of the document (*Changes Allowed → None*).[82] In most other cases, delivering your translation only as a PDF is not a good idea and a sure way to make your client unhappy. Your client most likely expects a workable document in a conveniently editable, unprotected format, much like a regular Word document, and this is where the second part of the problem starts.

While the inability to overwrite a PDF document is a common grievance for most translators, the implications of delivering a visibly inferior, though workable, Word file tend to be neglected in our profession. I would hope that after reading up to this point you would agree that it matters when your translation doesn't look sound or coherent (unfortunately, a typical Word translation of a PDF source file doesn't). A poorly formatted translation bears no visual proof of an outstanding piece of content work, nor any sign of your signature packaging. A translator's failure to produce a consistent, visually attractive document will not only negatively affect how it's perceived by the client, but will make the result close to unusable, especially for any further changes or edits. A chaos of paragraph styles, unmanageable columns, section breaks and incongruent, randomly scattered text boxes, so typical of Word documents generated by a PDF converter, is a problem if any changes need to be made in your translation at a later stage. The inner workings of a PDF conversion tool may be well beyond your control, but your deliverables shouldn't. Ideally, a diligent translator should seek to tackle both parts of the problem. We have to prepare the document so that we can work on it comfortably and efficiently. On the other hand, we need to provide the client with a visually consistent and practically usable output (better yet – including the packaging that speaks for itself and reflects the excellence of our product).

Though we cannot avoid speaking about software at this point, I stand true to my conviction that it's more helpful to learn a few basic principles than go

82 This would go beyond the scope of this chapter, but if you regularly work with PDFs, you might want to learn to "flatten" a PDF file, embed stamps or check accessibility (Chad Chelius' course "Creating accessible PDFs" on Lynda.com is a comprehensive source on the topic). A popular trick to make PDF uneditable is to print it using Adobe PDF as a printer, and a super-quick fix is to "sanitise" your document: activate *Protection* in the *Tools* and use *Sanitize Document* under the *Protection* tab.

into technicalities. Software changes very fast and different versions of the same tools exist. Some steps may be applicable to one specific version only, while other versions and programs provide similar features under different names. Rather than describing and memorising the exact "click path" that will change with another release, it's better to get a sense of direction – what is our purpose and which functions will be the best fit to get us there.

In the case of PDF conversion, the direction is straightforward. In fact, we have a classic input → process → output model. At the time of writing, there are a number of methods to transform the input into the output, but no one single method (or software) to get the perfect result. My basic idea is that, in order to improve the process, we have to pay more attention to **the input file**. Many colleagues swear by third-party programs that they use for their PDFs. You can try out Nitro, Foxit or Infix PDF editors – they all have their advantages. However, I prefer to work in the native Adobe Acrobat app, the Pro version, produced by the company that developed the PDF format. When talking to colleagues, I see that its many possibilities remain largely neglected or unexplored. (A caveat: the screenshots of the user interface in this chapter refer to Acrobat XI. The interface layout in the most recent version (DC 2019 at the time of writing) looks different, though the functions described are still there. You might have to look up the relevant features in the new interface and also customise the tool bar (right-click an empty space in the toolbar, choose *Customize Quick Tools*, select the tools and click the up arrow.)

When you start working on your PDF, it is a good idea to first look at the document properties (*File → Document Properties*). In my line of work, the field *Application* is typically either empty (meaning the file is a scanned PDF) or states something like this:

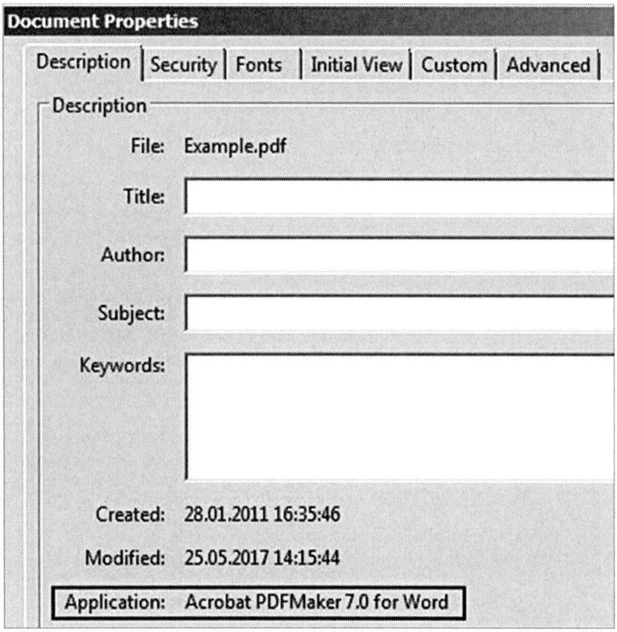

This is when it makes perfect sense to ask your client about the original document in the native file format (Word, PowerPoint or InDesign). Create a reusable email template to request an editable native file and to inform the client about the implications of working with a PDF – many clients aren't aware of them. I can advocate that translators should look through the eyes of their clients, however, it is unrealistic to expect our clients to reciprocate. If no native file can be provided, consider a policy to adjust the price you have quoted and mention it in your request. Don't leave this box unchecked before you get down to preparing the PDF file for translation.

Now to Adobe Acrobat workspace. In the right-hand part of the screen, you will find three tabs: *Tools – Sign – Comment* (you can adjust your workspace through *View → Show/Hide → Toolbar →Edit Current Tool Set*; press F8 and F9, if no toolbars are displayed). Make sure you have renamed the original PDF to make all changes on a file copy, then go to *Tools* and click on the *Content Editing* section:

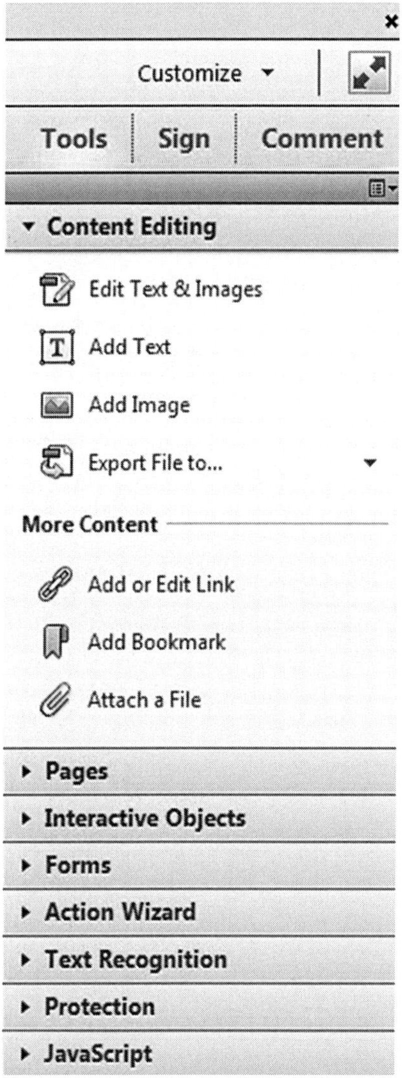

Select *Edit Text & Images*.[83] If you have a scanned, image-only document, Acrobat will respond with a prompt:

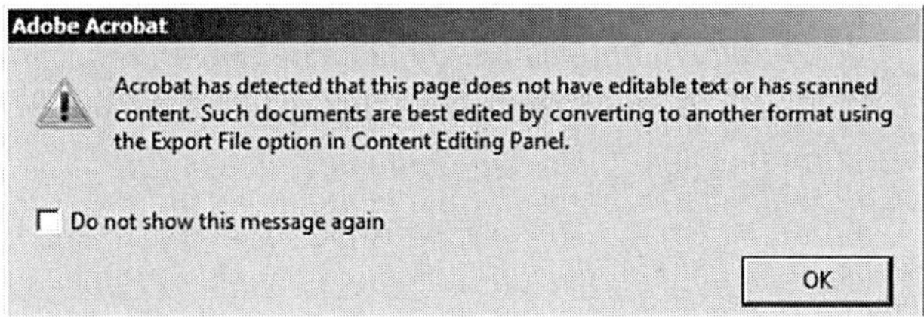

Now you have two options. You can do as told and convert the image into a Word document:

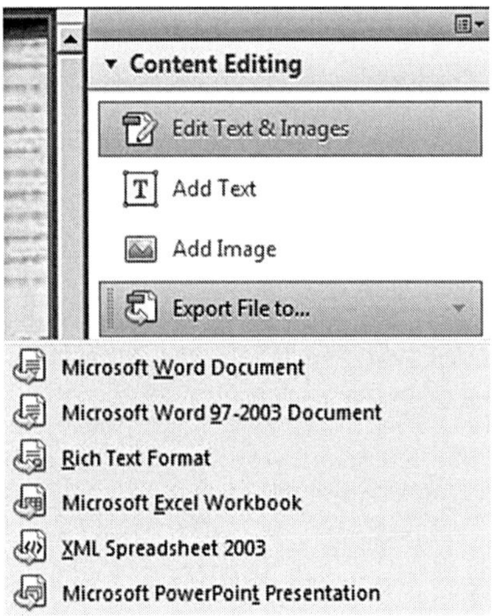

83 You can also access this function via *Edit → Edit Text & Images*.

In this case Acrobat will generate a Word file with the same name.[84] The other option is to take the OCR route. To do so, switch from *Content Editing* to *Text Recognition*. If *Text Recognition* is missing, go to *View → Tools → Text Recognition* to access it:

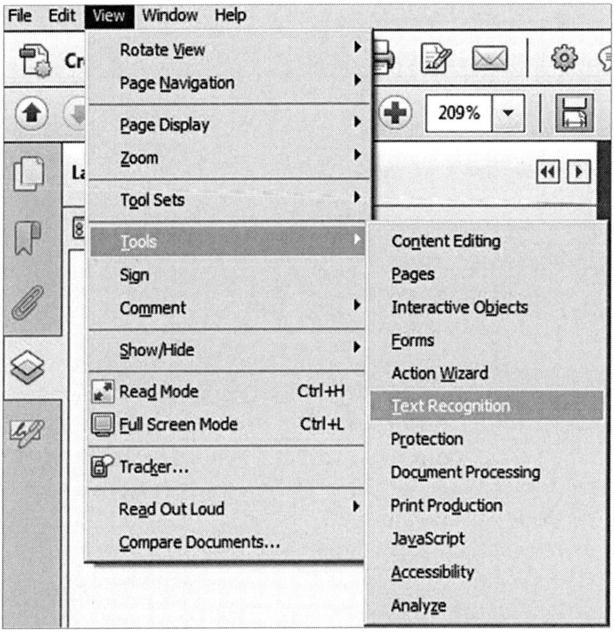

You can also access the *Text Recognition* feature through *Document Processing → Optimise Scanned PDFs → OCR Options*.[85] It is important to check and, if need be, adjust the settings, starting with the language. Since the OCR engines use language-specific dictionaries, the accuracy of conversion varies. Setting the correct language is the maximum you can do at this point.

The next setting – *PDF Output Style* – determines what kind of PDF your Acrobat software will produce.

84 Acrobat DX 2019 is more straightforward. Click *Export PDF* in the *Tools* panel on the right-hand side and choose Word (.docx) as the file format.

85 In Acrobat DX 2019, when exporting the document as a Word file, click on *Settings*, make sure the textbox *Recognize text* if needed is checked and then click the *Set language* button to choose the correct language.

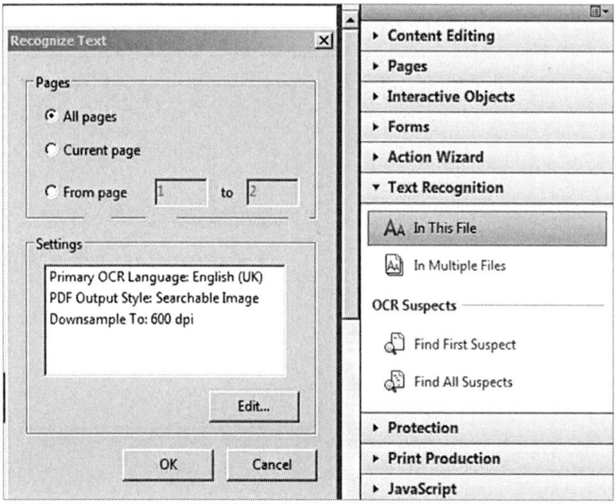

If you choose *Searchable Image*, the new file still remains largely an image, but now it has a rendered, that is to say selectable and searchable, text. An additional bonus of using this option is that Acrobat, while OCR-ing your document, will automatically straighten out ("deskew") scanned pages. On the contrary, *Searchable Image (Exact)* means that no visual "tweaking" will be made – if your pages were scanned askew, they will remain so after the text has been digitalised and captured. OCR-ing your document with the *Searchable Image* or *Searchable Image (Exact)* setting will produce the **second** – I tend to call it intermediate – type of PDF. A hidden text layer will be added to the document. Now you can, for example, select all the textual content (*Edit → Select All* or, as with many other programs, CTRL+A), copy and paste it into Word (e.g. to estimate the word count) or copy only a portion of the text. However, if you go to *Edit Text & Images*, you will find that you still cannot edit the text. (You can "erase" text fragments in the PDF document of this type, but it is not exactly deleting. Rather, you use a mask overlay to hide the unwanted pixels, be it text or graphics. More on it in a moment, when we look at the *Redact* feature.) To convert your document to yet another type of PDF, select *Editable Text & Images* as *PDF Output Style* (if this option isn't available in older versions of Acrobat, use *ClearScan*). This will produce an **editable** PDF that you can actually work with without leaving your program.

Now, if you select *Edit Text & Images* with the box *Outline Text & Images* checked, you will notice that Acrobat displays all visible elements in separate bordered frames.

- **Grant** oznacza każdą wpłatę dokonaną w odniesieniu do: (a) programów kształcenia PSZ, takich jak ustawiczne kształcenie medyczne (w tym koszty prelegentów, koszty najmu obiektów oraz skromnych posiłków dla słuchaczy), (b) edukacji pacjentów oraz grup wsparcia, badań przesiewowych stanu choroby lub konsumenckich targów medycznych, (c) finansowania uczestnictwa studentów medycyny, rezydentów oraz stypendystów w konferencjach edukacyjnych lub (d) niezależnych badań medycznych o celu naukowym.

- **Komisja ds. Grantów i Darowizn** oznacza komisję uprawnioną do rozpatrywania wniosków o granty i darowizny dotyczące pracownika służby zdrowia. GBU może zdecydować się na skorzystanie z usług niezależnej komisji lub pośrednika, by pełnił tę funkcję w jej imieniu. Wyznaczone osoby zatwierdzające dla każdej biznesowej jednostki lokalnej w kraju lub regionie mogą działać w charakterze Komisji ds. Grantów i Darowizn.

You will also notice many formatting options that became available for both text and image editing, including with external tools, such as Microsoft Paint or any other graphic editor available to you:

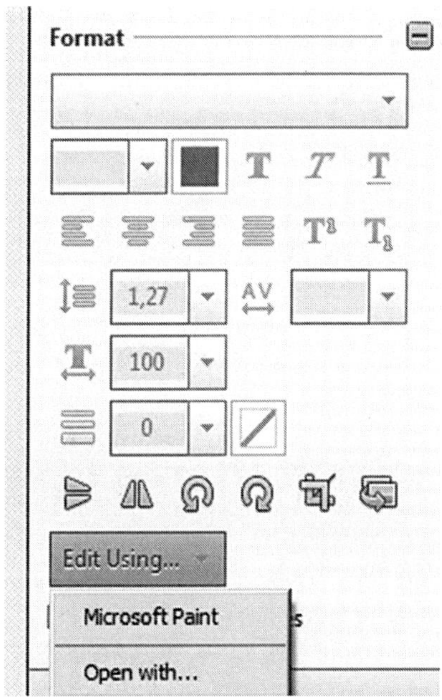

With *Editable Text & Images* (*ClearScan*), the result is as close to a native PDFs as it gets. A native PDF is the **third type** of a PDF document, a file generated in a PDF format by another program. You can work with text in such documents without exporting the content to Word. Overwriting the original text with your translation is possible, but still far less convenient than working in Word.

When you click in the text area, you will notice that each section of text is surrounded by a border. You can drag the text frames much like with text boxes in Word. When overwriting the text, you will find that text wrapping is also allowed, although not every text frame can automatically wrap the text and sometimes you will have to insert hard line breaks for new lines (use *Enter*). Though this type of PDF offers the ultimate flexibility within Acrobat, it is still not quite comparable with the result you get when preparing your PDF for export from within an advanced third-party OCR tool. For example, Acrobat doesn't allow splitting or merging the text boxes or changing their properties, a function available in ABBYY OCR applications.

No matter what software you use, the OCR process is a blanket operation. Which result you prefer – that of Acrobat, ABBYY, Nuance or any other third-party tool – depends largely on the specifics of your document and is, to a certain degree, a matter of taste. I dislike the text boxes in a Word file that ABBYY FineReader tends to scatter across the page when striving to recreate the native layout. Version 14 tends to produce noticeably fewer text boxes and a more natural feel, but the software still often fails to recognise human logic behind the layout of a typical Word page. As far as FineReader is concerned, there are further minor annoyances, such as footer and header margins that are too narrow or zero cell margins in tables (improved in version 14). Styles and fonts are usually messed up – it would be more reasonable for the developers to impose stricter rules on variation (and less variety as such) to produce a more sensible result. Some of the graphics might become displaced, even if you choose *Exact copy* in the *Document layout* menu. For example, a logo in the header of a page might slip to the top paragraph of the main text.

On the other hand, Acrobat tends to generate Word documents with unnecessary section or column breaks that may make the layout look similar to that of a native document, but result in much trouble when editing the content in between the breaks. Whether you use Acrobat, a third-party OCR tool or open a PDF document in Word directly, the resulting layout will never be perfect. That is why one of the general principles that I apply when converting PDFs is to minimise the area of recognition in order to minimise subsequent imperfections in the resulting Word file. For example, background graphics, such as watermarks in the Polish example above, are particularly hard to separate from the text. The same goes for signatures and stamps – when they overlap with your text, you are likely to be faced with gibberish on a Word page. This can be avoided only if you have a native PDF. In my experience, Acrobat does a better job separating and keeping layers (including watermarks in native PDF documents), while FineReader becomes more easily confused or tends to strip the background away. If you think the overlap will cause problems, I'd recommend removing the questionable part of the page altogether. The *Erase* tool in FineReader is an easy option, but the same effect can be achieved in Acrobat. As mentioned earlier, the software can cover up the unwanted pixels with a mask overlay. In Acrobat, you can use the *Redact* feature after you adjusted the *Redaction Tool Properties*, e.g. choose white as the *Redacted Area Fill Colour*:

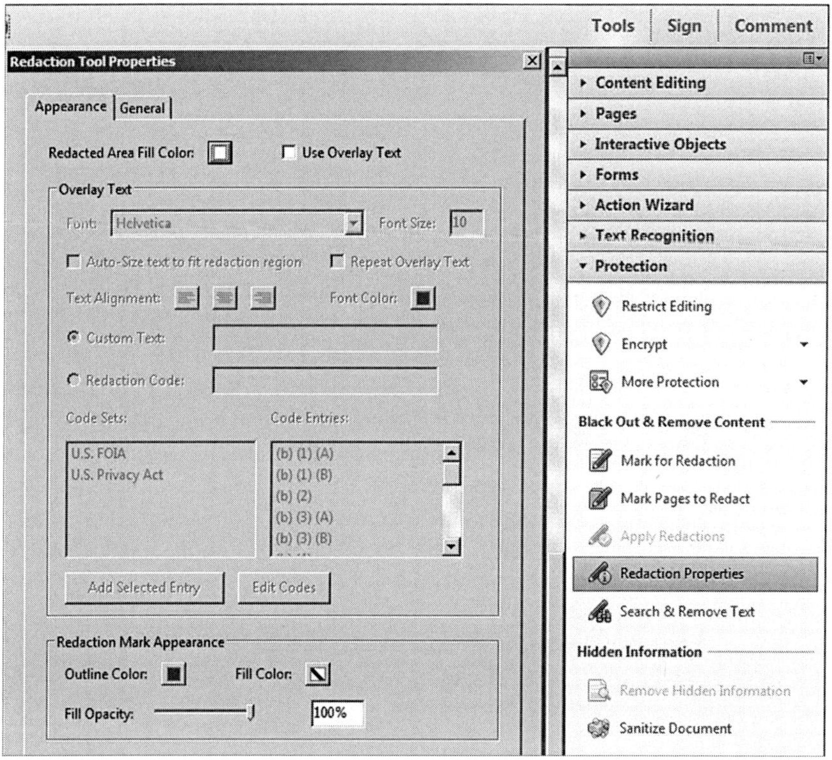

Or you can use the *Rectangle* drawing markup tool instead, having applied similar tool properties (solid white colour, line thickness 0 pt):

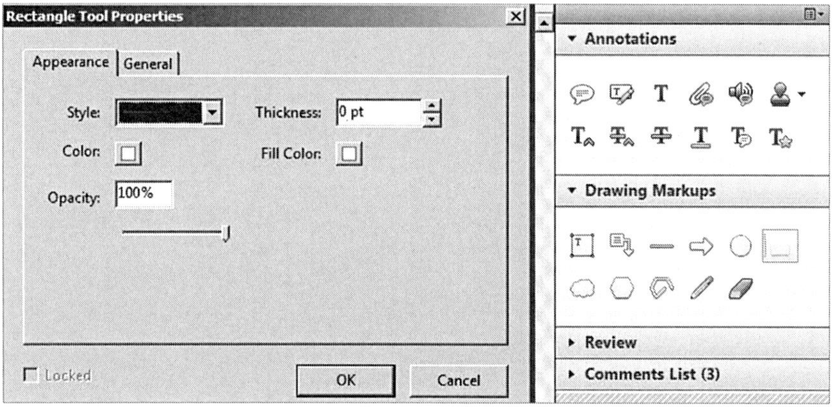

You can add the rectangle to the *Quick Tools Toolbar* and have it close at hand as a concealer. Whatever method you use to eliminate the problematic elements from the document, you will have less trouble adding the deleted pieces of text manually when working in Word. Do not let the software make guesses that are likely to result in multiple erratic sections, columns, text frames or undecipherable symbols and oversized letters in the middle of the text.

Another way to minimise the area of recognition is cropping your pages. It is useful with scanned, image-only, multiple-page PDFs, especially when the pages are uniformly laid out with headers and footers. Headers and footers tend to confuse the software and can be added manually at a later stage. Go to *Tools* → *Pages* → *Crop*:

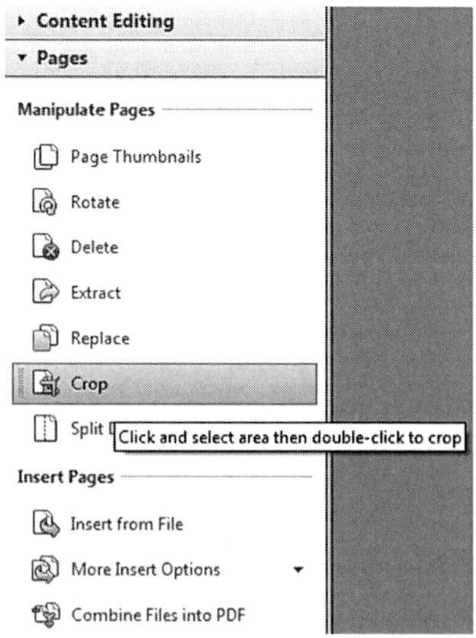

Then select and double-click the central area of the page that you want to keep intact. Double-click on the resulting frame and adjust the crop borders as needed. Select *All* under *Page Range* in the *Set Page Boxes* window to have all pages cropped at the same size.

I also recommend activating *Show Document Page Size* in *Preferences* under *Page Display*. The actual page size will be always displayed in the lower left corner. To change the page size, use the same *Crop* command (e.g. to choose the appropriate format before you export your PDF document to Word):

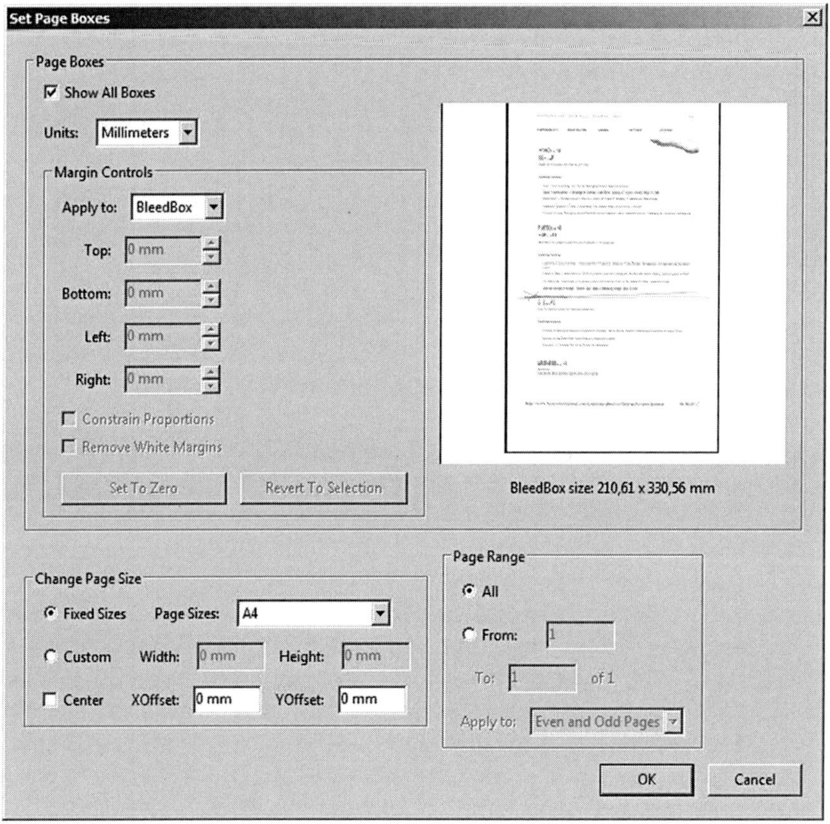

Given that Acrobat tends to produce a Word document with multiple sections, I find it easier to adjust the paper size while still in Acrobat rather than trying to fix it in Word afterwards.

I apply the same precision when processing PDFs in ABBYY applications. Everything that doesn't need to be translated (look through your client's eyes!) or that is likely to obscure the software output should be excluded from the process area. ABBYY software decomposes a page image into a number of rectangular areas and assigns them to various types of content – text, table, picture, background picture or barcode. You can change the area type (I find it most convenient to right-click on the area and use the *Change Area Type To* command), merge or separate areas, change the order of recognition, or "delete" the questionable areas, that is exclude them from processing to prevent potentially messy results.

Minimising the area of recognition illustrates a more general principle – more control against arbitrariness. You will get a cleaner result through marking (or unmarking) the areas before you save your document as a Word file.

Another means to vary the degree of control in ABBYY FineReader is to choose the mode you want to save the document in from the *Document layout* drop-down list:

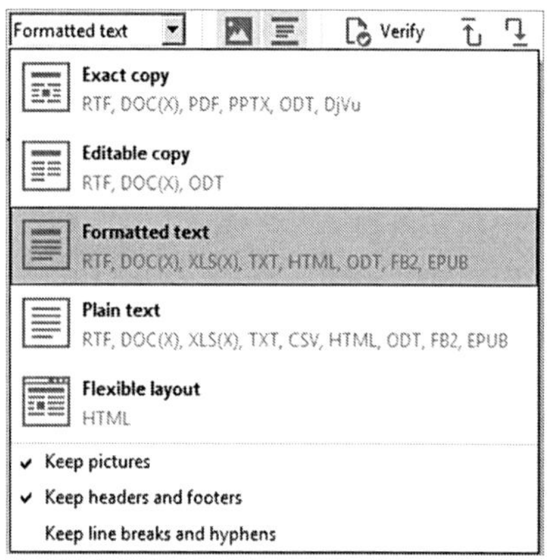

Similar formatting levels are provided by Nuance OmniPage – plain "decolumnised" text, formatted text "with styling" and TrueText to preserve "native formatting" as much as possible. Along with the possibility to choose and define zones similar to ABBYY's kinds of areas (text, table, graphic and form), OmniPage provides an additional layer of control through various layout templates such as single or multiple columns with or without tables, a spreadsheet, a form or a legal pleading, the last to help recognise and separate headers and footers. The results vary, so your judgement will depend on your source language, the type of document and, finally, your preferences and taste.

While a maximum degree of control is something I consider of utmost importance when converting PDFs, I don't think this control should be exerted to preserve and recover the formatting of the native document as accurately as possible. As far as design considerations are concerned, I can only second Chad Chelius. While he claims to be "the last person to tell you to sacrifice the design of your project", he advocates simple design and flowing text as two key things. Nine times out of ten, a client who send you a PDF doesn't expect you to return a

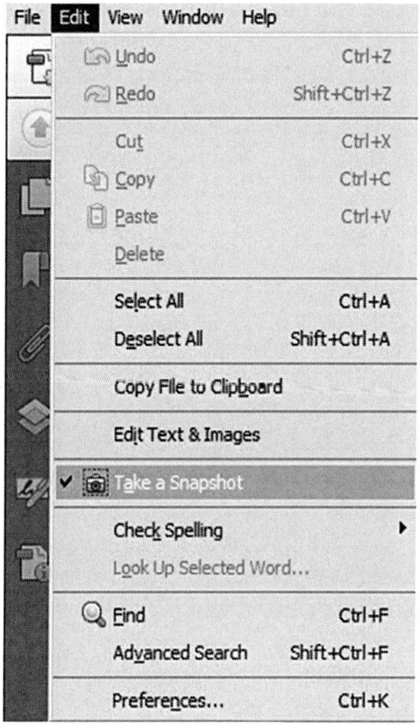

one-to-one formatted translation. On the other hand, they would benefit if your translation was formatted in a simple and consistent way. In fact, if you don't feel comfortable about the idea of using your own style guides and templates (see "Templatise your Word", p. 158), then dealing with PDF files may give you an impetus and justification to be flexible about page layout and design. For example, if the source PDF has a magazine-style layout with insets, pull quotes and sideheads, I don't see much point in trying to reproduce all the flourishes. Rather, you can note the location and function of a particular text element if it seems important (and use your own notes style to make the document more usable and mark your contribution to this process). As a matter of preference, I sometimes add borders to paragraphs instead of highlighting them in a more conventional way, such as through shading, bolding or italicising. Usually, this setting apart is sufficient as a signal of some layout quirk or structure in the original that the translator is careful to get across without overdoing the details. I also prefer to omit graphics when processing PDFs with OCR tools, for example exclude image areas or uncheck the *Keep pictures* option in FineReader. Instead, you can use Acrobat's *Snapshot* tool (I prefer to have it in my customised toolbar) to drag a rectangle around the area with the image you want to copy.[86] Simply release the mouse button for the image to be saved to the clipboard. When back in Word, place the cursor where you want your image to go and use CTRL+V.

A simple and consistent way of placing images is to insert them at the beginning of a new paragraph under the relevant text. You may or may not choose to centre the images, but it is a good idea to add captions. I believe captions de-

86 Using the *Snapshot* tool is not limited to images. It might be practical to copy whole bitmap segments of text for orientation, particularly for insets, pull quotes and the like. The result will be similar to a bilingual presentation which, in my experience, is always appreciated by translation clients.

serve their own style that should be applied consistently. Among various add-ins for Word, Kutools[87] is among the most useful ones. Among other things, it allows you to batch-insert captions to multiple pictures:

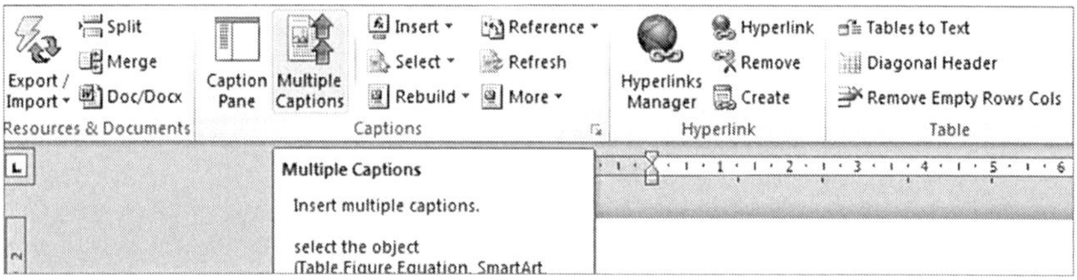

This kind of automation may seem an overkill if you have just a few images in your text, but it does enable a smart, consistent look across your translations. In other cases, when the left-to-right arrangement of text elements in the original PDF matters, the best tool to use is the *Table* tool in FineReader. I consider the *Draw Table Area* one of the most powerful and useful features of this software. There is no reason to limit its use to tables – it will be helpful whenever the layout is underlined by an invisible grid. The *Table* tool helps to construct this grid to separate the various elements and fix them relative to each other. It is definitely superior to tabs, columns, indents, spaces or any other formatting if you want to eliminate confusion and impose a clear, logical structure in your document.

Working with the *Table* tool is like applying the principle of **grid design** to your PDF translation. Any document with repetitive structural elements – that you typically find in data sheets, specifications or questionnaire forms – or with a list of arguments (bullet points!) can benefit from additional control enabled by this tool. The actual method is quite simple: select the *Table Area* tool from the toolbar of the *Image* pane and draw a rectangle around the area that should be rendered as a table. On top of this highlighted area you will see a horizontal pop-up toolbar:

Click on the *Analyze Table Structure* tool in the middle – a square with two circle arrows. The software may automatically guess how to split the area into rows and cells, however, you may want to tweak the result manually and add horizontal or vertical separators (the second and third tools on the toolbar above), delete wrongly placed lines (the fourth tool) or merge table cells and rows.

87 By Addin Technology <https://www.extendoffice.com/product/kutools-for-word.html>

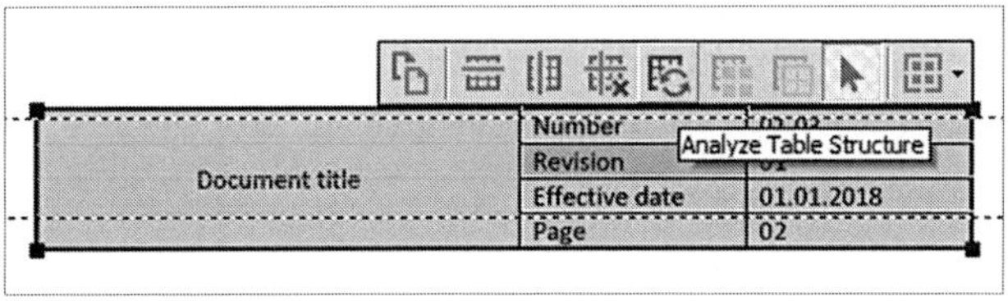

The process is pretty intuitive and, after a little practice, you will learn how to create perfect tables. You will still have to adjust your tables in Word, after you open the converted document. I find that the easiest way to post-process a table is to right-click on the table control icon in the upper-left corner and go to *Table Properties*. However, you may find it more convenient to use the *Table Tools* tabs (*Design* and *Layout*) on the ribbon. It makes sense to start with the *Design* tab to make separator rules invisible: choose *No Border* in the *Borders* group:

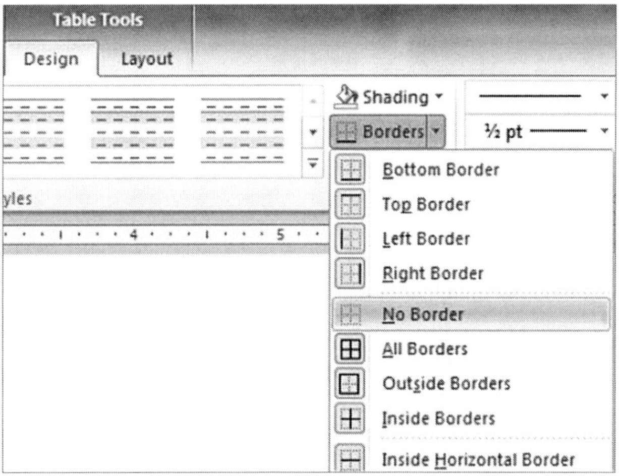

This is where your style guide for tables will come in handy, whether as a set of table properties to be applied manually (like I do) or templatised as a custom table style. For Word documents generated by OCR tools, it's usual to use macros to fix the generated file. Some translators swear by Dave Turner's CodeZapper macros, which have been around (without any recent updates) for many years. However, I would recommend TransTools (regularly improved and updated), in particular the formatting macros to clean documents produced by OCR software (reduce tags, remove excess spaces, fix paragraph and line breaks). In many cases, though, it is still worth considering Word's format eraser (the *Clear Formatting* button) and apply Word standard or your own custom styles and formats instead. The method you choose will depend on your PDF translation job, including the quality of the source text, its complexity and volume, your time constraints, and, above all, the purpose of the translation.

That said, we still have to accept that there is no one single push-button method if your goal is to produce a perfectly formatted Word document out of a client's PDF. In this chapter, I tried to show various methods that I personally favour when working on PDF files. These boil down to the following three steps:

1. Minimise the area of recognition to exclude all possible sources of OCR errors and problems – it will cost you less time and effort to manually add the missing pieces of text afterwards.
2. Maximise control over the OCR functions (e.g. select the *Table Area* tool to override any arbitrary software decisions) – both you and your client will be better served with a clear grid design than a smorgasbord of paragraph styles, columns, section breaks or random text boxes.
3. Apply simple, consistent formatting and a minimum number of styles in line with your own style guide – don't try to preserve the formatting of the source PDF, but deliver a Word document as a workable, self-contained solution: your client, in all likelihood, doesn't need a perfect copy of the original formatting in the translation (and doesn't need a half-baked product either, despite many translators believing their products still have to be refined by the client's mythical in-house "DTP professionals").

Besides these steps, I use another principle as a guideline that isn't limited to working with PDF files only: native software (along with the software that is used by our clients) is always preferable to third-party products. This certainly goes for CAT tools (or rather, against them and in favour of the client's software, as I showed in 2.9, p. 124). This goes for Adobe Acrobat – the software has a vast capacity for editing PDFs. The only advantage in using third-party OCR tools is where they can provide more control than Acrobat. Unfortunately, popular OCR tools such as FineReader or OmniPage, evolved toward fully-fledged alternatives to Acrobat rather than focusing on their own individualities and strengths. Every iteration typically brings ever more features along with a rather cosmetic upgrade of user interface, while the OCR core remains substantially unchanged.

■ ■ ■

Another topic worth touching upon is the "outsourcing" of converting PDFs into editable formats. What I term "outsourcing" in this context is any black-box process with the known input (PDF) and output (editable document in Word) – and a mystery in between. Such outsourcing options are plenty, starting with Adobe's own online conversion service (PDF to RTF). Then there are many far less reputable sites that invite you to upload your PDF and download an automatically converted Word file. A popular service among them is Zamsar. Obviously, you should consider the risk of confidentiality breach. If none, you can try other cloud-based services, such as CloudConvert, PDFCandy or easy PDFCloud. Another online option is Google Drive: when uploading a new file, check the option to *Convert uploaded files to Google Docs editor format*. Then right-click on the file and choose *Open with → Google Docs*. Now you can download the file as .docx, .rtf and other formats. Finally, if online conversion isn't appropriate for reasons of confidentiality, you can open your PDF in Word directly: the process is quick and the resulting Word document may be quite decent, comparable with that generated by a third-party PDF conversion tool.[88]

Another topic that goes beyond the scope of this chapter is using **professional** layout software for converting PDF into editable formats, in particular DTP software such as PDF2DTP by Markzware (to convert PDF into InDesign files).[89] The reason isn't only that this would ultimately extend beyond the boundaries of a translator's work, but mostly because your typical client would probably make little use of your translation if, to preserve the original PDF layout, you had to carefully reconstruct it in InDesign. However, if the document to be translated was **originally set** in InDesign, this is another topic altogether. Translating InDesign files doesn't necessarily shift the focus of work from that of a translator to that of a graphic designer. How to handle InDesign files is a subject relatively often raised in translators' fora nowadays, mostly with regard to how to open an InDesign file in CAT tools or how to get your client to extract the text and make it available for translation. In the next chapter, I will attempt to fill this gap and show how a translator can work in InDesign directly. This could mean not only a competitive advantage for translators, especially when working with high-end marketing and advertising clients, but also a more immediate, smoother workflow for the clients and

88 While the terms OCR tools and conversion tools are often used synonymously, it makes sense to differentiate between the two. For example, ABBYY's strong suit lay initially in OCR, while PDF conversion might be handled better by less known applications, such as PDF to Word Converter by Solid Documents. The latter produces quite decent results, while remaining essentially a black-box application with very few controls. A combination of two tools (one for OCR, one for the conversion) may be reasonable depending on the specifics of the source PDF.

89 < http://markzware.com/products/pdf2dtp/>

an overall better, organic, ready-for-publication translation, achieved through working in a "live" environment, while editing, adapting and fitting the text to the existing page layout.

3.5 InDesign: an off-the-book tutorial

There are lots of books and online courses for those who want to learn Adobe InDesign. Most proceed in a step-by-step manner, starting with the basic functions and moving on to explain all the features, palettes and tools of the software. For a translator, the idea of working on an InDesign document directly may be an intimidating prospect due to the sheer volume of information and the overwhelming amount of options that the software provides. The first piece of good news is that all these – both tutorials and the software options – are something you'll probably never need. Another piece of good news is that in the unlikely situation when you do encounter a specific "technical" problem, you can look it up on the Internet without having to absorb a tremendous mass of information first.

"Knowledge of some principles easily compensates the lack of knowledge of some facts", to quote the French philosopher Claude Adrien Helvétius. A translator who routinely works with Word, PowerPoint or Excel documents (let alone CAT tools) has sufficient knowledge of the general principles to cope with a regular InDesign file. As for "some facts" that are useful to know, the idea of this chapter is to compensate for the lack of more detailed knowledge of InDesign. I will also try to pinpoint the most typical problems and error messages that you may come across, starting with opening an InDesign file on your computer.

Professional translators aren't the target audience of the majority of InDesign books and tutorials. On the other hand, whenever the subject of translating an InDesign document comes up, it is invariably suggested that a translator should use a CAT tool to translate, i.e. to simply overwrite the text and deliver the document "as is" to her client, who will then carry out all the necessary adjustments. (The fact that the translator doesn't get to see the text as laid out on a page is blissfully ignored.) We've already discussed the advantages of working in a native format as opposed to CAT tools, but for the sake of completeness, let me summarise the two most important aspects here.

The first reason is quality. Doing your translation on an InDesign page enables you to see your content in a larger, more complex context, with all the nuances that would be lost if chunks of text were scattered randomly on a page, detached from accompanying images. It's true that today's CAT tools offer a preview function, but a preview is not an acceptable alternative to "the real thing"; it is rather a fragmented digital printout of text fragments similar to a text-only PDF.

Second, there are distinct advantages concerning workflow. You can fit your text to the space and lay it out properly as you work. You will spare your client's layouter (who might not know the language of the translation) the struggle with your text, which not infrequently results in being asked to make your translation shorter. Or, to better fit the text to the available space, change your translation to help get rid of the usual typographic widows and orphans (p. 84), adjust your headlines or captions and so on. Additionally, you will also be saved the trouble of having to revise your translation on a PDF, via notes and comments to the layouter. Such revisions may continue for several rounds and be quite stressful for everyone involved, which doesn't necessarily contribute to a better-quality product.

Both advantages – for the quality of your translation as well as for the communication with your client (or their graphic designer) – result from the immediacy and flexibility afforded by working directly in InDesign. I don't mean for a second that you should aspire to become a substitute layouter. Working in InDesign directly always refers to working on the content, not layout – you don't create new layout or make any substantial changes to it: any adjustments are limited to the text and affect the layout to a minimal degree, if at all, and only when it is strictly a requirement of the new language.

■ ■ ■

So you have received an InDesign file for translation. It makes sense to ask your client about the exact version of the software that the document was created in. InDesign is **backward compatible**, which means that if you have an older version of InDesign, you won't be able to open the document created in a newer version. On the other hand, your newer version of InDesign may produce a file incompatible with an older version used by your client. Trying to open a file created in a newer format brings up an error message: "Cannot open '<filename>', because it was saved with a newer version of Adobe InDesign (<version number>). You must use that version or later to open the file. To then enable it to be opened in this version, choose Save As InDesign (<version number>) or later, or export to IDML." As promised at the beginning of this chapter, you will do fine with no tutorials and no further information. The error message contains everything you have to know about the incompatibility issue and the solution to this problem: either install the most recent version of the software (and update any plugins you may also have) or request an IDML file from the client.[90]

The two InDesign file formats, INDD and IDML, differ in some respects, notably IDML files are conveniently smaller. The reason is that INDD files are usually saved with **image previews**. There is something important to understand about how InDesign handles images. Unlike the more familiar office formats (Word, PowerPoint or PDF) that **embed** images in a document, InDesign can both embed and **link back** to external images (this is the default setup). Graphic designers who produce professional publications keep the image files separately, usually in a folder called "Link" or "Assets". These folders are generated within an InDesign **package** that is automatically produced when the software gathers together copies of all the external resources such as images and fonts to be delivered to a publisher (or to a translator). The images you see in a file are references to external data. The actual graphics are needed for printing (including printing digitally to PDF). When working on an InDesign file on your computer, you deal with the visual references only – thumbnails of the actual graphics cached in the file or previews whose size can be configured in settings (*InDesign → Preferences → File Handling* (MacOS) or *Edit → Preferences → File Handling* (Windows), check the *Always Save Preview Images with Documents* box, select the page range (e.g. *All Pages*) and preview size (e.g. *Extra Large 1024×1024*)). So, an InDesign file with image previews is an INDD file (*.indd). The larger the previews, the larger the file. The same InDesign document saved as an IDML is smaller because it has no image previews: you will see grey boxes as placeholders (if you see images in an IDML file, it means they have been embedded).

90 IDML stands for InDesign Markup Language, a universally compatible format that can be opened and read by all InDesign versions from CS4 onward.

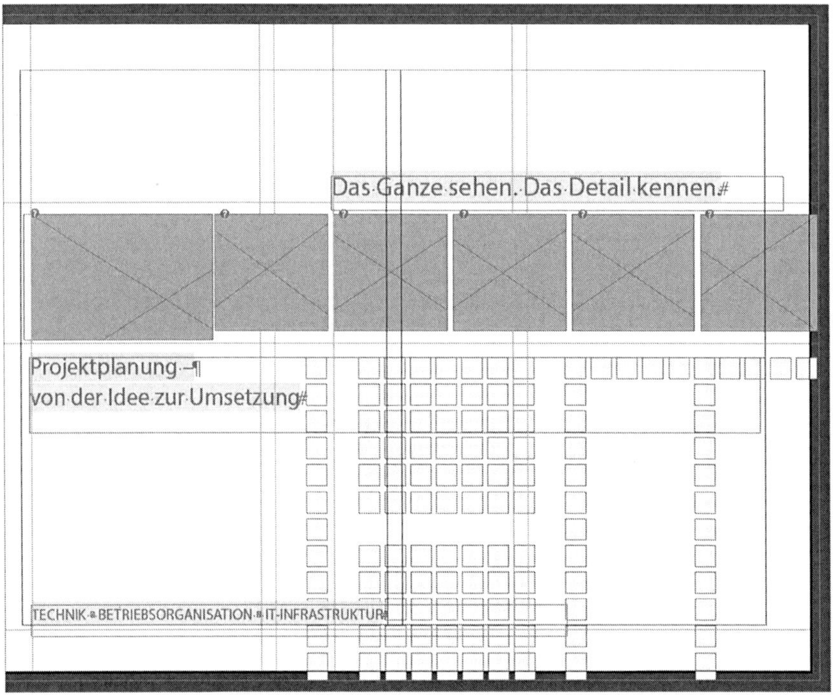

Translating your text on a page with grey boxes makes the whole idea of working in a visually rich layout moot. However, IDML is a convenient trade-off format: its primary function is to solve version incompatibility issues at the cost of stripping the file of cached resource data. You can think of IDML as "INDD light": this is a text-only InDesign document with placeholders for external graphic files. That is also one of the reasons IDML is **the** format your CAT tools will be most happy with. Practically speaking, if you plan to translate an InDesign document in a CAT tool, save it first as an .idml file. Then you can safely import it into your CAT tool. However, if you plan to translate your document in InDesign directly, IDML is still a reasonable trade-off. Although you will see no image previews, that doesn't mean that the graphics are gone. All you need to do is relink your images to the original graphic files (make sure you have received the "Links" folder) and they will pop up in place of the grey boxes.

You'll probably won't need a tutorial to fix the missing images. InDesign's default setting is *Check Links Before Opening Document* (enable this in *InDesign → Preferences → File Handling* (MacOS) or *Edit → Preferences → File Handling* (Windows). This ensures that when you open an .idml file, a warning will pop up:

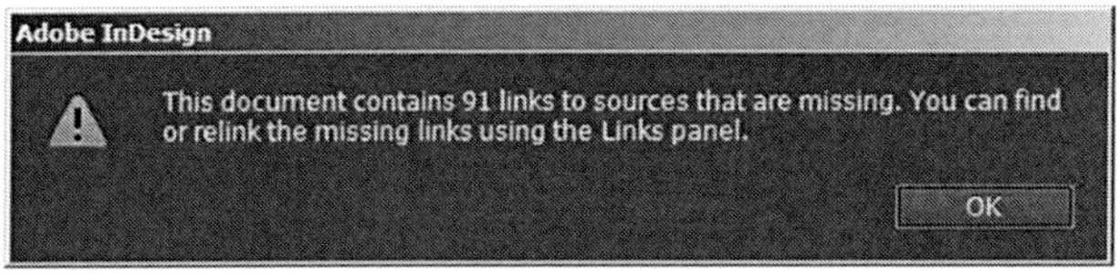

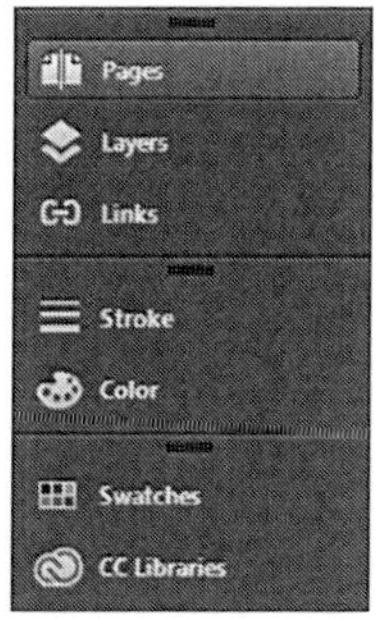

Like before, this notice instructs you what you have to do. Provided that a folder with all the resources is available, it can be done simply in a bulk action. In the top right corner of your InDesign workspace you will find this panel:

Click on *Links* to bring up a list of missing links:

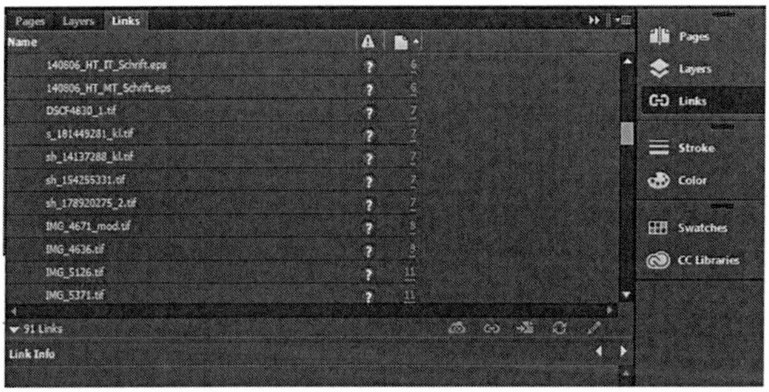

Select one of the links marked with the question mark icon and ALT-CLICK or OPTION-CLICK the *Update Link* button underneath:

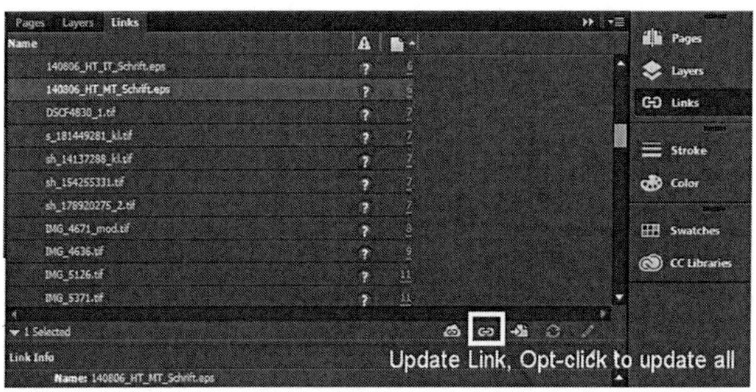

Specify the Links folder in a window that appears and make sure to check *Search for Missing Links in This Folder*:

Alternatively, you can right-click on one of the missing links, select *Relink* and then specify the path to the Links folder.

Missing images (or images that need to be relinked) is one of the two warnings that usually appear when you try to open an InDesign file from a client. The second warning is about fonts:

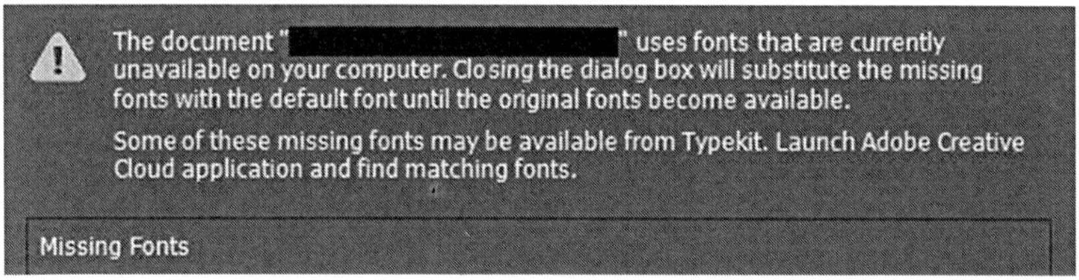

An InDesign file created on another computer has links to the fonts on that computer. If they are unavailable on your machine, the software will try to replace the missing fonts with those on your computer that it sees as default fonts. If you choose to ignore this message, InDesign will open the file, but highlight in pink the text with missing fonts (see the first picture in this chapter, p. 224). You can work with the highlighted text as usual, but all the formatting and fine typography will make no sense – your translation will get reformatted as soon as your client's designer opens the file on her machine and your fonts will be replaced by the originals. Instead of ignoring the message, first have a look into the package your client has sent you. If you have the fonts, you'll need to close InDesign and install them. In Windows, right-click the font files and choose *Install*. On a Mac, use Font Book – it will open a preview with the *Install Font* option at the bottom. Alternatively, you can manually copy the unzipped fonts to your Fonts folder: /Users/Your_Username/Library/Fonts. To identify the Fonts folder on a Mac, open the *Go* menu at the top of the screen and press OPTION+SHIFT: the menu list will be expanded and will include *Library*.

If you installed the fonts correctly, the software will find them when opening the file and the message about unavailable fonts should disappear. However, you can always check for missing fonts: go to *Type* and click on *Find Font*:

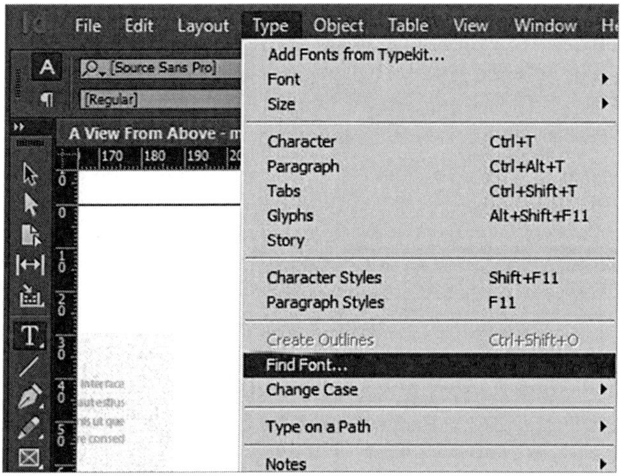

All the missing fonts will be marked with yellow warning triangles (note the *Replace With* option below):

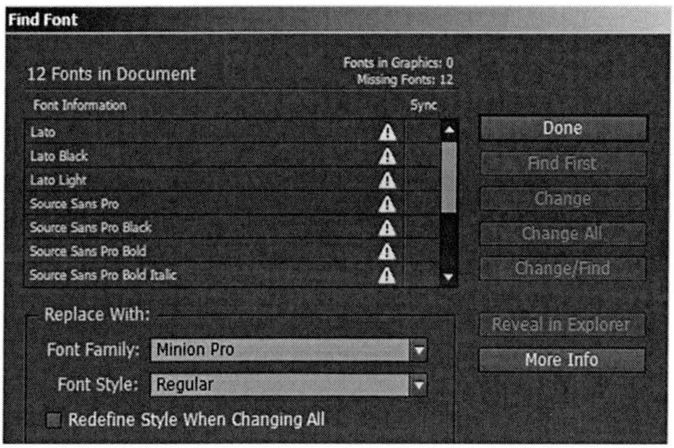

Generally, I strongly advise against replacing the original fonts with anything that InDesign will find on your computer or with fonts you think look alike. No matter how much two fonts may resemble each other, they are never identical. Designers choose a particular font for a reason, so the only ground that makes it appropriate to question their decision is the incompatibility between their chosen font and your language. Into-English translators have the least concern about the issue of incompatible fonts. Colleagues who work with Western European and Romance languages, such as Spanish or French, may be just as unaware of any font problems. However, the further east, the greater the chance that the font chosen by the designer doesn't contain all the accented characters and an extended character set. This is even more so for non-Latin languages, for instance Greek or Russian. Our Hebrew or Chinese colleagues don't need to be told about such problems – they may be used to actually **making recommendations** to their clients as regards writing systems, typography and fonts. However, Latvian, Turkish, Polish or Czech translators may have to look for an alternative to the original InDesign font. If your working language contains any special characters, it is helpful to be a bit more knowledgeable about fonts. Some may see it as a challenge or something that goes beyond their remit, but to me knowing the intricacies of our language is a competitive advantage that provides added value to our clients.

As soon as you discover a font incompatible with the target language in your InDesign document, provide feedback. In my opinion, pointing out a problem should go hand in hand with offering a workable solution. A safe bet is to recommend a Unicode or Open Type Pro font, and a better option is to suggest a specific, language-compatible font that is the best match in terms of typeface appearance (serif, sans serif), letter spacing, weight (light, regular, bold, black) and cut (italic, condensed). In my experience, the unique value of a translator as perceived by a client is often linked to her expertise and the ability to advise on possible choices. Therefore, it is definitely beneficial to gain this specialised knowledge and use it to serve your client and your own business.

An error message about unavailable fonts or images may pop up even if you do have them on your computer. This is usually due to broken links to these external resources, since InDesign uses absolute file paths. The absolute file references won't work if the files change location (such as when they are transferred to another machine). File paths are also handled differently on Mac and Windows computers. But that is practically all you need to know. Today, the differences between using a Mac or a Windows PC for InDesign are rather subjective. Designers prefer to use Macs, this being a matter of a long-standing tradition, but incompatibilities that plagued the interaction between graphic designers and their Windows colleagues are a thing of the past. So, whether your file was created on a Mac or a Windows computer, it'll be perfectly usable regardless of the system you work in.

Before installing the fonts, check the file size. Font files can get corrupted when emailed and if a Windows user zips the InDesign package, compression may reduce the font file size to 0. Make sure that the font files are intact both when receiving and when sending them back to your client.

■ ■ ■

If it currently seems that working with InDesign is a hassle, I hope that by the end of this chapter you'll be an InDesign convert. Let's start by getting a quick overview of an InDesign workspace:

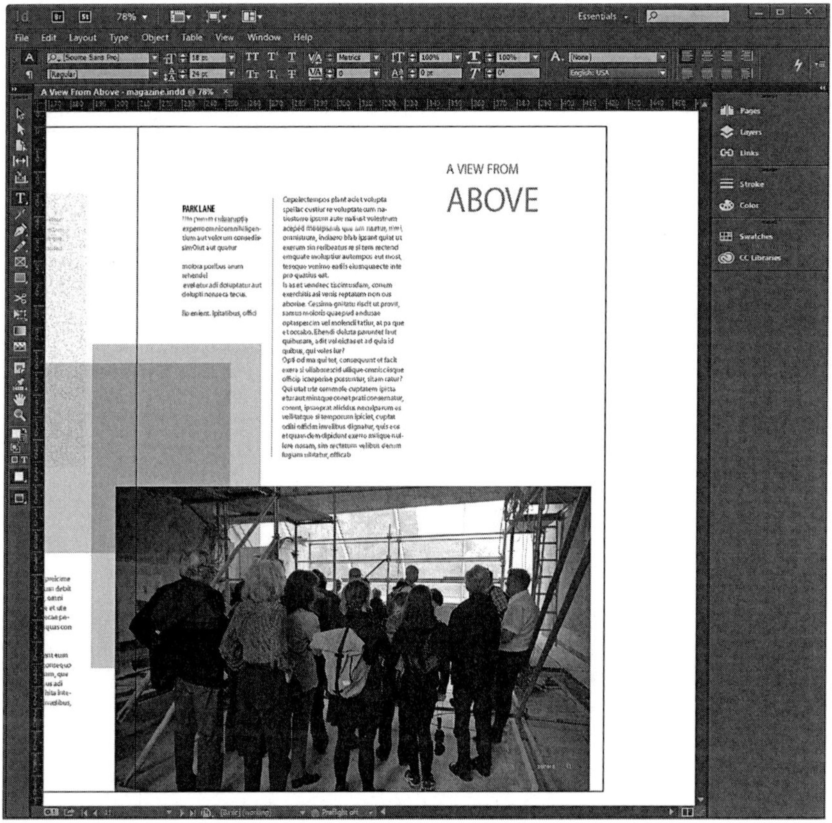

InDesign's default workspace may appear complex, but for the purposes of our work as translators, we'll need to familiarise ourselves with just a few functions. I would recommend starting with the *View* menu in the so-called *Application bar* at the top of the screen:

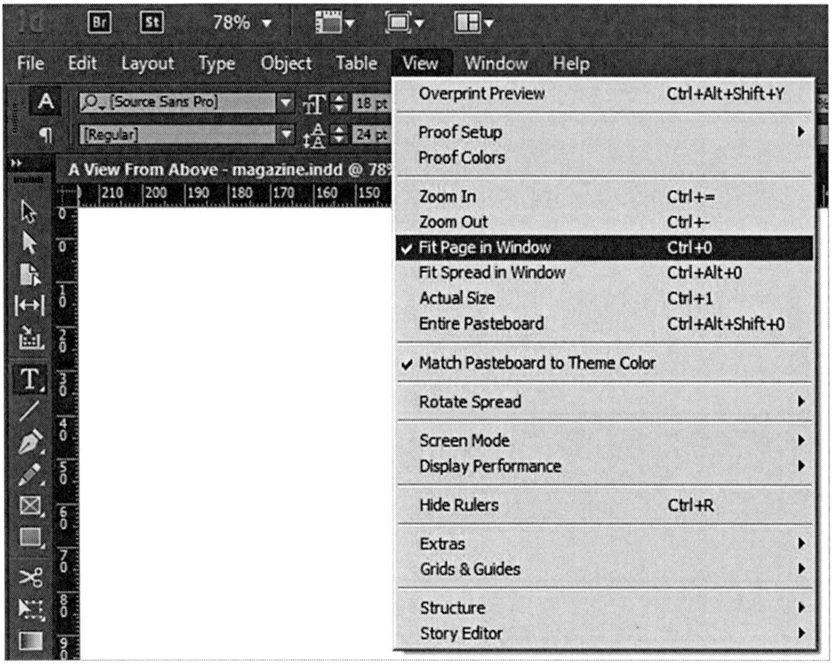

Here you will find links to convenient zoom tools (and even more convenient hot keys). If you zoom in and a part of the page or spread gets pushed outside the visible page area, you can use the horizontal and vertical bars to scroll across the page. These bars are used for navigation through your document, similar to Word and other familiar applications.

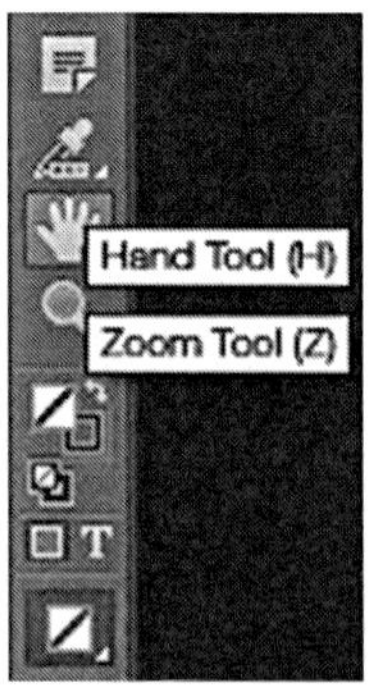

Next, have a look at the *Tools* panel, on a vertical bar on the left of the screen. Here you will find two very convenient tools – *Hand* (H) and *Zoom* (Z):

The *Zoom* tool allows you to adjust magnification: when you press ALT (OPT), the plus sign with the magnifying glass symbol changes to minus; click with the mouse to reduce the view size. With the *Hand* tool you can grab and drag the document in your workspace, which is a nice **alternative to navigation** with the vertical and horizontal scroll bars. You can simply press the H key, if you're not editing text. An even more useful shortcut is to hold down ALT (OPT)+SPACEBAR to get the grabber hand and move the document on the screen, and let go of the ALT (OPT) key and the spacebar to return to the previous mode (from here on, I will mostly omit references to Mac shortcuts, as they are identical with those on a Windows PC – feel free to translate CTRL as COMMAND and ALT as OPTION if you are an Apple user).

The black arrow at the very top of the vertical *Tools* panel is the *Selection Tool*, which is activated by default when you open your document. Structure-wise, an InDesign page is similar to a PowerPoint slide: it consists of various elements, such as images, shapes or text frames. Use the *Selection Tool* to select the text frame you want to edit, that is to overwrite the available text with your translation. Also, whenever it looks like the software doesn't behave like it should, first check what tool you're using. The active tool will be marked with a darker background. From here, you can go to the tool you'll probably use more often than anything else – the *Type Tool* (T). T stands for type, but for us it is equivalent to "text" or "translate". You will note that, depending on which tool from the *Tools* panel we choose, the appearance of the *Control* panel, the two-level space under the *Application* bar, will change accordingly. The *Control* panel is **context sensitive**: for example, as soon as you activate the *T* tool, it will change to display text edit options. Now the panel will look much like our familiar ribbon in Word:

The first two icons on the left are used to toggle between the character (top) and paragraph (bottom) formatting options. There is no need to go into details, since many of these options will be familiar or self-explanatory, but what is more important, you are well advised not to tamper with the character and paragraph styles already set. Before we move on to text editing options we will use while translating, I'll add a few comments about InDesign workspace.

A CTRL+Z shortcut will take you a step back. If you want to undo a step, use this shortcut or the *Undo* command in the *Edit* menu. InDesign doesn't have an "undo history": you can cancel only the most recent change. To remedy something that happened a few steps back, don't forget to save your work regularly. If you feel at a loss because something went wrong quite a few edits ago, use the *Revert* command (in the *File* menu) as a last resort to reopen the last saved version.

It is good practice to start working on your client's InDesign file by renaming it. As mentioned in the chapter on signing (p. 141), you can simply add your initials and your target language to the original file name. Better yet, use the option *Open as Copy* when opening the file to modify the file name on the spot: check *Copy* under the *Open* dialogue box used to navigate to the location of the file (*File* → *Open*). Also note that an .idml file will open as a new *Untitled* document that you'll have to name when saving as an .indd.

Another thing worth mentioning before moving on to text editing options is the *Pages* panel. Some elements of text may appear inaccessible when you try to select their container text frames. They may belong to a master page, similar to those in PowerPoint: to access them, go to the master pages (master slides in PowerPoint). The functionality of the *Pages* panel in InDesign matches that of PowerPoint in terms of how you switch between templates and normal slides or navigate through slides. The panel is located in the top right-hand corner, above the *Links* tab:

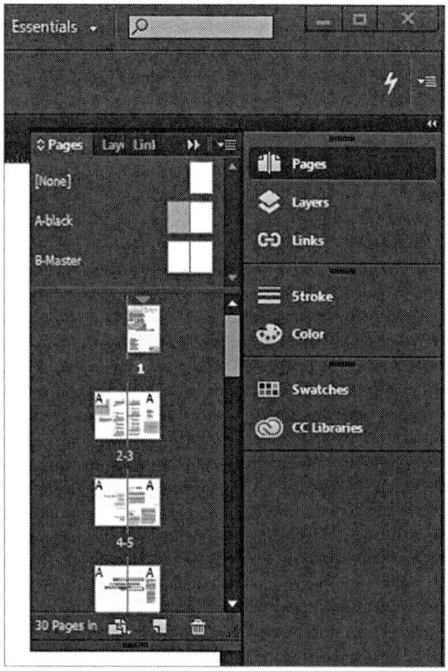

The regular page icons are marked with letters corresponding to the master pages. Double-click on an A or B master to display the master pages and edit the text elements that need to be translated.

The *Layers* panel under the *Pages* tab is the next place to look if you still cannot access some text elements – your text could have been rendered to graphics and can be edited only as an image, not as text. This is extremely rare, but may happen when a designer inserts a picture that already contains some text (e.g. a newspaper cut-out). To identify such images, uncheck the text layer – all text will disappear from your document pages and only the images will be displayed:

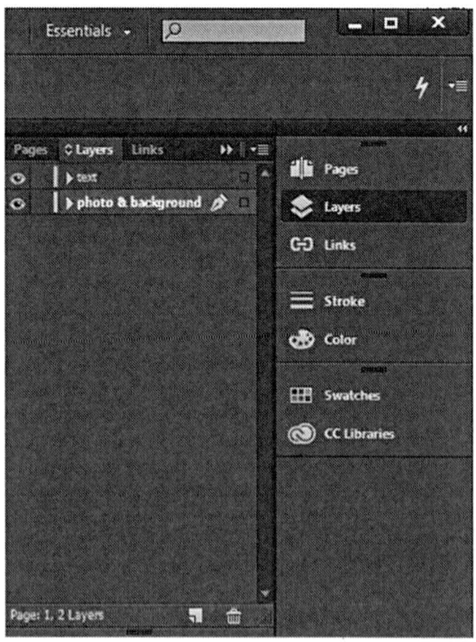

To toggle visibility, click on the eye symbol next to each layer. To focus on the text, you can make all graphics temporarily invisible. Don't forget to switch the layer back on before returning the translated document to the client.

The stacking order of the layers can be changed. When working with text, it is better when the text layer is placed above the image layer – you can move it upwards by simply dragging and dropping it.

In my experience, inaccessible text frames have been the most frustrating (if rare) challenge when translating in InDesign. The *Pages* and *Layers* tabs help to resolve the most obvious issues, however, there are other options to try when these don't work. Your text frame may be obscured by other objects or text frames on the page and so when trying to select it, something else will be selected instead. If that seems to be the case, right-click the object, as it may be that your text frame lies underneath. Check if the object is grouped together with other elements and if so, click *Ungroup* in the context menu:

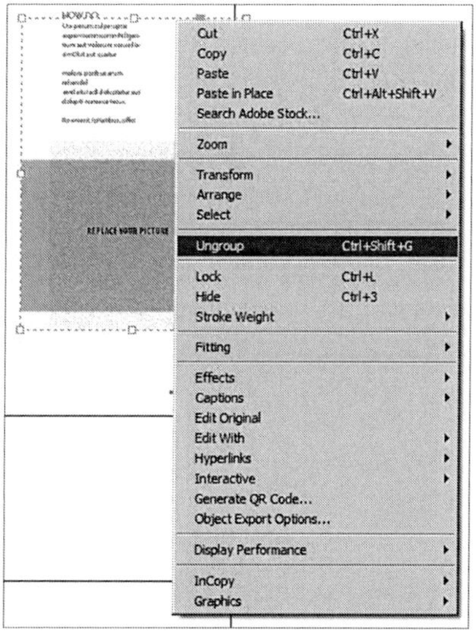

Another possibility is to use the *Arrange* and *Select* options: to gain access to your text frame, you may need to bring it to the front. Click on *Arrange* to use the *Bring to front* or *Bring forward* command. While *Bring forward* and *Send backward* are used to move the selected element forward or backward one click at a time, in front of or behind the next object in the stacking order, with *Bring to front* and *Send to back* you can place the object immediately on top or under **all** the other overlapping elements. With *Select*, you simply move from one object to another, without changing the stacking order.

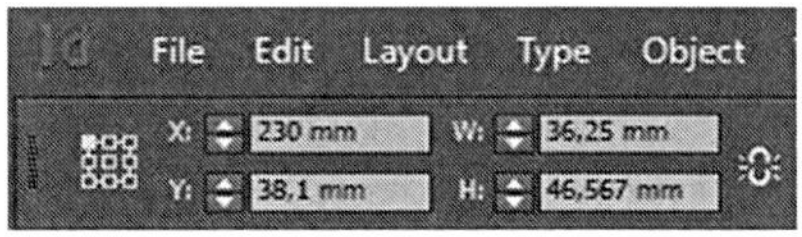

If the overlapping object isn't grouped (or you have already ungrouped it), try to drag it off your text frame. To make sure you will get it back into place intact, make a note of its coordinates. The context-sensitive *Control* panel for the *Selection Tool* provides a precise location of a selected object on the page, with up to three digits after the decimal point.

It may be a good idea to write down the X and Y values before dragging the object aside. To be completely on the safe side, pay attention to the square figure to the left of the X and Y coordinates (this figure is called *proxy*). Nine small squares are arranged in three rows and three columns and one of the squares is marked. This indicates which point of the selected object the coordinates refer to, like the top left coordinate in the example above. After you finished the translation in the now accessible text frame, select the misplaced object and enter the initial values to restore its original coordinates; it will move back into place over your text.

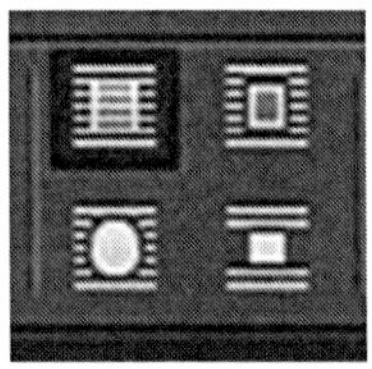

Just to mention it for completeness, in extremely rare cases when you move your text frame away from an interfering object, your text may suddenly disappear. This may be due to a collision with another object for which the *Text Wrap* feature has been activated. Select the conflicting object and check the *Control* panel. This time, instead of coordinates, pay attention to these four buttons approximately in the middle of the panel:

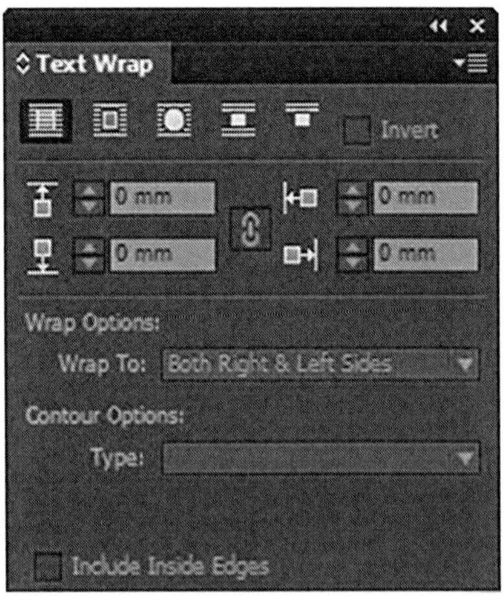

Make sure the first square is activated (you will see the prompt *No text wrap* if you hover over it with a mouse). Alternatively, go to *Window* in the Application bar, open the *Text Wrap* menu and click on the *No text wrap* button:

The issue of disappearing text may also have something to do with the next four buttons in the *Control* panel for the *Selection Tool*:

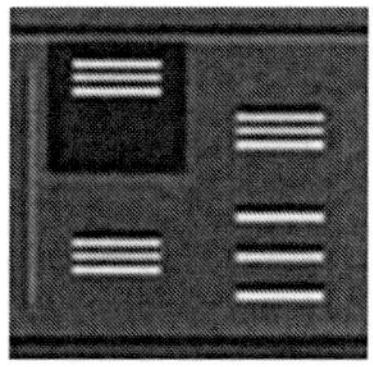

They control the vertical alignment of text in a text frame: *Align top*, *Align centre*, *Align bottom* and *Justify vertically*. When you switch to the *T* tool, the context-sensitive panel will provide you with two more options – *Do not align to baseline grid* (top) and *Align to baseline grid* (bottom):

Without going into too much detail about what may go wrong with these settings (it's not the translator's fault, just in case!), there is always a pragmatic, universal solution: open the original InDesign file in the source language and compare the settings.

■ ■ ■

Now that we've covered so much ground concerning the basic workspace and possible pitfalls, it's time to turn to the *Type* tool. After you selected a text frame (its border will become visible), click on *T*:

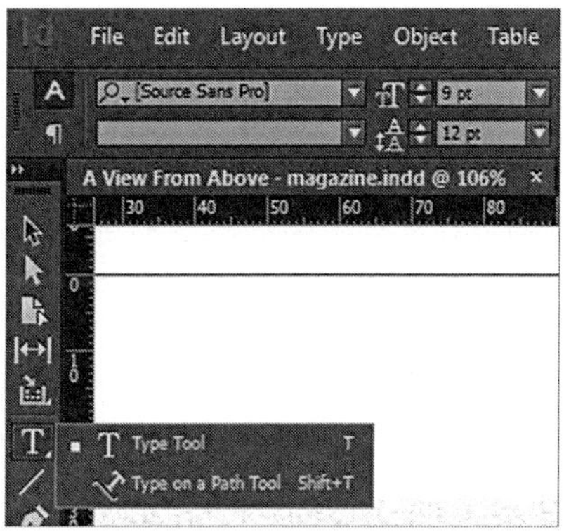

When you move your cursor into the text frame, its appearance will change to a vertical bar, much like the cursor in Word. You can start editing the text like you would in a text editor.

Besides the formatting options in the already mentioned *Control* bar, you will find a few useful settings in the *Type* menu of the *Application* bar at the top of the InDesign workspace:

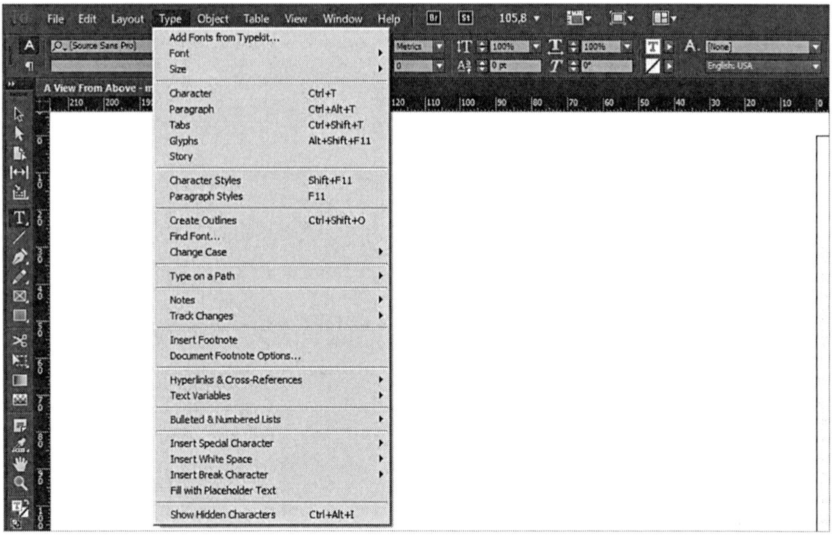

Since I prefer to see the formatting marks, my InDesign translation workflow usually starts with activating *Show Hidden Characters* (CTRL+ALT+I). As with Word, this will give you a good idea about how the original text was formatted. Check for hard returns (they should be used to start new paragraphs, not new lines), excessive spaces, tabs, bulleted and numbered lists (see "Setting type", p. 49). You don't necessarily have to fix any problems prior to translating, but you can take care of typography flaws while overwriting the text.

If you're used to using non-breaking spaces when working in Word, then the InDesign type menu will offer you a whole range of more sophisticated options:

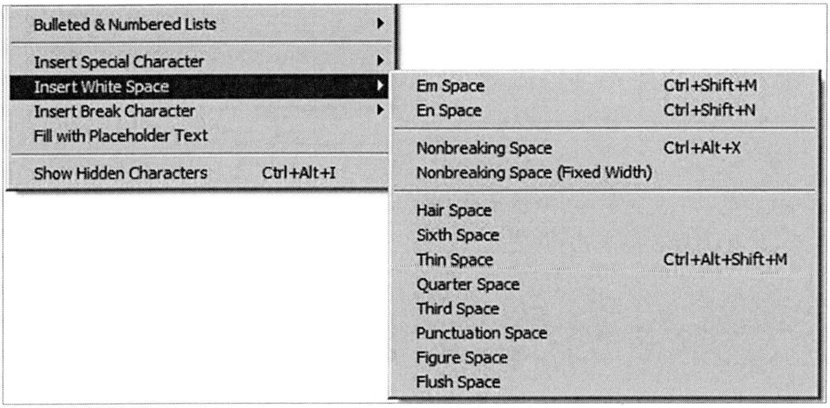

You'll do fine with just the most useful ones, such as a non-breaking space (CTRL+ALT+X), a non-breaking hyphen (CTRL+ALT+-) and a discretionary (soft) hyphen if you don't want to use automatic hyphenation (CTRL+SHIFT+-). You'll also find other subtleties, like dashes (*Insert Special Character → Hyphens and Dashes*) or quotation marks (*Insert Special Character → Quotation Marks*) to further refine and personalise your signature style.

Along with activating *Show Hidden Characters*, the moment I start translating in InDesign I set my **target language**: with the cursor in the text frame, press CTRL+A (*Select All*) to select all text and choose your language from the *Type* tool control panel.

You don't have to select text frames one after another. For (relatively) long running text, the text boxes will be linked or, to use InDesign terminology, **threaded**. The text will flow freely from frame to frame, sometimes spanning multiple columns or pages. With the CTRL+A shortcut you can select the contents of all connected text frames in one go. It is helpful to be able to recognise threaded frames – both through using the *Select All* function which highlights linked text and also by paying attention to the little details in the frame borders. The small square in the top left corner of the frame, visible when you select the frame with the *Selection Tool*, is called an "in port". If the square is empty, the frame isn't linked to any previous frame, but if the square contains an arrow, the text begins elsewhere. A square near the bottom right corner of the frame is called an "out port" and indicates whether the text ends here (empty) or flows into another frame (arrow):

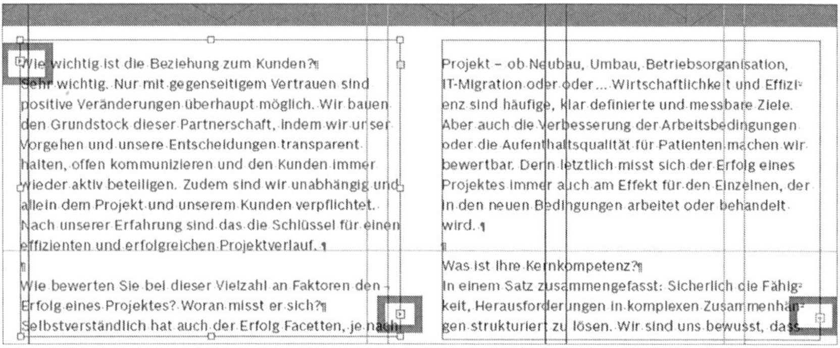

If you click into this small square, the cursor will change into a broken chain link with text in very small type. This may be practical for a designer who is going to place the following text elsewhere, but it is highly impractical for a translator. Press *Escape* instead of clicking the mouse button again for the small type to disappear (and also to prevent the unlinking of the connected text frames).

The in port and out port in the frame border are visible if the frame is selected with the *Selection Tool* and hidden when you use the *T* tool to edit the text. There is an exception, though. The out port may be marked **red** and contain a **plus sign** instead of an arrow. This is a warning that you must pay attention to at all times!

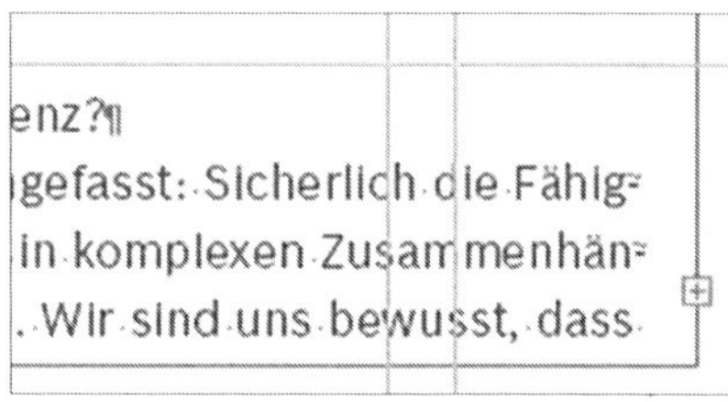

For a translator working on an InDesign file, one of the most important side aspects to deal with are oversets. **Overset text** occurs when there is more text than the text frame can contain and there is no other threaded frame to accommodate the excess – part of your translation (longer than the source) disappears. It is unlikely that you will encounter the overset problem if you do your translation directly in InDesign. After all, it's hardly possible to overwrite the existing text in a text frame without being aware of the frame boundaries. Otherwise, as many graphic designers know, a translated text tends to get longer than the original one. If the translator didn't pay attention to the actual text position and length on the page – which does happen if the source text is exported to another application, such as a CAT tool – a typical upshot will be overset text.

The red warning sign is useful because it enables us to detect hidden elements, but it can easily be overlooked. That is why both the universal remedy and also an important step in the workflow is to export your InDesign document as a PDF (more on that later). Before generating a PDF, the software will warn you and provide specific information about any oversets:

I can think of four ways to handle oversets. First, if you click the red plus with the *Selection Tool*, the cursor will change from a black arrow to a mini frame filled with the overset text:

That means you have grabbed the content of the frame and can paste it somewhere else. If you don't choose any specific text frame, a new one with the excess text will be automatically created anywhere you click on the page. However, not only is a new text frame unwanted, it will probably mess up the page layout. If you release the text into an existing text frame, you will end up with a mess in terms of both layout and content. What you can do, is to draw an empty text frame, either on the page or, preferably, somewhere **off the page** (you can also move the cursor with the text away from the page and click there). As a default option, the new text frame will be "threaded", i.e. linked with the previous one, so the excess text will flow from the first text frame into the new one, like in the picture below, where the new frame was set up just to the left of the page:

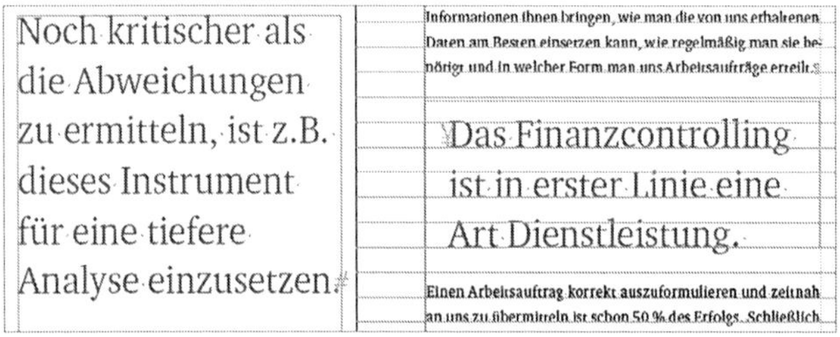

The advantage of using a provisional text frame outside the document page is the opportunity to have everything in sight while editing your translation. Deleting your text in any of the preceding connected frames will affect the content of all the ones that follow. For example, while shortening your text in the connected frames visible on the page, you can monitor the progressive reduction of the excess text in the frame off the page until it completely disappears, meaning you have fixed the overset (and can delete the now empty frame).

To have a visual cue for threaded text frames, especially if you have some off the page, it is recommended to activate, at least temporarily, the *Show Text Threads* feature (*View → Extras → Show Text Threads*). With this option activated, you will see diagonal lines connecting the out ports and the in ports on the threaded text frames:

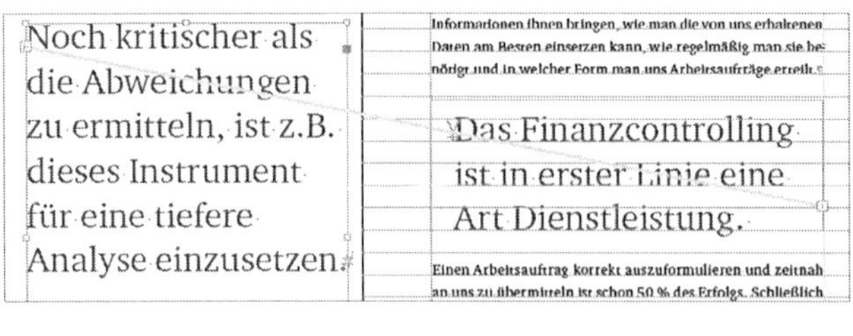

The second method of fixing overset text is to adjust the text format. You can use a smaller font size or reduce line spacing, but there are also more sophisticated, automated or semi-automated tools, such as the Fit Text script by Id-Extras. However, as the last thing you'll want to do is make serious changes to the design, such as changing the font size or line spacing, this isn't a recommended approach.

The third, and most appropriate method, is copyfitting – fitting your translation into the space set by the designer. Copyfitting or "text fitting" may be the most adequate notion for your job description and something to refer to when you communicate the value of your work in InDesign to your client. Rather than using any "technical" tricks, you translate the original content while minding the visual constraints of the page layout and accommodating the information to get the best communication effect. If your translation has become longer than the original text and needs shortening, using a provisional text frame outside the document, as described above, is a practical way to copyfit.

I'd like to also mention the fourth technique of working with overset text. The concept of copyfitting is based on the assumption that the layout is fixed and inviolable, never to be changed by anyone but the graphic designer. In practice, though, there may be some flexibility around this. Whenever you deal with a thoughtfully constructed and well-designed document, it is a good idea to become aware of what exactly creates the perception of thoughtfully constructed design. More often than not, it is an underlying, consistent system or logic that guides how content, both verbal and visual, is organised. In the context of InDesign, the ultimate tool to create structure from chaos is a document template based on a layout grid. Grids ensure structure, hierarchy, consistency and rhythm – all elements of good design. Essentially, a layout grid is a set of non-printing vertical columns, horizontal guides and baselines to help accurately position objects on the page. The so-called baseline grid is used to align text lines. Guides are critical for alignment and orientation – without a grid, a document page would appear as a haphazard arrangement of text and graphics. To make sure a layout grid behind your InDesign pages is visible, activate the *Show Document Grid* feature: go to *View → Grids & Guides → Show/Hide Document Grid*. You may also want to have a look at master pages which, while stripped of text and graphic elements, are the template for your InDesign document.

One of the things you may want to do is adjust a text frame, provided this won't interfere with the layout grid and that there is enough white space.[91] To make sure you comply with the existing layout, check vertical justification. The default setting is *Top*, but to align text frames near the bottom of the page the designer might have chosen another option. With the *Type* tool activated, right-click to go to *Text Frame Options* (CTRL+B). This setting, for example, means that whenever you add new lines to an "unthreaded" text frame, the frame will "grow" upwards, while the last line remains snapped to the bottom edge of the frame:

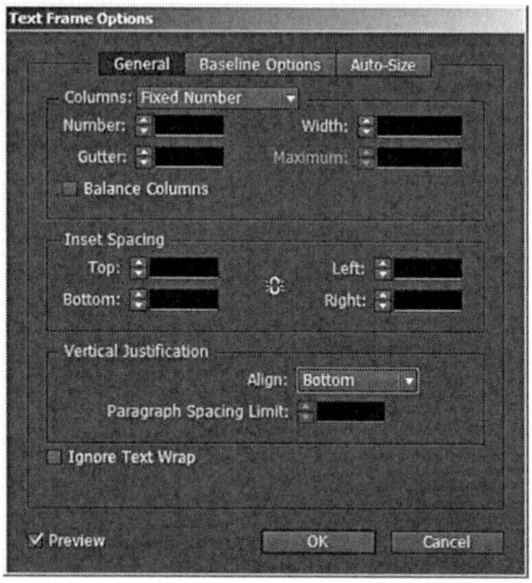

Also check the column alignment setting chosen by the designer (this should be kept unchanged):

To resize a text frame, drag any of the frame handles with the *Selection Tool*. You can also access the frame handles while using the *Type* tool: press and hold down CTRL. Be careful when using the corner handles though, as they allow resizing frames both vertically and horizontally at the same time – the risk of inadvertently neglecting the grids and guides doubles.

I would also recommend staying away from automatic resize options, even if InDesign conveniently offers such. When you right-click on a text frame with

91 Perhaps I should explain what I mean when I think of adjusting text frames. Provided there is enough space on the page, it is possible to expand text frames while adhering to the existing guides and grids. If a text frame fits smugly into a column, but is a bit too small to contain your translated text, you can expand its height. Or, if the designer chose a text frame that was just big enough for the original headline, but is definitely too tight to accommodate your translation, you can expand its width up to the next logical vertical line.

the *Selection Tool*, you will see a feature that does the job very easily: *Fitting → Fit Frame to Content*. Alternatively, you might be tempted to use one of the more precise frame fitting options:

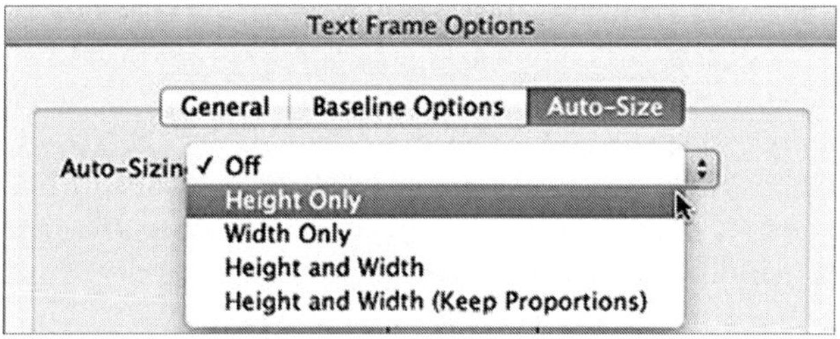

However, I think that layout changes, even if minor, should be a conscious choice and done manually. Text frame adjustments will always remain an exception and you won't save much time or be more efficient by going on autopilot.

Resizing text boxes seems to be the opposite of copyfitting, but only if we define it too narrowly. There must be a reasonable limit to adapting your translation to the available space. Sometimes, it simply doesn't make sense to sacrifice the new content for the sake of sticking to an old, no longer useful, randomly fixed number of lines. When you are at a loss about what else to change in your translation or when you feel strongly that any further change will inevitably mean a change for the worse, try to adopt a graphic designer's mindset. Had the graphic designer built in plenty of white space for future translations, you wouldn't be struggling with tight text frames. On the other hand, if she was dealing with a larger body of text (**your** translation), she would be adapting the design to the text, not the other way around. Copyfitting in a broader sense means fitting your text to the existing layout **logic**, not just to the existing text frames. That is why, in my view, copyfitting requires becoming familiar with grids and guides, and may include, wherever appropriate, adjusting the available text areas. Sometimes, this calls for expanding text boxes and sometimes adjusting image frames is worth considering.

The idea of a translator meddling with graphics is probably the most controversial for a "translator, not a graphic designer", but adjusting the size of an image frame isn't necessarily meddling if you know your way around InDesign. I have worked with quite a few graphic designers over the years and find that fairly often, the size of an image is chosen more or less randomly, as long as it fits in the overall design. A graphic designer would start the layouting by arranging blocks of text and then accommodate the graphics to fill in the remaining space. In general, it is easier to adjust an image than it is to edit the text to fit the layout grid.

If you need to readjust the images to make room for the text, keep in mind the layout grid and pay attention to the arrangement of images throughout the document (size, shape, margins, alignment, etc.). Images can be resized while maintaining the aspect ratio or by changing one dimension, width or height, separately – there is no universal recipe for modifying picture frames. In any case, make sure to check the options chosen by the designer. The image itself and the image frame aren't always identical, they can have different sizes. To check the size, position and scale of the image, go to *Object → Fitting* with the frame selected or right-click the frame:

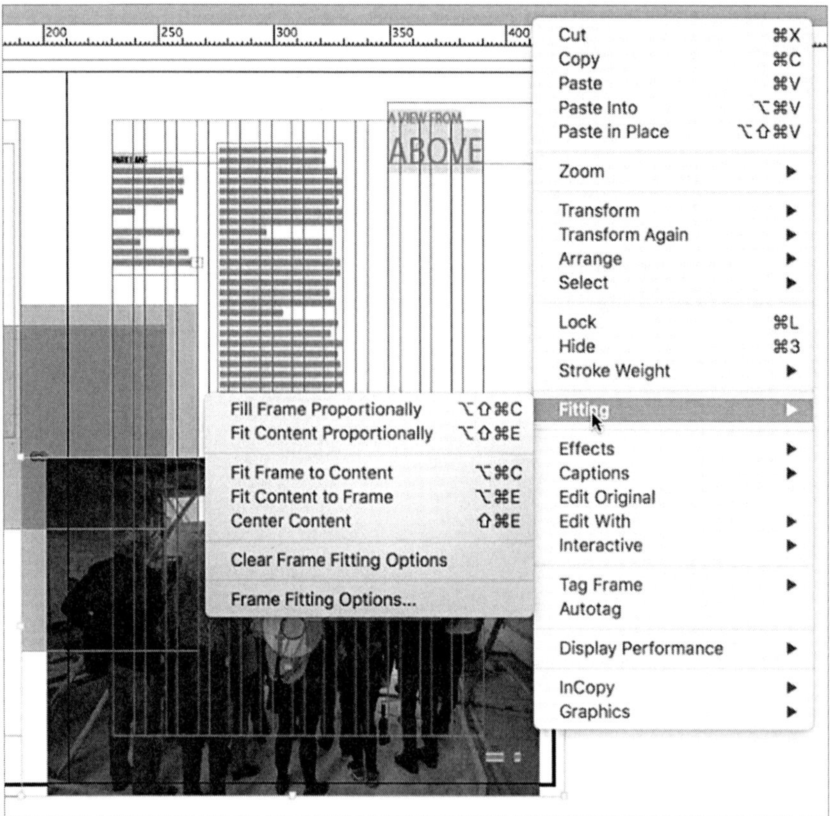

To switch back and forth between the frame content and the frame itself, double-click on the image (if you work on a text frame, double-click to switch to the *Type* tool). The shape of the cursor will toggle between arrow and hand; the latter allows you to move the image within the frame (for example, if only a fragment of the original image should be made visible).

■ ■ ■

As mentioned a few pages back, my workflow for translating in InDesign usually starts with selecting the target language. This is important if you want to check and correct spelling as you go. InDesign has decent spell-checking capabilities, including suggested corrections and user dictionaries (*Edit* → *Spelling* or Ctrl+I):

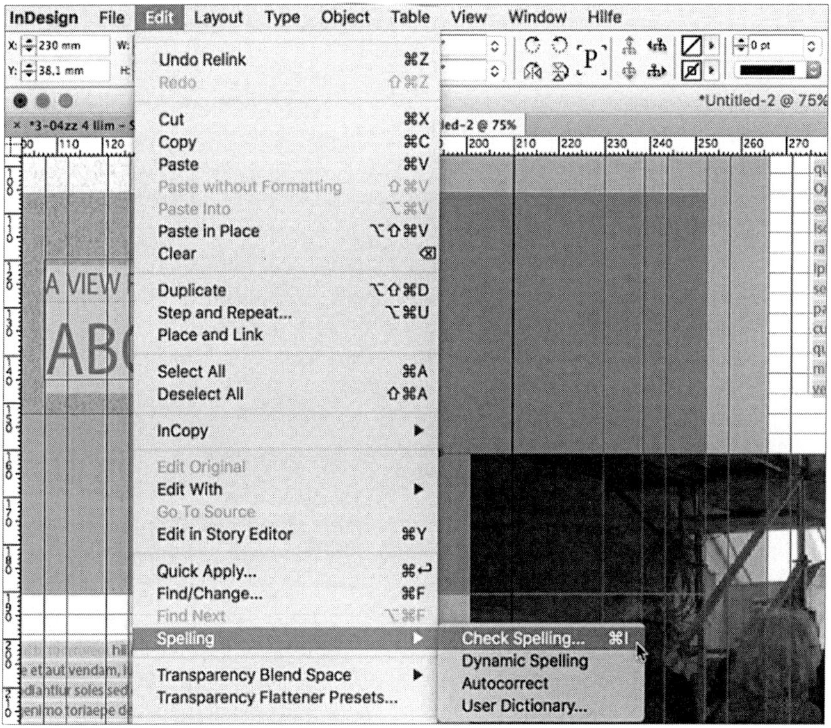

Selecting the right language, besides spell-checking, is the prerequisite for proper hyphenation. Hyphenation is a feature that should not be underestimated when working with text in InDesign. Given that graphic designers set up a layout a grid to space and align content, text is probably arranged in multiple columns. Unlike Microsoft Word documents, where you seldom use columns to format text, setting up a new document in InDesign immediately presents you with an opportunity to select the number of columns:

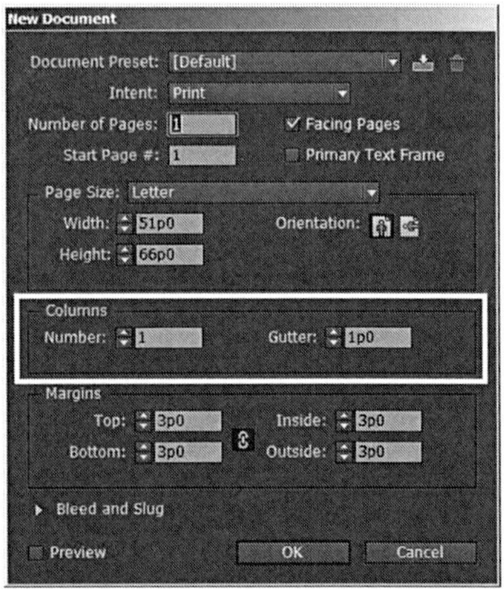

In contrast to a typical Word document, text in InDesign wouldn't span an entire page. It would be set in relatively narrow columns with a line width hardly exceeding Emil Ruder's "sweet point" of 50 to 60 characters (see p. 67). This makes the point about justification we raised earlier ("never use right margin justification") debatable. Besides, your designer might have had her reasons for full justification that doesn't necessarily have to look all that bad, given the text frames and the layout grid. This is the case when I really don't think a translator should go against a designer's choice.

To make sure your block of text looks good typography-wise, it is important to use hyphenation. Otherwise you risk winding up with big gaps between words, "cascading rivers of white space" or lines uncomfortably crunched together. They would look even more unbefitting against the backdrop of a thoughtfully planned layout. To achieve even lines and a consistent spacing in your body of text, InDesign offers very reasonable default settings as well as all kinds of options to adjust or override automatic hyphenation, e.g. applying no-break commands or manually adding regular, discretionary (soft) and non-breaking hyphens. To access global settings for hyphenation, go to *Preferences → Type → Dictionary*. To fine-tune automatic hyphenation options for selected blocks of text, use the *Paragraph* panel menu:

You may want to uncheck *Hyphenate Last Word* or *Hyphenate Capitalized Words* and uncheck hyphenation completely for titles and headlines. You may also need to edit the other hyphenation settings for your paragraph styles to bring them in line with your style guide and the rules of typography of your target language.

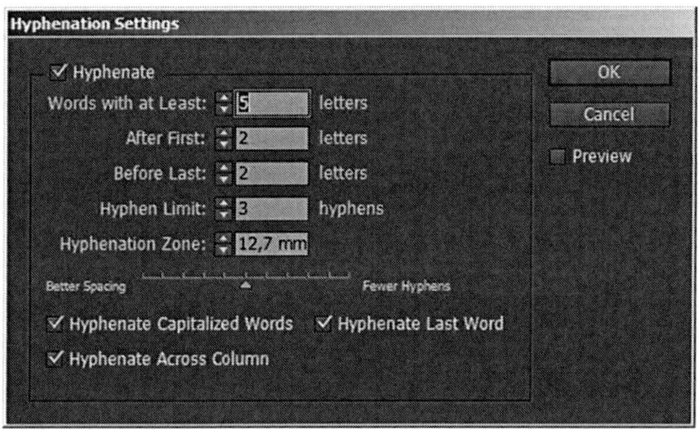

■ ■ ■

There are only two more points to make before finishing this chapter. The first is about editing your translation.

For editing and reviewing, one good piece of advice is to try to view your translation from another angle. For example, try printing it out or temporarily changing the font or formatting while going through it on screen. When the words look different, you will have a better chance to spot errors in spelling, punctuation and grammar. Seeing your translation in a new layout is like being given a fresh pair of eyes to recognise what can be improved to bring about a more effective message.

InDesign has a powerful feature for editing and revising your text – Story Editor. It allows you to see the translation without the distraction of the visuals. Select the text frame with the *Selection Tool* (or click with the *Type* tool inside the frame) and go to *Edit → Edit in Story Editor* (COMMAND+Y). A new floating window will appear in the workspace:

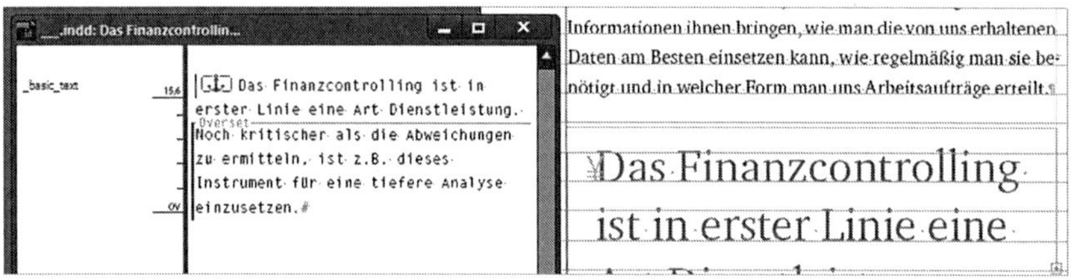

You can change the position and dimensions of the panel – the Story Editor will automatically wrap the text. To turn off the default left hand column which shows the applied styles and the depth of the text (I personally find them distracting), go to *View → Story Editor → Hide Style Name Column*:

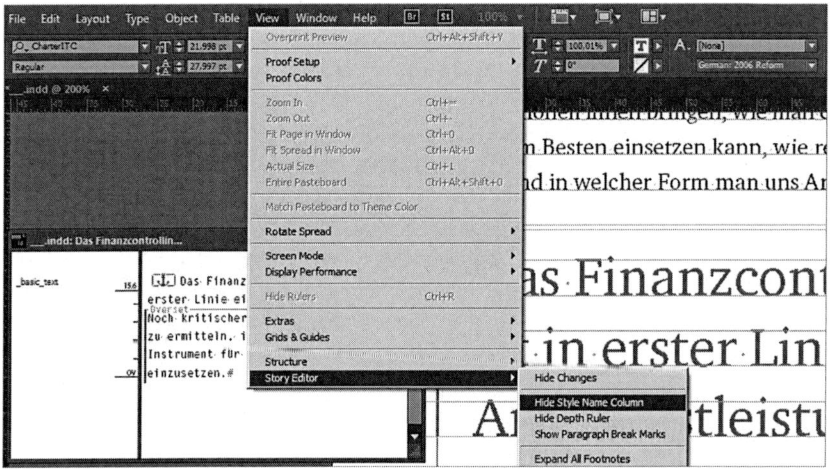

You can also customise the font, font size, spacing and colour of the Story Editor display, if the default settings don't work for you: go to *Edit → Preferences → Story Editor Display*. Any text edits you make while reviewing your translation in the Story Editor panel will be mirrored within the document.

The last point concerns delivering your InDesign translation to your client. You don't need to create a package folder for the final output if you only used the InDesign files supplied by the client – these are the only files that your client will need. If you had to use any fonts other than those in the original document, let the client know which ones and where you obtained them (and make sure they have signed that off before using the fonts). You are on the safe side if you deliver both files – .imdd. and .idml, to ensure your client doesn't run into any issues with version compatibility. Besides, it is good practice to include a PDF file. My preferred modus operandi with direct clients who need final files, whether for print or web, is to provide two PDF files. Here's why.

To generate a PDF as a digital print of your InDesign file, go to *File → Export*, enter the file name and location and choose *Adobe PDF (Print)* under *Format*. A dialogue box with several control options will appear:

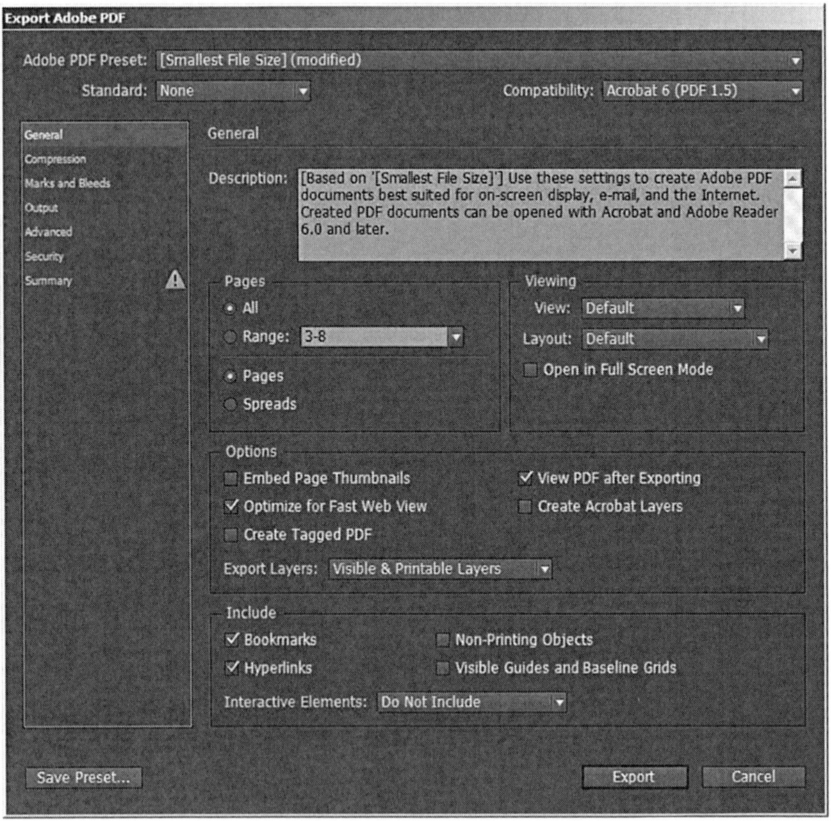

The only type of options needed for our purpose is *General*. I usually select *Smallest File Size* in the Adobe PDF preset menu and press *Export*. In the picture above, the preset is automatically assigned the attribute (modified) whenever you check any additional options, such as *Include Hyperlinks* (which makes sense when the document contains a table of contents with hyperlinks or any other internal or external links). After you press *Export*, the software will check the document for any possible flaws. If found, a warning will be displayed, for example, about unresolved cross-references, missing images or oversets. This is one bonus of exporting your InDesign file to PDF – you will get an opportunity to correct any technical errors before handing over your translation to the client.

The *Smallest File Size* setting will produce a text-editable PDF that can be viewed on screen. Your client can use it for editing or publishing online. To produce a print-ready PDF which in theory could go straight to press, opt for *High Quality Print*. This will result in the most professional-looking file, but also in a larger file size, especially if your document contains links to high-resolution images. Other than that, both PDF files are identical content-wise. When working with corporate clients from industries other than media or advertising, it is a good idea to provide a short note about the difference between the PDF files as regards their purpose and the visuals – I regard this as a value-adding part of my job. It doesn't feel like the extra mile, but is a rather rewarding experience.

3.6 A job for Photoshop

I can imagine you thinking "Tis chapter must be the least relevant in this whole book. Photoshop? I don't have it and there is no way in hell I would ever lay my hands on it, especially for translation!" For me, it was the idea for this chapter – showing how a translator can use image editing tools – that started me thinking about writing this book a few years ago. At the time, within a month I translated a corporate brochure and two or three presentations with lots of infographics. No legends for the information contained in the pictures were possible or would make much sense. My usual methods of overlaying the picture with comments (see p. 178) wouldn't work either: additional explanations would have destroyed the immediacy of the images and resulted in a mess. A Photoshop edit was the answer. Now I can also imagine you thinking "But wait, wasn't that a job for the designer or whoever did the infographics for your clients?" In that particular situation no designers were available and the job just needed to get done – that is often the only thing that matters for our clients. Also at that time, another client sent me a few completed forms where only a number of fields needed a translation. It would have been a waste of time and effort to apply OCR software to the scans. In the good old days of working on paper someone would've momentarily solved the problem with Tipp-Ex and a pen. Today, you are far better served by Photoshop. It requires not much more time and sometimes less effort. The process is smooth and seamless, and the result nicer.

Then a colleague asked me about Paintbrush. She had just bought a new Mackintosh and found out that an image editing application could be a real help for her technical translations – manuals and specifications with densely annotated drawings and schematic diagrams. I told her about my ways of working with non-editable text as a graphic for translation, and so the idea was born. The colleague suggested that I should write a blog post about my experience with image editors and her example would serve as an illustration to prove how easily the method works – even for those who think working on graphics is the last thing they can imagine doing. Then we both realised one example wouldn't be enough. Before we got into details and broke down the methodology, we would first need to provide a few decent arguments why a typical translator shouldn't treat an image editor as something not to be touched with a bargepole. Or why working with graphics might be good for their business. And so, a blog post turned into a book chapter.

I should explain that Photoshop is one among a huge variety of image editing software available (e.g. GIMP, Pixlr, Paint.NET, PhotoScape), but it is one I am most familiar with. If you are more comfortable with another application, feel free to stick to it. If my workflow described in this chapter makes sense to you, you'd just need to look for similar functions and features in your preferred software. That said, Photoshop is **the software of choice** for most professionals in the area of graphic design.

The example I chose to demonstrate the how-to process has nothing to do with the initial illustration suggested by my colleague. I chose it deliberately – there is actually very little text to translate, but the text is set as graphics and is non-editable with a text tool such as Word. The pieces of text are very short and placed quite close to the objects they refer to, with little place to move them. Before we get down to the process in all its steps and details, here is a short introduction to the Photoshop workspace. If you've already read the previous chapter on InDesign, what you'll see on the screen in Photoshop will look familiar.

Photoshop allows you to select one of the pre-set workspaces. I usually stick to the default *Essentials* workspace, but it might be a good idea to select *Typography*, in particular if you need to insert special characters (*Window → Workspace → Typography*):

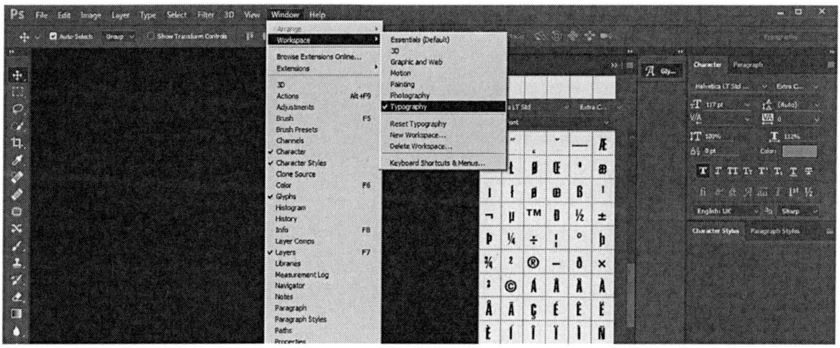

An important element is the vertical *Tools* palette on the left. The double-arrow button is used to toggle between a single-column or a two-column view:

or

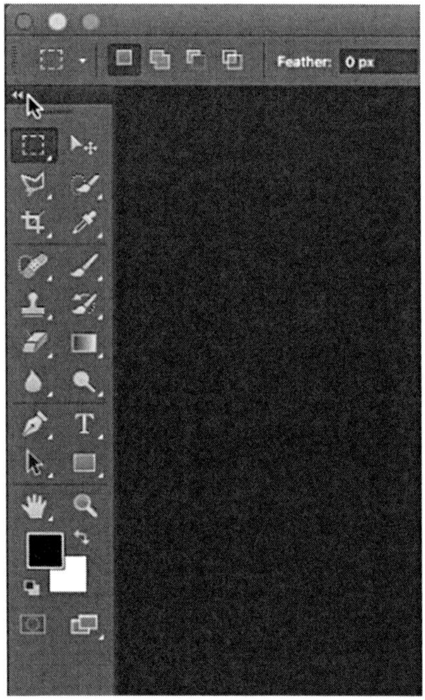

Some tool icons have a tiny triangle in the bottom-right corner. This means that more tools are grouped together under this icon, which shows the tool which was used last. Right-click on the icon to expand it and access the hidden tools. The name of the tool appears below the cursor when you hover over the icon.

Like in InDesign, always pay attention to which tool you currently have in hand – the icon for the active tool will look "pressed down". The horizontal *Options* bar under the menu at the top of the screen is context-sensitive – it changes depending on which tool you select. For example, the *T* icon lets you access a group of nested text tools, though in 99.9% of cases you'll need only the regular "horizontal" type tool:

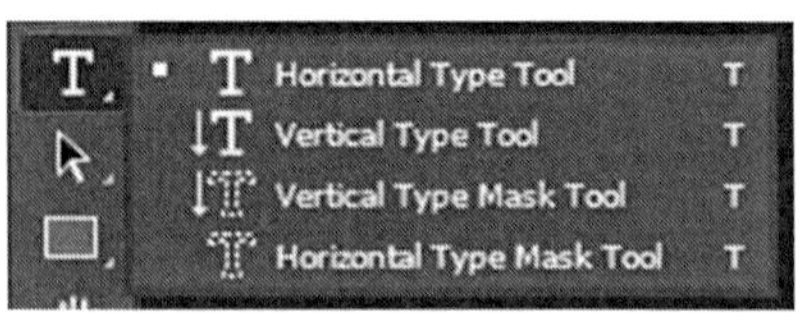

With *T* activated, you will find the usual formatting choices in the *Options* bar, including paragraph options like *Left align text*, *Centre text* and *Right align text*:

When working with text, it is a good practice to display both *Character* and *Paragraph* panels: *Window → Character* and *Window → Paragraph* or click the *Panel* button – the last icon on the right edge of the *Options* bar:

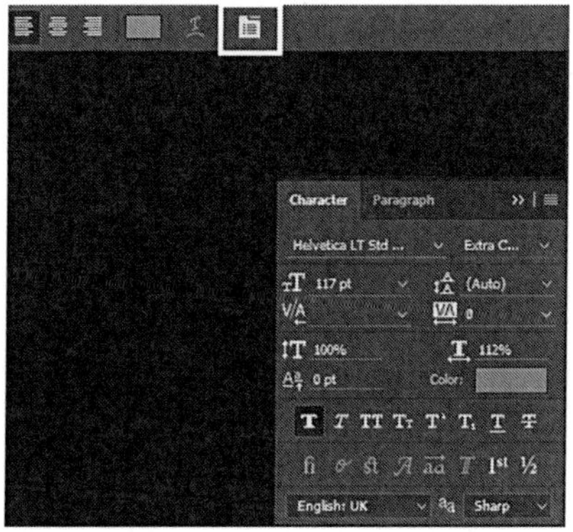

The navigation features are self-explanatory. To zoom in, press CTRL+ and to zoom out, press CTRL-. When you press and hold down the spacebar, the cursor changes to a hand symbol – now you can drag the image around instead of using the scroll bars.

Whenever Photoshop doesn't seem to respond like you expect it to, check which tool is currently active and, when in doubt, press the uppermost icon on the *Tools* bar, the *Move* tool, to go back to square one. I'd also recommend displaying the *History* panel (*Window → History*). This is an advanced Undo/Redo feature that lists all the actions that you've carried out so far. If you think something has gone wrong, use the *History* panel to check your steps, undo changes and go back to any previous state in your workflow.

The last and perhaps most important panel is *Layers*. When open (*Window → Layers*), it will reside in the bottom right of the screen. *Layers* might be one key feature that marks a crucial difference between Photoshop and any non-pro or semi-pro photo editors. The idea of layers is rather simple and by and large not new. As an interpreter, I did a fair share of work at workshops and seminars where an overhead projector was very much in use. This old-school technology had its benefits for presentations. The lecturer usually printed the presentation materials on transparency papers and put them, in the course of the seminar, on the projector's glass bed.

Very often, while the image or text was being projected, a new, blank transparency was placed on it as an overlay. This was used to draw over the printed image, to highlight a bullet point or encircle an element of a diagram, without leaving any marks on the transparency below. Sometimes, the lecturer would superimpose the first transparency with two or three new ones, this technique being a low-tech precursor to PowerPoint animations.

The layers mechanism in Photoshop allows you to build up a stack of transparencies in a similarly non-destructive way. To edit their shot without damaging the original image, photographers may add a number of adjustment layers to the initial, so-called "background" level. Graphic designers and illustrators compose pictures from several layers combined together. The *Layers* panel lets you create and modify new layers, control and change the stacking order (the layer above becomes an overlay for the layer below) and do tons of other things. To list them, I'd probably need to write another book. Instead, I'll try to cover the basics which will be important when working with text.

First, always keep in mind which layer you are working on at the moment – all changes that you make will affect only the currently selected layer. Second, it is good to know that once you applied the *T* tool to the image area, a new text layer is created. To edit the existing text, you must choose its text layer. (That means that if you have a hard time "getting at" the visible piece of text, first make sure the correct text layer is active and then grab the text tool.)

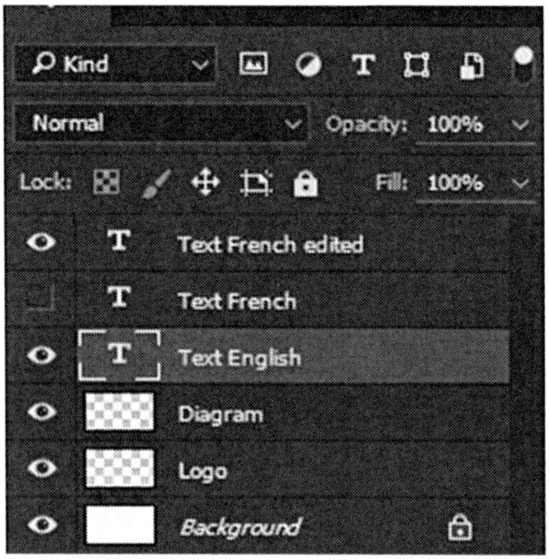

In the example of the *Layers* panel above, the active layer is called "Text English" (it is a good practice to give each layer a clear label; double-click on the automatically generated label to rename it). "Text English" may be overlayed by a layer called "Text French edited", if the positions of both layers in the image coincide or overlap. You can rearrange the stack order: click on the layer title in the panel and drag it below or above the current position. The layer called "Text French" isn't visible in our image, it's hidden – to show and hide a layer, click the eye icon on the left.

When you get to know Photoshop layers, you might start to miss this feature in other applications. For example, a seemingly "inaccessible" text element on a

PowerPoint slide may get you all worked up before you realise you have to switch to one of the slide masters. A *Layers* panel would save you time and trouble.

■ ■ ■

Now let's get down to work. In the following case study, I assigned myself a task to replace non-editable pieces of the source text with translations. The workflow steps described below are limited to what is needed to solve the problem. The limitation is intentional: the amount of information, in print and online, on everything that Photoshop can be used for is limitless. My example is purely fictitious, serving the purpose of illustration. I selected a language in which most of us wouldn't easily guess the word meanings, so translation is necessary. For various reasons beyond our control, no annotations, legends or comments to the picture are acceptable. We just have to reproduce the original picture with the planet names in the target language:

Bright colours are also chosen largely for the sake of illustration. In real life, it is rather unlikely that you'll have to consider colour when dealing with text and even less so colourful background. Also, the text shape is a bit of a challenge. But I actually came across some odd cases of curved text in my translations, so I've decided to include it here for an extra challenge. The picture might typically be embedded in a Word document or a PowerPoint presentation. Before we switch to Photoshop, there is only one thing we must do while still in Word or PowerPoint: select the picture and click CTRL+C (COMMAND+C) to copy it to the clipboard.[92]

Now to Photoshop. First, create a new document: go to *File → New* or CTRL+N (COMMAND+N; as most Mac shortcuts are identical to Windows shortcuts, I will omit them from now on). Photoshop opens a dialogue box where you can choose a file name and other attributes.

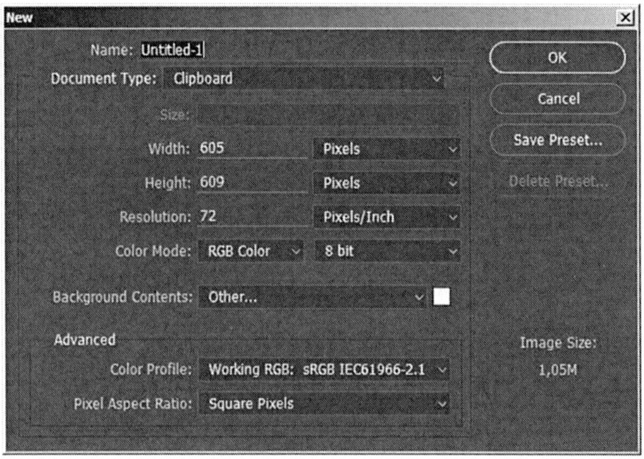

By default, the dimensions of the image saved to the clipboard will appear in the dialogue box, so type in a name for your new file and click OK. Photoshop will create a blank area of the size of the image you've just copied. Now paste it into your file: *Edit → Paste* or CTRL+V. (Some versions of Photoshop have an option *File → New From Clipboard* that will produce the same result in one go.)

92 Useful tip: if you have difficulty with copying an embedded picture in your Word or PowerPoint or if you have multiple pictures you'd like to retrieve as original image files in one go, make a copy of your .docx or .pptx file and rename it into .zip. Unpack the .zip file or simply double-click on it: your .zip extractor will automatically create a new folder or display its content. Look for another folder within it, called either "word" (for a Word document) or "ppt" (for PowerPoint). Open it: find a folder called "media". It'll contain all the original image files used in your document, listed one by one.

With the image opened in Photoshop, go to the bottom-right part of the workspace, where you'll find *Layers* (if the feature is missing, activate it in *Window → Layers* or by pressing F7). Now create a copy of the original image where all the adjustments, including replacement of the original text with your translation, will take place. In the *Layers* panel, grab the *Background* layer with your mouse and drag it onto the *Create a new layer* icon, which is to the left of the trash can:

Alternatively, right-click on the *Background* layer in the *Layers* panel, choose *Duplicate Layer* and type in a name for the new layer, e.g. "Translation" or "Target". For the sake of convenience, it might be a good idea to rename the background e.g. to "Source" or, as in our example, "Greek Original". Click on the eye symbol of the source layer to make it temporarily invisible and select the translation layer. This is how your *Layers* panel should look now:

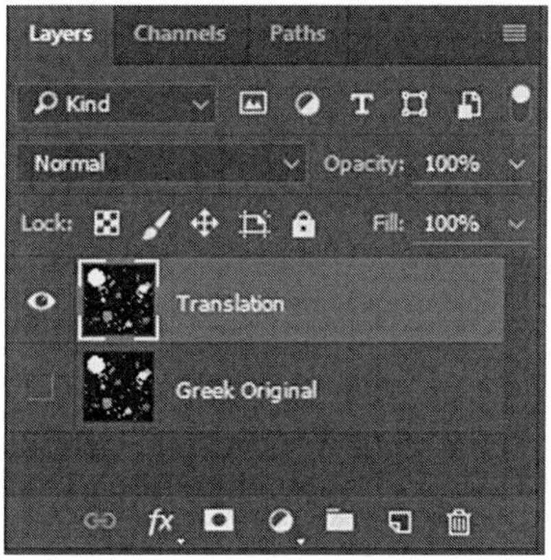

Save your file; the file extension will be .psd (native Photoshop file). The next step is to erase the source text. When we say that the text is "non-editable", we usually mean that it is rasterised, i.e. turned into a bitmap that consists of pixels. The opposite of bitmap graphics is vector graphics; in fact, when we'll type our translation with the *Text* tool later, we will create vector layers and will be able to edit the text like in an ordinary text editor.

In order to erase the original text before we type in the translation we have to replace the pixels which compose the Greek letters with the pixels similar to those of the background. There are several ways to do so. I'll start with the easiest option.

First, we need to select the area with the text to be erased. Photoshop provides various selection options. In this case, we'll use the *Lasso Tool* or the *Po-*

lygonal Lasso Tool – they are grouped together on the *Tools* bar; right-click to choose one (or press the *L* key to grab the default *Lasso Tool*):

With the *Lasso Tool* selected, the cursor will turn to a small lasso icon. Zoom in on the image to make it easier to drag the cursor on the screen. Click somewhere close to the first Greek word and draw a freehand outline around the text; when you return to the starting point, release the mouse button. Now your text is contained in an area surrounded by a contour line:

You don't have to be very precise. In case you missed a few pixels or captured too much of the area, the *Options* bar provides ways to add to or subtract from the current selection. I also like to use the *Smooth*, *Expand* or *Contract* options (*Select* → *Modify* → *Smooth*) to iron out any border problems instead of ditching the selection and giving the lasso (and my freehand drawing) another try:

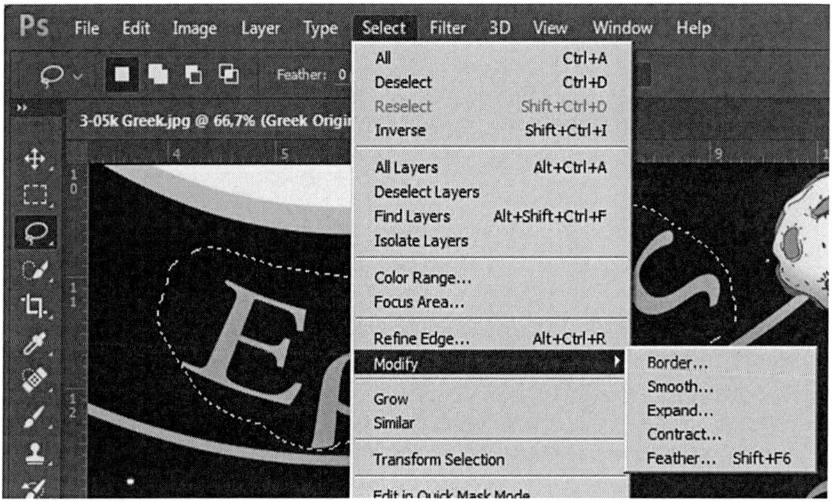

Make sure you're still on the correct layer, that is "Translation" and not "Greek Original", otherwise many menu options will be greyed out and inaccessible. Take another tool from the *Tool* panel – the *Eyedropper* (or simply press the *I* key):

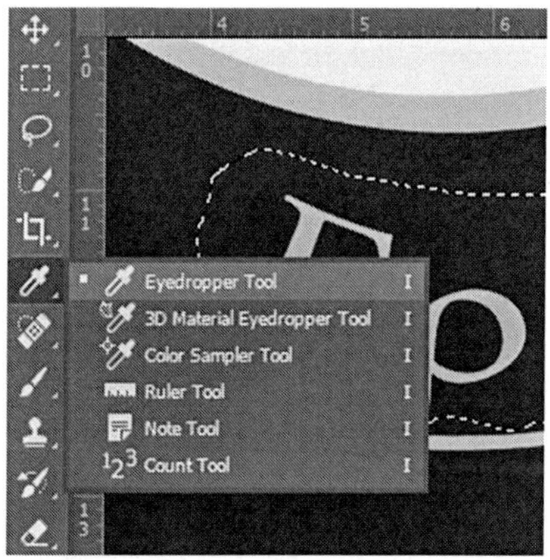

The *Eyedropper*'s purpose is to pick a colour in the image. Once picked, the colour can be applied to another area or element in the image. To get a good sample of the background colour, click the dark area around the letters with the *Eyedropper* tool. Now go to *Edit* → *Fill*. Choose the *Foreground Colour* as *Contents*, making sure the blending options below are as default (blending mode: normal; opacity: 100%) and press *OK*:

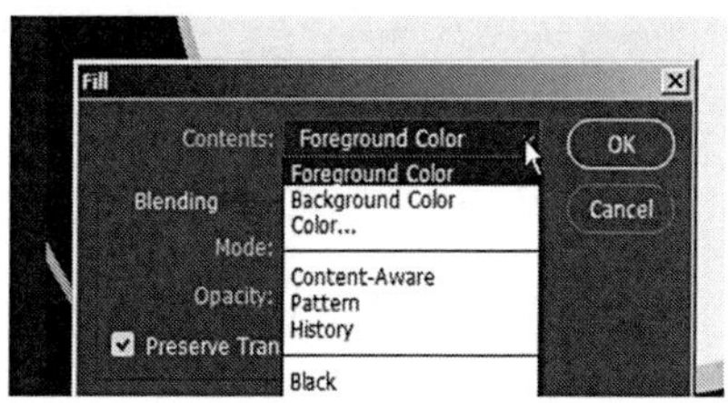

A super simple way to reach the same effect is the ALT+BACKSPACE shortcut. Professional graphic artists often use it to fill a selection with the foreground colour in one go.

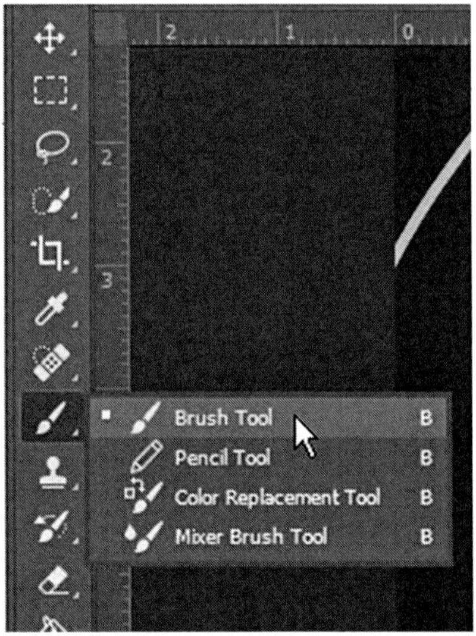

Now that the selected area is filled with the chosen colour and the orange letters are gone, press CTRL+D for deselecting (or go to *Select → Deselect*). This gets you back to working on the entire layer instead of a selection within the "marching ants" contour. Using the *Fill* option is perhaps the easiest way to make the text disappear. But it isn't the only one. You can also choose the *Brush* from the *Tools* panel (or press *B*):

This is a basic painting tool for applying colour using strokes. You will probably make do with the default settings, but if you feel like experimenting, have a look at the *Options* bar where you'll find different kinds of brushes; you can change the shape, hardness or diameter of the brush tip (you can also quickly change the brush size and shape by right-clicking on the image):

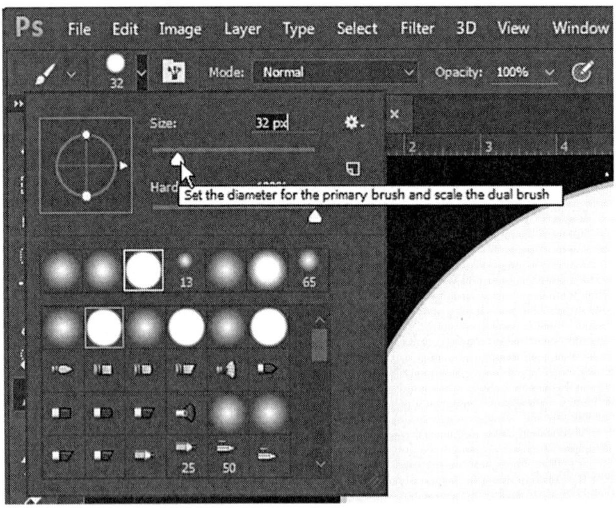

If using the *Brush* tool, you can forego selecting an area with the *Lasso* tool (or any other selection tool) and simply paint over the text. Remember to use CTRL+Z or the *History* panel to go back a step or two if your brush touched an element (like the orbit lines in the picture) that you'd rather keep intact. Alternatively, instead of the *Brush* tool, you can use the *Paint Bucket* tool – select an area to fill with a colour using the *Lasso* tool and then click inside it with the *Paint Bucket* selected. A small caveat is that both the *Brush* and the *Bucket* tools work well with solid colour. In all other cases things may get out of hand.

If your text is placed against a textured or complex background in such a way that no clear separation of text and image is possible, there are two ways to reconstruct the background that got erased or damaged while removing the text. First, select the required area (e.g. with the *Lasso* selection tool like described above) and once again, go to *Edit* → *Fill*. This time, choose *Content-Aware* instead of *Foreground Colour* from the *Contents* drop-down menu, and press *OK*:

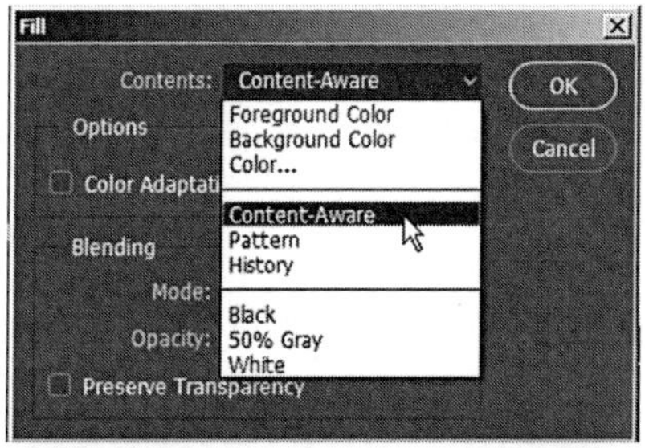

Content-Aware Fill lets us replace unwanted areas of the image and automatically blend it with the surrounding pixels. You may need to apply the *Content-Aware Fill* a few more times to get the result you're happy with. You may also try Photoshop's retouching tools: *Healing Brush*, *Spot Healing Brush* or *Patch*. These are grouped together under the *Eyedropper* icon in the *Tools* panel:

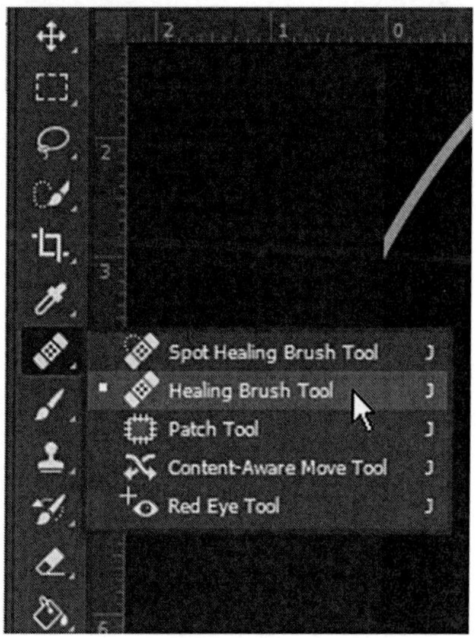

However, the most popular technique is probably using the *Clone Stamp* tool. It works similarly to the retouching tools, while offering maximum control and precision. First, select the *Clone Stamp* tool from the *Tools* panel or with the *S* key. Use the *Options* bar or right-click to adjust the tool size and shape, opacity etc. like with the *Brush* tool. Now press ALT (the cursor will become a target) and click an area to copy or "clone", in our case the dark background. Then drag the cursor over the text to paint over the letters. You'll work more precisely if you toggle between ALT-clicking the source areas and then clicking and moving your cursor over the area to be replaced. The *Options* bar has a setting to either clone the source pixels automatically, following the cursor movement in the destination area, or replace the pixels in the destination area only with those you picked while pressing the ALT key:

When the *Aligned* checkbox is ticked, you can duplicate entire areas – copying and pasting the source pixels with mouse clicks as you move over the target area.

■ ■ ■

Back to our image. Using one of the above techniques, replace the remaining pieces of text, one by one, with the dark background (use the *Clone Stamp* tool to add a few random stars to make it more realistic, or for training purposes). You should end up with a pristine sky with all text removed:

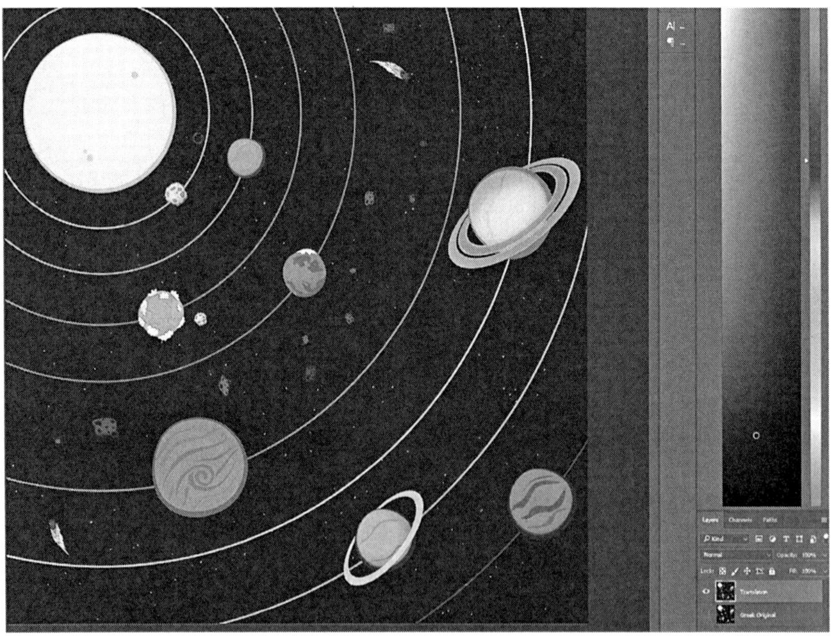

Now let's give the planets back their names. Start by bringing back the "Greek Original" layer (click the visibility icon – the eye symbol appears) and hiding the "Translation" layer (uncheck its eye icon). You can also keep both layers visible, but it's best to swap them around – drag the "Greek Original" layer over the "Translation" layer to make it visible and drag it later to the bottom to hide it again. I find it more convenient to toggle the eye icons. Now that the layers' visibility is swapped, the original is back up again:

Go to the "Greek Original" layer and pick the *Eyedropper* tool. Click one of the Greek letters with the tool to sample its colour. You will notice that the foreground – the first of the two overlapping colour squares below the magnifying glass near the bottom of the *Tools* panel – has changed to match the colour you've just picked:

Take the *Type* tool, making sure the type colour in the *Options* bar matches the foreground colour. If it doesn't, click the foreground colour box and confirm the selected colour simply by clicking *OK* in the dialogue box that will appear:

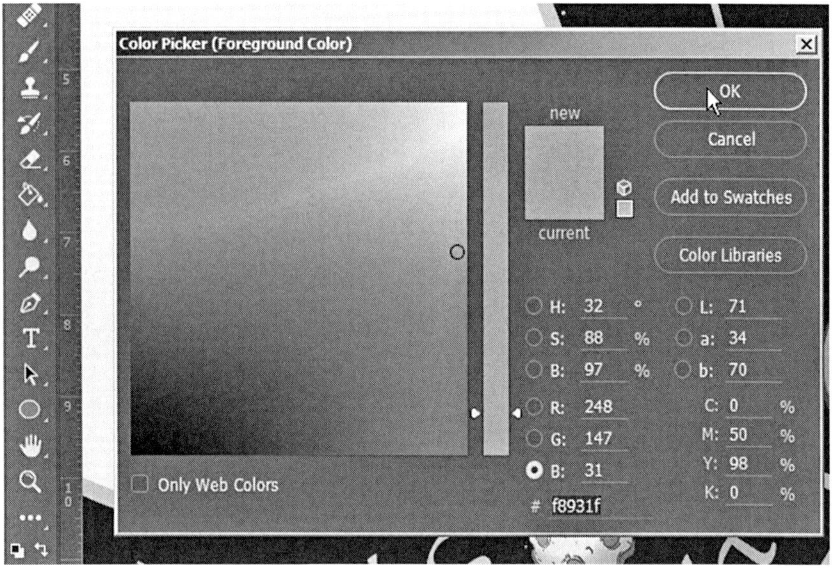

Type your translation over the Greek word. Because you've used the *Type* tool, a new text layer will be automatically created over the currently active one:

Drag the "Mercury" layer in the *Layers* panel to stack it above the "Translation":

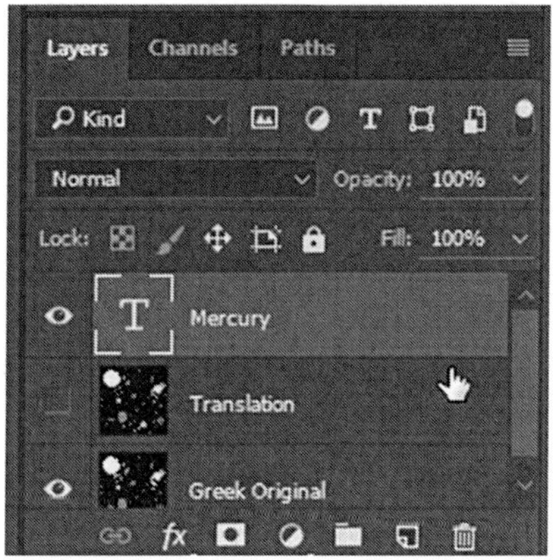

With the *Type* tool selected, you can use the *Options* bar to adjust text formatting. For example, to resize your font, select the text and click into the font size area:

You can enter a different value or smoothly make your font larger and smaller with the scroll wheel of your mouse. To adjust the position of the text, select the *Move* tool – the very first icon in the *Tools* panel. With it selected, you can drag the whole text layer anywhere in the image or, using the keyboard arrow keys, move it pixel by pixel in each direction.

It is generally a good idea to try to choose a font style similar to that of the original, but in practice it is seldom worth the bother. The rule is to try and look at it through the client's eyes and more often than not, the font style won't matter for the client. Regarding the content, if you want to change something in your translation, go to the *Layers* panel and choose the relevant text layer in the stack. Then select the *Type* tool, hover over the existing text with your cursor and click into it. Now edit.

Proceed likewise with each planet, picking the right colour and placing your translation over the original text. Don't forget to save your file, at least occasionally! It is also a good practice to proceed by duplicating an existing text layer. You can create a copy of any text layer similar to how you did with the background layer at the beginning, by dragging the text layer onto the icon left to the trash can in the *Layers* panel. The icon stands for *Create a new layer*:

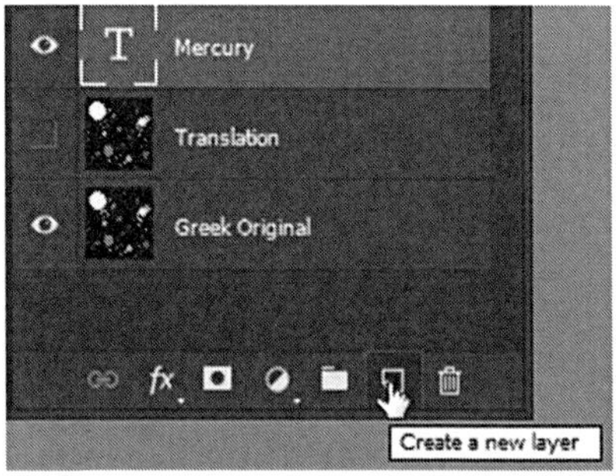

Choose the new text layer in the *Layers* panel (it will be named like the original one + "copy"), take the *Move* tool and place the text where it belongs. Then, select the *Type* tool, edit or overwrite the text and, if needed, modify its size and colour.

Whether or not you created all the text layers from scratch or duplicated and edited the first one several times, you will end up with a stack of text layers in the *Layers* panel. In our case, it looks like this:

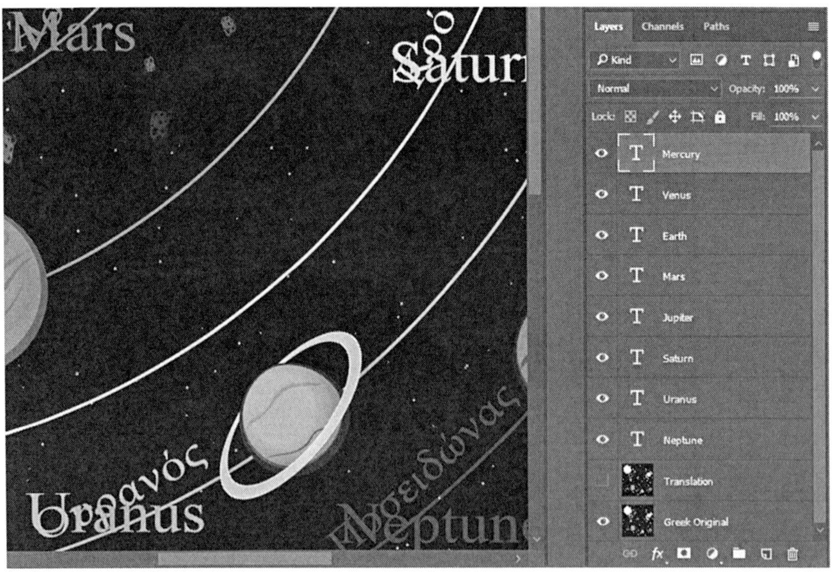

The picture for the Photoshop case study in this chapter is rather sophisticated if our task is to replace text. I chose it to raise the bar and cover more options. Multiple colours are one thing, but in real life, it is unlikely that you'll come across angled text (though vertically aligned text is more widespread; conveniently, Photoshop offers you a *Vertical Type* tool, on the *Type* button). To set your text at an angle, first choose the relevant text layer – I'll start with "Mercury". Go to *Edit* → *Transform* → *Rotate*. A bounding box will appear around the word Mercury. Hover your mouse over one of the corners – the cursor should change to double rotation arrows. Now turn the bounding box:

Alternatively, use the CTRL+T shortcut for free transform. When you've turned the picture, double-click into the bounding box or click the *Move* tool and press *Apply* when a dialogue box will ask "Apply the transformation?"

With the *Rotate* or *Free Transform* feature active, you can also use the *Options* bar. Here you can enter and modify the value of the angle precisely, while keeping an eye on how the bounding box with your text behaves in real time:

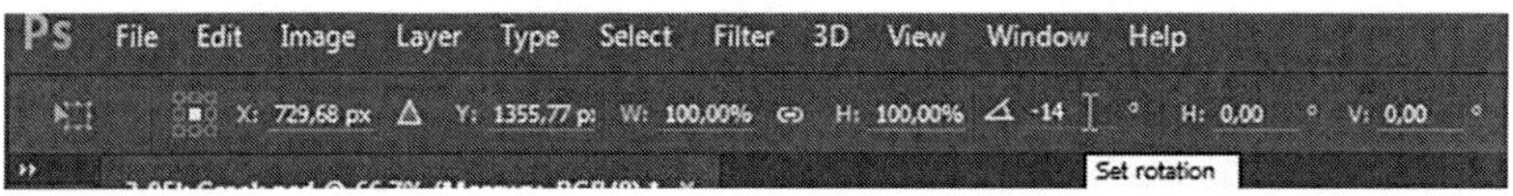

After rotating a word, it may be necessary to slightly adjust its position. Select the *Move* tool to drag it with the mouse or to move it with the keyboard arrow keys.

You'll notice that the Greek word for Mercury is already gone. It is up to you when you swap the visibility of the two levels – "Translation" and "Greek Original". I did it before changing the angle of the text layers, but you can do it later, after you adjusted the position of all the text layers if you don't mind the Greek words beneath. It may look busy, but that's very easy to clean up! Make sure that the "Translation" layer is stacked below all the text layers (otherwise your text won't be visible) and that its eye symbol is on.

Before:

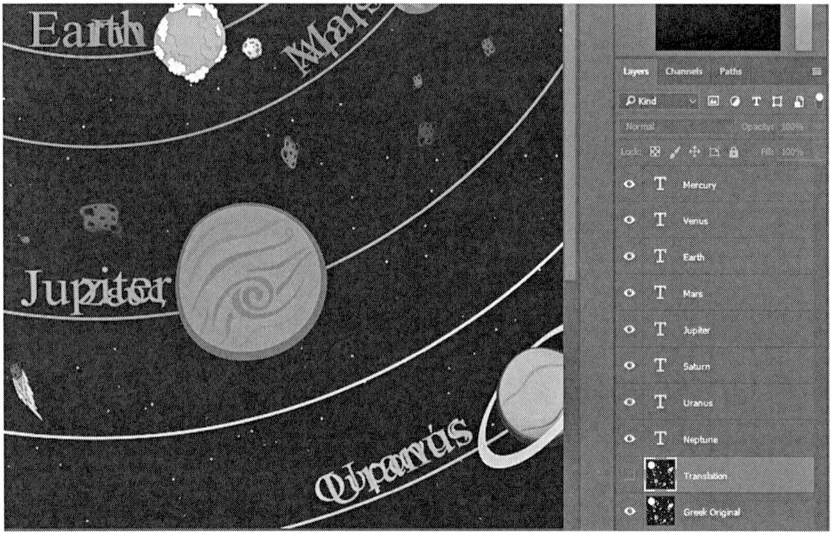

After:

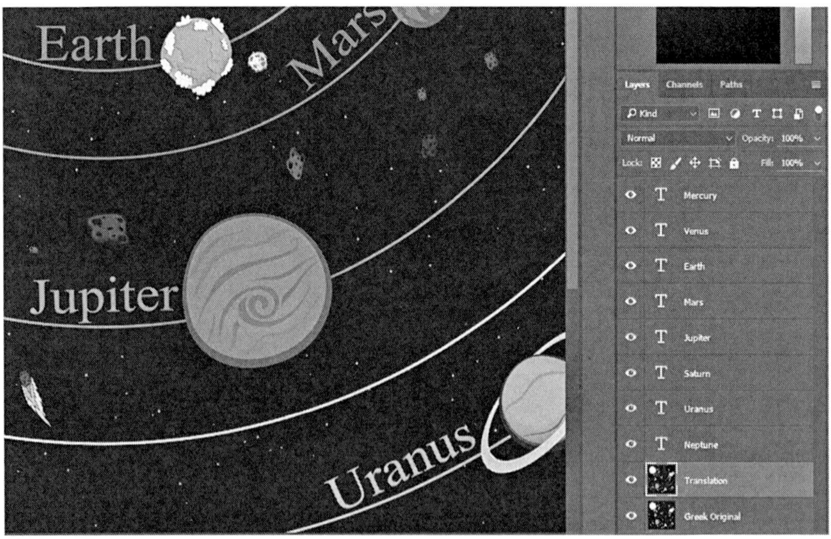

The final touch is to tweak the text shapes so that the words run smoothly along the circular lines. A quick method is to use the *Warp Text* tool in the *Options* bar. Start by selecting the text with the *Type* tool in the text layer:

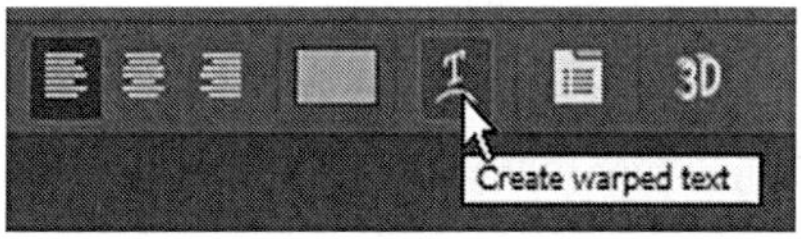

Choose the *Arc* style and shape the text with the *Bend* slider until the arc diameter appears to be in line with the diameter of the planet's orbit. This is more easily done than described. You may want to rotate or move the text a bit, but that also takes only a couple of seconds:

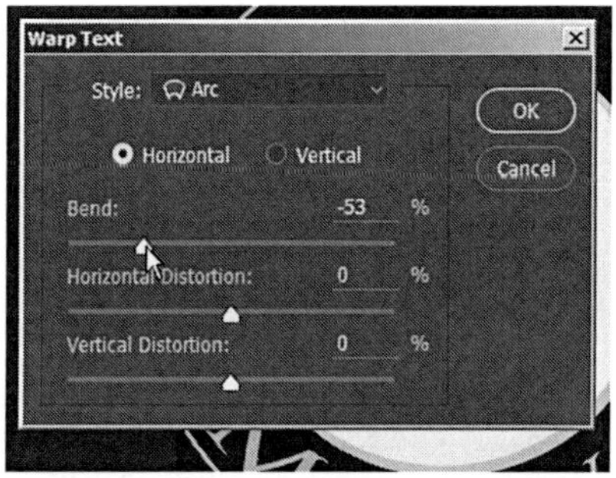

Repeat with the other words. The result will do nicely (and impress the client!), but it's also worth mentioning a proper way to wrap the text along a curved path: right-click the *Rectangle Tool* and select the *Ellipse Tool*:

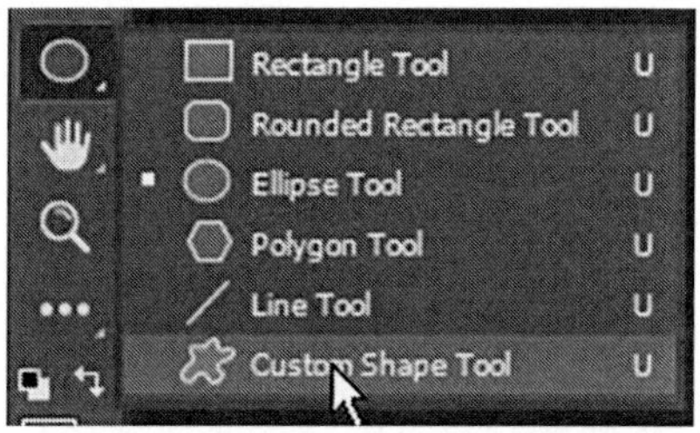

Choose *Path* in the Options bar:

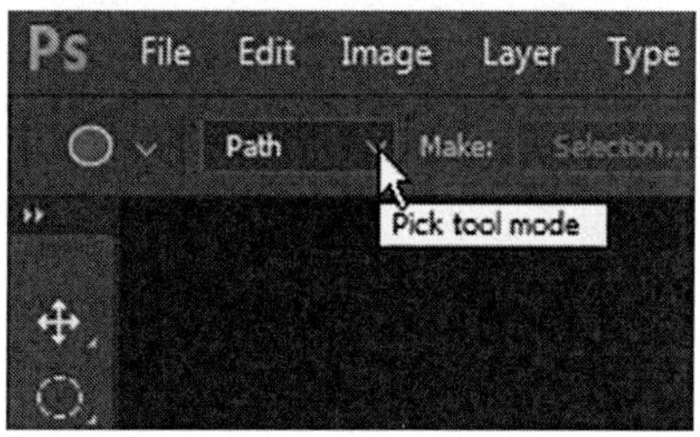

Draw a circle. To make sure that the circle follows the planet's orbit, first place the cursor in the centre of the Sun (where the orbits originate), click, press ALT (OPTION) and drag the mouse from the centre outward until you create a perfect circle outline. Select the *Type* and move the cursor to the circle outline where you want to start adding text. The text will automatically wrap around the circle and bend along the circular path.

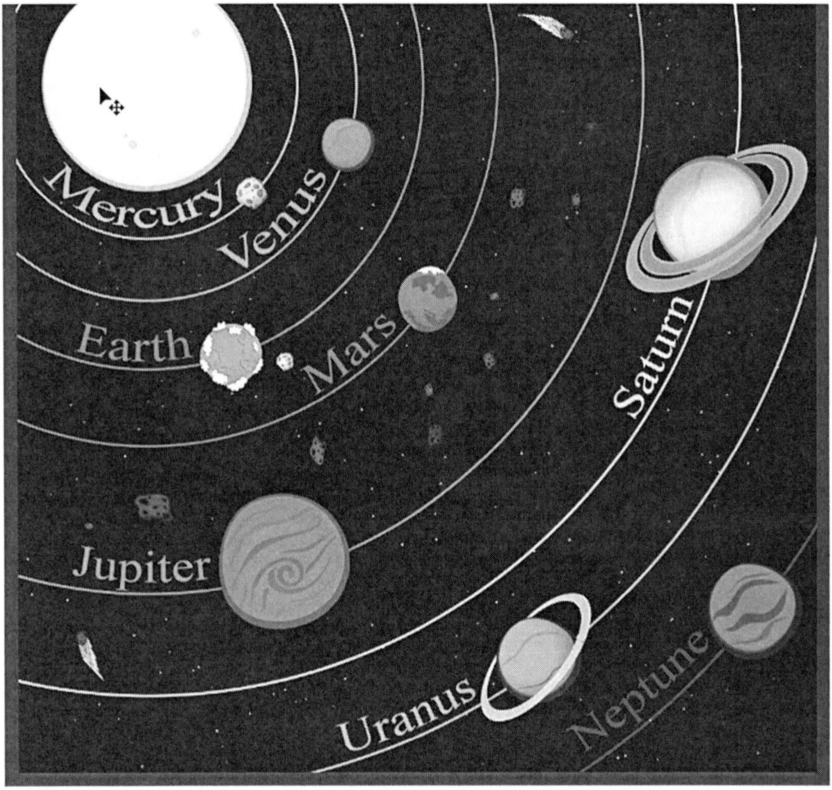

When you are done modifying your translation, save your image one last time. I would recommend keeping the .psd file in case you need to edit the text at a later stage. However, to insert the image in your Word or Power-Point document, you must also save it in a more conventional image format, such as .jpg. When saving your image as a .jpg, you will lose all your layers, but you'll end up with a relatively small and manageable file. Go to *Save as* and choose *JPEG* as the file format. In the dialogue box, choose from among several image options (Quality: 8 and High are usually a reasonable trade-off between image quality and file size).

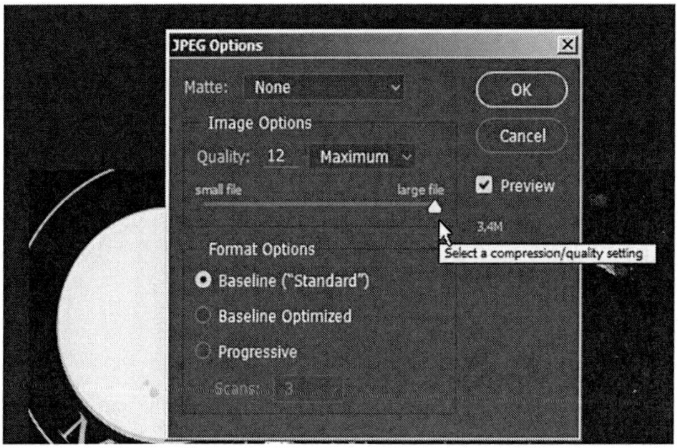

Your Photoshop job is done!

4 On the need to translate differently: a word to critics

> I understand what you're saying, and your comments are valuable, but I'm gonna ignore your advice.
>
> — Roald Dahl, *Fantastic Mr Fox*

This book would be incomplete if I wouldn't attempt to respond to some of the criticism that I envisage. "Translation is all about the meaning of a word, not about its appearance," a critic might say. "The book takes as an example a linguistically incompetent client who cannot make a direct judgement about the quality of a translation. Typically, such clients have to rely on the judgement of their target audience – in a utilitarian way: if the translation reaches the audience and serves its purpose, then it is a quality translation. For lack of an immediate feedback, such clients may be indeed prone to judge the quality of a translation by secondary, superficial factors, including appearance. However, this may apply only to a negligibly small number of translation clients and probably to a very small extent. The author puts too much focus on form – at the expense of substance."

That is true. I emphasise the form, because in my experience, non-verbal aspects of translation are usually undeservedly neglected by translators. To make up for this neglect, the book makes a point to show that appearance does matter. When your client doesn't understand the meaning of your written word, it is the look of that word that creates an impression. Quality, like beauty, lies in the eye of the beholder. And if you are a quality-driven translator, this can be made to work for you – to help communicate your professionalism and expertise, quality and care, whether or not your client is sensitive to both the verbal and the visual or only to the visual aspect.

This is the purpose of design – not to be beautiful, but to communicate effectively. Design is as much about strategy as it is about aesthetics. In the publishing business, translators often work hand in hand with graphic designers, but they rarely learn from designers and almost never apply the principles of good design to their work. In my opinion, it is not because translators have a hyperbolic attitude to substance over form or because they disparage graphic design. I rather think that all too often translators underrate the impact of the non-verbal component in their output and, generally, the power of a good first impression. And sometimes, they do have a hard time accepting that graphic design, much like translation, is about communication, not about "making things pretty" – so it's worth repeating here again.

"I am a translator, not a graphic designer" – I constantly heard this said in protest while working on the book and I tried to address it as best I could.

However, this is just one critical response that I can foresee. "The book seemingly encourages translators to pay more attention to presentation and be more 'creative' about it," may be another comment. "Is it allowed, or helpful, to take liberties with source documents such as making significant changes to the formatting? What good will it do?"

The book draws on my experience about how to produce better business translations, particularly for corporate clients – translations that serve the client's purpose and communicate their intent in an effective way. I also share my experience about how to make the quality of translation more obvious to clients – especially in view of the fact that clients very often cannot make a judgement about quality on their own. Being more "creative" is definitely part of the strategy, but "taking liberties" doesn't apply only to formatting. For better translations and for more success as a translator, as our industry moves forward, I am convinced that a different approach – call it "more creative" or liberal, for lack of a better word – should involve both form and substance, the visual and the verbal aspects of communication.

Unlike in the previous sections, the point of this chapter is to leave aside presentation and explore content as created by a translator. Once again, I imagine how a critical reader may raise an eyebrow at this statement ("Do translators create original content?"), but bear with me. What follows are my reflections on how we can benefit from this approach and how it may be relevant for the future of our business. True to the motto "more substance, less form," there will be almost no more pictures here of the sort of the previous sections. Though wait... "What is the use of a book without pictures and conversation?" asked Lewis Carroll's Alice. So, let me recount a conversation that I had a couple of years ago.

Once, while on an interpreting assignment at a conference, I spent my evening with conference participants. The conference took place in a resort and during dinner I spoke to an executive who was sitting next to me. It turned out that he was an assistant to the CEO of a large international company that hosted the conference. The company was my regular client, so I was quite familiar with the latest developments in the industry and the inner workings within the organisation. After some small talk and a bit of talking shop, the conversation turned to the specifics of my job. As usual, the first questions were about language in general and my working languages in particular. If I remember correctly, I tried to make a point that for me as a translator, my job was just as much about the subject matter as it was about the language (or even less about the latter), and that spurred more interest and appeared to resonate with my table neighbour. We talked about how I work with his company's documents, be it presentations or business reports, and what this work entailed. To our mutual surprise, this was also the core of his work and essentially not much different from what I was doing. The only difference was that he was limited to "translating" in the same language, while I had to deal with two or three languages at the same time.

For the CEO's assistant, preparing reports and presentations appeared similar to my translating them. Of course, the "source documents" were initially drafted and set out by their authors – his boss, heads of departments etc. – but his job was to "translate" them without switching the language. Apart from the organisational routines (consolidating reports, verifying figures or applying standardised guidelines), getting the message right often involved substantial work. Sometimes it meant recreating the original documents, writing more clearly, adjusting details or improving the line of argumentation. And sometimes he said he really had to get into the author's head to understand, paraphrase and adapt the message.

Whether staying within one language or working from one language into another, I don't think the word "creative" is really appropriate to describe this kind of activity: it offers little to no room for free interpretation or subjectivity, let alone mistakes. Like a conscientious and detail-oriented translator, the CEO's assistant's job was all about "getting the message right", though this might also entail actually developing the original idea, and elaborating and shaping the message. It was fun to discuss the specifics of his "monolingual translation", but this is not because his was such a particular case. Rather, this episode illustrates a fairly typical case.

At this point, it would be wise to add a caveat. I believe that "situational awareness", to borrow a military term, should be a core skill in a translator's toolkit. While I believe the situation from my anecdote to be far from unusual, it is neither universal nor predominant. The modus operandi – to which extent the described "creativity" is appropriate – should always depend on the situation. In business communication, translation serves a specific purpose:

it is usually the means, not the end. The translator aims for the translation to achieve the desired effect on the target audience and may, if appropriate, somewhat depart from the literal sense. The academic interest is different: it is the text itself that translation serves to interpret and understand, so creativity wouldn't be tolerated here. The same goes for legal contracts, witness testimonies or medical reports. Yet the example of "monolingual translation" deserves more attention.

It is naïve to expect that subject-matter experts will always produce well-written texts. For a translator, it is just as naïve to take the original text blindly for granted. A significant portion of what we get to translate could first do with a bit of "monolingual translation". The disconnect between what the author originally had in mind and how their original intention and purpose translated into the resulting text is as old as communication itself.

You can easily substitute "graphic designer" in the much-quoted statement from this book with "content creator". Because in my experience, a typical translator doesn't feel entitled to do anything much about her source text: "I am a translator, not the author and not the creator of the document at hand". The CEO's assistant clearly saw his job as that of facilitating communication within the organisation through better "translations", similar to my role. There is no comparison between his full-time employment and my freelance work. However, that is hardly the reason why translators don't usually take on the responsibility to create or recreate content in order to improve their clients' communication. "Doesn't this exceed our area of expertise, not to mention our job description?", would be another question. Which brings me to my next point and another related conversation.

In late 2013, I interviewed Don DePalma for my blog. His company, Common Sense Advisory (CSA), calls itself "the preeminent market research firm in the language services sector". Back then, I was driven by the idea that I could get CSA's founder and mastermind to confirm that his research was drawing on the information from large translation companies and was applicable to what is often referred to as the bulk translation market only, without paying due attention to translation professionals in the high-quality premium segment. After I posted the interview,[93] a colleague asked me what DePalma could have possibly meant when he spoke of "high quality, precision, professional trans-

93 Valerij Tomarenko. "Highs and lows of translation business: interview with Don DePalma, CSA" [blog]. *Translator's Notes*, published 11 November 2013 <https://anmerkungen-des-uebersetzers.com/2013/11/11/highs-and-lows-of-translation-business-interview-with-don-depalma-csa/> accessed 22 August 2018.

lations" as "opportunities for better translators" beyond the bulk language industry with its less-than-perfect, but cheap and readily available, output. What does "precision" in particular mean?, was my colleague's question. My guess is that DePalma used "high quality" and "precision" more or less synonymously, since precision or accuracy have long been one of the absolute criteria for judging the quality of translation.

Truth be told, I don't think that "precision" is the right term for the approach of the CEO's assistant in his role of a "monolingual translator". Neither do I think that "precision" is synonymous with high-quality translations produced by quality-driven, client-focused colleagues, at least not in the conventional sense of the word. We can argue about definitions, recall what "being true to the meaning" actually is and discuss the concept of faithfulness in translation. Yet I believe that equating quality with "precision" is a fallacy of a kind that disregards today's reality and the client's needs precisely in that high-quality, premium segment presumably not considered in the CSA research.

Staying within the topic of accuracy and precision, I'm going to throw in a couple of examples. For instance, if you're familiar with the best practice in editing and proofreading, you know that a fresh look at your text is recommended as it can help you to be more perceptive. You can print out your work and read it on paper. Or you can try to make the document look different by changing its typeface, font size and colour. A popular piece of advice is to read your text out loud or have someone read it to you. Recently, the last option has become much easier thanks to new text-to-speech (TTS) applications. You can have your news read to you from your phone while driving or exercising, and you can listen to your translation in order to review it, thanks to the *Speak* command in Microsoft Word and the *Read Out Loud* feature in Acrobat. If standard software sounds monotonous, there are more sophisticated applications with customisable voices, tone modulation and speed. It may seem an unrelated digression, but the reason I brought up TTS software is this: I have little doubt that a computer or another digital device ensures maximum accuracy and precision when creating an audio copy of the written word. Yet I have just as little doubt that a natural human voice, however less reliably reproducible and more error prone, would still be preferred by a typical listener. I believe it's reasonable to consider human preference a quality criterion. I don't think that making computer reading less monotonous or increasing the degree of sophistication in any other way would change something as substantial, though hard to specify precisely, as that.

Another example concerning precision (or, conversely, creativity or "taking liberties" with source matters) seems even less relevant for translators, but only at first sight – it is photography. I believe that one particular area of photography, namely commercial product photography, is in many respects not unlike translation. Both product photographers and translators work largely for the same type of customer, namely corporate clients for whom it is essential to present and market their products. Whether visual or verbal presentation, the communication intent roughly overlaps. With a stretch of imagination, one can even draw a parallel between products for photographers and their textual descriptions for translators – both serve as "sources" to be processed, converted and reproduced. Given the ubiquity of high-quality, easy-to-use cameras, it seems strange that professional product photographers haven't been all made redundant yet – another parallel with translators, who are particularly uncertain about the future of the profession. The actual task of a product photographer is not to display creativity, but to produce high-quality, high-precision images in an objective, highly accurate and reproducible way. With modern digital technology, it may seem that making such images should be no more difficult than producing a perfectly recited audio version of the written text, in other words no more difficult than pressing the metaphorical button.

I chose these examples because they both illustrate a notable disconnect. On the one hand, shooting photos and converting written text into speech (or into another language) has become a utility: something that is extremely common, undoubtedly useful and widely available at a low-to-zero cost. On the other hand, the fact that everyone can have easy access to this utility cannot eliminate a need for highly skilled, highly specialised professionals. No serious publishing house would use TTS software to produce audio books or audio versions of newspaper and magazine publications. Though DIY product photography has found its place (on eBay and other consumer-to-consumer sales websites), high-value professional skills are still in demand when high-value audiences are the target. What makes an Audible narrator or a product photographer indispensable? The relatively small success of TTS technology is a more clear-cut case: this is a human versus machine competition in which the human still wins. As for product photography, I'm not sure it can be explained by a difference in technical skills. Of course, if we compare the work of a professional product photographer with a picture taken by someone who merely knows how to use a camera, the difference in results will be obvious. But so would the difference in the results produced by different photographers, if we broaden our comparison. In the area of commercial photography success depends on two things. First, it has something to do with the intrinsic limitation of technology, no matter how advanced and state-of-the-art it is: a camera cannot read the client's mind. To translate the client's idea into a great visual product, technology doesn't suffice. This is what a photographer is needed for. The first key to success is the photographer's skill in working out what the client intends and needs, and use specialist knowledge, technology and techniques to realise that intent. Second, it is the photographer's own authentic vision, individuality, his or her way to stand out from the crowd. This is a quality that makes one photographer different from another. It is something intangible and elusive, yet very specific and powerful enough to impact the client's preferences and choice.

I see in this an analogy to translation. Ming Thein, one of the most accomplished commercial photographers and the former chief of strategy at Hasselblad, has captured it well:

> The expectation of a photograph is that it is an unmodified accurate and complete representation of what we'd see if we were there. There's a problem with this, however: what two observers see might be the same, but what they notice is probably going to be very different.[94]

A very similar expectation is held for translation. Don DePalma's statement reflects very well how "precision" is nested within the idea of "high-quality translation". But what should quality translation "precisely" represent? To paraphrase Ming Thein, translation can be expected to be an "accurate and complete representation of what we'd see if we were there", in other words, of what we'd see if we were able to look at the subject through the client's eyes. And to continue with the analogy, two different translators would produce two different representations exactly because of the two factors that I mentioned above. First, the result would depend on what each of them discovered and observed, and second, the result would be different depending on each translator's "vision", individuality and writing skills.

With the same caveat in mind, namely that "situational awareness" is critical (there are situations and environments where one's personal touch might be completely out of place), this is something that translators can definitely learn from product photographers. Throughout this book, I have argued that designers and photographers are more aware of their clients' expectations than translators are. They are aware of the fact they are hired to apply their talents and skills – not only to operate the camera and set up lighting properly, but to read their clients' minds and translate their ideas using their own authentic visual language. Designers and photographers know their clients may be ex-

94 Ming Thein. "Crystal ball gazing: Predicting the photographic ecosystem in 10 years, part II" [blog]. *Ming Thein Photographer*, published 19 June 2017 <https://blog.mingthein.com/2017/06/19/10-year-predictions-part-ii> accessed 22 August 2018.

cited and knowledgeable about their products, but that they should be wary about what the clients actually suggest. Chase Jarvis, a well-known photographer and educator, puts it in bluntly:

> Clients cannot tell you what they need [...] They need a great visual representation of something, a solution. They think they know the best way to photograph something, but they don't really. That's why they hire you. Take their suggestions to heart, because they definitely know their brand, product, their vision – perhaps even shoot a few versions of the images they THINK they want to see first – but then go nuts with own vision. Add value. Show them something they didn't expect. Don't be a monkey with a finger.[95]

I have seen it again and again how many translators are slavishly dependent on their clients' texts. More experienced translators know that their job is to go beyond the "source text" – to explore a broader context. Above all, we need to explore what our clients intended to reach and express with their texts and adapt them to the audience they are intended for. If we get the impression that a text fails to communicate clearly and connect with the audience, we know we have to ask questions. What we can learn from designers and photographers is that we shouldn't take all the information we get from clients at face value. Clients think "they know the best way [...] but they don't really": I believe this advice is applicable to communicators such as ourselves.

That doesn't mean that a translator, even a highly specialised one with insider knowledge of the client's industry, is smarter than her client. A healthily critical attitude to information that we receive from our clients is needed due to the very same problem – that of communication. It is not only that subject-matter experts don't always produce well-written texts; they often cannot articulate their needs and intentions. In *The Design Method*, Eric Karjaluoto stresses the importance of the "discovery stage". When asking questions, his advice is "to start with what your clients need to achieve. Determine not only what they want to create, but also what they need to make happen".[96] I think that this utilitarian approach – the purpose prevails – is particularly valid for high-quality, client-focused translators.

■ ■ ■

95 Chase Jarvis. "10 things every creative person (that's you) must learn" [blog]. *Chasejarvis.com*, published 2017 <http://www.chasejarvis.com/blog/ten-things-every-creative-person-must-learn> accessed 22 August 2018.

96 Karjaluoto, *The Design Method*.

If we agree about the two success factors from the example of commercial photography, that should be our first takeaway – work out what the client has intended. Now, let us turn to the second piece of advice, our individual "vision" or "voice".

I don't think the importance of a unique voice is only born out of the necessity to market oneself and stand out from the competitors. I believe that if we take to heart the first principle – identify the purpose of our clients' writing and prioritise the intent – then the outcome of our work will be necessarily different from the majority of today's translations. The bulk industry favours those who churn out text by text, sentence by sentence or, assisted by CAT tools, segment by segment. A questioning approach is reserved exclusively for post-editing machine translations (PEMT), though a careful, critical assessment of the source texts instead of the machine-translated output could sometimes bring more benefits to our clients. At the risk of repeating myself ad nauseam, subject-matter experts are not necessarily talented writers and effective communicators.

An article about changes and challenges in the translation industry published in "Johnson", *The Economist*'s column that covers language matters, states:

> [M]ost work is in commercial translation, but that is a kind of writing too. Executives sometimes reject a translation of a speech or a letter because it doesn't look enough like their original. But a good translator needs to rethink a text, rewording important pieces, breaking up or merging sentences, and so on. Translation software can be accurate, but it translates sentence-by-sentence. Since languages have different rhythms and different expectations for what counts as a good sentence, that approach can result in a mess. So it is often best simply to rewrite after thinking about the intended meaning.[97]

This is all the more true given the abundance of poorly worded content in business communications. If that is the case, we can only help by applying the approach advocated in *The Economist*. The resulting translation will be different not only from the majority of today's translations, but also from the supposedly unquestionable and incorrigible original. A translator who realised that her client "hadn't a clue how to say what she wanted to say even in

97 Johnson. "Why translators have the blues: A profession under pressure". *The Economist*, 27 May 2017 <https://www.economist.com/news/books-and-arts/21722609-profession-under-pressure-why-translators-have-blues> accessed 22 August 2018.

her native language", as a colleague once put it, finds herself in a situation not entirely different from that of the CEO assistant mentioned earlier. I'm certainly not suggesting this for each and every case, but it is often up to the translator to make a whole lot of difference, literally and figuratively.

The rewriting approach describes pretty well how subject-matter experts treat their "source text" when they occasionally take on the role of translators. From a typical translator's perspective, they are not afraid to break the rules of "high-quality, precision translation". Yet the result is effective and to the point, as I observed in many cases. This is part of what I'm trying to convey by advocating having a "distinctive voice" as a translator: it entails not only superior verbal skills, but also "situational awareness" and the ability to adapt the content in the best interest of the client. ISO 17100, a translation industry standard, places emphasis on revision as an obligatory part of the translation process. Perhaps it might be an idea to extend the principle of revision to the source text. That – and this is the second takeaway from this chapter – is the starting point for differentiation. If there are "opportunities for better translators", in DePalma's words, differentiation is what I'd rather replace "precision" with.

When considering changes or deviations from the original document, these are usually referred to as "improvements". While not every translator recognises that a translation can and should be better than the source text, it is a more significant insight to realise that translations need to be different and unique, especially those at the high end of the market. The word "different" sounds radical, but it is definitely more motivating than "better". I'm tempted to paraphrase Chase Jarvis and say "Add value. Don't be a monkey with your CAT tool". To continue the quote from Jarvis, this is something to keep in mind:

> Don't aim for "better", aim for "different". It's funny how related "better" and "different" are. If you aim for "better" that usually means you're walking in the footsteps of someone else. [...] But if you target being different [...] then you are blazing your own trail. And in blazing your own trail, making your own footprints, you are far more likely to find yourself being "better" without even trying.[98]

■ ■ ■

98 Jarvis, "10 things every creative person (that's you) must learn".

"This is all so wrong I don't know where to begin!", a critic might say. "Finally, the author is effectively arguing against faithfulness to the original. It's like throwing the very essence of translation to the wind. Where is all this going?"

If you are under the impression that I advocate creativity in translation, I didn't think about this when I started out on this chapter. In fact, I feel ambivalent about such an approach. On the one hand, I don't favour any particularly creative attitude *per se*, definitely not for its own sake. But at the same time, I think that as translators our choice is limited. In the field of commercial language services, translation "as is" – I would call it a conventionally faithful translation of clients' documents taken at their face value – becomes increasingly an unsustainable business. Simply converting "source texts" to "target texts" like in former times stops being good enough, both for us and for our clients. It is no longer a solid basis for the future of our profession. Granted, reproducing clients' texts in another language is a professional translator's core competence. However, being competent is no guarantee for being competitive, especially in this day and age. I place emphasis on limited choices, because I think of the usual business constraints.

We seldom think about why we refer to translations as *projects*. Most of the time, it may be just an empty phrase. However, when I hear the word, I automatically visualise the so-called project triangle (also known as the "project management triangle" or the "triple constraint"). Various models exist that show an interrelation between the variables of time, scope, quality, cost, performance and people. My favourite one maps out the critical elements of a translation project like this:

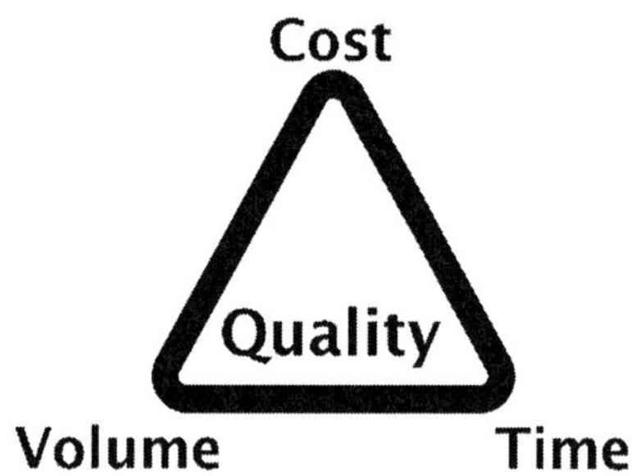

For the moment, let's leave aside the question whether the core part of the triangle is taken by *translation* quality or translation *project* quality. I would not want to equate them, though for commercial translators translations matter only as long as the project variables are in place. It is these variables that leave us with a limited choice.

Volume is usually a variable beyond our control. As for the other constraints, I don't think we can reasonably compete on price and time. Given the growing availability of translations, volumes are reported to be increasing, while prices are dropping and time frames are getting tighter. With automation technology – machine translation of any kind, with or without human revision (PEMT) – conventional translation is on the way to being turned into utility. There may be other triple constraints, with *customer service* another possible variable. However, I doubt any other factors can balance out cost and time, if the product itself – a ready-made text in another language – can be had at the snap of a finger, virtually for free or at a vanishingly low price. That leaves only one thing that makes our future less precarious and competition a bit healthier – translation quality. Unlike the other elements in the triangle, quality defies quantification, hence its problematic nature. To begin with, a client's judgement of translation quality, unlike translation project quality, may lack objectivity and immediacy. And, seeing that translations are essentially translation projects, translation quality *per se* is only one, not necessarily central, element in a project with all its classical constraints.

If we assume that the quality of machine translation will continue improving, competing on quality will become more and more of a challenge. Whether they are aware of it or not, translators are already competing against machine translation today. They will lose the battle tomorrow, if they abide by the parochial definition of translation as "replacement of textual material in one language by equivalent textual material in another language".[99] Whatever productivity-boosting techniques they may hope to use, the machine will always beat them on cost and time.

Today, the biggest deficiency of machine translation is seen in its proneness to mistakes. The second biggest fault is that the translation still largely comes out unclear and unnatural. We can reasonably assume that eventually, the degree of accuracy and also naturalness of machine translation will significantly improve. Nevertheless, the ultimate best that machine translation is likely to achieve one day in terms of translation quality will be more or less close to the output of today's average translator. In other words, the most it can hope to lay claim to will be similar to today's low- and average-standard translations produced as copies of source texts in another language taken "as is", segment by segment. My personal analogy to this kind of quality is the quality of text-to-speech systems. Like TTS, machine translation has the potential to be highly useful and readily available. The problem, however, is that machine translation output, similar to TTS read-out, cannot possibly overcome its ho-hum nature. The area of application, therefore, will remain limited: the purpose of converting the written word to another language with machine translation or to speech with TTS is best described as "for information only".

99 Anne Schjoldager. *Understanding Translation* (Academica, 2008: p. 17).

This is the area where the future of human translation is at its most precarious. Already today, machine translation occasionally does a better job of translating "for information only" (or an average human translator fails to meet the quality standards better than machine translation can). It is in this area where human translators are in trouble as they see their jobs falling to machine translation or PEMT and complain of a race to the bottom. They have little choice but to start to translate differently. "If you don't want to be replaced by a machine, don't act like one", as the saying goes.

Specialisation is widely recognised as the way to counter the trend. Specialisation derives from subject-matter expertise. Being a subject-matter expert, you are likely to produce translations that most accurately convey the author's idea, while not necessarily being close to the author's text. As a consequence, differences are inevitable. Translations by subject-matter experts tend to be more like paraphrase and adaptation, and are marked by greater individual freedom of expression. That is how they become different – both from the source text and from the typical result of an average translation, let alone a machine translation, so they "stand out from the crowd". Specialisation as subject-matter expertise and compelling writing to engage with the target audience are the well-known ingredients of a translator's recipe for success. But finally, if we don't want to be replaced by machines (or blend in with a crowd of those who deliver nothing better or different than machine-translatable work), the answer is to focus on those things where you can make a difference, because it is there that a machine fails. Take the photography analogy: no camera can look through the client's eyes. No machine translation system can read the client's mind to work out the communicative intent and adapt the client's text for its audience and to its purpose. In order to go beyond what is explicitly stated in the client's document, specialisation and excellent writing skills need to be paired with situational awareness and a talent for discovery and research (Karjaluoto's *The Design Method*).

If my example with the CEO's assistant as a "monolingual translator" struck you as an argument for taking menial, uncreative tasks alongside your translation, this may be the point to bring back the idea of creativity in translation, after all. No machine can create truly original content. As I wrote a few years ago, machine translation, like stock photography, "is all about finding new uses for already existing stock texts [...] it recycles residuals of past communication".[100] To focus on a future-proof area that isn't vulnerable to machine translation, we have no choice but to consider creating fresh content for our clients while still working on their source texts. For me, this is how we can be different and influence quality among the other project constraints. So my attitude toward "creativity in translation" is leaning in favour of being more liberal and less secretarial, simply on the grounds that the more distinct and individual your approach to translation, the lesser the chance you can be replaced by something as uncreative as a machine.

■ ■ ■

A final question I expect some of you to ask at this point is something like this: "All this talk about how to translate differently and create content as a translator is rather confusing and not in line with how translation is generally understood. Is it really translation we are talking about?" That is a good question. In fact, discussions about various types and strategies of translation have been underway for quite a while, in the academia, at conferences and in translators' groups on social media. To mention a few examples, there is a technical translation school and a technical translation company in Russia, both founded by Israil Shalyt, that have been the subject of controversy among professionals for years. When translating English technical manuals into Russian, Shalyt proposes an adaptation approach to make the translated documents compliant with the technical documentation standards applicable and relevant to the Russian audience. As a result, the source and target texts may differ considerably. That makes a translation by Shalyt's tech-savvy translation company very unlike that by an average translator, too. The controversy is partially due to the fact that Shalyt insists on his approach being extremely rare, if not outright unique. The issue is therefore about definitions. Is it translation, localisation, adaptation or technical rewriting? Remarkably, quite a few professionals claim that, while an average, standard or substandard translation would definitely come up much closer to the source text, it is actually the kind of translation as that taught and practised by Israil Shalyt that deserves its true name.

From my own experience, I remember an author who contributed to a compilation of articles on business communication. I was asked for an expert opinion on several translations of her article in different languages. All were

100 Valerij Tomarenko. "What is left behind" [blog]. *International Association of Professional Translators and Interpreters* <https://www.iapti.org/articles/art32-what-is-left-behind-valerij-tomarenko.html> accessed 22 August 2018.

produced by professional native-speaker translators and were perfectly okay, but the author was dissatisfied with all of them. Finally, she told the publisher that no translator was capable of doing a good job. She'd rather write her article anew in the target language, which she could only read but not write in, hence the predicament! I quote this example because to me it shows that translation, at least in the conventional sense or when done by a typical translator, is sometimes seen as a questionable way of creating content in another language. This is discussed by Wayne Bourland, director of the global localisation team at Dell's. In his article "Why we shouldn't translate marketing… and why we do it anyway",[101] he also refers to the usual project constraints:

> We invest all of this effort [a few weeks' time, involving several peer and executive reviews – V.T.] into creating beautiful marketing copy in English (or whatever your source is), and then turn it over to the translation team – and expect the same level of quality at a fraction of the cost and delivered within a few days.

Project constraints aside, Bourland still sees an intrinsic problem with translation. If a company needs a marketing copy in another language, he argues, it should use either its own employees in the target market or an ad agency with experience in that local market, but not translate. The local copy as produced by own staff or by a carefully chosen marketing agency "will be inconsistent, as a matter of fact, you won't even recognise the product in the [local] copy. BUT, it will likely be of great quality, engaging, and locally meaningful: far superior to what you would have gotten from the translation process." It is remarkable that Dell's director of translation won't even entertain the notion that such a copy can result from translation. Although the way he talks about it – "of great quality, engaging, and locally meaningful" while radically dissimilar from the source, perfectly describes the quality work of many high-end translators. It is exactly the kind of work that requires to "translate differently and create content".

Maybe the answer is to find the right – and catchy – definition for this kind of translation, largely unknown outside the profession and considered rare and unique even within the industry. This is how the term *transcreation* was invented – to carve out a niche and stand out against the mainstream. It is normally applied to creative, marketing-focused copy only. Arguably, it would be

101 Wayne Bourland. "Why we shouldn't translate marketing… and why we do it anyway". *Brand Quarterly*, published 13 August 2018 <http://www.brandquarterly.com/why-we-shouldnt-translate-marketing-and-why-we-do-it-anyway> accessed 22 August 2018.

useless and counterproductive for business or technical translations of the kind that Israil Shalyt's company specialises in. The Italian communications professional Claudia Benetello specialises in copywriting and transcreation along with translation and interpreting. In her presentation on the multiple roles she plays as an interpreter in the music industry, she comes up with the term "hybrid interpretation".[102] "Translating in itself is only one part of the job", she observes. A hybrid interpreter goes beyond translating her "source text", for instance when interpreting for an artist. This may include "personally asking the artist further questions if the answers given are not exhaustive" or even adding information, "especially when the artist is not very articulate". This resonates well with how the CEO's assistant described his job during our memorable conversation and how I understand adding value as a professional translator. Benetello's approach "may appear unorthodox or disconcerting to some". However, it is justified by the value it creates "for the audience and clients alike". Benetello concludes in her presentation that "delivering a service that goes beyond interpreting as we know it allows the interpreter to better serve the needs of the audience and thus ensure quality". The same can be said for translation, particularly in view of the ever-tightening distance between "orthodox" translation and machine translation.

■ ■ ■

"I write because I don't know what I think until I read what I say" – this confession from Flannery O'Connor illustrates just how I feel about this last section. As translators, we create value for our customers through creating content. The problem is that the quality of our content may not be immediately apparent for the client. People trust their eyes more than they trust words, least of all words in a language they don't master. Hence the idea of this book. In previous chapters, I tried to show how to make quality work more visible and show that we are not "just" translating, but thinking of the best ways to communicate and achieve the client's goals. I cannot hope this advice will be heeded by everyone, but I do hope that it can serve as food for thought.

We are experts working with verbal content. But in the end, lessons from visual communicators are essential, too. They help us uncover the client's intent and develop a distinctive voice. If you learn to see the client's world through the client's eyes, you will get there. I believe we have no other choice.

---

102 Claudia Benetello. "A hybrid within a hybrid: the interpreter-journalist for the music industry. A professional's perspective". In: ICIQ. Third International Conference on Interpreting Quality, Granada 5–7 October 2017. *Book of Abstracts*, p. 33 [PDF]. <http://qinv.ugr.es/iciq3_boa.pdf> accessed 22 August 2018.

Recommended reading

Airey, David. *Logo Design Love: A Guide to Creating Iconic Brand Identities* (Peachpit Press, 2014).

Beckwith, Harry. *Selling the Invisible: A Field Guide to Modern Marketing* (Grand Central Publishing, 2012).

Bringhurst, Robert. *The Elements of Typographic Style: Version 4.0*, 20th Anniversary Edition (Hartley and Marks Publishers, 2013).

Cordisco, Mikaela, Emilia Di Martino, Emine Bogenç Demirel, Jean-Yves Le Disez, Fabio Regattin and Segers, Winibert (eds). *Exploring Creativity in Translation across Cultures / Créativité et traduction à travers les cultures* (Aracne Editrice, 2017).

Durban, Chris. *The Prosperous Translator* (FA&WB Press, 2010).

Friedman, Anthony. *Writing for Visual Media* (Focal Press, 2010).

Gabrielle, Bruce R. *Speaking PowerPoint: The New Language of Business* (Insights Publishing, 2010).

Kapterev, Alexei. *Presentation Secrets: Do What You Never Thought Possible with Your Presentations* (Wiley, 2011).

Karjaluoto, Eric. *Speak Human: Outmarket the Big Guys by Getting Personal* (smashLAB Inc, 2009).

Karjaluoto, Eric. *The Design Method: A Philosophy and Process for Functional Visual Communication* (New Riders, 2013).

Lupton, Ellen. *Thinking with Type: A Critical Guide for Designers, Writers, Editors and Students* (Princeton Architectural Press, 2010).

Lupton, Ellen. *Type on Screen: A Critical Guide for Designers, Writers, Developers and Students* (Design Briefs, 2014).

Malamed, Connie. *Visual Language for Designers: Principles for Creating Graphics that People Understand* (Rockport Publishers, 2011).

Provost, Gary. *100 Ways to Improve Your Writing: Proven Professional Techniques for Writing with Style and Power* (Berkley, 1985).

Reynolds, Garr. *Presentation Zen: Simple Ideas on Presentation Design and Delivery*, 2nd Edition (New Riders, 2011).

Rushkoff, Douglas. *Program or Be Programmed: Ten Commands for a Digital Age* (Soft Skull Press, 2011).

Schopp, Jürgen. Translation und Typographie (facultas Universitätsverlag, 2011).

Spiekermann, Eric. *Stop Stealing Sheep & Find Out How Type Works* (Adobe Press, 2013).

Strunk, William, Jr. *The Elements of Style*, 4th Edition (Pearson, 1999).

Sugarman, Joseph. *The Adweek Copywriting Handbook: The Ultimate Guide to Writing Powerful Advertising and Marketing Copy from One of America's Top Copywriters* (Wiley, 2006).

Vinh, Khoi. *Ordering Disorder: Grid Principles for Web Design* (New Riders, 2010).

Wheeler, Alina. *Designing Brand Identity: An Essential Guide for the Whole Branding Team*, 3rd Edition (Wiley, 2009).

Williams, Robin. *Non Designer's Design Book* (Peachpit Press, 2008).

WLF Think Tank. *101 Things a Translator Needs to Know* (WLF 101 Publishing, 2014).

Index

M

N

O

P

Q

R

S

T

V

W

Essrich, Ricarda: Positionierung als freiberuflicher Übersetzer – Spezialisierung oder Diversifikation? Umfang: 120 Seiten, ISBN: 978-3-938430-87-3, Erscheinungsjahr: 2017, Preis: 27,00 €

„Der Weg zum Erfolg als freiberuflicher Übersetzer führt über die Spezialisierung", behaupten die einen. „Ohne Diversifikation geht es nicht", die anderen. Doch wer hat Recht? Sollte man sich auf ein möglichst winziges exotisches Fachgebiet konzentrieren oder lieber möglichst viel aus möglichst unterschiedlichen Sparten anbieten, um viele Kunden bedienen zu können? Oder liegt die Lösung vielleicht irgendwo dazwischen?

Ricarda Essrich macht sich in ihrem Buch auf die Suche nach Antworten auf diese Fragen. Dabei lässt sie in eingestreuten Interviews einige erfolgreiche Kolleginnen und Kollegen zu Wort kommen, die erzählen, wie sie sich als Übersetzer oder Dolmetscher positioniert haben.

Nur durch eine geschickte Positionierung – die meist mit einer Spezialisierung einhergeht – können Sprachmittler langfristig wirtschaftlich erfolgreich sein. Die Autorin zeigt in diesem Buch, wie man sich spezialisiert, was Spezialisierung bedeutet und wie man trotz Spezialisierung das eigene Portfolio verbreitert, um Risiken zu reduzieren und Wachstumspotenziale zu nutzen.

Die Konzentration auf bestimmte Fachgebiete oder Fähigkeiten könnte für etliche Sprachmittler der Weg zu deutlich mehr Erfolg am Markt sein. Wie das gehen kann, zeigt das Buch.

Sattler-Hovdar, Nina: Translation – Transkreation. Vom Über-Setzen zum Über-Texten, Umfang: 169 Seiten, ISBN: 978-3-938430-73-6, Erscheinungsjahr: 2016, Preis: 31,00 €

Marketing-Übersetzung, adaptive Übersetzung, „freie" Übersetzung, kreative Adaption, Copy-Editing, druckreifes Übersetzen, oder auch einfach nur „eine Übersetzung, die sich irgendwie griffiger liest" – kommt Ihnen das bekannt vor? Gemeinsam ist ihnen allen, dass sie eine Dienstleistung erfordern, die unter der Bezeichnung „Transkreation" anschaulich zusammengefasst werden kann. Allerdings existiert bislang wenig praxisbezogene Literatur zum Thema Transkreation – einem Markt, der stark unterschätzt wird, dabei ein hohes Zukunftspotenzial besitzt.

Transkreation ist eine Form des übersetzenden Textens, einer Kombination aus Übersetzen und Texten. Dies ist besonders bei Marketing-, PR- und Werbetexten gefragt, generell jedoch bei jeder Art von Texten, die direkt oder indirekt das Image und den Umsatz eines Unternehmens steigern sollen. Viel zu wenigen Auftraggebern und auch Auftragnehmern ist bislang klar, worin der Unterschied liegt und welcher Aufwand dahinter steckt.

Dieses Buch bietet nun endlich Abhilfe. Auftragnehmer erhalten zahlreiche Tipps, wie sie effizienter und effektiver an die Arbeit herangehen und nachhaltigen Erfolg erzielen können. Auftraggeber erfahren, wie sie ein optimales Ergebnis zum bestmöglichen Preis-Leistungs-Verhältnis erhalten. Die Lektüreempfehlung für Übersetzer aller Genres und Auftraggeber aller Branchen.

Braun, Manfred (Hrsg.): Wissensmanagement für Sprachmittler im Überblick und Detail, Umfang: 133 Seiten, ISBN: 978-3-946702-00-9, Erscheinungsjahr: 2018, Preis: 25,00 €

Das Thema Wissensmanagement lässt sich zwischen zwei Buchdeckeln kaum erschöpfend abhandeln. Intention des Sammelbands ist es daher, nach einer theoretischen Einführung in die Materie, einige Aspekte beim Umgang mit Wissen darzustellen, die für Sprachmittler besonders wichtig und interessant sind.

Übersetzer und Dolmetscher sehen sich jeden Tag mit der Aufgabe konfrontiert, Wissen und Fakten möglichst schnell und effektiv zu recherchieren, zu bewerten, zu verwenden und bestenfalls auch zu archivieren, damit es bei zukünftigen Arbeitsaufträgen wieder aufgefunden werden kann.

Während wir früher Wissen, über das wir nicht selbst verfügten, nur in gedruckter Form in Büchern und Zeitschriften zugänglich machen konnten, haben wir dank des Internets heute die Möglichkeit, innerhalb von Millisekunden auf das geballte Wissen oder Nichtwissen der ganzen Welt zuzugreifen. Wie häufig wir dies tun, fällt uns erst auf, wenn der Internetzugang gestört oder zu langsam ist oder ein Stromausfall oder ein defekter Computer uns vom weltweiten Wissen abschneidet.

Wir sollten daher regelmäßig unseren Umgang mit Wissen überprüfen und überlegen, wie wir unsere Arbeitsweise optimieren können. Die Beiträge des Sammelbands bieten hierfür nützliche Anregungen.

Ottmann, Angelika (Hrsg.): Best Practices – Übersetzen und Dolmetschen. Ein Nachschlagewerk aus der Praxis für Sprachmittler und Auftraggeber, Umfang: 398 Seiten, ISBN: 978-3-938430-78-1, Erscheinungsjahr: 2017, Preis: 31,00 €

Best Practices sind bewährte Verfahrensweisen, d. h. Methoden, Prozesse, Arbeitsweisen und Modelle, die sich in der Praxis bewährt haben und von einem Großteil der Praktiker angewendet und unterstützt werden. In diesem Sinne wendet sich das Werk an alle, die mit den Dienstleistungen Übersetzen und Dolmetschen befasst sind, sei es als Ausführende (Übersetzer, Dolmetscher), als Vermittler (Agenturen) oder als Auftraggeber (Unternehmen, Behörden, Institutionen).

Mit den Best Practices für Übersetzen und Dolmetschen bekommen Auftraggeber verlässliche Kriterien für die Ausschreibung und Abwicklung von Übersetzungs- und Dolmetschaufträgen an die Hand, Sprachmittler können die Best Practices für ihre Verhandlungen mit den Auftraggebern nutzen, um Missverständnisse zu vermeiden, die der Komplexität der Abläufe geschuldet sind, und alle Beteiligten erhalten nützliche Tipps für ihre tägliche Arbeit.

Das Buch ist ist ein Nachschlagewerk und Referenzhandbuch für alle, die Antworten auf Ihre speziellen Fragen suchen, für alle, die wissen möchten, welche Anforderungen ihr Gegenüber hat, für alle, die über den Tellerrand ihrer Tätigkeit hinausblicken und sehen wollen, wie andere es machen.

Alle Preise sind Bruttopreise und verstehen sich zzgl. Porto und Verpackung (ab 2,50 €). Bestellungen erbitten wir bevorzugt über unsere Internetseite: www.bdue-fachverlag.de. Dort finden Sie außerdem Leseproben zum kostenlosen Download.